Jewish Business Ethics

Jewish Business Ethics

The Firm and Its Stakeholders

edited by
Aaron Levine
Moses Pava

Robert S. Hirt, Series Editor

The Orthodox Forum Series
A Project of the Rabbi Isaac Elchanan Theological Seminary
An Affiliate of Yeshiva University

JASON ARONSON INC.
Northvale, New Jersey
Jerusalem

This book was set in 11 pt. Goudy Oldstyle by Alpha Graphics of Pittsfield, NH and printed and bound by Book-mart Press, Inc. of North Bergen, NJ.

10 9 8 7 6 5 4 3 2 1

Library of Congress Cataloging-in-Publication Data

Jewish business ethics : the firm and its stakeholder / edited by
Aaron Levine and Moses Pava.
p. cm.
"The Orthodox Forum series."
Papers presented at the 8th conference of the Orthodox Forum, held
Apr. 28–29, 1996, in New York City.
Includes bibliographical references and index.
ISBN 0-7657-6056-8
1. Commercial law (Jewish law) Congresses. 2. Business ethics
Congresses. 3. Ethics, Jewish Congresses. 4. Business—Religious
aspects—Judaism Congresses. I. Pava, Moses L. II. Levine, Aaron.
III. Orthodox Forum (8th : 1996 : New York, N.Y.)
LAW
296.3'644—DC21 98-36490
CIP

Printed in the United States of America on acid-free paper. For information and catalog write to Jason Aronson Inc., 230 Livingston Street, Northvale, NJ 07647-1726, or visit our website: www.aronson.com

THE ORTHODOX FORUM

The Orthodox Forum, convened by Dr. Norman Lamm, President of Yeshiva University, meets each year to consider major issues of concern to the Jewish community. Forum participants from throughout the world, including academicians in both Jewish and secular fields, rabbis, *rashei yeshiva*, Jewish educators, and Jewish communal professionals, gather in conference as a think tank to discuss and critique each other's original papers, examining different aspects of a central theme. The purpose of the Forum is to create and disseminate a new and vibrant Torah literature addressing the critical issues facing Jewry today.

The Orthodox Forum
gratefully acknowledges the support
of the Joseph J. and Bertha K. Green Memorial Fund
at the Rabbi Isaac Elchanan Theological Seminary
established by Morris L. Green, of blessed memory.

Other Volumes in the Orthodox Forum Series

Rabbinic Authority and Personal Autonomy
edited by
Moshe Z. Sokol

Jewish Tradition and the Non-Traditional Jew
edited by
Jacob J. Schacter

Israel as a Religious Reality
edited by
Chaim I. Waxman

Modern Scholarship in the Study of Torah
Contributions and Limitations
edited by
Shalom Carmy

Tikkun Olam
Social Responsibility in Jewish Thought and Law
edited by
David Shatz, Chaim I. Waxman, and Nathan J. Diament

Engaging Modernity
Rabbinic Leaders and the Challenge of the Twentieth Century
edited by
Moshe Z. Sokol

Jewish Perspectives on the Experience of Suffering
edited by
Shalom Carmy

THE ORTHODOX FORUM
EIGHTH CONFERENCE

April 28–29, 1996
9–10 Iyar 5756
Congregation Shearith Israel
New York City

LIST OF PARTICIPANTS

Dr. Norman Adler, Yeshiva University
Rabbi Marc Angel, Congregation Shearith Israel
Dr. David Berger, Brooklyn College & Yeshiva University
Rabbi Yitzhak Berger, Yeshiva University
Mr. Ari Bergmann, Bankers Trust Company
Rabbi Saul J. Berman, Yeshiva University
Rabbi Jack Bieler, Hebrew Academy of Greater Washington
Dr. Rivkah Blau, Shevrach High School
Rabbi Yosef Blau, RIETS/Yeshiva University
Dr. Judith Bleich, Touro College
Dr. D. Barry Bressler, Staten Island College
Rabbi Michael J. Broyde, Emory University
Professor Jeffrey Callen, Stern School of Business–NYU
Rabbi Sahlom Carmy, Yeshiva University
Rabbi Zevulun Charlop, RIETS/Yeshiva University
Rabbi Mark Dratch, Shaarei Shomayim Congregation, Toronto
Rabbi Barry Freundel, Kesher Israel Synagogue, Georgetown
Rabbi Robert S. Hirt, RIETS/Yeshiva University
Dr. Avery M. Horowitz, Yeshiva University
Dr. Ephraim Kanarfogel, Yeshiva University
Dr. Eliyahu Kanovsky, Yeshiva University

Dr. Eugene Korn, Hartman Institute
Dr. Joshua Krausz, Yeshiva University
Dr. Norman Lamm, Yeshiva University
Mr. Shalom E. Lamm, Lion & Lamm
Dr. Aaron Levine, Yeshiva University
Mr. Nathan Lewin, Miller, Cassidy, Lorroca & Lewin
Dr. Yehoshua Liebermann, Bar Ilan University
Dr. Gershon Mamlak, City University of New York
Mr. Leon M. Metzger, Paloma Partners Company L.L.C.
Dr. Israel Miller, Yeshiva University
Dr. Harold Nierenberg, Yeshiva University
Dr. Moses L. Pava, Yeshiva University
Mr. Jay Pomrenze, Bankers Trust
Dr. Jonas Prager, New York University
Rabbi Daniel Rapp, RIETS/Yeshiva University
Rabbi Michael Rosensweig, RIETS/Yeshiva University
Dr. Alvin I. Schiff, Yeshiva University
Dr. David J. Schnall, Yeshiva University
Dr. David Shatz, Yeshiva University
Dr. Michael D. Shmidman, Yeshiva University
Dr. Moshe Z. Sokol, Touro College
Mr. Marc D. Stern, American Jewish Congress
Rabbi Moshe D. Tendler, RIETS/Yeshiva University
Dr. Chaim Waxman, Rutgers University & Yeshiva University
Rabbi Mordechai Willig, RIETS/Yeshiva University
Dr. Joel B. Wolowelsky, Yeshivah of Flatbush High School
Rabbi Walter S. Wurzburger, Yeshiva University

Contents

Prologue: What Is Jewish Business Ethics? xi
Moses L. Pava

1 Moral Markets: Two Cheers for Stakeholder Theory 1
Moses L. Pava

2 Convenantal Morality in Business 27
Walter S. Wurzburger

3 The Employee as Corporate Stakeholder: Exploring the Relationship between Jewish Tradition and Contemporary Business Ethics 45
David J. Schnall

4 Aspects of the Firm's Responsibility to Its Customers: Pharmaceutical Pricing and Consumer Pricing 75
Aaron Levine

5 Balancing the Scales: *Halakhah*, the Firm, and Information Asymmetries 123
Jonas Prager

6 Responsibility of the Firm to the Environment 147
Yehoshua Liebermann

7 Ethical Investment: The Responsibility of Ownership in Jewish Law 175
D. B. Bressler

8 The Corporate Veil and Halakhah:
A Still Shrouded Concept 203
Michael J. Broyde and Steven H. Resnicoff

Epilogue 273
Aaron Levine

Contributors 317

Index 319

Prologue: What Is Jewish Business Ethics?

Moses L. Pava

The core idea upon which this book is built is that the power and success of business is ultimately dependent on mangers' beliefs about life's meaning. It is no exaggeration to suggest that corporate success is set in motion and encouraged by a set of core ethical values shared by managers, employees, and stakeholders. It is our unflinching belief that traditional Jewish sources provide useful and practical paradigms and solutions to many of the important issues facing the modern business manager. Jewish business ethics must begin by taking both business and Jewish ethics seriously.

Granted there is an important and dynamic literature focusing its attention on the halakhic responsibilities of the individual business man or woman, but business ethics decisions are often different in kind from personal ethical choices. How so? The moral dilemmas faced by the modern business organization often do not resemble those faced by the isolated individual. Individuals can rarely, if ever, affect the lives of thousands of people with a single decision. For corporations, unfortunately, the decision to lay off huge numbers of employees is becoming uncomfortably routine. Similarly, few individuals have the ability to irreversibly pollute the environment as quickly as the Exxon Corporation or Union Carbide. Wal-Mart's recent choice not to stock record albums that contain what they perceive as offensive lyrics carries with it huge social impacts, as Wal-Mart is of one the largest players in the CD market.

Understanding the responsibilities of business to society requires an understanding of the business entity as such. A Jewish business ethics, properly understood, needs to explicitly recognize the real-world situations of our students and young business people. Students must honestly confront what it means to be a part of a pluralistic, modern business institution embedded in a democratic polity. A Jewish business ethics designed only for a hypothetical world in which *halakhah* guides our public and private institutions—but which ignores business realities—is an interesting intellectual exercise, but fails to provide guidance in the here and now. If a Jewish business ethics is going to have practical import (i.e., impact on behavior), we must begin the process by understanding and interpreting traditional and authoritative Jewish sources, but we must also grapple with the meaning of business in contemporary society. Therefore, this book is an attempt to interpret traditional normative texts and apply these texts to the modern situation. The focus of the analysis is at the level of the organization. Each of the authors in this volume views both aspects of this process earnestly.

The task of interpreting and applying a Jewish business ethics is an important and timely one because the nature of business is changing at a dramatic pace. The size, power, and influence of the modern business corporation are unprecedented in human history. Business transactions are novel, and decision-making is more complex and nuanced than ever. In this constantly evolving environment, top business executives and the best global corporations are increasingly aware of the existence of business responsibilities not only to shareholders to increase profits, but also to various other groups affected by business decisions. Top businesses explicitly articulate social responsibilities to various groups, including employees, customers, local and national communities, and stockholders. Admittedly the recognition is often hazy and ill-defined, but this marked change in attitude on the part of business executives nevertheless represents an important and evolving social trend. An overriding concern of this book is to articulate a Jewish perspective on business responsibilities. The chapters in this book represent an important step in the continuing process of developing and clarifying a meaningful Jewish business ethics.

THE BOOK'S STRUCTURE

The structure of this book is built around the idea that the business firm is best understood by examining the relationships among the various stakeholder groups which define the modern corporation. The term *stakeholder* is a play on the word stockholder. While more traditional views of the corporation emphasize managers' responsibilities to maximize profits to stockholders, the stakeholder theory encourages us to take a larger and more expansive view of business. While it remains true that the corporation must take seriously its responsibility to "increase" profits to stockholders, the theory explicitly recognizes responsibilities to various other groups which make up the corporation. In theory, at least, it is possible that a corporation's responsibilities to employees, say, will trump responsibilities to stockholders, or that environmental concerns will limit profit-seeking behavior.

This particular structure was chosen for four distinct reasons: First, the stakeholder theory has emerged as an important theory in the secular business ethics literature. To date, there are more than a hundred academic articles and a dozen books on the topic. Thus, evaluating the stakeholder theory from a Jewish perspective is in itself an important and overriding concern. Second, stakeholder theory reflects a view of decision making consistent with a religious worldview. Stakeholder theory suggests that before human beings promote their own individual or group preferences, human beings need a framework to critique and alter those preferences. The more traditional views of the corporation which emphasize profit maximization, to the extent that they are founded solely on a self-serving view of decision making, are at odds with the vast majority of Jewish sources. This thesis is elaborated in my introductory remarks on stakeholder theory (Chapter 1). Third, structuring the discussion around the stakeholder theory emphasizes and underlines our belief that the most important modern business ethics concerns are best framed as organizational issues as opposed to personal ones. The stakeholder theory is first and foremost an organizational theory, and by sticking to stakeholder theory, the focus of the discussion remains fixed precisely where it should be. Fourth, and perhaps most important, the theory provides a natural way to think about and group traditional Jewish business ethics sources. A well-grounded fear when embarking on a project such as this, where one of the implicit goals is to integrate secular and religious worldviews, is the very real danger of ending up by trying to force a square peg into a round hole. I believe a careful reading of the papers included in this volume will demonstrate that our initial optimism about the stakeholder theory and its potential consistency with Jewish sources was not disappointed. This is not to say that Jewish values and stakeholder theory are one, but rather that stakeholder theory is sufficiently robust to provide a starting point to structure an interesting and constructive discussion and debate centering on what Jewish business ethics might entail.

AN OVERVIEW

In Chapter 1, I provide a general discussion of stakeholder theory and a critique of the theory from a religious perspective. Walter Wurzburger continues this broad theme in Chapter 2. He notes that "for Judaism, enhancement of one's own material well-being represents a positive value," but carefully adds the important caveat that individual and corporate economic satisfaction can only be attained through "activities which represent a worthwhile contribution to societal well-being." This succinct formulation of Jewish business ethics provides a powerful measuring rod by which to begin the entire discussion. Wurzburger argues for the appropriateness of the notion of corporate social responsibility from the perspective of what he labels "Jewish Covenantal ethics." Judaism, according to his view, is both a legal system and a moral system "which imposes requirements for social responsibility upon business organizations." His explicit recognition of ethical responsibilities beyond strictly halakhic requirements provides the foundation upon which a meaningful Jewish business ethics might be built. The fact that business ethics, properly understood, is not identical to business law (whether one is talking about secular or religious law) is a necessary starting point if a realistic and practical business ethics is to eventually emerge.

If the first two chapters take a macro approach, Chapters 3, 4, 5, and 6 apply a micro view. Each of these chapters examines business responsibilities in the context of a particular stakeholder group. These chapters cover business responsibilities to employees (Chapter 3), to consumers (Chapters 4 and 5), and to the environment (Chapter 6).

In Chapter 3, David Schnall harnesses a number of important sources dealing with the responsibilities of the firm with regard to employees.

Specifically, his paper examines selected areas including the administration of pay and benefits, occupational safety, and collective bargaining. His final conclusion, which suggests that classic Jewish thought posits a clear responsibility upon the employer to consider the needs of his workforce beyond bottom-line considerations, seems indisputable. Importantly, Schnall also points out that while Judaism "favors a concern for and an obligation to the needs of the workforce," other normative sources stress a balance in work relationships. He writes, for example, that employees who incur damages in the normal execution of their jobs may not necessarily be entitled to compensation paid by the firm. This point is worth emphasizing. Business ethics in general, and Jewish business ethics in particular, are not a one-way street where the firm takes on ever-increasing responsibilities toward society and all other stakeholder groups are passive beneficiaries. Rather, a full-blown theory would need to articulate both the corporate responsibilities and the reciprocal responsibilities of stakeholder groups toward the corporation. This is not to say that both parties have the same responsibilities, but simply that both parties have some responsibilities.

Aaron Levine in Chapter 4 and Jonas Prager in chapter 5 examine Jewish texts in light of corporate responsibilities to consumers. Specifically, Levine examines the legitimacy of allowing market forces to set pharmaceutical prices and the responsibility of the firm not to violate the privacy of its customers. In both instances, Levine cites glaring market failures obviously at odds with important and normative Jewish legal texts. For example, Levine notes that Johnson & Johnson was charging between $1,250 and $1,500 for a year's supply of Ergamisol while its nearly identical veterinary version was selling a year's supply for as low as $14.95. Whether or not one agrees with Levine's conclusion that these particular examples of corporate abuse require government solutions and sanctions (in this case Levine suggests a government-imposed "opportunity cost" price ceiling), his analysis clearly demonstrates that, at least potentially *halakhah* could endorse increased government regulation in the marketplace. While it is undeniable that Jewish sources recognize the potential for acting for reasons beyond self-interest as the previous chapters would emphasize, Jewish sources do not always expect everyone, when given the chance, to do so.

It is worth emphasizing that Levine's essay suggests an important question: In general, under what circumstances would a Jewish business ethics rely on voluntarism and under what circumstances are government solutions called for? At minimum, as Levine himself suggests elsewhere,[1] an answer to this question requires us to clearly define the context. Is the goal of a Jewish business ethics to describe the characteristics of an ideal Jewish state organized around Jewish Law, or is it to provide practical "guideposts" for a pluralistic and democratic society? If the primary goal is the latter, as many believe, some may feel uncomfortable imposing government solutions on the basis of religious law, especially in the absence of any articulated theory about the relationship between state and religion. The point is simply that a solution appropriate for a halakhic state may or may not be appropriate for a secular state.

Jonas Prager (Chapter 5) extends the discussion of corporate responsibility to consumers by examining the information asymmetries which often characterize the relationship between sellers and buyers. According to Prager, sellers are typically better informed about product quality and sales practices than are purchasers, and thus might be tempted to exploit their superior knowledge to deceive buyers. After detailing some pragmatic solutions endorsed in the economic literature, Prager suggests that an ethical perspective shapes the halachic outlook. His integration of economic concepts with the rabbinic material represents the core methodology of a Jewish business ethics. Similarly, his substantive conclusion is consistent with the central insights of a Jewish business ethics: "It is the underlying moral standard that distinguishes the halakhic perspective toward firm behavior from the pure economic or economic-legal attitude. "'Do the right thing, not the expedient one' is the message Judaism sends to the firm's decision makers."

Yehoshua Lieberman (Chapter 6) introduces the reader to some important talmudic sources which, either explicitly or implicitly, deal with business responsibilities toward the environment. He asks, How can business firms engaged in profit-seeking activities be expected to contribute to society's welfare, including concern for the environment? His attempt to link Coase's famous theorem with the assumptions of Jewish law is an interesting intellectual exercise and demonstrates the diversity and range of thought which characterize this volume.

---

[1]See Aaron Levine, "Response to Peter J. Hill," *Cultural Dynamics* 7 (3) (1995): 387–398.

Finally, Chapters 7 and 8 return to some of the broad issues foreshadowed in the opening two chapters. Barry Bressler (Chapter 7) examines in some detail the parameters of investors' responsibilities. The question of socially responsible investing, as he sees it, hinges on the nature of the corporation as viewed in Jewish law. His suggestion that individual stockholders (with a small percentage share of total outstanding stock and little or no ability to affect corporate decision-making) in large, publicly traded corporations may not share the same level of responsibility as corporate directors and executives deserves attention. That there exist different levels of responsibility depending on one's relationship to the corporation is an important result with general applicability. His introduction of the concepts of *lifnei iver* (abetting moral misconduct) and *mesaya l'yiday ov'rei aveira* (assisting moral misconduct) represents an important contribution to the business ethics debate. Both of these ethical concepts have much to teach about investors' responsibility, and business ethics more generally conceived. Bressler's provocative conclusions will no doubt engender additional constructive debate.

Michael Broyde and Steven Resnicoff's topic and coverage complements Bressler's perspective. In Chapter 8, Brodye and Resnicoff once again raise fundamental questions about the precise nature of the corporation as seen through traditional Jewish sources. Specifically, they ask whether *halakhah* can recognize the secular structure which gives corporations a legal existence different from that of shareholders which make up the corporation. Or does *halakhah* adopt the posture that the secular corporate veil is of no significance and treat the corporation as it would treat a partnership? Their comprehensive discussion, which compares modern American legal concepts with traditional halakhic thinking, underscores the desirability of integrating the two systems, but also highlights some of the conceptual difficulties encountered in a serious and honest attempt to do so. Here, I refer specifically to their final agnosticism about whether or not Jewish law can accommodate secular innovations that create categories unheard of in Jewish law. In their words, "None of the Jewish law theories of a corporation is entirely satisfying or compelling."

All of the papers that constitute this book were presented and discussed in turn by the participants at the Eighth Conference of the Orthodox Forum held in New York City on April 28th and 29th, 1996; the papers were revised as a result of the discussion at the conference. In an epilogue to this volume, Aaron Levine reflects on some of the issues raised during our two days of meetings. His comments, by no means meant to be exhaustive, capture some of the flavor and texture of these lively deliberations. In addition, Aaron Levine and I would like to thank formally Jay Pomrenze and Ari Bergmann, both of Bankers Trust, for leading a discussion from the perspective of the religiously observant practitioner. The session was chaired by Nat Lewin, to whom we are grateful. We particularly appreciated their honesty and forthrightness in not sugar-coating their presentation and discussion. They painted a realistic picture of the business culture and indicated the difficulty of integrating ivory-tower theorizing with the real-world practice of business.

It is a distinct pleasure for us to thank Dr. Norman Lamm, President of Yeshiva University, for convening the Orthodox Forum and seeing the need for a serious discussion of Jewish business ethics. His participation in the deliberations of the forum was greatly appreciated and added immeasurably to the quality of the discussion.

Thanks are also due to the Steering Committee of the Forum for helping us formulate the questions and paper topics addressed in this volume. Special thanks are reserved for Rabbi Robert Hirt, vice president for Administration and Professional Education of the Rabbi Isaac Elchanan Theological Seminary, an affiliate of Yeshiva University, and the editor of the Orthodox Forum Series, for overseeing the work of the Orthodox Forum with sincerity and consummate skill. His managerial philosophy represents a case study of the best of the stakeholder approach. Mrs. Marcia Schwartz of M.S.D.C.S. (Max Stem Division of Communal Services) greatly facilitated both the planning and execution of the conference and the preparation of this volume. Mareleyn Schneider and Leonard Brandwein provided valuable computer assistance. Thanks also to Dror Barber, Elisha Graeff, Chaim Herman, and Yakir Levin who ably helped us prepare the articles for publication.

THE STATE OF THE ART

In conclusion, I would like to return to the title: What is Jewish business ethics?

A pervasive belief in our society (apparently even among many religious thinkers) is to think of business as a human invention which stands apart. We often justify questionable commercial actions by smiling reassuringly and stating, "Well, it's just business." According to this somewhat cynical view, just as it is meaningless to talk about an ethics of poker or an ethics of chess, so too business ethics in general, and Jewish business ethics in particular, is a useless enterprise. Business and ethics each have their own sets of rules, and mixing the metaphors of business with the metaphors of ethics produces a shrill poem. This criticism is disturbing, especially when it is launched from a religious perspective. If the following papers prove anything, they certainly undercut the notion that Jewish sources are, or have ever been, indifferent to economic arrangements. Jewish business ethics, far from being an innovative activity, grows naturally out of the central and historic concerns of the Jewish community.

For a business ethics to affect behavior, as Walter Wurzburger and others have noted, the proposition that human beings (at least on occasion) can make decisions in ways other than pure self-interest must not only be true, but must also be accepted by business men and women. This theme is a recurrent one in the following chapters, and if it is not unique to a Jewish worldview, it is certainly central to a Jewish way of thinking. Social scientists and business ethicists who adopt the "orthodox" economic view of human behavior during the six working days and embrace a religious view on the seventh day suffer a kind of intellectual schizophrenia. One of the important lessons that emerges here is that such schizophrenia is unnecessary. An intellectually rigorous model of human behavior can be successfully married to an uncompromising religious faith.

Perhaps the cliché "business is business" will ultimately prove false. A Jewish business ethics is integral to centrist orthodoxy, in the final analysis, because of its potential to transform the status quo. A Jewish business ethics tantalizingly suggests that, at least someday, business might be conceived of as one more expression of man's Highest concern. Judaism is antithetical to the business-is-business mentality. A business ethics which explores the possibility of advancing the way we think about business—a business ethics which combines the necessary freedom to creatively pursue physical well-being with the traditional view of man as created in God's image—will ultimately be worthy of being described as a Jewish business ethics.

At the level of the individual, Rabbi Joseph B. Soloveitchik has promised us that the Jewish concept of *teshuva* (literally "to return," but usually translated as repentance) is not only about altering one's actions, but more importantly, can be understood as a kind of personal transformation. In describing the *teshuva* process, Rabbi Soloveitchik writes:

> It is a precept whose essence is not in the performance of certain acts or deeds, but rather in a process that at times extends over a whole lifetime, a process that begins with remorse, with a sense of guilt, with man's increasing awareness that there is no purpose to his life, with a feeling of isolation, of being lost and adrift in a vacuum, of spiritual bankruptcy, of frustration and failure—and the road one travels is very long, until the goal of repentance is actually achieved. Repentance is not a function of a single, decisive act, but grows and gains in size slowly and gradually, until the pentinent undergoes a complete metamorphosis, and then, after becoming a new person, and only then, does repentance take place.[2]

Ideally, according to this view, the *mitzvah* of *teshuva* is only fulfilled after one becomes "a new person." Ultimately, Jewish business ethics is important because it offers a similar promise at the level of the organizations in which we spend so much of our time.

[2]Peli, Pinchus (1980). *On Repentance: In the Thought and Oral Discourses of Rabbi Joseph B. Soloveitchik*. Jerusalem: Oroth.

1

Moral Markets: Two Cheers for Stakeholder Theory

Moses L. Pava

And he took the book of the covenant, and read in the ears of the people: and they said, all that the Eternal has spoken, we will do, and we will listen (na-aseh ve-nishma).

—*Exodus* 24:7

When the Israelites gave precedence to "we will do" over "we will hearken" a Heavenly voice went forth and exclaimed to them, who revealed to My children this secret which is employed by the ministering angels . . .

—*Shabbat* 88a

There was a certain Sadducee who . . . exclaimed: "Ye rash people who gave precedence to your mouth over your ears: ye still persist in rashness. First ye should have listened, if within your powers, accept, if not, ye should have not accepted." Said Raba to him: "We who walked in integrity, of us it is written 'The integrity of the upright shall guide them . . .'"

—*Shabbat* 88a

Business ethics, and even a Jewish business ethics, are, above all, a practical enterprise. One begins by acknowledging the pluralistic nature of the modern business organization. Business men and women, by virtue of their choice to participate in the modern corporation, accept either explicitly or implicitly the concept of pluralism. Given this preliminary assumption, the business ethics discussion begins by recognizing and attempting to understand current social, political, and business realities. A Jewish business ethics designed to operate in a Torah society only, where one can assume at the outset a universal acceptance of Jewish law as binding, is an interesting and important academic (and perhaps religious) exercise, but is not particularly useful to contemporary business executives and students, Jewish or otherwise. However, as this paper demonstrates, recognition and understanding of current realities need not imply full acceptance of the status quo. A Jewish business ethics that attempts to integrate fully the best of an ever-growing secular literature on business ethics with traditional Jewish sources provides both a realistic starting point and the critical tools necessary to enter into the business ethics debate.

The specific purpose of this paper is to both describe and critique from a Jewish perspective an important area of business ethics known as stakeholder theory. To date, there are more than a hundred academic articles and a dozen books on the topic.[1] My conclusion, hinted at in the title of this paper, is that on the one hand, stakeholder theory represents an important advance over competing theories of how business should be conducted. By clearly invoking the language of ethics and responsibility as a foundation of modern business, stakeholder theory reminds us of the predominant biblical vision that "Man does not live by bread alone, but by everything that proceedeth out of the mouth of the Lord doth man live."[2] Stakeholder theory provides strong and persuasive arguments against the traditional view of business, which asserts that the sole goal of the corporation is to maximize profits. On the other hand, care must be taken to distance ourselves from some of the most recent and much more radical pronouncements of a minority of stakeholder theorists. Some advocates of stakeholder theory now recommend that we "create" our own ethics because, in the final

[1]Thomas Donaldson and Lee E. Preston, "The Stakeholder Theory of the Corporation: Concepts, Evidence, and Implications," *Academy of Management Review* 20:1 (1995): 65–91.

[2]Deuteronomy 8:3.

analysis, it is "just us" (and there is no "justice" as has been traditionally understood). Obviously, this radical strain of stakeholder theory is inconsistent with the fundamental message and method of Jewish business ethics. In spite of this last point, on balance, stakeholder theory is a positive and ethically significant development.

I. WHAT IS THE STAKEHOLDER THEORY OF THE FIRM?

The first task of this paper is to provide a clear description of the theory. The chore is made more difficult because of a lack of consensus among business ethicists on this basic issue. Perhaps the best place to begin the discussion of stakeholder theory is not with the academic literature at all, but with a document found hanging on the office walls of corporate executives at Johnson & Johnson. Because of its singular importance, we quote Johnson & Johnson's business "credo" in full. The credo states that the goals of the corporation are as follows:

> We believe our first responsibility is to the doctors, nurses and patients, to mothers and fathers and all others who use our products and services. In meeting their needs everything we do must be of high quality. We must constantly strive to reduce our costs in order to maintain reasonable prices. Customers' orders must be serviced promptly and accurately. Our suppliers and distributors must have an opportunity to make a fair profit.
>
> We are responsible to our employees, the men and women who work with us throughout the world. We must respect their dignity and recognize their merit. They must have a sense of security in their jobs. Compensation must be fair and adequate, and working conditions clean, orderly, and safe. We must be mindful of ways to help our employees fulfill their family responsibilities. Employees must feel free to make suggestions and complaints. There must be equal opportunity for employment, development and advancement for those qualified. We must provide competent management, and their actions must be just and ethical.
>
> We are responsible to the communities in which we live and work and to the world community as well. We must be good citizens—support good works and charities and bear our fair share of taxes. We must encourage civic improvements and better health and education. We must maintain in good order the property we are privileged to use, protecting the environment and natural resources.

> Our final responsibility is to our stockholders. Business must make a sound profit. We must experiment with new ideas. Research must be carried on, innovative programs developed and mistakes paid for. New equipment must be purchased, new facilities provided and new products launched. Reserves must be created to provide for adverse times. When we operate according to these principles, the stockholders should realize a fair return.[3]

Johnson & Johnson clearly articulates its belief that the corporation has responsibilities to meet the needs of many different groups of people. These groups which "have a stake in or claim on the firm"[4] are called stakeholders. Johnson & Johnson explicitly includes the following groups among its stakeholders: customers, suppliers, employees, managers, local and world communities, and stockholders. The twin themes of "fairness" and "responsibility" permeate the document. The term "fair," although not defined, is used four times, and some form of the word "responsibility" is used five times. Importantly, the traditional notion of "profit maximization" is replaced by the admittedly fuzzy idea of a "sound profit."

In an important review paper, Donaldson and Preston[5] have carefully noted that stakeholder theory can serve three distinct (although usually consistent) purposes. According to the authors, stakeholder theory has been variously invoked as a *descriptive*, as an *instrumental*, and as a *normative* theory. Their paper correctly suggests that care must be taken to distinguish among the uses of the theory.

A. Stakeholder Theory as Descriptive

Donaldson and Preston write that "The stakeholder theory is unarguably *descriptive*. It presents a model describing what the corporation is. It describes the corporation as a constellation of cooperative and competi-

---

[3]Johnson & Johnson, 1998 Annual Report to Shareholders.

[4]William M. Evan and R. Edward Freeman, "The Stakeholder Theory of the Corporation: Concepts, Evidence, and Implications," in *Business Ethics*, ed. W. Michael Hoffman and Robert E. Frederick (New York: McGraw-Hill, 1995), p. 146.

[5]Donaldson and Preston, pp. 65–91.

tive interests possessing intrinsic value."[6] Johnson & Johnson's credo is also unarguably descriptive and illustrates Donaldson and Preston's first point nicely. The first purpose of the credo is to describe the nature of the corporation known as Johnson & Johnson. The credo comes to answer the question, What is the corporation? By explicitly recognizing the corporation's responsibilities to its various stakeholders, the corporation itself suggests that it is to be defined through its numerous relationships. No one group (whether they be shareholders, employees, or managers) can claim that they alone are identical to the corporation. A basic axiom of stakeholder theory suggests that the corporation, as a whole, is distinct from, and greater than the sum of its constituent parts.

Evan and Freeman, in their path-finding paper, describe stakeholder theory as follows:

> The concept of stakeholders is a generalization of the notion of stockholders, who themselves have some special claim on the firm. Just as stockholders have a right to demand certain actions by management, so do other stakeholders have a right to make claims. The exact nature of these claims is a difficult question that we shall address, but the logic is identical to that of the stockholder theory. Stakes require actions of a certain sort, and conflicting stakes require methods of resolution . . . "[7]

Johnson & Johnson's credo is an attempt to specify with some degree of precision the "exact nature of these claims." Thus, for example, the document states that the corporation has responsibilities (1) to produce "high quality" products, (2) to insure suppliers "make a fair profit," (3) to create an environment where employees "have a sense of security in their jobs," (4) to protect the environment, and (5) to earn a "sound profit" or a "fair return."

What is Johnson & Johnson? It is not just the shareholders (or "owners"), it is not just the managers, and it is not just employees. Ultimately, Johnson & Johnson is defined by the special relationships (including both relationships defined by explicit contracts, for example, shareholders and managers, and those defined by implicit contracts, such as managers and local communities) among the di-

[6] Ibid., p. 66.

[7] Evan and Freeman, p. 149.

verse groups which participate in and are affected by the activities of the corporation.

B. Stakeholder Theory as Instrumental

The purpose of stakeholder theory is not merely to describe the environment impartially. The theory also suggests that firms which carefully follow the advice of stakeholder strategists will outperform (in terms of financial measures) other firms which are managed under more traditional views. Stakeholder theory

> establishes a framework for examining the connections, if any, between the practice of stakeholder management and the achievement of various corporate performance goals. The principal focus of interest here has been the proposition that corporations practicing stakeholder management will, other things being equal, be relatively successful in conventional performance terms (profitability, stability, growth, etc.).[8]

The Johnson & Johnson credo also captures this second aspect of the theory. The very last line explicitly links "principles" to profits. "When we operate according to these principles, the stockholders should realize a fair return." There now exists a sizeable literature on this specific question that supports the hypothesis of a positive association between perceived corporate social responsibility and financial performance.[9] This aspect of the theory lends strong credence to the often-heard cliché that good ethics is good business.

No doubt, this cliché is almost always true. However, it should be emphasized that the ultimate justification for stakeholder theory is not dependent on the promise of a "fair return" to shareholders. Rather, a "fair return" is the happy outcome of following the "principles" of stakeholder theory. The principles, themselves, however, need independent justification. This leads us to the third, and most important, purpose of stakeholder theory.

---

[8]Donaldson and Preston, pp. 66–67.

[9]Moses L. Pava and Joshua Krausz, *Corporate Responsibilities and Financial Performance: The Paradox of Social Cost* (Westport, CT: Quorum Books, 1995).

C. Stakeholder Theory as Normative

After describing stakeholder theory as both descriptive and instrumental, Donaldson and Preston conclude that

> the fundamental basis [of stakeholder theory] is *normative* and involves acceptance of the following ideas:
>
> (a) Stakeholders are persons or groups with legitimate interests in procedural and/or substantive aspects of corporate activity. Stakeholders are identified by *their* interests in the corporation, whether the corporation has any corresponding functional interest in *them*.
>
> (b) The interests of all stakeholders are of *intrinsic value*. That is, each group of stakeholders merits consideration for its own sake and not merely because of its ability to further the interests of some other group, such as the shareowners.[10]

In other words, stakeholder theory not only describes the corporation as it exists, but provides guidelines as to what the corporation potentially could and *should* be. "The theory is used to interpret the function of the corporation . . . "[11]

Unlike the instrumental aspect of the theory, rules are prescribed not because they necessarily enhance financial performance, but because the rules are inherently "right." "The normative approach, in contrast, is not hypothetical but categorical; it says, in effect. 'Do (Don't Do) this because it is the right (wrong) thing to do.'"[12] Johnson & Johnson's credo and its explicit use of such terms as "just" and "ethical" clearly and unambiguously invokes a normative stance. Its professed responsibilities to suppliers to earn a "fair profit," to employees to help them fulfill their "family responsibilities," and to local communities to support charities, will often require justification beyond increased profits to shareholders.

---

[10]Donaldson and Preston, p. 67. Italic text added for emphasis.

[11]Ibid., p. 71.

[12]Ibid., p. 72.

II. WHAT THE STAKEHOLDER THEORY OF THE FIRM IS NOT: THE AUSTERE THEORY

It is this last aspect of stakeholder theory, its normative aspirations, that make the theory important, controversial, and interesting. To more fully understand stakeholder theory, it is necessary to compare it to its main competitor, or to what Clarence Walton terms the "austere" theory of the firm.[13]

Milton Friedman is most closely associated with this more traditional view of the corporation. His position can be summarized as follows: Business managers have a responsibility to stockholders—the owners of the corporation—to maximize firm value. Managers, acting as agents of the stockholders, have no mandate to embark on socially responsible projects that do not enhance the income generating ability of the firm. In addition, managers should not refrain from profitable investments which satisfy all legal constraints but do not conform to managers' own personal social agendas. Rather, as Friedman put it, "The social responsibility of business is to increase profits." He further emphasized, "Few trends would so thoroughly undermine the very foundations of our free society as the acceptance by corporate officials of a social responsibility other than to make as much money for their stockholders as they possibly can. This is a fundamentally subversive doctrine."[14]

Friedman's primary assumption, which leads to his conclusion that social responsibility is a "subversive doctrine," is his belief that the term *social responsibility* as applied to the corporate context, if it means anything at all, implies that the business manager "must act in some way that is not in the interest of his employers."[15] Thus managers who act out of a sense of social responsibility are engaging in a form of taxation without representation. Further, Friedman believes that business managers have no comparative advantage when it comes to implement-

[13]Clarence C. Walton, *Corporate Social Responsibilities* (Belmont, CA: Wadsworth Publishing Co., 1967).

[14]Milton Friedman, *Capitalism and Freedom* (Chicago: The University of Chicago Press, 1962), p. 133.

[15]Milton Friedman, "A Friedman Doctrine—The Social Responsibility of Business Is to Increase Its Profits," *New York Times Magazine* (September 30, 1970): 33.

ing social programs. Managers are experts in producing products, selling them, or financing them. Management has no necessary expertise in fighting social ills.

His voice, although the loudest, clearest, and least apologetic, is by no means solitary. Numerous economists, accountants, sociologists, corporate executives, and social critics either explicitly or implicitly accept a similar view of the corporation. Theodore Levitt, for example, articulates the following vision:

> The trouble (with our society today) is that all major functional groups—business, labor, agriculture, and government—are trying piously to out-do the other in intruding themselves in what should be our private lives . . . Welfare and society are not the corporation's business; its business is money-making and this is their sweet music. The same goes for unions. Their business is bread-and-butter and job rights. In a free enterprise system, welfare is supposed to be automatic; and where it is not, it becomes the government's job. . . .
>
> The only political function of business, labor, and agriculture is to fight each other so that none becomes or remains dominant for long.[16]

According to Clarence Walton, himself a critic of the theory, the traditional view is predicated on the following four factors:

> (a) large numbers of owners who are willing to commit their resources in risk-taking ventures for profit; (b) competitive markets for all products; (c) ability to substitute one resource for another when the competitively set cost–price equation makes another form of resource combination more profitable; (d) acceptance by all of the owners of the principle of self-interest as the motivating force in all economic activity.[17]

Each of the four elements that justify the traditional view has been subject to severe scrutiny. For example, the assumption of perfectly competitive markets, which ignores the existence of externalities (e.g., pollution), is controversial and now difficult to assert fully. Nevertheless, the single most important element of the austere theory for the present purposes is Walton's fourth factor. Walton suggests that the

[16]Theodore Levitt, "The Dangers of Social Responsibility," *Harvard Business Review* (September–October 1958): 41–50.

[17]Walton, p. 128.

austere theory ultimately rests upon one particular view of human decision making. James March has recently described this view of human decision making as the "rational" model.[18]

In his comprehensive coverage of the topic, he suggests that standard theories of choice in economic thought always assume decision processes are both *consequential* and *preference-based.* Actions, taken today, are dependent on the anticipated consequences of those actions. Decision processes are preference based in the sense that anticipated consequences are always valued exclusively in terms of personal preferences. Alternative actions are judged in terms of the extent to which their expected future consequences are perceived to serve the preferences of the decision maker.

March efficiently summarizes his discussion of the rational model as follows:

> A rational procedure is one that pursues a logic of consequence. It makes a choice conditional on the answers to four basic questions:
>
> 1. The question of *alternatives*: What actions are possible?
> 2. The question of *expectations*: What future consequences might follow from each alternative? How likely is each possible consequence, assuming that alternative is chosen?
> 3. The question of *preferences*: How valuable (to the decision maker) are the consequences associated with each of the alternatives?
> 4. The question of the *decision rule*: How is a choice to be made among the alternatives in terms of the values of the consequences?[19]

Walton's linking of the austere theory of the firm with the rational model of decision making is worth consideration, especially from the perspective of a religiously grounded business ethics. He is not alone in his suggestion that the rational model provides one of the necessary foundations for the austere theory. For example, Christopher Stone, another important critic of the austere theory, similarly notes:

---

[18]James March with the assistance of Chip Heath, *A Primer on Decision Making: How Decisions Happen* (New York: Free Press, 1994).

[19]Ibid., pp. 2–3.

> Underlying the polestar argument are a number of assumptions—some express and some implied. There is, I suspect, an implicit positivism among its supporters—a feeling (whether its proponents own up to it or not) that moral judgments are peculiar, arbitrary, or vague—perhaps even "meaningless" in the philosophic sense of not being amenable to rational discussion. To those who take this position, profits (or sales, or price–earnings ratios) at least provide some solid, tangible standard by which participants in the organization can measure their successes and failures, with some efficiency, in the narrow sense, resulting for the entire group . . . [20]

Supporters of the austere theory are often just as likely to make the connection. In spite of Friedman's use of the term "ethical custom,"[21] I believe one is still justified in entertaining a lingering doubt as to whether he is using the term in its traditional sense. Friedman's rhetorical question: "If businessmen do have social responsibility other than maximizing profits for stockholders, how are they to know what it is?"[22] would seem to suggest that the only available model of decision-making is the rational model, which puts personal preferences at the center. The implied assumption being that personal preferences are clear, consistent, and real, while social responsibilities are vague, ill-defined, and therefore, less than real. Further, his more recent defense of "enlightened" self-interest also seems to support Walton's view. For example, in his book (co-authored with Rose Friedman) the authors further elaborated:

> Narrow preoccupation with the economic market has led to a narrow interpretation of self-interest as myopic selfishness, as exclusive concern with immediate material rewards. Economics has been berated for allegedly drawing far-reaching conclusions from a wholly unrealistic "economic man" who is

---

[20]Christopher Stone, "Where the Law Ends: The Social Control of Corporate Behavior," in *Business Ethics*, ed. W. Michael Hoffman and Robert E. Frederick (New York: McGraw-Hill, 1995), p. 145.

[21]Friedman has written that the responsibility of management is to conduct the business in accordance with the desires of stockholders, "which generally will be to make as much money as possible *while conforming to the basic rules of the society, both those embodied in law and those embodied in ethical custom*" (Friedman 1970, p. 33, emphasis added).

[22]Walton, p. 133.

> little more than a calculating machine, responding only to monetary stimuli. That is a great mistake. Self-interest is not myopic selfishness. It is whatever it is that interests the participants, whatever they value, whatever goals they pursue.[23]

While the notion of enlightened self-interest provides a helpful clarification of Friedman's view, enlightened self-interest, which continues to insist that personal preferences serve as the sole criterion for decision-making, is still best understood as an example of the rational model.

Even if Friedman himself is somewhat less than pellucid on this critical issue, more recent advocates of the austere theory are crystal clear. Jensen and Meckling are nothing if not "pure" rationalists. With no detectable irony whatsoever, Jensen and Meckling unveil a "set of characteristics that captures the essence of human nature, but no more."[24] They label their model of human behavior *REMM*: the Resourceful, Evaluative, Maximizing Model. The process of discovering this model is described by the authors as follows: "REMM is the product of over 200 years of research and debate in economics, the other social sciences, and philosophy. As a result, REMM is now defined in very precise terms . . . "[25] Included among the so-called scientific discoveries is the following "postulate":

> REMM is always willing to make trade-offs and substitutions. Each individual is always willing to give up some sufficiently small amount of any particular good (oranges, water, air, housing, honesty, or safety) for some sufficiently large quantity of other goods. Furthermore, valuation is relative in the sense that the value of a unit of any particular good decreases as the individual enjoys more of it relative to other goods . . . [26]

The most important implication of REMM for our purposes is the following:

---

[23]Milton Friedman and Rose Friedman, *Free to Choose* (New York: Avon Books, 1980), p. 18.

[24]Michael C. Jensen and William H. Meckling, "The Nature of Man," *Journal of Applied Corporate Finance* 7(2) (1994): 4.

[25]Ibid., p. 5.

[26]Ibid., p. 5.

> Like it or not, individuals are willing to sacrifice a little of almost anything we care to name, even reputation or morality, for a sufficiently large quantity of other desired things, and these things do not have to be money or even material goods . . . [27]

It thus follows that referring to human needs—or one might add, responsibilities—is simply semantic trickery. Therefore, the authors are able to conclude that there really are no housing, education, food, or energy needs. Rather needs should be exposed for what they are—human desires. Further, given this discovery, it can be shown (and the authors do show) that employees' values and beliefs can easily be manipulated by changing the corporate reward structure. If certain attitudes, values, and customs are rewarded in the workplace, employees will come to accept them as their own.

If the critics (Walton and Stone) and the friends (Friedman, Jensen, and Meckling) of the austere theory are correct, we can now identify a fundamental distinction between the stakeholder and austere theories. While the austere theory is linked to the rational model of decision-making, the stakeholder theory necessarily entails an alternative model of human decision making for support. March calls this alternative the model of appropriateness.

III. AN ALTERNATIVE VISION: THE LOGIC OF APPROPRIATENESS

According to March, the logic of appropriateness, like the rational model, can be summarized by a set of questions:

Decision makers are imagined to ask (explicitly or implicitly) three questions:

> 1. The question of *recognition*: What kind of situation is this?
> 2. The question of *identity*. What kind of a person am I? Or what kind of organization is this?
> 3. The question of *rules*: What does a person such as I, or an organization such as this, do in a situation such as this?[28] (emphasis added)

---

[27]Ibid., p. 7.

[28]March, p. 58.

The essence of the logic of appropriateness is the notion that decision making is ultimately not only about promoting one's immediate self-interest, but is better envisaged as understanding, interpreting, and accepting ethical principles or rules of behavior. This perspective asserts that it is meaningful to talk about behavior as if behavior is meaningful (independent of personal preferences). As March himself makes explicit, "Decision makers can violate a logic of consequence and be considered stupid or naive, but if they violate the moral obligations of identity, they will be considered lacking in elementary virtue."[29]

To be sure, a logic of appropriateness recognizes that some behavior is dictated by individual self-interest, but the domain where self-interest commands jurisdiction is ultimately bounded by rules of appropriateness. According to the model of appropriateness, principles trump self-interest. The Johnson & Johnson credo, and stakeholder theory more generally, must necessarily be grounded in this alternative vision of human decision-making. For example, advocates of the rational model have no vocabulary by which to explain Johnson & Johnson's use of terms such as "responsibility," "fairness," and human "dignity," other than explaining them as a cynical attempt by management to manipulate and fool its constituencies for its own personal gain. To understand these terms as an honest attempt to communicate corporate and management "ideals" one must abandon the rational model as the single model of human decision-making in favor of something like the logic of appropriateness. In fact, the Johnson & Johnson credo reads as if it is a literal attempt to answer March's last two questions concerning identity and rules.

---

[29]Ibid., p. 65. Amartya Sen's *On Ethics and Economics* (New York: Basic Blackwell, 1987) makes a similar point as follows: "There is an essential and irreducible 'duality' in the conception of a person in ethical calculation. We can see the person, in terms of agency, recognizing and respecting his or her ability to form goals, commitments, values, etc., and we can also see the person in terms of well-being, which too calls for attention. This dichotomy is lost in a model of exclusively self-interested motivation, in which a person's agency must be entirely geared to his own well-being" (p. 41).

With respect to stakeholder theorists, Evan and Freeman and Bowie have attempted to justify the theory in terms closest to the model of appropriateness. For example, Evan and Freeman write, "stakeholder theory must be consistent with the following two principles. The corporation and its managers may not violate the legitimate rights of others to determine their own future. The corporation and its managers are responsible for the effects of their actions on others."[30]

The stakeholder theory thus asserts the existence of "legitimate rights" as axiomatic. Bowie is even more explicit in his rejection of the rational model and an acceptance of "the moral point of view." He writes

> The main difference between the classic economic point of view and the moral point of view lay in the assumption by most economists that people behave egoistically while the business ethicists insists that people can—at least on occasion—behave non-egoistically. The economist accepts human preferences and the choices made on the basis of them (revealed preference theory) while the business ethicist serves to judge human preferences and the choices made on the basis of them.[31]

Stakeholder theory makes sense, according to Bowie, only to the extent that the model of appropriateness has validity. Again in his words, "a Friedmanite will respect the needs and rights of other stakeholders to increase profits for the stockholders. But for a genuine stakeholder theorist, the needs and rights of the various stakeholders take priority. Management acts in response to those needs: profits are often the happy result."[32]

It thus seems that among the most important distinctions between the stakeholder and austere theories are the very different models of decision-making that ultimately justify the two theories. The austere

---

[30]Evan and Freeman, p. 149.

[31]Norman E. Bowie, "Challenging the Egoistic Paradigm," *Business Ethics Quarterly* 1(1) (1991(b)): 3.

[32]Norman E. Bowie, "New Directions in Corporate Social Responsibility," in *Business Ethics*, ed. W. Michael Hoffman and Robert E. Frederick (New York: McGraw-Hill, 1995), p. 601.

theory is inextricably linked to the rational model, while the stakeholder theory is justified through the model of appropriateness. If this is true, a fundamental question for a Jewish business ethics emerges. Can we can critically distinguish between the rational model and the model of appropriateness? Is one model somehow "more correct" than the other? An answer to this question would provide an important key in distinguishing between the stakeholder and austere theories of the firm.

March suggests that the question of which view of decision making is ultimately primary and which is derivative is an empirical one. If so, he is correct in finally maintaining an agnostic position on this important question. However, for a business ethics grounded in traditional Jewish sources the question is more appropriately thought of not as an empirical one, but as a question of faith. The thesis of this paper is that from a religious perspective, particularly a perspective founded on Jewish sources, the model of appropriateness *must* subsume the rational model. One way of restating this point is as follows: from a Jewish perspective, decision makers not only can choose from among a complete set of known acts, but decision makers can choose between alternative modes of decision making. Psychologists describe this latter ability as "framing of decisions."[33] If so, the religious perspective is consistent with the stakeholder theory, and must necessarily reject the austere theory.

IV. A JEWISH PERSPECTIVE ON STAKEHOLDER THEORY

True proponents of self-interest believe that ultimately the model of appropriateness can be folded back into the rational model. The view does not deny ethics outright, but suggests that, ultimately, self-interest explains the existence of ethical principles. According to this view, self-interest is the independent variable, and ethics is the dependent variable. In this sense, the rational model subsumes the model

[33] Amos Tversky and Daniel Kahneman, "The Framing of Decisions and the Psychology of Choice," *Science* 211 (January 1981): 453–458.

of appropriateness. It is readily acknowledged that ethics (and even a religiously grounded ethics) promote material benefits. The following observation is not unusual: "Truth, trust, acceptance, restraint, obligation—these are among the social virtues grounded in religious belief which are also now seen to play a central role in the functioning of an individualistic, contractual economy."[34]

It can even be admitted that the maximum material benefits only accrue to those who internalize the logic of appropriateness. Even so, advocates of this position continue to insist that it makes sense to speak of ethics as being motivated by a pure self-interest. This view has been given its clearest modern articulation by the economist George Akerlof.

Akerlof imagines a world where employers will pay honest employees more than dishonest employees. Honest employees are not expected to embezzle, and therefore employers can afford to pay them a higher salary. In such a world, parents will choose to make their children honest if, and only if, the cost of doing so is sufficiently small. In such a way, parents ensure the economic well-being of their offspring. "According to the model here, it pays persons to bond themselves by acquiring traits that cause them to appear honest. And the cheapest way to acquire such traits according to our model is, in fact, to be honest!"[35]

In Akerlof's world, it makes sense to think of human beings as choosing values solely for the purpose of promoting long-run material interests. In his words:

> Most persons attempt to choose values for their children (and perhaps also for themselves) according to their economic opportunities that allow them to get along economically . . . not only the wealthy . . . but also the poorest of the poor—immigrants, sharecroppers, and mountaineers—consciously teach their children values aimed at leading them best to survive economically.[36]

---

[34]Fred Hirsch, *Social Limits to Growth* (Cambridge, MA: Harvard University Press, 1976), p. 141.

[35]George A. Akerlof, "Loyalty Filters," *American Economic Review* 73(1) (1983): 56.

[36]Ibid., p. 54.

Akerlof's view is not only that ethical principles are *consistent* with the promotion of material well-being, but that the acceptance of ethical principles is always *motivated* by self-interest. The model suggests that individual decision-makers choose to purchase "ethics" as a result of exactly the same process which explains why consumers choose to buy, say, potatoes for tonight's dinner. Ethics is just one more commodity.

In Akerlof's view it is possible that honesty becomes a goal to pursue for its own sake, but he is careful to note that such behavior is dysfunctional.

> In my model of childrearing, honesty may begin as a means for economic betterment, but then there is a displacement of goals so that the person so trained will refrain from embezzlement where there is no penalty. Psychological experiments with animals show similarly that animals may quite easily be trained to have dysfunctional behavior.[37]

Akerlof implicitly suggests that if parents could teach their children to feign honesty at a low cost, rational parents would choose to do so.

It is precisely here that religiously grounded views contrast sharply with the self-interest model. From a religious perspective, in the final analysis, ethics (although consistent with the rational model) cannot be fully explained through the rational model. Although choosing to live an ethical life often promotes material interests, the reason for choosing ethics is not self-interest. Rather the choice is ultimately made in attempt to understand life as meaningful beyond the satisfaction of material comforts. In answering March's questions, "What kind of a person am I?" and "What does a person such as I . . . do in a situation such as this?"[38] one must find a place for one's own preferences, but one must also be able to critique and alter those very same preferences. It is beyond dispute that, from the Jewish perspective, the acceptance of ethical principles by the individual or community is ideally not motivated through the calculus of material self-interest. Abraham Joshua Heschel dramatically makes this point as follows:

[37]Ibid., p. 57.

[38]Ibid., p. 58.

> The most precious thing that has ever been on earth were the Two Tablets of stone which Moses received upon Mount Sinai; they were priceless beyond compare. He had gone up into the Mount to receive them; there he abode forty days and forty nights; he did neither eat bread nor drink water. And the Lord delivered unto him the Two Tablets of stone, and on them were written the Ten Commandments, the words which the Lord spoke with the people of Israel in the Mount out of the midst of fire. But when coming down the Mount at the end of forty days and forty nights—the Two Tablets in his hands—Moses saw the people dance around the Golden Calf, he cast the Tablets out of his hands and broke them before their eyes.[39]

Even the most "precious thing" in the world, according to Heschel's view, the tablets of stone containing God's own writing, are ephemeral. The law itself takes precedence. Religious views begin with the model of appropriateness as axiomatic, and it is rationality which is derivative.

An important and fundamental articulation of this view is the following rabbinic *midrash* where, before God gives the Torah to Israel, He approaches every tribe and nation:

> He appeared to the children of Esau the wicked and said to them: Will you accept the Torah? They said to Him: What is written in it? He said to them: "Thou shalt not murder." They said to Him: The very heritage which our father left us was: "And by thy sword shalt thou live." He then appeared to the children of Amon and Moab. He said to them: Will you accept the Torah? They said to Him: What is written in it? He said to them: "Thou shalt not commit adultery." They, however, said to Him that they were all of them children of adulterers, as it is said: "Thus were both the daughters of Lot with child by their father." Then He appeared to the chilren of Ishmael. He said to them: Will you accept the Torah? They said to Him: What is written in it? He said to them: "Thou shalt not steal." They said to Him: The very blessing that had been pronounced upon our father was: "And he shall be as a wild ass of a man: his hand shall be upon everything." . . . But when He came to the Israelites and: "At His right hand was a fiery law unto them," they all opened their mouths and said: "All that the Lord hath spoken will we do and obey (*na-aseh ve-nishma*)."[40]

---

[39]Abraham Joshua Heschel, *The Sabbath: Its Meaning for Modern Man* (New York: Farrar, 1951), p. 96.

[40]*Mekilta de-Rabbi Ishmael* (Philadelphia: The Jewish Publication Society of America, 1961), pp. 234–235.

In this rabbinic embellishment, the rabbis expand on the strange phrasing at Exodus 24:7. This biblical verse, on which the *midrash* is based, quotes the children of Israel at the foot of Mount Sinai. As the entire nation enters into and accepts the Divine covenant, the people promise to God—"*na-aseh ve-nishma*"—which literally translated means we will do and we will hear. The priority of *doing* the commandments over *hearing* the commandments deeply puzzled the rabbis and required explanation. Logically, of course, one must hear the commandments before one can do them. In the above quoted *midrash* the seemingly strange and impossible promise of the children of Israel is imaginatively compared to other hypothetical answers to God's invitation. The common feature to each of the other responses is the insistence on viewing the decision to accept the covenant as an opportunity to promote self-interest. The other nations are given the specific content of a commandment and respond to God that the distinctive content of the commandment is inconsistent with their own preconceived preferences and identity. The children of Israel, by contrast, at the crucial moment of the founding of the nation, recognize that their identity from that point on is defined through their acceptance of the Divine commandments. According to the rabbinic imagination, it would make no sense whatsoever for the Israelites to ask about and evaluate the specific contents of the Divine revelation before their acceptance. The general promise of the existence of the 613 commandments is sufficient. In this *midrash*, the rabbis recognized that the search for meaning as exemplified in faith (*na-aseh*) must come before its actual discovery (*nishma*). Returning to the language of this paper, we can restate this observation as follows: from a religious perspective the logic of appropriateness must subsume the logic of self-interest. We can summarize this discussion by simply noting that economists are correct to point out that it would often pay to purchase a conscience. But what they have failed to notice is the obvious fact that consciences are not for sale.

A Jewish business ethics is therefore inconsistent with the traditional theory of the firm. As argued above, even advocates of the austere model ultimately justify it by invoking the rational model of decision-making. The stakeholder theory, by contrast, is justified through an alternative vision of human decision-making, a vision consistent with a religious worldview. Hence, two cheers for stakeholder theory.

WHY WITHHOLD THE THIRD CHEER?

In spite of the fact that Jewish sources are more consistent with the stakeholder than the austere view, the endorsement here is only partial. In part, some of the traditional opposition to stakeholder theory has grown out of a healthy and intuitive fear of a perceived risk inherent in the stakeholder approach. The fear is that as the list of stakeholders continually grows to include groups more and more tangential to the core economic mission of the corporation, the entire notion of moral responsibility becomes blurred. There is clearly a kernel of truth to Andrew Singer's question, "Can a Company Be Too Ethical?"[41] If managers have a direct responsibility to everyone and everything (animals and even the inanimate earth), then the notion of responsibility becomes so diluted that in essence the corporation retains responsibilities to no one. Corporations become like the humanitarian who proclaims a love to all men and women, but in reality is incapable of loving particular men and women. In the present context, if the corporation has responsibilities to everyone, one wonders, do they really have responsibilities to anyone? One is left with the ironic result that a theory that began its life as an "ethical" theory develops into a purely "relativistic" theory. I think this fear is implicit, for example, in Levine's rejection of corporate philanthropy on halakhic grounds,[42] and is more explicit in Goodpaster's[43] critique of stakeholder theory.

The fear has proven well-warranted. Freeman, who is usually acknowledged as a leading spokesperson for stakeholder theory, now writes:

> Seeing the stakeholder idea as replacing some shopworn metaphors of business with new ones—such as stakeholders for stockholders, humans as moral beings

[41]Andrew Singer, "Can A Company Be Too Ethical?" in *Business Ethics*, ed. W. Michael Hoffman and Robert E. Frederick (New York: McGraw-Hill, 1995), pp. 590–597.

[42]Aaron Levine, "Aspects of Ideology of Capitalism and Judaism," presented at 1994 Orthodox Forum, New York.

[43]Kenneth E. Goodpaster, "Business Ethics and Stakeholder Analysis," *Business Ethics Quarterly* 1(1) (1991): 53–74, and "In Defense of a Paradox," *Business Ethics Quarterly* 4(4) (1994): 423–429.

> for humans as economic beings, and the Doctrine of Fair Contracts for the current panoply of corporate chartering laws—is to give up the role of finding some moral bedrock for business. Finding such bedrock . . . is especially fruitless on pragmatist grounds for there are no foundations for either business or ethics. All we have is our own history, culture, institutions, and our imaginations. For the pragmatist it is "just us" rather than "justice" or "justification" in any sense of foundational bedrock. The cash value of our metaphors and narratives just is how they enable us to live, and the proof is in the living.[44]

Stakeholder theory that began as an attempt to understand corporate behavior in terms of accepted moral principles is now to be judged solely by "the cash value of our metaphors" as there "are no foundations for either business or ethics."[45] A theory that originally rejected the rational model as the fundamental model of decision-making is now understood by one of its leading thinkers in terms perilously close to Friedman, Jensen, and Meckling. The thrust of the stakeholder theory, and its appeal from a religious perspective has been, and will continue to be, its insistence that there exist interpretive methods to judge business other than in terms of the "cash value." Freeman's call to invent a new business ethics is rejected outright by religious business ethicists.

In reading Freeman's recent revision of stakeholder theory one is reminded of Michael Walzer's trenchant critique of "invention" as a mode of moral criticism:

> We do not have to discover the moral world because we have always lived there. We do not have to invent it because it has already been invented—though not in accordance with any philosophical method. No design procedure has governed its design, and the result no doubt is disorganized and uncertain. It is also very dense: the moral world has a lived-in quality, like a home occupied by a single family over many generations, with unplanned additions here and there, and all the available space filled with memory-laden objects and artifacts. The whole thing, taken as a whole, lends itself less to abstract modeling than to thick

---

[44]Freeman, p. 418.

[45]See also Andrew C. Wicks, Daniel R. Gilbert, and Edward R. Freeman, "A Feminist Reinterpretation of the Stakeholder Concept," *Business Ethics Quarterly* 4(4) (1994): 475–498.

> description. Moral argument in such a setting is interpretive in character, closely resembling the work of a lawyer or judge who struggles to find meaning in a morass of conflicting laws and precedents.[46]

Discovery and invention are attempts at escape. The only method that corresponds to our experiences as moral agents is the path of interpretation. As a general description, perhaps Walzer's statement is too far-reaching. But, without question, the Jewish ethicist immediately recognizes Walzer's metaphor of the moral world as a "home occupied by a single family over many generations" as his own. Ethical arguments from a Jewish perspective must of necessity have a "lived-in quality" and always make reference to and are based on the "memory-laden objects and artifacts."

Walzer's description of the interpretive mode of moral inquiry is consistent with the customary, text-centered, Jewish approach to ethics. The traditionally schooled Jew is not taught to begin anew, as if he or she is to originate the moral discussion, but is educated about what came before. All of us, in a very real sense, are like the potential convert to Judaism in the following talmudic narrative:

> Our Rabbis taught: A certain heathen once came before Shammai and asked him, "How many *Torot* have you?" "Two," he replied: "the Written Torah and the Oral Torah." "I believe you with respect to the Written, but not with respect to the Oral Torah; make me a proselyte on condition that you teach me the Written Torah [only]." [But] he scolded and repulsed him as a proselyte. When he went before Hillel, he accepted him as a proselyte. On the first day he taught him *alef, bet, gimmel, daled*, the following day he reversed [them] to him. "But yesterday you did not teach them me thus," he protested. "Must you then not rely upon me? Then rely upon me with respect to the Oral [Torah] too."[47]

The potential convert is initially only willing to accept the authority of the written Torah. Although Shammai rejects the request, Hillel embraces the potential convert and begins teaching him the ABCs. Hillel's acceptance of the potential convert is based on his insightful

---

[46]Michael Walzer, *Interpretation and Social Criticism* (Cambridge, MA, and London: Harvard University Press, 1987), p. 20.

[47]*Shabbat* 31a.

realization that acceptance of any written document as authoritative necessarily implies a prior acceptance of an oral tradition of interpretation. Hillel demonstrates this point to the convert by reversing the ABCs on the second day. The alphabet, the very key to the written Torah, is itself part of the oral Torah. The story demonstrates that in order to read the written text one must be part of a continuing tradition of interpretation. Hillel's belief was that the convert's willingness to accept the written Torah implied a willingness to accept the oral tradition, even if the convert himself did not yet realize this.

Interpretation is what makes traditional approaches traditional. This approach, while less radical than invention, is hardly passive. Interpretation is not merely a handing down of traditional institutions and texts from one generation to the next. As R. Joseph Soloveitchik put it, "Halakhic man received the Torah from Sinai not as a simple recipient but as a creator of worlds, as a partner with the Almighty in the act of creation. The power of creative interpretation (*hiddush*) is the very foundation of the received tradition."[48] Interpretation, according to this view, marries intellectual authority to principles of tradition. This union creates a positive tension, but no inherent contradiction.[49]

If Freeman's new stakeholder theory was the last word on this topic, there would be no way (or desire) to integrate the theory with traditional Jewish sources. Kenneth Goodpaster reminds us, however, that the original stakeholder theory, which insists on the model of appropriateness as fundamental, is still alive and well. According to Goodpaster, stakeholder theory "is *not* an expansion of the list of principals, but a gloss on the principal–agent relationship itself. Whatever the structure of the principal–agent relationship, neither principal nor agent can ever claim that an agent has 'moral immunity' from the basic obligations that would apply to any human being toward other members of the community."[50]

---

[48]Joseph Soloveitchik, *Halakhic Man* (Philadelphia: Jewish Publication Society of America, 1983), p. 81.

[49]For additional discussion see Moses L. Pava, *The Foundations of Jewish Business Ethics* (Hoboken, NJ: Ktav, 1997), Chapter 5.

[50]Goodpaster, 1991, p. 68, emphasis added.

Goodpaster's more moderate stance, which underscores the primacy of the principal–agent relationship, reflects a deep concern with the problem of moral relativism which is now fully explicit in Freeman's view. He has recently articulated his position more fully. Consider the following somewhat paradoxical description of stakeholder theory:

> It may appear that management both does and does not have primary (noninstrumental) obligations to stakeholders other than shareholders and the corporation. But this appearance is seen to be misleading when we understand that *nonfiduciary* obligations are owed to some and *fiduciary* obligations to others. . . . Directors and officers must see themselves as both trusted servants of the corporation and its shareholders (a kind of partiality) *and* as members of a wider community also inhabited by the corporation, its shareholders, and many other stockholder groups."[51]

Again, Goodpaster's stakeholder theory reflects the healthy skepticism that a pure "multifiduciary" stakeholder approach tends to lead eventually to moral relativism. Goodpaster concludes, "we believe that the paradox is best left to directors and officers who are experienced enough in both private and public life to understand it—and wise enough to manage it."[52] Thus, in the end, stakeholder theory (or at least one version of the theory) puts corporations in a familiar position. On the one hand, corporate executives possess the freedom to choose appropriate business goals, but, on the other, the freedom entails social and moral responsibilities as traditionally understood. Corporations are distinct entities, but, like individual human beings, the behavior of the corporation is subject to ethical principles.

CONCLUSION

Stakeholder theory strictly speaking is more than a single theory. In its original form, and in its more moderate formulations, it reflects a view of decision-making consistent with the religious worldview. Be-

[51]Goodpaster, 1994, p. 428, emphasis added.
[52]Ibid., p. 429.

fore human beings promote their own preferences, human beings need a framework to critique and alter those preferences. The austere theory of the firm, to the extent that it relies on the rational view of decision making, is at odds with the vast majority of Jewish sources. In the final analysis, it is impossible to believe that business ethics will ultimately be improved by a more intense focus on corporate profits as the austere theory promises. Stakeholder theory, warts and all, continues to inspire hope.

Rabbi Shimon, in the year 130, correctly criticized the Roman Empire. In response to Rabbi Judah's declaration, "How fine are the works of this people! They have made roads and market places, they have built bridges, they have erected bath houses," he boldly retorted, "All that they made they made for themselves."[53] The pursuit of material wealth, when viewed as an end in and of itself, is summarily rejected. Rabbi Shimon and his son, rather than keeping quiet as Rabbi Jose did, went into seclusion for twelve years. They willingly returned to civilization only after they saw an old man running with two myrtles in his hand to greet the *Shabbat*. It was this sight that reminded them that the Roman model was not the only one. Economic activities, if they are pursued properly, can ultimately serve a Higher purpose. "If I am not for myself, who will be for me, but being for myself what am I?"[54]

At last count, at least twenty-nine states have adopted statutes, consistent with the stakeholder theory, that extend the range of permissible concern by boards of directors to a host of nonshareowner constituencies, including employees, creditors, suppliers, customers, and local communities.[55] At the same time, many major United States corporations are adopting goals similar to the goals described in the Johnson & Johnson credo.[56] This evolution in corporate law and management thought suggests an increasing acceptance of the stakeholder view. It deserves at least two cheers from a Jewish perspective.

---

[53]*Shabbat* 33b.

[54]*Avot* 1:14.

[55]E. W. Orts, "Beyond Shareholders: Interpreting Coporate Constituency Statutes," *The George Washington Law Review* 61 (1) (1992): 14–135.

[56]Moses L. Pava and Joshua Krausz, *Corporate Responsibilities and Financial Performance: The Paradox of Social Cost* (Westport, CT: Qurum Books, 1995).

2

Covenantal Morality in Business

Walter S. Wurzburger

In our free market economy, business organizations make a far greater impact upon the general welfare of society than do individuals acting purely as individuals. Against the background of the enormous power wielded by corporations, it is widely debated whether they are morally justified in pursuing only their economic self-interest or whether they should also concern themselves with the effects of their actions upon societal welfare.

In my *Ethics of Responsibility*[1] I have argued for a Jewish Covenantal ethics that makes demands which go beyond strictly halakhic requirements. Proceeding from the principles and guidelines developed there, I shall discuss whether and to what extent a Jewish moral system imposes requirements for social responsibility upon business organizations.

Before addressing this issue, it is important to point out that, from a Jewish point of view, the pursuit of economic self-interest—the linchpin of the capitalistic system—is perfectly legitimate. This does not imply that capitalism is the only halakhically acceptable economic system. No particular economic system, be it feudalism, mercantilism, capitalism, or socialism, can claim a monopoly on Jewish authenticity. The

[1]Wurzburger, Walter S. *Ethics of Responsibility* (Philadelphia: Jewish Publication Society of America, 1994).

history of *halakhah* (Jewish law) abounds with evidence that Jewish civil law has been operative in a variety of economic systems and has adapted itself to numerous changes in the socioeconomic and political order. The principle *hefker beit din hefker*, giving the courts the power to confiscate property, has afforded enormous latitude and discretion to rabbinic authorities in all matters pertaining to the regulation of the economy. It is only when one engages in what Walter Kaufmann branded "theological gerrymandering" that one can provide religious endorsement for any particular economic order. As long as the institutions of a society are just and compassionate, *halakhah* is completely neutral with regard to whatever particular socioeconomic or political systems are adopted.

This by no means implies indifference to the conditions prevailing within the sociopolitical realm. On the contrary, far from advocating the privatization of faith, Judaism mandates the establishment of a moral society. The Torah summons not only the Israelites individually but the people of Israel collectively to constitute "a kingdom of priests and a holy people."[2] This is why *halakhah* addresses not merely individuals but also the community as a distinctive entity. Whitehead's definition of religion as "what man does with his solitariness" is totally inappropriate as a characterization of Judaism with its ideal of *tikkun ha-olam* (social order) and its numerous ordinances aiming at the establishment of a just sociopolitical order. Niebuhr's *Moral Man and Immoral Society* may reflect Christian categories of thought, but the kind of dichotomy advanced there is completely out of tune with the basic communal thrust of Jewish piety.[3]

It also must be emphasized that, for Judaism, enhancement of one's own material well-being represents a positive value, provided that it is attained through activities that represent a worthwhile contribution to societal well-being. According to a talmudic opinion, the mere fact that a professional gambler does not contribute to *yishuv ha-olam* (settlement of the world) disqualifies him from serving as a witness.[4] This ethos stands in sharp contrast with more otherworldly oriented religions, which look

---

[2]Exodus 19:6.

[3]Nieburn, Reinhold, *Moral Man and Immoral Society* (New York: Charles Scribner and Sons, 1932).

[4]B. T. *Sanhedrin* 24b.

askance at the pursuit of affluence or wealth as a manifestation of greed and avarice.

To be sure, Judaism is fully aware of the spiritual hazards of affluence. The Torah points to these dangers when it warns "Jeshurun waxed fat and kicked . . . and forsook God."[5] Moreover, the Talmud contends that "poverty is becoming to Jews."[6] These declarations are not condemnations of the possession of wealth as such, but rather point to the many dangers to our spiritual well-being posed by affluence. Poverty is not an ideal. On the contrary, lest one become impoverished, the rabbis imposed a limit on the percentage of one's resources that one may contribute to charity.[7]

Far from being treated as a spiritual handicap, the possession of wealth is regarded as a genuine blessing and, according to the Talmud, a prerequisite for the attainment of prophecy, which is the highest possible state of spiritual perfection.[8] Hence, the pursuit of one's own material well-being is a desirable objective, provided that it does not degenerate into a one-sided preoccupation at the expense of the pursuit of other worthwhile interests.

In his "Lonely Man of Faith," Rabbi Joseph B. Soloveitchik emphasized the religious importance of human efforts to harness the forces of nature through technology, thereby enhancing the material well-being of society.[9] Moreover, there are explicit commandments such as *tzedakah* (charity) and *gemilut hasadim* (performance of kindness) as well as the general mandate to participate in *yishuv ha-olam* that obligate us to transcend considerations of self-interest and be concerned with the overall welfare of society. It hardly makes sense to exempt business executives from these obligations. Why should a moral requirement for altruistic conduct be imposed upon private individuals, but not upon corporate officials, when their decisions and activities have far greater repercussions for the well-being of society?

---

[5]Deuteronomy 32:16.

[6]B.T. *Hagigah* 9b.

[7]B.T. *Ketubot* 16b.

[8]B.T. *Nedarim* 38a.

[9]Joseph B. Soloveitchik, "The Lonely Man of Faith," *Tradition* 7:2 (Summer 1965).

Not only society suffers when company officials are exempted from all social responsibility in the discharge of their official duties. As I have shown in my *Ethics of Responsibility*,[10] agent-morality is a vital component of Jewish ethics. Considerable emphasis is placed upon the cultivation of desirable traits of character. In the opinion of Maimonides, we acquire virtuous dispositions through the repeated performance of good actions, which eventually generate desirable character traits. Thus the repeated performance of charitable acts will in the long run produce the kind of charitable person for whom giving has become second nature. Conversely, the character development of company officials would suffer if their corporate ethos steered them to focus exclusively upon the bottom line, with utter disdain for altruistic considerations.

Another important factor in favor of corporate social responsibility relates to Judaism's emphasis upon the all-inclusive nature of the demands entailed by the service of God. In the words of Hillel's classic formulation, "Let all your actions be performed for the sake of Heaven."[11] Since business activities are included in this maxim, one cannot claim that "business is business." Hence, company officials, acting in their official capacity, cannot be exempted from ethico-religious responsibilities toward their fellow human beings.

Doctrinaire free-market economists, on the other hand, are unequivocally opposed to the notion of corporate social responsibility. Adhering to the classical position of Adam Smith, they maintain that, in the long run, the pursuit of self-interest is bound to bring about the greatest common good. A good businessman is not a person who conducts his business with the objective of doing good for society but one who succeeds in maximizing the profits of the business. According to Milton Friedman, the intrusion of any other considerations would be counterproductive with respect to social utility, since, allegedly, "The competitive pursuit of profit within the law will in itself direct business to do what is best for society."[12] This being the case, "The social

[10]See especially Chapter V, pp. 67–86.

[11]*Avot* 2:12.

[12]Thomas Mulligan, "A Critique of Friedman's Essay: 'The Social Responsibility of Business Is to Increase Its Profits'," *Journal of Business Ethics* 5 (1986): 265–269.

responsibility of business is to increase its profits."[13] In Friedman's view, while it is desirable that all businesses, even those privately owned, should be conducted exclusively with the objective of profit maximization, there are additional *moral* reasons why corporate officials have no right to pay attention to considerations of social responsibility. Since a corporation belongs to the stockholders, its officers, directors, managers, or employees would be derelict in their duty if, in the discharge of their responsibilities, they allowed themselves to be influenced by any other factors than the bottom line.

Proponents of corporate social responsibility concede that from a strictly legal point of view, corporations are owned by their shareholders. But they insist that, from a moral point of view, they belong not only to stockholders but also to various other stakeholders, which include their employees and the consumers of the corporation's products or services, as well as the community at large. Hence, it is not sufficient for corporations to operate in conformity with legal requirements, but, in addition, they must also respond to the moral obligation of advancing the total welfare of all those affected by their operations.

While it is generally agreed that individuals acting for themselves are subject to both legal and moral constraints, it is a matter of controversy whether or to what extent individuals acting as agents or representatives of business organizations are obligated or even permitted to be concerned with moral considerations of social responsibility. Just as legal ethics demands that a lawyer serve the best interests of his or her client (barring illegal or blatantly immoral conduct) without regard to the overall interests of society, so, it is widely believed, a member of a business firm should act only for the self-interest of the business organization and pay no attention to social consequences. This position, however, runs counter to the view that an autonomous person cannot divest himself or herself of all moral responsibility for his or her actions, especially when they cause harm to others, simply by accepting the role of an agent or a representative of someone else. This, incidentally, is in keeping with the halakhic axiom, *ein shaliach li-devar aveirah* ("There is no deputy for an illegal act"; that is, the responsibility for an illegal act cannot be shifted to the employer).

---

[13]*New York Times*, 1980.

To be sure, corporate structures as such pose a special problem. Whether the legal fiction of a corporation as a legal person is recognized by *halakhah*[14] or whether Jewish law considers a corporation merely as the joint property of its owners is a matter of controversy. In the latter case, it is evident that a corporation cannot enjoy moral immunity. After all, its directors, managers, and employees are natural persons who are agents or representatives not of artificial persons, but other natural persons, who are also subject to moral requirements.

But even if Jewish law considered a corporation as a legal person, one could still argue that a corporation should also be subject to moral requirements, notwithstanding the fact that artificial persons do not possess the characteristics that make natural persons subject to moral requirements. We have previously noted that *halakhah* contains numerous laws governing not individuals but corporate entities such as the *tzibur* (the corporate entity). Were one to contend that only autonomous natural persons can be subject to the moral law, then one might ask how the legal system can assign various rights to corporations, since (with the exception of the advocates of animal rights) it is usually agreed that only autonomous persons can be the recipients or grantors of rights. If corporations can have rights, they should also have duties. Obviously, a corporate entity can exercise its rights only through the agency of natural persons. Similarly, the moral obligations devolving upon a corporation can only be discharged through the agency of natural persons. As Richard T. DeGeorge put it,

> As long as the ends for which corporations are formed are not immoral and as long as the means by which those ends are pursued are not immoral, corporations are not bound by the large range of moral rules that bind natural persons. . . . they are organizations run by human beings, and as such, have a moral status that makes them amenable to moral evaluation, even though they are not moral persons *per se*.[15]

It must be pointed out that there is no support whatsoever for Adam Smith's thesis that the common good is best served when individuals ex-

[14]Hayyim David Regensberg, *Sefer Mishmeret Hayyim* (Philadelphia: Jewish Publication Society of America, 1966), pp. 124–137.

[15]Richard T. DeGeorge, *Business Ethics* (New York: Macmillan, 1986), p. 96.

clusively pursue their own self-interest. There is no evidence for the operation of the invisible hand, which supposedly guarantees that reliance on the profit motive will result in the greatest possible social good. Perhaps in an ideal world the maximization of profit would automatically maximize the public good. But in the real world, this does not hold true. We cannot avoid possible conflict between personal and public interests. This is why Judaism has never endorsed an unadulterated capitalism nor favored a radical laissez faire policy. Professor Levine[16] and Dr. Tamari[17] have adduced ample evidence from halakhic sources that the intervention of governmental agencies with the operation of the free market is absolutely necessary for securing the common good.

There is another reason that the exclusive pursuit of self-interest as advocated by Adam Smith runs counter to the Jewish value system. Numerous classical sources establish direct linkage between personal financial gain and the adoption of altruistic policies. Thus Ecclesiastes recommends, "Cast thy bread upon the waters, for thou shalt find it in many days."[18] According to the Talmud, giving of charity enables one to keep one's wealth. In a similar vein, the Sages admonish "Pay the tithe in order to become rich."[19] While one may interpret such statements merely as claiming that charitable acts will be rewarded by God, Maimonides establishes a direct causal link between the performance of socially beneficial actions and the personal well-being of their agents. In a well-known comment, he observes that, whereas the performance of ritual commandments earns only spiritual rewards in the hereafter, benevolent actions merit both spiritual and material rewards. According to Maimonides, the reason for this difference is that the performance of benevolent actions automatically produces benefits for society at large, which, in turn, will redound to the advantage of the agent.[20] Similarly *Tosafot* considered the giving of charity as one of the commandments that yield this-worldly

---

[16]Aaron Levine, *Free Enterprise and Jewish Law* (New York: Ktav, 1980), pp. 131–160.

[17]Meir Tamari, *With All Your Possessions: Jewish Ethicsand Economic Life* (New York: Free Press, 1987), pp. 83–125, 209–241.

[18]Ecclesiastes 11:1.

[19]B.T. *Shabbat* 119a, B. T. *Taanit* 9a.

[20]Maimonides, *Mishneh Commentary* to *Pe'ah* 1:1.

benefits to those obeying it.[21] It is revealing that Professor Nozick, who on libertarian grounds objects to the expenditure of any taxation revenue for welfare projects, believes that, in the absence of coercion by governmental authorities, the same objectives could be more efficiently attained by individuals who would be persuaded by considerations of self-interest to voluntarily engage in philanthropic pursuits.[22]

Proceeding from this premise, we may reverse Adam Smith's thesis and claim that it is the pursuit of the common good rather than of self-interest that in the long run will maximize our individual welfare. One therefore might plausibly argue against Milton Friedman that prudential considerations of enlightened self-interest warrant the exercise of social corporate responsibility.

Recent empirical studies cited by Professors Pava and Krausz[23] seem to corroborate this thesis. There appears to be some correlation between the profitability and the degree of corporate social responsibility displayed by a business organization. The much publicized and highly commended decision of the proprietors of the Malden Mills to rebuild their factory in Massachusetts after a devastating fire provided a most inspiring illustration of Corporate Social Responsibility. Although for all practical purposes the textile industry has abandoned the Northeast and has relocated in the South and in the Orient, the owners of the company felt responsible for the welfare of their employees and their community and were prepared to forego the short-range economic benefits of relocation. They not only continued to pay the salaries of their employees but resumed operation in the same location. The owners are convinced that in the long run their social responsibility will result in increased profitability for the firm.[24]

To be sure, the statistical data adduced to demonstrate that corporate social responsibility engenders profitability represent far from con-

---

[21]B. T. *Bava Batra* 8b, s.v. *Matan Sekharah*.

[22]Nozick, Robert, *Anarchy, State, and Utopia* (New York: Basic Books, 1974).

[23]Moses L. Pava and Joshua Krausz, "The Association Between Corporate Social Responsibility and Financial Performance: The Paradox of Social Cost," *Journal of Business Ethics* 15 (1996): 2321–357.

[24]Personal communication to the author from Aaron Feuerstein, president of Malden Mills.

vincing evidence. It could be argued that the more successful firms owed their profitability to other factors. Conceivably, their success was achieved not because of but in spite of their practice of corporate social responsibility. Had they not been handicapped by ethical restraints, the bottom line would have been even more impressive.

It is, therefore, highly dubious whether corporate social responsibility can be justified, apart from strictly moral considerations, also on the basis of enlightened self-interest. It is far from certain that good ethics is good business. Contrary to proverbial wisdom, honesty may not be the best policy. As Plato already pointed out, it is not justice but the *appearance* of justice that matters most in the quest for personal success. What is ethically desirable may not conform to prudential requirements. Under contemporary conditions, a sales manager would not go far were he to insist that the sales force refrain from making any kind of unsubstantiated claims for the superiority of the products offered. Similarly, most advertisements are at least guilty of creating artificial wants, if not of outright concealment of relevant information. Candor and truthfulness are completely out of place in the business world, where *caveat emptor* is the guiding principle. As the employees of a large securities firm were told by a company official, "we are not selling truth."[25]

It has been argued that business can be compared to a poker game. One can participate only when one is willing to play by its rules, which involve bluffing. By the same token, some ethicists contend that the rules of the business game stipulate that one does not show one's hand in negotiations. They claim that just as the telling of a white lie constitutes morally acceptable conduct, concealment of one's true intentions in a business negotiation is perfectly proper. Ethical scruples are, therefore, liabilities rather than assets in the business world. Were it really the case that morality goes hand in hand with commercial success, we would not witness as many scandalous infractions of the moral law (not to mention even criminal conduct) as we do in our time.

It therefore seems extremely dubious that one could make a convincing case for corporate social responsibility solely on the grounds of enlightened self-interest. But, as we indicated previously, one could argue that,

---

[25]Robert F. O'Neiland and Darken A. Proust, "Economic Criteria and Ethical Criteria," *Journal of Business Ethics* 13 (1994): 76.

even when self-interest cannot be invoked, there are at least some moral obligations which should bind business organizations. After all, the halakhic system addresses a number of religious imperatives to the *tzibbur* rather than to individuals. Irving Kristol's contention that there is no such thing as social justice, because only autonomous individuals can be just, runs counter to the entire thrust of the Jewish tradition, with its many provisions designed to promote public welfare and a just social order. As Professor Levine has shown, even the religious ideal of *imitatio dei*, which many authorities consider an outright Halakhic imperative, applies not only to individuals but it also has a social dimension which is supposed to guide communal affairs and public life.[26]

This, however, by no means implies that the moral obligations of corporations must be identical with those of individual persons. In *Ethics of Responsibility*, I have advocated a pluralistic ethics, which makes it possible to distinguish between various types of morality, with different requirements for personal and political morality. I pointed out that, while sovereign states are also subject to the moral law, their moral obligations are different from those incumbent upon individuals.

Even Milton Friedman, for all his opposition to corporate social responsibility, demands that corporate conduct conform to the basic rules of society as embodied in the law and in the ethical customs of society. It can be taken for granted that he would frown upon the use of "shark repellents" to prevent unfriendly takeovers, when such methods are employed to protect the interests of management rather than of the shareholders. These strategies may be extremely costly to the owners, who are less interested in the survival of the company than in the best possible return on their investments.

Friedman acknowledges that some ethical restraints, though not legally enforceable, apply to corporate entities. He stipulates that corporations not merely abide by the law but also play by the rules of fair competition and refrain from resorting to deception and fraud. It appears that what he primarily objects to is for business to adopt a "do-good" policy, because, in his view, that is none of its business.

---

[26]Aaron Levine, *Economic Public Policy and Jewish Law* (New York: Ktav, 1993), pp. 14–15.

Although he does not specify what kind of moral restraints are applicable to corporations, it appears that in his opinion they should be subject to at least *some* negative duties and refrain from outright fraud or breaking of promises even when not resulting in legal liability. He would probably also disapprove of such unethical conduct as resorting to bankruptcy to win leverage for a company. It is, however, extremely doubtful whether he would go so far as to mandate that, unless intended to forestall public pressure for governmental regulation, corporations voluntarily compensate injured parties for indirectly caused damage (*gerama* or *dina de-garmi*) when restitution is not legally enforceable but constitutes only a moral obligation (*hayyav be-dinei shamayim*).

As against this minimalist conception of ethical restraints, DeGeorge unequivocally declares that corporations "are bound not to harm others."[27] In his view, mere compliance with the law does not satisfy moral obligations. Justice is a dynamic rather than static concept. As the *Maggid Mishneh* (Vidal Yom Tov of Tolosa, 14th century) pointed out,[28] in the course of time human perceptions about the requirements of justice are bound to change. Hence, a legislative lag between the emergence of beliefs regarding moral propriety and the enactment of laws designed to assure compliance with newly recognized moral requirements is unavoidable. Moreover, there are aspects of moralities of aspiration that unlike the provisions of contractual morality, are not reinforced by legal sanctions.

Paralleling the Kantian distinction between perfect and imperfect duties, DeGeorge draws a sharp line of demarcation between positive and negative duties. Only the latter are unconditionally applicable to corporations. They are enjoined from harmful activities such as polluting the environment, producing defective or unsafe equipment, or from perpetrating other forms of deception or fraud such as misrepresenting the quality of a product or withholding relevant information from a client.

Undoubtedly, a Jewish business ethics would prohibit such activities. Misrepresenting merchandise and misleading advertisements unques-

---

[27]DeGeorge, p.152.

[28]*Maggid Mishneh* ad *Hilkhot Shekhenim*, 14:5.

tionably constitute transgressions of the outright halakhic prohibition against *geneivat da'at* (creating a false impression). *Halakhah* would also forbid lewd advertisements, which are frequently utilized for sales promotion. Similarly, strictly halakhic prohibitions like *lifnei iver* (offering ill-suited advice), *lo ta-sim damim be-veitekha* ("Do not bring blood upon your house," Deuteronomy 22:8) or *lo ta-amod al dam rei'akha* ("Do not stand idly by the blood of your neighbor," Leviticus 19:16) may be invoked to forbid cost-cutting procedures which expose employees to avoidable risks or the sick to unsafe equipment such as flawed dialysis machines (such as those that were responsible for many fatalities). Also, the withholding of superior products (for example, automobiles equipped with better brakes) from the market in order to promote the sale of older, less-safe models could hardly qualify for halakhic approval. For that matter, *halakhah* must object to the industrial practice of built-in obsolescence because it would come under the rubric of the prohibition of *bal ta-shlit* (the prohibition against wasteful destruction). Classical Jewish sources obviously did not deal with a problem of such recent vintage as ecology, a term which until a few years ago was totally unknown. Hence, it may be more difficult to adduce outright halakhic prohibitions against causing environmental damage. As I pointed out in *Ethics of Responsibility*, it should be feasible to extrapolate an environmental ethics from halakhic data. There can be little doubt that it would be proper for Jewish communal authorities to issue outright prohibitions against the most flagrant sources of irreparable environmental damage. During periods when Jewish communities enjoyed autonomy with respect to internal affairs, enactments of *takkanot tzibur* (measures for the public welfare) designed to insure compliance with socially beneficial practices were commonplace.

It would be difficult to claim that the growing of tobacco or the manufacture of tobacco products constitutes a direct technical violation of *lifnei iver*, even if smoking were forbidden by *halakhah*. But a good case can be made that such activities are incompatible with the requirements of Jewish Covenantal morality. One could say that following the precedent of the rabbinic prohibition against the sale of arms to non-Jews, which was enacted to avoid responsibility for bloodshed, one should also refrain from providing products which are injurious to the health of individuals. One may also invoke the formal prohibition against engaging on a regular basis in commercial activities with merchandise that may not be consumed by Jews. Although the production or sale of tobacco or harmful drugs would not be halakhically forbidden, such activities definitely run counter to the spirit of Jewish law.

There is no reason why corporate executives should be bound solely by outright halakhic norms, but not by the imperative of acting *lifnim mi-shurat ha-din* (conducting oneself beyond the strict letter of the law as both claimant and defendant).[29] After all, even Milton Friedman maintains that corporations are subject to some ethical restraints, even if they are not subject to legal sanctions. In view of the overall attitude of Jewish law to at least preventing harm to others, it is evident that Jewish covenantal ethics mandates concern for the requirements of *lifnim mi-shurat ha-din*. According to some halakhic authorities provisions of *li-fnim mi-shurat ha-din* may even be enforceable by a *beit din* (Jewish court).[30]

So far we have limited ourselves to ethical considerations pertaining to the requirements of justice. The halakhic principle *ein shaliah li-devar aveirah* can be invoked when company executives, in pursuit of maximization of profit for their corporation, violate the rights of others by causing them harm directly or indirectly. Under such circumstances they cannot claim moral immunity on the ground that as agents of the shareholders they are duty-bound to concern themselves exclusively with the profitability of their operations. This is not true because we are confronted with a case of conflicting obligations; there is no doubt that here the duty not to harm others overrides the obligation to maximize the profit of the shareholders.

In a similar vein, Jewish ethics cannot condone investments in countries that engage in repressive practices and violate basic human rights. *Halakhah* provides ample precedence for proscribing activities that come within the purview of *me-sayei'a yedei ovrei aveirah* (aiding and abetting transgressors of the law). Business executives are morally obligated to subordinate considerations of profitability to the requirement not to engage in practices that would strengthen the forces of evil.

---

[29]See Moses L. Pava, "The Talmudic Concept of 'Beyond the Letter of the Law,'" *Journal of Business Ethics* 15 (1996): 941–950.

[30]Hayyim Hizkiyahu Medini, *Sedei Hemed ha-Shalem* (Benei Barak: Beit ha-Sofer), vol. 4, p. 53.

Positive duties of corporations represent an entirely different story. There is far more room for debate on the extent to which corporate social responsibility should include altruistic policies that cannot be justified on the ground of self-interest (such as public relations benefits). According to DeGeorge, the nature and scope of positive duties "depend on their [the corporations'] ends . . . and the sociopolitical environment in which they are organized and operate."[31]

Among the most obvious candidates for inclusion in the list of a company's positive duties are making available health care for employees and their dependents, day-care centers for their children, and scholarships for members of their families. These practices may even be justified in terms of the enlightened self-interest of the sponsoring corporation, since they inspire greater loyalty to the company and are therefore likely to lead to increased productivity.

Less clear-cut are corporate social responsibilities arising from the relocation of a plant to an economically more attractive site or from making companies "leaner and meaner" through layoffs. Although both the employees and the community in which the company was located lose many benefits as the result of these measures, they are not entitled to compensation on the ground that they suffered harm. We must distinguish between failure to provide benefits and actually causing harm. This being the case, relocation of a company cannot be treated as the violation of a negative duty. Whatever social responsibility will devolve upon a corporation will be in the category of positive duties. But since the loss of jobs amounts to the withdrawal of benefits from stakeholders (i.e., employees and the community affected), it should be taken into consideration as *a* factor in the decision making of the company. Undoubtedly, the economic feasibility of continuing operations in the present location is of paramount importance. But it does not follow that the maximization of profit for stockholders should be the only consideration. A good case could be made that corporate executives should sacrifice some profit of the shareholders in order to accommodate the interest of the rest of the affected stakeholders. Moreover, even if the survival of the corporation depends upon relocation or layoffs, the company has, as Meir Tamari maintains,[32] a moral

---

[31]DeGeorge, *loc. cit.*

[32]Meir Tamari, "Social Responsibility of the Jewish Individual," in *Tikkun Olam: Social Responsibility in Jewish Thought*, edited by David Shatz, Chaim I. Waxman, and Nathan J. Diament (Northvale, NJ: Jason Aronson, 1997).

obligation to retrain dismissed workers in order to enable them to secure other employment.

Far more problematic is the question whether corporate funds should be disbursed for the purpose of subsidizing general education, when such expenditures cannot be justified in terms of gaining good will for the firm. Professor Levine insists this represents the kind of philanthropic activity which, in his opinion, represents a breach of the fiduciary responsibilities of corporate officials.[33] Although we shall later on challenge Professor Levine's position, at this point we shall insist that, even from his position, a distinction should be made between subsidizing a better school system and other purely philanthropic measures. With the advance of technology and automation and the disappearance of the need for most unskilled labor, an educated workforce becomes increasingly necessary for the viability of a company. Moreover, a company cannot function without consumers of its goods or services. Poor education translates itself into lower earnings and a reduced standard of living, resulting in a shrinking market for goods and services. Hence, the self-interest of the corporation is served by raising the educational standards of the community. We would, therefore, be justified in claiming that expenditures for education should be regarded as part of the cost of maintaining the "enabling conditions" which are indispensable to the functioning of corporations.[34]

We still have to deal with the issue of corporate philanthropy. American law recognizes this increasingly widely adopted practice as a legitimate expenditure of corporate funds. There is no doubt that, viewed from an ethical perspective, negative duties must take precedence over positive duties. Thus it would be morally wrong for a company to set aside funds for the support of a museum, while taking advantage of legal technicali-

---

[33]Aaron Levine, "Aspects of the Ideology of Capitalism and Judaism," in *Tikkun Olam: Social Responsibility in Jewish Thought*, edited by David Shatz, Chaim I. Waxman, and Nathan J. Diament (Northvale, NJ: Jason Aronson, 1997). I am delighted to note that in the meanwhile I received a supplement to Professor Levine's original draft (pp. 24–25) in which he indicates that his strictures against corporate philanthropy apply only to "small business organized as a closely held corporation" and that his objections "may not apply to the publicly traded corporation."

[34]James B. Wilbur, *The Moral Foundations of Business Practice* (Lanham, MD: University Press of America, 1992), p. 32.

ties in order to avoid compensation for environmental damage caused by its operations or refusing to take steps to minimize exposure of its employees to avoidable health risks.

When dealing with the positive moral duties of a corporation, we should apply the principle that proximity creates a special set of obligations. Jewish law stipulates that "the poor of your city take precedence over the poor of another city"[35] and that members of one's family come before strangers. In keeping with these guidelines, the needs of the stakeholders should be assigned priority over those of the general public.

This moral consideration reinforces another factor that should influence management or directors in the allocation of corporate funds for philanthropic purposes. A corporation is more likely to reap material rewards from charitable contributions benefitting its stakeholders than from those made to other worthwhile causes. It must be admitted that these considerations tend to be ignored by corporate executives, who, unfortunately, in many cases base decisions concerning philanthropy on considerations of self-interest (e.g., social advancement, peer pressure) rather than concern for the common good.

The fact that the discretion enjoyed by management over disbursement of charitable funds lends itself to abuse does not, however, discredit such practice altogether. It basically amounts to an additional perk granted to company officials. The personal benefits accruing to company officials from corporate giving qualify as *tovat hana'ah* (the benefit of a pleasure, that is, the satisfaction of obligating somebody), which has been legitimately conferred upon them as part of their compensation package. There is no need to throw out the baby with the dirty bathwater. Company officials should not be categorically barred from corporate giving, but should be sensitized to approach this task with a high degree of moral responsibility.

Professor Levine argues that, as a matter of principle, any type of corporate philanthropy is illegitimate, because company officials are not authorized to practice charity at the expense of the shareholders.[36] It appears to me, however, that since corporate philanthropy is a widely adopted practice, it should come under the rubric of *minhag ha-medinah* (the usage or conduct of the country) or *minhag ha-soharim* (the usage or conduct of

[35]B.T. *Bava Metziah* 71a.

[36]Aaron Levine, *loc. cit.*

merchants). For this reason, we can assume the tacit consent of shareholders that management rely upon their own judgment as to the channels for charitable expenditures. If high-ranking company officials are authorized to allocate themselves exorbitant salaries (witness the current pay scales of CEOs) even at a time when shrinking profits dictate dismissals of employees, why should disbursements of funds for charitable purposes be viewed as a violation of fiduciary responsibility?

We shall now turn to another objection which Professor Levine has raised against corporate philanthropy. He contends that it basically amounts to compelling shareholders to give up some of their rightful possessions. Since exerting pressure upon an individual even to sell an article involves the violation of *lo ta-hmod* ("Thou shalt not covet," Exodus 19:14), it is alleged that pressuring stockholders to consent to the allocation of funds to charities is also included in this biblical prohibition. Were Professor Levine's analysis correct, then all professional fund-raising by charitable institutions should also be forbidden, because successful solicitation depends upon a solicitor's ability to overcome by persuasion (or by manipulation) a potential donor's resistance to making a requested contribution. It therefore appears that the objections raised against corporate philanthropy are invalid.[37]

We therefore conclude that Jewish Covenantal ethics with its overall commitment to the practice of *hesed* encourages corporate philanthropy, with the proviso that it does not conflict with the discharge of more pressing duties of social responsibility toward stakeholders.

---

[37]It may be argued that these considerations apply only to large corporations but not to closely held corporations with only a small number of shareholders. I am delighted to note that, in the addendum to the original draft of his paper, Professor Levine explicitly states that his categorical objection to corporate philanthropy does not apply to publicly traded corporations. It is significant that both of us proceeded from different starting points. While he primarily had in mind closely held corporations, the major focus of my paper was publicly traded companies. It therefore seems that what originally appeared to be a major controversy between us, has by now been reduced to a minor difference in emphasis. See also above, footnote 33.

3

The Employee as Corporate Stakeholder: Exploring the Relationship between Jewish Tradition and Contemporary Business Ethics*

David J. Schnall

I. A STAKEHOLDER PRIMER

Neoclassic economic theory posits a simple doctrine regarding the ethics of business organization: those involved in the marketplace have a singular obligation to increase profits. With the advent of the corporation, the introduction of public investment, and the separation of ownership from management, this obligation is transferred to the operating officers of the firm. As agents of those who own stock, they hold a fiduciary responsibility to increase the value of their holdings and maximize profits, with little concern for the broader social consequences of their

*This paper is dedicated to the blessed memory of my beloved parents, Mr. and Mrs. Harry Schnall, A"H.

actions. Accountability is the sole province of corporate principals whose assessments are based in profitability and growth.

This perspective was clearly articulated by Milton Friedman, for whom the suggestion that managers have a broader social responsibility was nothing less than "subversive." The "business of business is business" he argued. Those who advocate a "social conscience" to provide employment, overcome discrimination or avoid pollution "are preaching pure and unadulterated socialism. . . . " he concluded.[1]

Absent the ideological rhetoric, a similar indifference to the broad implications of corporate action was articulated more recently by Robert Allen, then chairman of AT&T. In the wake of the decision to cut some 40,000 jobs, AT&T stock rose by $7 per share, increasing corporate value by approximately $11 billion and Allen's personal stock holdings and options by some $5 million. Responding to suspicious questions, Allen said: "Increasing shareholder value is the right incentive for me to have at AT&T. Is it the right incentive for me to affect 40,000 people? Hell, I don't know . . . Is it fair? Hell, I don't know if it's fair. I don't make the rules."[2]

Notwithstanding, there is ample evidence to suggest that early on, many corporate leaders sensed obligations to constituencies other than shareholders, if only as a modality for increased profit. Preston cites a Depression Era commitment by the General Electric Corporation to satisfying the needs of four major groups: shareholders, employees, customers, and the general public. So too, Robert Johnson, president of Johnson & Johnson in 1947, identified the company's primary clientele as customers, employees, managers, and stockholders, while Robert Wood, CEO of Sears in 1950, argued that profit would best result from satisfy-

[1]Milton Friedman, "The Social Responsibility of Business Is to Increase Its Profits," *New York Times Magazine* (September 13, 1970), pp. 32–33, 123–126, see also Milton Friedman, *Capitalism and Freedom* (Chicago: University of Chicago Press, 1962), J. C. Shepard, *The Law of Fiduciaries* (Toronto: Carswell Company, 1981), and Oscar Williamson, *The Law Of Discretionary Behavior* (London: Kershaw Publishing Company, 1965).

[2]Quoted in Allan Sloan, "For Whom the Bell Tolls," *Newsweek* (January 15, 1996): 37.

ing corporate responsibilities to employees, customers, and society-at-large.[3]

Such anecdotal evidence from captains of industry is confirmed by empirical studies of corporate leadership over the past three decades. Surveys of upper-level managers suggest that large majorities believe it is unethical for corporations to ignore the needs of customers and employees in favor of stockholders. In practice, they tend to identify their role as satisfying a broad clientele, including shareholders.[4]

This tendency, and the moral basis that is its underpinning, was succinctly articulated as "stakeholder theory" by R. Edward Freeman. Building upon earlier work in the area of corporate social responsibility, governance, and performance, Freeman originated a systematic framework for assessing the role of multiple constituencies affected by corporate decisions, whose needs and interests must be accommodated in commercial policy and management strategy.[5] Over the past decade, his frame-

---

[3]Lee E. Preston and H.J. Sapeinza,"Stakeholder Management and Corporate Performance," *Journal of Behavioral Economics* 19(4) (1990): 361–375; J. C. Worthy, *Shaping an American Institution: Robert E. Wood and Sears, Roebuck* (Urbana, IL: University of Illinois, 1984).

[4]See, for example, Richard Baumhart, *An Honest Profit: What Businessmen Say About Ethics in Business* (New York: Holt, Rinehart & Winston), and B. Z. Posner and William H. Schmidt, "Values and the American Manager," *California Management Review* 26(3) (1984): 202–216.

[5]R. Edward Freeman, *Strategic Management: A Stakeholder Approach* (Boston: Pitman, 1984); R. Edward Freeman and D. L. Reed, "Stockholders and Stakeholders: A New Perspective on Corporate Governance," *California Management Review* 25(3) (1983): 88–106; R. Edward Freeman and D. R. Gilbert, "Managing Stakeholder Relationships" in *Business and Society*, ed. S. P. Sethi and C. M. Falbe (Lexington: Lexington Books, 1987); William Evan and R. Edward Freeman, "A Stakeholder Theory of the Modern Corporation: Kantian Economics," in *Ethical Theory and Business*, ed. Tom Beauchamp and Norman Bowie (Englewood Cliffs, NJ: Prentice-Hall, 1988); R. Edward Freeman and William Evan, "Corporate Governance: A Stakeholder Interpretation," *Journal of Behavioral Economics* 19(4) (1990): 337–359; R. Edward Freeman, "The Politics of Stakeholder Theory: Some Future Directions," *Business Ethics Quarterly* 4(4) (1994): 409–421.

work has been elaborated and refined, subjected to deconstructionist analysis and feminist theory, reduced to a series of research propositions, and applied to policy concerns beyond the scope of business and commercial strategy.[6]

In a most fruitful attempt to distinguish stakeholder theory from other strains in the literature linking business, ethics, and society, Donaldson and Preston have identified alternative perspectives for its application: descriptive, instrumental, and normative.[7] In its first formulation, considering multiple constituencies is something managers do from an intuitive sense of fair play. It is encouraged by their legal and social operating context and the faith that such considerations will support their strategic objectives. As such, stakeholder theory becomes a value-free description of managerial reality awaiting empirical confirmation.

At a second level, stakeholder theory is instrumental, that is, a prescriptive for effectively pursuing commercial strategy. Here the essential mission of the corporation remains profitability and increased shareholder value. Attending to the needs of other stakeholders, however, is a quick and efficient means of reaching these goals. It increases sales, it helps to hold down costs, and it reduces liability and the demand for external regulation.

Finally, normative principles sit at the core of stakeholder theory. Concern for the full scope of social interest represented by any and all who are affected by managerial strategy is an ethical and moral requirement

[6]See, for example, Thomas M. Jones, et al., "The Toronto Conference: Reflections on Stakeholder Theory," *Business and Society* 33(1) (1994): 82–131; Bruce Langtry, "Stakeholders and the Moral Responsibility of Business," *Business Ethics Quarterly* 4(4) (1994): 431–443; Andrew Wicks, et al., "A Feminist Reinterpretation of the Stakeholder Concept," *Business Ethics Quarterly* 4(4) (1994): 475–497; Thomas M. Jones, "Instrumental Stakeholder Theory: A Synthesis of Ethics and Economics," *Academy Of Management Review* 20(2) (1995): 404–437; John Altman, "Toward a Stakeholder-Based Policy Process," *Policy Sciences* 27(1) (1994): 37–51; Robert A. Reineke, "Stakeholder Involvement in Evaluation: Suggestions for Practice," *Evaluation Practice* 12(1) (1991): 39–44.

[7]Thomas Donaldson and Lee E. Preston, *Academy of Management Review* 20(1) (1995): 65–91.

regardless of whether it appears reasonable to corporate officers or increases their profit. Managers are fiduciaries and agents, to be sure, but they represent the interests of all upon whom their decisions impact. They should be held accountable to this broad-based set of constituencies or to the public agencies who are their advocates.

Among those who may hold no corporate stock but who are directly affected by managerial policy, employees rank high in any assessment. Osigweh places them within the "internal environment" of commercial activity, alongside managers and shareholders, and closer to the heart of corporate organization than customers and suppliers.[8] Clarkson suggests that employees have many more concerns and are more frequently affected by corporate strategy than any other stakeholder. He counts no fewer than twenty such policy areas that impact upon employees, at least twice as many as any other group. These range from compensation and benefits to unionization and collective action, from dismissal, layoff, and appeal to occupational safety and health.[9] What follows is an exploration of classic Jewish texts and sources regarding the obligations of employers toward their workforce. In the main, it will focus upon normative decision and juridical finding (i.e., *halakhah* and *p'sak*) rather than homily and moral discourse (*aggadah* and *d'rush*). The intent is to consider the general status of employees as "stakeholders" of the firm and the demands of Jewish tradition regarding their rights in selected areas, including the administration of pay and benefits, occupational safety, and collective bargaining. A closing section will place these findings within the context of stakeholder theory. In general theme and method, this essay follows the author's prior attempts to match contemporary organizational theory and behavior with that

[8]C. A. B. Osigweh (1994), "A Stakeholder Perspective of Employee Responsibilities and Rights," *Employee Responsibilities and Rights Journal* 7(4) (1994): 279–296; also C. A. B. Osigweh, "Toward an Employee Rights and Responsibilities Paradigm," *Human Relations* 43(12) (1991): 1277–1309 and C. A. B. Osigweh, "Elements of an Employee Rights and Responsibilities Paradigm," *Journal of Management* 16(4) (1990): 835–850.

[9]Max Clarkson, "A Stakeholder Framework for Analyzing and Evaluating Corporate Social Performance," *Academy Of Management Review* 20(1) (1995): 92–117.

which emerges from normative Jewish sources, especially in the context of employee relations.[10]

II. LABOR AND EMPLOYMENT IN CLASSIC JEWISH THOUGHT

Classic Jewish orientations regarding responsibility toward employees derive from several sources: the status of work and the worker, the employment relationship, analogous legislation, especially that which regulates indentured servitude, and the presence of *minhag*, here defined as accepted business practice. What follows is a brief overview of these various elements.[11]

As is well-known, labor is introduced to Adam in Scripture (Genesis 3:17–19) as a scourge and punishment. For his iniquity and disobedience, the land would be cursed before man, who would earn his bread only "by the sweat of [his] brow." While not ignoring the plain sense of the text,

---

[10]Also add David J. Schnall, "Baigley Umanut: Organized Labor and the Jewish Tradition," in Yaakov Elman and Jeffrey S. Gurock (eds.), *Hazon Nahum: Studies in Jewish Law, Thought and History Presented to Dr. Norman Lamm on the Occastion of his Seventieth Birthday* (New York: Yeshiva University Press, 1997), pp. 627–642. See for example, David J. Schnall, "An Alternative Source for Contemporary Public Administration: Classic Jewish Attitudes toward Municipal Employment," *Administration and Society* 29(1) 1997:3–17; David J. Schnall, "Faithfully Occupied with the Public Need," *Journal of Jewish Communal Service* 71(4) (1995): 315–324; David J. Schnall, "By the Light of the Moon: Interfacing *Halakhah* and Employee Relations," *Torah U-Maddah Journal* 4 (1993):175–186; David J. Schnall, "Exploratory Notes on Employee Productivity and Accountability in Classic Jewish Sources," *Journal of Business Ethics* 12(6) (1993):485–491.

[11]Normative Jewish texts recognize two categories of workers: *kablanim*, roughly equivalent to independent contractors, and *po'alim*, analogous to full-time employees. Important legal principles are derived from the distinction, as in R. Jacob b. Asher (Germany, 1270–1343), *Tur, Hoshen Mishpat* 333:2. By contrast, some of the literature cited here makes no such distinctions. It should be understood, therefore, that the focus of this exploration is upon the *po'el* as the closest analogy to the corporate employee considered in stakeholder theory.

classic commentaries chose not to transfer its meaning to labor generally, however. For some it serves as evidence that man is sustained only by the grace of the Lord. Others wrest the verse from its context, inferring from it the medicinal value of perspiration and the sage advice that food is best consumed after exercise.[12] By contrast, the bulk of rabbinic sources treat labor as an ennobling requisite to the process of moral development. For example, Rabbi Yehudah declares "work brings honor to its master"; for Ulla, one who benefits from the work of his hands outshines those who fear heaven, while Rabbi Yirmiah proclaims it more dear than noble ancestry. Similarly, a father is obliged to teach his son a trade lest he teach him robbery, and numerous religious duties are relaxed or modified to allow those steeped in work to continue their productivity with minimal disturbance.[13]

Mannheim and Sella reviewed some 900 "work-related statements" appearing in both the Babylonian and Jerusalem Talmud, the *Tosefta*, and nineteen compendia of the *midrash*. They executed a content analysis to assess and classify the norms and values represented by these statements. Their results suggest that of all "ideational references" to the value of labor in these texts, 84 percent were positive, reflecting a "high esteem of work and craft." Further, regarding the interaction between gainful employment and religious study—the primary value in Jewish life—fully 65 percent of all references "prescribed that the learning of Torah and work should be pursued jointly."[14]

However, the Rabbis also exhibit concern for those who toil in the employ of another. Such workers were generally presumed to be impoverished, vulnerable, and in need of social and legislative protection. It was early established that, in contrast to his employer, a laborer retained

---

[12]*Genesis Rabbah* 20:9–10, *Berakhot* 57b, and R. Ephraim Solomon b. Aaron (Luntshits, 1550–1619), *Klei Yakkar*, Genesis 3:19, s.v. *bezey'at appekha*.

[13]The references derive from *Berakhot* 8a, 45–46, *Nedarim* 49b, *Hullin Genesis Rabbah* 74:12, and *Kiddushin* 29a and 33a, *Hullin* 54b; *Tur, Hoshen Mishpat* 337:20; Rav Yosef Caro (Safed, 1488–1575), *Shulkhan Arukh, Hoshen Mishpat* 337:20.

[14]Bilha Mannheim and Avraham Sella, "Work Values in the Oral Torah," *Journal of Psychology and Judaism* 15 (4) (1991): 241–260. *Kiddushin* 82 provides a good overview of the talmudic discussion regarding the interface between employment and study.

the right to rescind the terms of his employment, "even in midday." To do otherwise would relegate him to a status akin to slavery, violating the Biblical declaration (Leviticus 25:55) that the Children of Israel be servants of the Lord, and, by implication, not the servants of others.[15]

To the minds of talmudic sages, workers never lose their dignity and social integrity. Employers are expected to extend kindness and compassion toward them, even beyond the prescriptions of the law's strict letter. Consider the following two anecdotes as illustration. Rabbi Yohanan ben Massya was alarmed that his son had contracted to provide meals for their employees. He urged that before any work was begun, they specify that these be meager repast only. Otherwise, he opined, "my son, even if you provide a meal fit for king Solomon you will not have fulfilled your obligation, for they are the children of Abraham, Isaac, and Jacob. . . . "[16]

In another incident, porters damaged the wares of Rabbah Bar Hanan (by some readings "Bar Hanah" or "Bar Rav Huna") and he confiscated their clothes against his loss. On the grounds that they were indigent and in need, the workers petitioned Rav not only to retrieve their clothes but also to extract their wages, notwithstanding the damage they had caused. Rav ruled in their favor on both counts. Pressed as to whether this conformed to the law, he cited from the Book of Proverbs (2:20): "that you may walk the good road and guard the pathways of the righteous," implying an enforceable claim for compassion resting on moral rather than purely legal grounds.[17]

---

[15]*Bava Kamma* 117b, *Bava Metziah* 10a, Maimonides (Egypt, 1135–1204), *Yad, Sekhirut* 9:4 and *Shulkhan Arukh, Hoshen Mishpat* 333:3–5. It should be noted that this right to retract from a contractual agreement was not unlimited. If the employer suffered an irretrievable loss by consequence, and if the worker was not motivated by personal emergency, such as illness or bereavement, then the latter would be held liable.

[16]*Bava Metziah* 83a.

[17]*Bava Metziah*, 83a. Talmudic commentaries are much exercised by the ruling of Rav. Some, for example, R. Asher b. Jehiel (Germany, 1250–1327), *Rosh*, record it as *halakhah*, while most, including Maimonides, *Tur*, and R. Yosef Caro, do not. Still others, such as R. Yitzhak b. Jacob Alfasi (Algeria, 1013–1103), *Rif*, and R. Nissim Gerondi (Barcelona, 1310–1375), *Ran*, appear to excise those words in the talmudic passages that imply Rav's intent to read compassion as a basic part of the legal structure.

Legal mandates governing the indentured Hebrew servant stand as yet another source for employee relations generally. Though not without exception, the presumption appears to be that those benefits or prerogatives due such a servant should generally be extended to all workers. By complement, workers should be protected from the legal debilities characteristic of the Hebrew servant, as already suggested.

The reasoning is succinctly stated in rulings issued by Rabbi Meir Rottenburg b. Barukh of Rottenburg (*Maharam* Rottenburg, ca. 1215–1293), and applied broadly elsewhere. Scripture expressly provides for indentured servitude, whether as restitution for criminal behavior (Exodus 21:2–7), or by consequence of overriding debt (Leviticus 2:39–47). Nevertheless, religious tradition frowns upon the practice even among those in dire straits. Freedom is the natural state of the Jews; they may serve no one but the Deity. Consequently, Rabbi Meir concludes: "All that is lenient for a Hebrew servant is extended to the laborer, a fortiori. For the Hebrew servant has transgressed and nevertheless the Merciful One has been lenient." Therefore certainly a laborer who has not so transgressed has the same benefit.

In addition, Scripture (Deuteronomy 16:18) refers to the efforts of the Hebrew servant as "double the hire" of a worker. Since the normal term of indenture is six years, Rabbi Meir further ruled that the life of an employment contract may not extend beyond three years, lest the worker be "enslaved" by its conditions. Though written in response to

---

In an ingeneous interpretation of the proceedings, Rabbi Solomon Eliezer b. Judah ha-Levi Ideles (Poland 1555–1631), *Maharsha*, argues that the verse from Proverbs was intended as legal citation by metaphor. To be held liable for damage porters must be permitted to travel the safest path, that which presents least risk, that is, " . . . the good road . . . " as provided in the substance of immediately preceding Talmudic discussion. By implication, Rabbah had not been a fastidious employer in this regard, he had not "guarded the righteous pathway," and was subject to a judgment against him.

Nevertheless, the principle of an employer being required to extend compassion beyond the demands of the law has continued as a religious precedent in labor relations, as well as in numerous other contexts. For a review, see, for example, Shmuel Shilo, "On One Aspect of Law and Morals in Jewish Law: *Lifnim me-Shurat ha-Din*," *Israel Law Review* 13 (1978): 359–390.

a petition regarding liability for a teacher's sick-days, the principle also has been invoked as precedent for retirement benefits and severance pay.[18]

Yet another source contributing to the parameters of employee relations is *minhag*, that is, general practice. This may be global, or defined by locale or by industry. Its impact is not peculiar to issues relating to employment or to those of commercial activity generally. Rather it inheres in the broad scope of social and communal relations in Jewish tradition. As is well-known, within these specific parameters, that which is designated *minhag* may take precedence over enacted legislation, rabbinic ruling, and, within sharp limitations, even over scriptural mandate.

A specific example in the realm of employee relations may help elaborate the point. The *Mishneh* tells us:

> One who hires laborers and demands that they rise early and work late, in a place where it is not the custom [*minhag*] he may not force them. Where it is the custom to provide food, he must provide food, to offer fruit refreshments, he must offer fruit refreshments. Everything [is measured] by the custom of the locality.

In a following discussion, the Talmud derives from biblical writ (Psalms 104:22–23) that the workday commences with the first rays of sun and continues until nightfall. Nevertheless, local custom supersedes such a practice and unless stated otherwise, employees can presume that the terms of their hire conform to local *minhag*. By some interpretations, the

[18]Rabbi Meir b. Barukh of Rottenburg (Rothenburg, ca. 1215–1293), *Responsa Maharam Ben Rav Barukh*, Prague Edition (Tel Aviv, Sternberg, 1969), Items 72 and 85. Rabbi Meir modifies his latter position in yet another ruling, suggesting that only workers who reside with their employers and are "sustained at their table" should limit the span of their work contracts. See his ruling cited in the commentary of Rabbi Mordekhai b. Hillel ha Kohen (1240?–1298) to *Bava Metziah*, Items 459–460; see also Rabbi Moshe Isserles (Poland, 1525 or 1530–1572), *Rema*, in a note to *Hoshen Mishpat* 333:3. Using much the same reasoning, Rabbi Moshe Sofer (Germany, 1762–1839) concludes that terms of employment may range beyond three years but not exceed six years, the normal span of indenture, *Responsa Hatam Sofer, Orah Hayyim*, Item 206.

latter is understood to fully abrogate the precedent of *halakhah*. At the very least, it becomes a presumed, though unstated, clause to the employment contract, subject to contrary stipulation.[19]

III. THE ADMINISTRATION OF PAY

Among the best-known elements of an employer's responsibility to his workforce are compensation management and distribution of pay. Scripture demands that every effort be made to pay workers punctually. Employers are warned that "... the wages of a hired servant shall not abide with you until morning" (Leviticus 19:13). Equally,

> you shall not oppress a hired servant who is poor and needy, whether he be of your brethren or of your strangers who are in your land and your gates. In his day shall you give him his hire, nor shall the sun go down upon it, for he is poor and to that he sets his spirit; lest he cry to the Lord against you and it be a sin in you."[20]

This particular concern for timely payment is summarized under the general descriptor, *lo talin*, after a Hebrew phrase in the text of the first reference. With these as base, the Talmud and *Midrash* declare, and Maimonides (Egypt, 1135–1204) rules, that an employer who maliciously withholds payment may be liable for as many as five transgressions.[21]

More specifically, wages are due within hours of the completion of a shift. For an employee whose workday ends after nightfall, this means before daybreak. For an overnight worker, this means before the fol-

---

[19]*Bava Metziah* 83a–b; *Talmud Yerushalmi, Bava Metziah* 7:1; Maimonides, *Yad, Sekhirut* 9:1; *Shulkhan Arukh, Hoshen Mishpat* 331:1. For an early application of *minhag* to the matter of a worker's right to supplementary employment, that is, "moonlighting," see Rabbi Gershom Me'or ha-Golah (France, 960–1040), *Teshuvot Rabbenu Gershom Me'or ha-Golah* (New York: Yeshiva University, 1955), Item 92. For a broad discussion of *minhag* in Jewish Law, see Menachem Elon, *Ha-Mishpat ha-Ivri: Toldotav, Mekorotav, ve-Ikronotav* (Tel Aviv: Yavneh, 1978), I:739ff.

[20]Deuteronomy 24:14–15.

[21]*Bava Metziah* 110–111; *Sifrei Ki Tetzeh* 145; *Yad, Sekhirut* 11:2.

lowing nightfall—whether this ends a day, a week, or even a year of hire.[22]

The reasoning that undergirds this stringent demand for punctuality is twofold. The predominant rationale is a presumption of poverty grounded in the phrases "you shall not oppress a hired servant who is poor and needy" and "nor shall the sun go down upon it [his hire] for he is poor," cited above. Biblical commentary underscores the point. For example, Nahmanides (Spain, 1194–1270) explains that without his pay, an employee will scarcely feed his hungry family that very night. "He is poor," Nahmanides concludes, "as are most who give themselves for hire." Similarly, R. Aaron ha-Levi (Barcelona, 13th century), the presumed author of *Sefer ha-Hinukh*, notes: "All workers, or most, require their pay for their food." Therefore it is improper to delay to him his food, and in this vein it is written: "for he is poor. . . ."[23]

Given a presumption of poverty, the demand for prompt payment of wages appears as a function of broader charitable impulses, beyond the context of the workplace. Consequently, it is reasonable that employer liability be relaxed in regard to more affluent employees. This eventuality is considered in the Talmud, though largely by implication.

In its analysis of biblical sources, such terms as "poor" and "needy" are understood to demonstrate that if an employer has insufficient funds to meet his entire payroll, needy workers have first claim. In principle, however, it appears that even wealthy employees can claim prompt payment under the provisions of *lo talin*. The point is elaborated explicitly in the *Zohar*.[24]

This forms a second prop to the scriptural mandate. Workers, including even those who cannot demonstrate need, depend upon prompt payment, nevertheless. It is toward that end that they extend themselves,

---

[22]*Yad* ibid; *Tur, Hoshen Mishpat* 339:1–4; *Shulkhan Arukh, Hoshen Mishpat* 339:1–3.

[23]Nahmanides (Spain, ca. 1195–c. 1270), commentary to Deuteronomy 24:15; R. Aaron ha-Levi (Barcelona, 13th century), *Sefer ha-Hinukh*, Item 588.

[24]*Bava Metziah* 111b; *Zohar, Kedoshim* 29, Item 86; also, see R. Menahem b. Solomon Meiri (Perpignan, ca. 1249–1306), *Beit ha-Behira* (Jerusalem: Makhon Ha-Talmud, 1965), commentary to *Bava Metziah* 111a. There support is marshaled from the Biblical phrase "to it [his wages] he sets his spirit."

often assuming personal risk while executing their tasks and responsibilities. In the language of the Talmud: "Why does he ascend upon a ladder, suspend himself from a tree and place himself at risk of death [if] not for his wage. . . . One who withholds the pay of a worker it is as if he takes from him, his spirit."[25]

Thus, apart from their subjective levels of need, employees have a claim to immediate pay that is rooted in the effort and the time invested in their jobs.

The point is amplified by a related talmudic discussion. There is little question that wages are due upon the completion of a shift. Still, at several junctures, the Rabbis carry on a lively, if abstract debate regarding the theoretical essence of pay. Rabbi Meir argues that the total wage is due upon the completion of a job; the Sages held that pay was cumulative, accruing with the completion of each intermediary task. By their assessment, wages remained with the employer as a loan that came due upon completion of the job.

This latter position is confirmed by most authorities, though its implications are few and distant from current concerns. However, it may serve to reinforce the claim of an affluent employee. Loans must be repaid in a timely fashion, without regard to the financial status of the creditor. So too the financial status of a worker, a creditor of sorts in relation to his wage, is not directly relevant to the liability of an employer to meet his obligations punctually.[26]

In a related gesture on behalf of employees, Jewish tradition also facilitates their claims in payroll disputes. Under normal circumstances, defendants in a civil case who make partial admission to the existence of a debt are required to take an oath against the remainder. In the original formulation, those who fully deny its existence are free of any liability, though at a later point in talmudic history, a special oath was introduced for them as well.[27]

Disputes over pay, however, represent the first of a handful of instances in which initiative is shifted to the claimant. Workers at the completion

---

[25]*Bava Metziah* 112a.

[26]*Bava Kamma* 99a; *Kiddushin* 48a; *Avodah Zarah* 19b. For its applications see *Yad, Ishut* 5:19–20 and *Shulhan Arukh, Even ha-Ezer* 38:13.

[27]*Shavu'ot* 44–46. Regarding *Shevu'at Heset*, the additional oath, see for example, the commentary of *Tosafot* to *Shavu'ot* 45a, s.v. *ik'ruha rabbanan*.

of a shift, whose hire is stipulated but who claim that they have yet to be paid, are permitted to take an oath to that effect and collect their due, no matter their employer's counterclaim.

The Talmud[28] debates the legal basis for this shift of initiative. Its instinct is to assign this innovation to the more general tilt in favor of worker rights. In the words of Rabbi Nahman, the oath was "transferred to the worker because of his livelihood." An objection is raised regarding what amounts to a legal disadvantage for the employer, based on an abstract concern for the protection of wages. Numerous arguments are mounted to illustrate that the employer is so taken with his financial and commercial responsibilities that he implicitly concedes this initiative if but to protect his integrity and his credibility with the workforce.

Details of this lengthy discussion notwithstanding, most commentary suggests that the Talmud never strays from its initial direction, that is, whether this oath was instituted to substantiate fact or to set at ease the mind of the employer, its basis lies in a concern for the well-being of workers and the protection of their wage.

However, both in meeting payroll punctually and in confirming worker claims of nonpayment, exemptions are provided to facilitate extenuating circumstance and to assure that the concern for the prerogatives of labor should not interfere unduly with the pursuit of normal enterprise. For example, if particular accounts receivable must be settled before regular payroll can be covered, an extension is automatically granted the employer as an implicit aspect of the employment contract. So too, if the time required to complete wage calculations extends beyond the provisions of *lo talin*.

In cases where the employer has no available funds to cover payroll, an extension also is provided until such funds are available. At that point, employee claims precede those of other creditors. Several authorities suggest that an employer is, at least morally, obligated to dispose of other assets or to seek loans elsewhere to cover his payroll and fulfill his commitments to his employees. Further, he would be wise to stipulate, as

[28]See *Shavu'ot* 45b and commentary thereto of *Rif*, *Ran*, s.v. *ik'ruha*; and commentary of *Rosh*; also *Yad, Sekhirut* 11:6; R. Jehiel Michel Epstein (Belorussia, 1829–1908), *Arukh ha-Shulkhan, Hoshen Mishpat* (Jerusalem: Wagshal, 1987) 89:2.

part of the original employment contract, that he be held blameless should fiscal circumstance conspire to prevent him from meeting his payroll.[29]

IV. SEVERANCE BENEFITS

Severance pay is an interesting study in applying the several sources for responsibility to employees in normative Jewish thought. Some have sought precedent for these benefits, in the requirement to provide *ha-a'nakah*, a gratuity or bonus to the indentured Hebrew, normally upon the completion of his six-year term of service. Scripture declares:

> And when you let him go free from you, you shall not let him go empty. You shall furnish him liberally of your flock and of your threshing-floor and of your wine-press; of that which the Lord your God has blessed you, shall you give to him.[30]

The Talmud and its commentaries, and authors of later codes, record numerous debates over the details of this benefit. Was this due any Hebrew servant or only those indentured by virtue of their criminal guilt? Was this a philanthropic gesture on the part of the master, or an integral aspect of remuneration to the servant, for additional services rendered during the term of indenture? Was it a flat-rate bonus or calculated pro rata to the prosperity enjoyed during the term of indenture?[31]

---

[29]*Bava Metziah* 111–112; *Yad, Sekhirut* 11:4; *Tur, Hoshen Mishpat* 339:8–9, and commentary of *Beit Yosef*, s.v. *sakhir*; *Shulkhan Arukh, Hoshen Mishpat* 339:9–10 and commentary of *Rema* 339:10 and R. Abraham Danzig (1748–1820), *Pithei Teshuva* 339:8.

[30]Deuteronomy 15:12–14.

[31]*Kiddushin* 14–15; commentary of *Tosafot*, s.v. *ve-iydakh*; *Yad, Avaddim* 3:12; commentary of R. Shabbetai b. Meir ha-Kohen (Poland, 1621–1662), *Shakh* to *Hoshen Mishpat* 86:3 and of R. Joshua ha-Kohen Falk (Poland, 1555–1614), *S'ma, Hoshen Mishpat* 86:2; commentary of *Meiri* to *Kiddushin* 15a; *Ha-a'nakah* in R. Shlomo Zevin, ed., *Encyclopedia Talmudit* (Jerusalem: Yad Harav Herzog, 1971) 9:774–787.

Such issues aside, the author of *Sefer ha-Hinukh* strikes new ground in extending *ha-a'nakah* to workplace relations generally. He concedes that the institution of the Hebrew servant, along with practices related to it, were all linked to the Jubilee year and consequently, discontinued with the destruction of the Second Holy Temple.

> Nevertheless, even at this time, "let the wise one listen and add wisdom" (Proverbs 1:5). Should [he] hire one from among the Children of Israel, and he work for him for a long time, or even a brief while, when he leaves him, let [the employer] give *ha-a'nakah* from that which the Lord has blessed him.[32]

As its language suggests, the comment was subsequently understood in a moral rather than a legal context. Yet some contemporary authorities have attempted to match it with the earlier-noted ruling of Rabbi Meir of Rottenburg and thus give it the power of law. All benefits that accrue to a Hebrew servant who has violated God's law by indenturing himself, are therefore also due the typical employee who is guilty of no such trespass. By extension, *ha-a'nakah* severance benefits should accrue to the typical worker upon termination, based on precedent from the Hebrew servant.[33]

However, while the analogy between the Hebrew servant and the employee is intriguing, it is not compelling, and its use as a basis for legally enforceable employee benefits has not been undisputed. By consequence, severance pay has also been rooted in the more general obligation for employers to deal equitably with their workers. This, in turn, emerges from the precedent of Rabbah Bar Hanan who was enjoined to pay the wages of his porters even though it was he who suffered loss by their work. As noted above, Rav cited the verse "so that you walk the good road and guard the pathways of the righteous" as proof-text in issuing this ruling. The incident thus becomes a call for understanding and generosity even when employees are found to be negligent or incompetent.

But is such compassion to be legally imposed? The issue turns on a broad debate over judicial assertiveness in the context of legal disposi-

---

[32]*Sefer ha-Hinukh* (Jerusalem: Eshkol, 1946), Item 483.

[33]*Responsa Mahaharam me-Rottenburg ibid.*, especially Item 85. See the decision in *Kaiserman v. Derenfeld, Piskei Din Rabbaniyim* 3:287, cited in Wahrhaftig 647n and Elon 750n.

tion. At its heart is the legal status of moral obligation in juridical action, a matter that much exercised numerous medieval Jewish authorities. For some it was a "simple" matter, based on early precedent, that moral obligation, that is, that which is clearly above the line of the law, cannot be imposed by the courts. By contrast, interlocutors among both talmudic commentaries and jurists suggest that when one party is financially able, or when there is no immediate financial loss, the courts have the right to set aside a judgment and, in the name of compassion and equity, find on behalf of a needy petitioner, even when the inclination of the law appears to the contrary.[34]

The latter has found contemporary expression in the thinking of Rabbi Ben Zion Ouziel (Israel, 1880–1953), in support of employee benefits. Thus:

> It is the responsibility of the employer not to act harshly with his employees and managers but to the contrary, with a pleasant eye and open heart. He must fulfill "and guard the pathways of the righteous. . . . "
>
> The court has the power to attach funds from an employer on behalf of his workers in all instances that it deems within the context of "so that you walk the good road and guard the pathways of the righteous." This according to its assessment of the status of the employer and of the workers, and the circumstances of the termination.[35]

The principle was later invoked in an award of severance pay by the Rabbinical Court of Haifa.

Finally, employers have also been held liable for severance pay based on the existence of *minhag*, that is, that such is a usual and customary labor practice. In this sense, the benefit accrues to the employee not from

---

[34]See the commentary of Rabbi Mordekhai Ben Hillel to *Bava Metziah*, Item 257; *Beit Yosef, Hoshen Mishpat* 12:8, and Rabbi Yoel Sirkus (Poland, 1561–1650), *Bayit Haddash*, on *Tur Hoshen Mishpat* 12:5. Curiously, Rabbi Yosef Caro refrains from recording his opposition to such judicial assertiveness while Rabbi Moshe Isserles simply records both positions: *Shulkhan Arukh, Hoshen Mishpat* 12:2.

[35]Rabbi Ben Zion Ouziel (Israel, 1880–1953), *Mishpatei Ouziel* (Tel Aviv: Bezalel, 1944) Item 41; cited in Rabbi Moshe Findling, *Te-Hukat ha-Avodah* (Jerusalem: Schreiber, 1941), p. 133; See *Lev v. Hinukh Azmai Council of Kfar Ata, Piskei Din Rabbaniyim* 3:95.

a sense of moral obligation imposed by the court nor from analogy with a defunct institution, but from that which is implicit in the conditions of employment.

In general, to be imbued with the legal power of a *minhag*, a practice must be both "spread throughout all the lands" and "common and employed frequently." Thus, Rabbi Ouziel hesitated to base his aforementioned ruling on an extant *minhag* of severance benefits to workers. To his mind, "the practice has not yet been accepted throughout the land and it is not common save in specific instances."[36]

However, in his treatment of the issue some years later, Rabbi Eliezer Judah Waldenberg found sufficient reason to believe that a *minhag* had developed along these lines and stood prepared to employ it in his ruling. He notes the moral precedent implicit in *ha-a'nakah* for a Hebrew servant and even enters the debate over the details of its implementation. Still, his finding in favor of the employee is based on contemporary labor practices, even to the size of the benefit due the petitioner. In his words:

> There exists a general *minhag* in the country to pay severance benefits to workers and managers of various categories, in the form of one month [pay] for each year of service, by the most recent annual salary rate. . . . This is rooted in the country for decades with no distinction between full-time or part-time workers. Therefore it certainly was with this in mind that [the employer] engaged the petitioner.[37]

V. COLLECTIVE ORGANIZATION AND THE RIGHT TO STRIKE

In addition to setting conditions favorable to employee salaries and benefits, Jewish tradition also provides for their right to organize and to act

---

[36]*Yad, Ishut* 23:12; *Rema, Hoshen Mishpat* 331:1. Based on a ruling of Rabbi Isaac b. Sheshet (1326–1408), *Rivash*, Shillem Wahrhaftig also adds that a *minhag* must be public knowledge and clear. This is cited by *Rema* though this element is not included in his ruling.

[37]Rabbi Eliezer Judah Waldenberg, *Tzitz Eliezer* (Jerusalem: Waldenberg, 1985), 7:48, Item 10.

collectively. This principle derives from the basic powers extended to the board or council of any community. The Talmud records that "the townsfolk may set weights and measures, fix the wages of workers, and penalize against infraction."

Labor collectives were seen as a sub-set of such communal administration. The *Tosefta* offers the following illustrations:

> Textile workers and dyers may decide that all material brought into town will be processed collectively. Bakers may establish their work shifts and donkey drivers may say, "to whomsoever [among us] a donkey dies, we will replace it for him." If it dies through negligence, they are not required to replace it. . . . Merchant seamen may say, "to whomsoever [among us] a ship is lost, we will replace it for him" . . . And if he went to a place where no one goes, they need not replace it for him.[38]

Apparently, these groups of laborers could collectively apportion work, set hours, and organize programs of insurance against loss in trades where such eventualities were common, such as transport and shipping. As with civil administration, these groups also could "penalize against infraction," that is, they had limited powers of adjudication and enforcement.

To illustrate, the same talmudic discussion records a dispute among the butchers of a town over their right to regulate work hours and reduce competition. Rava, the presiding authority, ruled against the sanctions they had imposed upon one of their number who had violated the regulation. In support, Rabbi Papa explained that true to their analogy with a town board, worker collectives may set independent standards only "if there is no important person in the town. . . . " Regulations set by worker groups do not require managerial stipulation. However, to be valid and enforceable, they must be confirmed before a Sage versed in law and custom, empowered to "correct the actions of the state and bring success to the path of its residents," that is, one appointed not just as a religious authority but also as a municipal executive whose mandate is to oversee the public interest.[39]

---

[38]*Bava Batra* 8b; *Tosefta, Bava Metziah* 11:12.

[39]*Bava Batra* 9a and commentaries of R. Asher b. Jehiel and *Meiri*; also *Yad, Sekhirut* 14:11; *Beit Yosef, Hoshen Mishpat* 231:30 and *Shulkhan Arukh, Hoshen Mishpat* 231:28.

This restriction on worker initiative is relatively narrow. Most authorities hold that even in the presence of an "important person," workers are free to set purely internal standards without interference. Validation is required only for initiatives that bear directly upon the public interest, loosely defined as any departure from generally accepted business practice with direct financial impact upon the consumer, though not upon the employer. The case of the butchers cited above was subject to validation because limiting competition among members of a trade results in artificially higher prices. By contrast, the collective insurance arrangements, noted earlier, are matters of internal administration and require no executive validation.[40]

Aside from their right to organize and to impose internal standards, most authorities also confirm that workers may engage in strikes and job actions in pursuit of their collective interest. The Talmud details a precedent among Temple priests. The House of Garmu, bakers of the "shewbread," and the House of Abtinas, charged with sifting the incense, both refused to train others in their delicate craft. More amenable artisans were summoned from Alexandria but the skills of these early "strikebreakers" proved inadequate. The Sages subsequently were forced to double the wages of the recalcitrant priests before they would return to work, enjoying their newfound affluence with impunity.[41]

It is revealing that the incident occurs among "public employees." Those who toil for the common weal may be held to unusually high standards of quality, productivity, and personal ethic. They also may have a special claim to job security. However, unlike their equivalent in much of American labor relations, they appear to suffer no special restrictions upon their collective action for their public commission.[42]

The right to strike, and related considerations, were largely ignored among medieval Jewish thinkers, suggesting the absence of any persis-

---

[40]Commentary of Rabbi Nissim Gerondi, *Ran* to *Bava Batra* 9a; *Beit Yosef, Hoshen Mishpat* 231:30 and Rabbi Moshe Isserles (*Rema*), *Shulhan Arukh, Hoshen Mishpat* 231:30 and 272:16,18; also *Yad Gezeilah* 12:12,15.

[41]*Yoma* 38a, *Shekalim* 14a, *Tosefta, Yoma* 2:5; *Yerushalmi, Yoma* 3:9.

[42]*Yad, Sekhirut* 10:7 and *Klei Mikdash* 4:21; *Beit Yosef, Hoshen Mishpat* 306:12. Also, commentary of Rabbi Yom Tov Ishbili (Spain, ca. 1270–1342), *Ritva* to Makkot 13a.

tent or systematic pressure in that direction. Modern authorities have attended to these issues, however, especially given the emergence of large and assertive trade unions and the importance of labor ideology as a foundation of Zionism and the State of Israel. Within limits, most have supported the rights of employees to strike, to impose discipline among members, to prevent "strikebreaking," and to keep employers from using nonunion labor. Within these broad junctures, however, opinion diverges.

For example, Rabbi Ben Zion Ouziel found no inherent right for workers to take unilateral action; strikes cause damage and loss to all concerned. The appropriate course of action is to have both sides appear before a properly constituted court or some mutually acceptable system of binding arbitration, with no interruption of work and productivity. His colleague, Rabbi Abraham Isaac Kook (Israel, 1865–1935), agreed that disputes between workers and management should be submitted to arbitration, as a corollary to executive approval for any labor decisions that impact upon the public. However, he found that if management refuses to appear or fails to uphold a subsequent ruling, then a union is within its right to call a strike.[43]

Others are still more liberal. Rabbi Eliezer Judah Waldenberg has invoked the long-standing tradition of unilateral action without court approval as precedent. He suggests that if management violates a contractual agreement, a legal obligation or a long-standing employment practice, employees may call a strike without first resorting to arbitration. Rabbi Moshe Feinstein ruled further that strikes were permissible in the United States regardless of the point of contention or the circumstances of negotiations. Since no "important person" has been empowered, and since American law legitimates job-stoppage as a labor strategy, decisions made by unions to strike are legal and binding.[44]

---

[43]*Mishpatei Ouziel* 42:6; R. Kook (Israel, 1865–1935) is cited in Kasriel Tkhursh, "Dinei Shevitot Be-Halakhah," *Shanah be-Shanah* (1963), p. 241.

[44]*Tzitz Eliezer* 2:23; talmudic precedents for unilateral action in civil law are to be found in *Bava Kamma* 27b; *Yad, Sanhedrin* 2:12; Rabbi Asher b. Jehiel, *Rosh, Piskei ha-Rosh: Bava Kamma* 3:3; *Tur, Hoshen Mishpat* 4:1; *Shulkhan Arukh, Hoshen Mishpat* 4:1. The ruling of Rabbi Moshe Feinstein is found in *Iggerot Moshe, Hoshen Mishpat* (Brooklyn: Moriah, 1954), Item 59.

VI. PERQUISITES, EXPENSES, AND WORKER COMPENSATION

Aside from wages, Jewish tradition also concerns itself with the variety of benefits to which workers may be entitled as a condition of their employment. Perhaps best known is their right to eat of the produce of any field in which they are currently occupied. In biblical language:

> When you shall enter the vineyard of your fellow, you may eat grapes until you are content in your spirit, but you shall not put any in your vessel. When you shall enter the standing corn of your fellow, then you may pluck the ears with your hand, but you shall not move a sickle to his standing corn.[45]

There is no reference to an employee here and one authority unsuccessfully attempted to infer a general license for visitors in a field to help themselves. However, the Talmud concludes that the biblical intent is to allow field hands to eat of their master's crop. Such benefits are provided even to the beast of burden (Deuteronomy 25:4). It would be cruel and unnatural to expect workers to harvest produce without enjoying some of it and to restrict them only serves to encourage theft.

Consequently, the right is limited to agricultural workers involved in harvesting fresh produce and vegetation at the time of their shift, and it is not transferable to family members. Further, while there is no formal limit to the amount or the value they may consume, such workers are warned not to abuse this privilege, lest their maintenance outweigh their labor and their service not be renewed.[46]

Such applications appear far afield to a discussion of employer responsibilities, especially in nonagrarian concerns. Nevertheless, they may have keen application, if only in the breach. Apparently, aside from this example, Jewish tradition does not require employers to provide food, maintenance, and related expenses, unless (1) they were stipulated in the original employment contract, or (2) they are a customary adjunct to the employee's wage. In this way, benefits to the worker deviate from those provided to an indentured Hebrew.

---

[45]Deuteronomy 23:25–26.

[46]*Bava Metziah* 92a; *Yerushalmi, Ma'asrot* 82:6–7; *Yad, Sekhirut* 12:1–3, 11–13; *Tur, Hoshen Mishpat* 337:1–3, 12, 17.

For the latter, the Talmud understands the biblical text "for [the servant's life] is good with you" (Leviticus 25:40) to suggest that a householder be expected to provide support for both the Hebrew servant and his family. However, in the words of one commentary:

> It appears that this is specifically for a Hebrew slave, whom, in the verse, is set free after six [years]. However, a worker for a year, a month a week, or a day, we do not say this, as it is said in [*Bava Metziah* 83a] " . . . everything goes by local custom. . . . "[47]

Similarly, employees are not entitled to recompense for travel, living expenses, or per diem maintenance unless all this has been previously stipulated or such reimbursement is already a generally accepted employment practice. The point derives from the adjudication of several disputes involving sales representatives, business agents—even partners to a transaction—in which no provisions were made for these expenses. In each case, the rulings suggest that, absent customary procedure to the contrary, the employee is entitled only to the salary agreed upon. Where such practice was customary, it appears that custom also will dictate the normal per-diem rate to which employees are entitled even if their actual expenses are lower.[48]

However, in several medieval rulings an employer is found liable for costs above those normally related to the execution of the task itself, particularly regarding emergency circumstances related to the perils of travel in foreign lands. Employers are expected to cover costs and damages that result from greater risk and exposure than an employee normally might be expected to assume. Noted examples include imprisonment for trading in contraband, suits related to product liability, and a variety of taxes.[49]

---

[47]*Kiddushin* 22a and commentary of R. Asher b. Jehiel, *Rosh,* thereto.

[48]See Rabbi Samuel b. Abraham Adret (Spain, ca. 1235–1310), *Responsa Rashba* (Tel Aviv: Gittler, 1958) 3:140; Rabbi Yair Bachrach (Germany, 1638–1702), *Havvat Yair* (New York: Reich, 195?), Item 154; Rabbi Yisrael Isserlien, *Terumat ha-Deshen* (Warsaw: Schriftgeissen (Original 1882, rereleased 1957). Item 323.

[49]See Rabbi Moshe Trani (Venice, 1568–1639), *Responsa Mabit* (Lvov: Flecker, 1861, 1955) 3:156 and 3:188; Rabbi Yosef Colon (1420–1480), *Responsa Maharik* (Warsaw: Fiscus, 1884, 1967), Item 153; also the commentary of Rabbi Mordekhai

Custom also weighs heavily on liabilities for work-related injury. It goes without saying that employers are expected to maintain a safe and secure workplace, even as shopkeepers must protect the safety of their customers and householders are admonished to make their homes secure for visitors, "that you bring not blood upon it" (Deuteronomy 22:8). Beyond that, however, workers who suffer damages due to the normal execution of their task are not due compensation, their risk being a presumption of the job. Thus

> it is written "and to [his wage] he sets his spirit" (Deuteronomy 24:15). We derive that for his wage does he scale a wall or suspend himself from a tree [and] this means that occasionally he may fall and be killed. He has put himself at risk for his pay.[50]

Only when the negligence of an employer contributes to worker injury will a claim for compensation be considered. And once again, negligence is determined by deviation from customary employment practice. For an example, the talmudic Sage Samkhus records in the name of Rabbi Meir that a porter injured on the job may claim compensation if his burden were one *kab* heavier than customary. Since the talmudic norm for such labor is 1:30 *kab*, it is inferred that employers are held negligent for injury resulting from a workload increase of 1/30. At the same time, employees are held partially responsible for not objecting to the increased burden and consequently, may be compensated for damages only, but not for related benefits normally included in such suits.[51]

---

b. Hillel to *Bava Metziah*, Item 359. While there may be no formal claim to compensation, in case of an employee's death while on the job, many authorities required compensation to the heirs of the deceased as a form of penitence for the employer, even if no negligence was involved. See, for example, Rabbi Jacob Weil (Germany, d. before 1456), *Responsa Maharyoh* (Jerusalem: Schtitzberg, 1959), Item 125; R. Samuel Medina (1506–1589), *Responsa Maharashdam* (Lemberg: Balaban, original 1862, rereleased 1958), Item 435.

[50]Nahmanides, *Teshuvot ha-Rashba ha-Meyuhasot la-Ramban* (Tel Aviv: Gittler, 1958), Item 20. Regarding the responsibilities of a householder or shopkeeper for the safety of visitors and clients, see *Bava Kamma* 16b, 32a–b; *Yad, Rotzeah* 11:4, and *Nizkei Mammon* 10:11.

[51]*Tosefta, Bava Metziah* 7:10; *Bava Metziah* 80b; *Yad, Sekhirut* 4:7; R. Meir Abulafia (ca. 1180–1244), *Ramah*, cited in *Tur Hoshen Mishpat* 308:8; *Shulkhan*

VII. JEWISH SOURCES AND STAKEHOLDER THEORY

There can be little doubt that classic Jewish thought posits a clear responsibility upon the employer to consider the needs of his workforce. As demonstrated here, regarding disputes over the administration of the payroll, benefits due upon severance, or the right to organize and to collective action, employers must be mindful of their obligations to labor; they will be held liable and accountable in the breach. As demonstrated elsewhere, similar obligations accrue in such areas as sick leave and retirement benefits.[52]

Though beyond the scope of this presentation, it also should be understood that normative Jewish sources exhibit clear intent to provide balance in work relationships, thereby helping to secure the pursuit of commercial interests. For example, exemptions are available to employers who are temporarily constrained from fulfilling Scriptural demands regarding payroll. Similarly, beyond the basic requirements of workplace safety, workers are expected to take responsibility for their health and security. Those who incur expenses or damages in the normal execution of their jobs may not be entitled to reimbursement. Jewish texts also oblige employees to work to their fullest capacity, lest they be guilty of theft in accepting wages for less than an honest effort.[53]

Nevertheless, there is an evident tilt in favor of workers, for example, by creating for them a special oath in support of disputed claims or by declaring an obligation to treat them with compassion. On the assumption of their poverty and vulnerability they are provided special standing in relation to their employers. There is much in common with stakeholder theory in that both appreciate a responsibility toward those impacted by managerial decisions—employees being among the most immediate—beyond the interests of profit.

Yet, the parallels are limited and imperfect. Jewish values have a vision of society as a corporate whole. Business pursuits and commercial

---

Arukh, Hoshen Mishpat 308:7 and the commentaries thereto of *S'ma* 308:12, R. Jacob me-Lissa (d. 1832), *Netivot Mishpat* 8:3 and R. Aryeh Leib (Stry, 1745?-1813), *Ketzot ha-Hoshen* 308:2.

[52]See, for example, Wahrhaftig, pp. 509–532.

[53]*Yad, Sekhirut* 13:7; also, see, for example, Schnall, *ibid.*, "Exploratory Notes . . . " and "By the Light . . . "

strategies are but one element in a web of relationships that must conform to the more general sense of obligation and responsibility. By contrast, stakeholder theory appears still to presume the autonomy of the business enterprise, separate and apart from commitment to the broader social milieu. For this reason, responsibility to other constituencies can be perceived as little more than an instrumental strategy, ultimately focused on profit—the carrot rather than the stick.

The point bespeaks important conceptual lacunae. Mired in a tradition of self-conscious corporate autonomy that must struggle to justify social responsibility, managers are ignored as independent and assertive stakeholders themselves. Yet there is evidence to suggest that often they pursue selfish concerns, attempting to increase their own discretion with arrogant indifference not only to the needs of multiple constituencies, but even to the narrow interests of shareholders.

Consider the "governance" movement and its various "shareholder revolts" within Fortune 500 corporations over the past decade. These have been focused on increasing both influence over management policy and responsiveness to shareholder needs. Large investors, notably public and union-based pension funds, have demanded greater accountability among managers and board members, even suggesting that executive compensation be linked to corporate performance. By 1996 this trend had spread to smaller companies whose management was no less indifferent. Apparently, shareholders must be protected along with other stakeholders.[54]

In this vein, it is instructive to consider an oft-noted stylistic and substantive contrast between Western and Jewish ethical thought.[55] The former is defined largely by its emphasis upon individual rights, both enumerated and reserved. The individual, and by extension the corporation, is legally and morally sovereign and has a primary claim to unrestricted

[54]*New York Times* (February 6, 1996) D:1, 8.

[55]See, for example, Robert Cover, "Obligation: A Jewish Jurisprudence of the Social Order," *Journal of Law And Religion* 5 (1987): 65–90; Steven Friedell, "The Different Voice in Jewish Law: Some Parallels to a Feminist Jurisprudence," *Indiana Law Journal* 67 (1992): 915–949; Aaron Schreiber, *Jewish Law and Decision Making: A Study Through Time* (Philadelphia: Temple University, 1979); Suzanne Stone, "In Pursuit of the Counter Text: The Turn to the Jewish Legal Model in Contemporary American Legal Theory," *Harvard Law Review* 106 (1993): 813–894.

liberty and privacy. Regulation bears the burden of moral justification in an ethical arena that is inherently adversarial. From this emerges the controversial suggestion that the corporation and those who sit at its helm have a responsibility that extends beyond their profit statements.

By contrast, normative Jewish tradition presupposes obligation and accountability to a larger social or moral entity. Thus, indenture is discouraged because freedom is the natural human condition, yet one remains free to be a servant of the Lord. Similarly, while a healthy respect for private property and initiative is evident, with management and ownership come conservatory and custodial responsibilities in a network of relationships, ordained and cemented from above. The tradition venerates neither a struggle for individual freedom nor an inherent individual sovereignty, both of which contribute to the adversarial flavor of American legal and economic culture. By consequence, no moral battle must be waged over responsibility to the employee. The issues are operational and logistical; they deal with adjudicating equity when obligation to a network of multiple constituencies is given.

This leads to yet another important distinction. Contemporary stakeholder theory represents and important attempt to create a systematic conceptual base that may respond to what has been the norm in Western culture and is now being restated as "neoclassical" economics. By contrast, Jewish tradition is precisely that: a tradition. It has emerged through millennia of practice, its values often must be inferred from a host of varying sources, and it displays a commitment to evolutionary change in response to secular usage and local custom.

Consequently, while the thrust of the argument favoring obligations to the workforce remains consistent, its specific manifestations are not rooted in the sources of Jewish tradition with equal clarity. Some, such as the punctuality of pay, are plainly stated in Scripture. They are the most obviously authoritative, emerging as they do from the earliest and purest Jewish expressions of social equity and the ethics of the workplace. Others derive from analogous social relationships, as between master and indentured servant. These cannot command the same authority; the analogies are imperfect and the institutions from which they derive are obsolete. Still others emerge from a call to generosity and compassion toward those more vulnerable. Though morally commendable, the legal status of such principles has been called to question by numerous Jewish thinkers.

Finally, and most to the point, many are borrowed from that which is usual and customary in contemporary business practice. They have little claim as characteristically Jewish formulations, excepting that when an insistence upon fastidious application would hamper the free flow of social or economic intercourse, the tradition generally stands aside, and incorporates local usage. Secular advances in responsibility to the workforce are thus automatically appended to the body of Jewish tradition, though a pure and original linkage is difficult to establish beyond the commitment to facilitate social and economic enterprise.

Herein resides one more caveat in the linkage between our two models. Langtry takes Freeman et al to task for assuming a unitary view of their theoretical foil, Milton Friedman and his neoclassical corporation. Yet by their own admission, business leaders and executives have noted a moral and practical concern for the needs of multiple clientele. Langtry calls this "tinged stockholder theory": the primary responsibility of the firm is to those who own its stock; however, this obligation must operate

> subject not only to legal constraints but also to moral or social obligations. These might be, for example, grounded in moral rights possessed by people generally or by specific categories of people such as employees of the firm; or there might be moral duties of beneficence not grounded in rights of the recipients.[56]

Goodpaster[57] makes a similar point. A firm may have a compelling responsibility toward multiple constituencies whose well-being is affected by its decisions. However, these remain "nonfiduciary." To expect corporate executives to act with equanimity toward all who hold a "stake" in their decisions robs the fiduciary relationship of its moral power and turns the modern private corporation into a public institution. Perhaps this summarizes what emerges from a review of Jewish sources regarding employee relations.

---

[56]Bruce Langtry, "Stakeholders and the Moral Responsibilities of Business," *Business Ethics Quarterly* 4 (1994): 431–443.

[57]Kenneth Goodpaster, "Business Ethics and Stakeholder Analysis," *Business Ethics Quarterly* 1 (1991): 61–70.

Clearly, Jewish tradition favors a concern for and an obligation to the needs of the workforce. This is variously grounded in economic need, inequities of status, investment and risk on behalf of the job, general compassion, a concern for those more vulnerable, and an obligation to fulfill the word of God. Still, this not nearly the same as positing a fiduciary responsibility to protect the interests of such stakeholders, equal to or beyond the pursuit of profit and gain. To suggest corporate employers bear a responsibility to their workers equal in force as that which guides their relations with principals, is to misunderstand what drives both our models.

4

Aspects of the Firm's Responsibility to Its Customers: Pharmaceutical Pricing and Consumer Privacy

*Aaron Levine**

INTRODUCTION

Our purpose here will be to investigate aspects of the responsibility *halakhah* imposes on the firm in dealing with its customers. First, we will take up the pricing policy *halakhah* calls for in the sale of pharmaceutical drugs. We will then address the issue of the responsibility of the firm not to violate the privacy of its customers. In each instance, we will demonstrate that the profit motive cannot be relied upon to bring about the conduct and the institutional arrangement *halakhah* desires.

---

*My thanks to Dr. Moses Pava, Rabbi Shalom Carmy, and Nat Lewin for their comments on an earlier draft of this paper. My gratitude to Elisha Graff for his technical assistance and meticulous work in validating the sources cited in this paper.

The Pricing of Pharmaceuticals

In recent years, pharmaceutical companies have been under attack for their pricing policies. Within the framework of the current unregulated price environment, drug companies have consistently demonstrated their willingness to charge for life's necessities whatever the market will bear. To cite but a few examples:

Ceradose, a drug used to treat Goucher's disease, costs an average of $250,000 per year. Taxol, a drug used by women with advanced ovarian cancer, was initially priced in the $3,000 to $4,000 range. Betaseron, a new drug for the treatment of multiple sclerosis, was initially priced at $10,000 per year.[1]

Looking beyond the astronomical prices of individual drugs, a report prepared by a United States Senate Committee found that pharmaceutical price inflation was six times that of the general rate of inflation for the period 1980–1992. It is not surprising that the same report found that profit margins for pharmaceutical companies were four times that of the average Fortune 500 company.[2]

Critics call for price regulation of the drug industry. In rebuttal, the industry insists that its potential for high profits is necessary to attract the capital needed to do research and development on new drugs. Without a constant stream of new, patent-worthy products, brand-name companies would eventually go out of business.

The Pricing of Pharmaceuticals and *Halakhah*

In his work *Torat ha-Adam*, Nahmanides (Spain, 1194–1270) clearly enunciates a prohibition against earning windfall profits in the sale of pharmaceuticals. In making the moral case against the practice, Nahmanides begins with the dictum that providing medication to someone in need is an aspect of the *mitzvah* of restoring lost property to its rightful owner (*hashavat*

[1]Baruch A. Brody, *Ethical Issues in Drug Testing, Approval, and Pricing* (New York: Oxford University Press, 1995), p. 230.

[2]*Earning a Failing Grade: A Report Card on 1992 Drug Manufacturer Price Inflation*, Staff of Senate Special Commission on Aging, 103 Cong., 1st Sess., p. 3, note 2.

avedah). Specifically, making the medication available restores a sick person to himself (*hashavat gufo*). Since the taking of a fee for the performance of a *mitzvah* is generally prohibited, restriction on the pricing policy for a seller of drugs follows. Accordingly, should *A* be in possession of herbs which *B* needs for medication, it is unethical for *A* to take advantage of *B*'s need and hike up their price more than warranted (*yoter min ha-ra'uy*). The practice is unethical *whether the herbs are available elsewhere or not.*

The restrictions *halakhah* places on *A*'s pricing policy go beyond ethical guideposts. Since it is *B*'s desperation that makes him agree to the excessive price, the stipulation is not legally binding. *B* escapes the extra payment by merely claiming that his stipulation was made in jest (*mashteh ani bakh*). This holds whether the herbs were available elsewhere or not.[3]

In the sale of medication, Nahmanides entitles the seller to only their *damim*. What exactly Nahmanides means by this phrase can be seen from the conceptual linkage he makes between the price constraint a seller of medication is subject to and the price constraint a doctor is subject to. In respect to the latter, Nahmanides posits that a physician is entitled to no more than compensation for lost earnings and a fee for his toil and effort. It is, however, unethical for a physician to charge a fee for either the diagnosis or treatment program he offers.[4]

Nahmanides's guideposts for medical fees provide a basis to extrapolate *halakhah*'s view on price regulation in the pharmaceutical industry. Before a formulation can be arrived at, however, it must be noted that Nahmanides's analysis evidently deals with a part-time physician who earns his livelihood primarily outside the medical profession. What level of earning is a doctor entitled to if he devotes himself full-time to the medical profession? Resolution of this issue will provide the guidepost for price constraint for the monopolist pharmaceutical dealer.

---

[3]Nahmanides, *Torat-ha-Adam, Inyan ha-Sakanah*, pp. 44–45. Nahmanides's ruling is adopted by R. Jacob b. Asher (Toledo, 1270–1340), *Tur, Yoreh De'ah* 336:3; R. Joseph Cairo (Safed, 1448–1575), *Shulkhan Arukh, Yoreh De'ah* 336:3; R. Jehiel Michel Epstein (Belorussia, 1829–1908), *Arukh ha-Shulkhan,Yoreh De'ah* 336:3–4.

[4]Nahmanides, op. cit., *Tur*, op. cit. *Shulkhan Arukh*, op. Cit.; *Arukh ha-Shulkhan*, op. cit, 336:3.

Addressing himself to the issue of medical fees, R. Hayyim David ha-Levi draws a parallel from the compensation full-time teachers of Torah are entitled to. Teaching Torah is a *mitzvah*. As such, the teacher is entitled only to compensation for lost earnings. But if an individual forsakes the pursuit of a livelihood and devotes himself full-time to Torah teaching, R. Asher b. Jehiel (Germany, ca. 1250–1327, *Bekhorot* 4:5) entitles him to a salary. In a similar vein, the Talmud (*Ketubot* 105a) records that the civil judges of Jerusalem were compensated ninety-nine *maneh* out of Temple funds. Since assuming the judicial role is an aspect of teaching Torah, compensation should obtain only when an individual abandons his work to take on a case. R. Isaac of Dampierre (1120–1200, *Tosafot*, ad loc.) justifies the judges' salaries on the grounds that they made themselves available on a standby basis and the community was therefore bound to support them.

R. Hayyim David ha-Levi equates a medical practitioner with a teacher of Torah. Accordingly, if a doctor devotes himself full-time to his profession, he is entitled to a salary. Given both the high social standing of the doctor and the likelihood that he could command a relatively high earning outside the medical profession, R. Hayyim David ha-Levi finds no moral issue with very comfortable medical profession salaries.[5]

R. Hayyim David ha-Levi's thesis requires further clarification. The legitimacy of a full-time doctor earning a salary rests on the talmudic dictum that the civil judges of Jerusalem were given ninety-nine *maneh*[6] for their salary. R. Hayyim David ha-Levi regards salary as calculated to equal what these judges could earn elsewhere. Economists call this alternative compensation *opportunity cost* earnings. This assumption can, however, be questioned. In rationalizing this payment, *Tosafot* merely state that the prohibition of accepting payment for the *mitzvah* of teaching Torah is *inoperative* when the individual devotes himself full-time to his profession. In respect to the salary of judges, the Talmud comments (*Ketubot* 105a) that in the event it proved inadequate, for example, the

---

[5]R. Hayyim David ha-Levi, "Tashlum Sekhar ha-Rofeh ba-Halakhah," *Shevilim*, Kislev 5737 (1977): 22–29.

[6]Daniel Sperber (*Roman Palestine*, 2nd ed., Ramat Gan; Bar-Ilan University Press, 1991), pp. 35–37, 241, note 8) posits that the ninety-nine *maneh* was a daily stipend.

judge's family increased in size, the stipend was increased. The ninety-nine *maneh* hence was calculated to provide an *adequate* support level and was not an opportunity cost payment.

In his treatment of medical fees, R. Solomon Zalman Auerbach posits that a full-time doctor is entitled to an opportunity cost payment. Opportunity cost should be based, in his view, only on *current* alternative employment opportunities, such as a job in medical research. Opportunity cost should, however, not be calculated on the basis of what the doctor could now earn had he not trained himself for the medical profession.[7]

The guideposts that *poskim* have formulated for medical fees for full-time physicians should equally apply for price regulation of the monopolist pharmaceutical dealer. What is indicated is that the vendor of medications is entitled to no more than opportunity cost earnings.

Attitude of *Halakhah* Toward Windfall Profits in Essential Goods

Reinforcing the assertion that *halakhah* rejects a free-market approach to the pricing of pharmaceuticals is the general attitude it takes regarding windfall profits in respect to items which are essential to a minimum standard of living.

Talmudic Sages expressed a deep concern that commodities essential to life should be available in the marketplace at the lowest possible price. Toward this end, the talmudic Sages engaged in a variety of efforts designed to reduce windfall profits of sellers. These measures ranged from jawboning, policies designed to depress the demand side of the marketplace, and, in the case of essential foodstuffs, a one-sixth profit rate constraint. The following is a brief description of these interventions.

An instance of the use of the jawboning technique as a means of lowering price on a ritual item is recorded at *Sukkah* 34b. Here, we are told that Samuel warned the sellers of *hadassim* not to raise the price of undamaged branches, or he would publicize that clipped *hadassim* are also acceptable. Samuel, in fact, held that clipped *hadassim* were acceptable.

---

[7]R. Solomon Zalman Auerbach, quoted by A. S. Abraham in *Nishmat Avraham, Hilkhot Bikkur Holim*, p. 234.

Promulgating this leniency would have shifted the demand curve for undamaged *hadassim* downward and hence *forced* a price reduction on the sellers. Why Samuel opted for the weaker measure of merely bluffing the sellers is explained by *Tosafot* (ad loc.) as stemming from the circumstances that use of undamaged *hadassim* constitutes an enhancement of the *mitzvah* (*hiddur mitzvah*). Samuel's policy was designed to achieve a dual objective. On the one hand, he wanted to encourage lower prices for a ritual item. But, on the other hand, he did not want to discourage the purchase of undamaged *hadassim*, as their use constitutes *hiddur mitzvah*. Striking a balance between the two objectives led him to merely bluff the sellers rather than promulgate his lenient ruling.

Samuel is once again found taking up the cause of consumers in his fight against price gauging by vendors of earthenware pots. Following the rabbinic view that earthenware pots cooked with *chametz* before Passover and held over the holiday were forbidden to be used after the holiday, the pubic bought new earthenware pots after Passover. Capitalizing on this new surge of demand, the vendors raised the prices for their pots. Disturbed by the price hike, Samuel threatened the vendors that unless they reduced the price of their wares to the pre-Passover level, he would issue a ruling that the old pots could be used after Passover. The only thing that stopped him from actually issuing such a ruling was that the price gauging took place in Rav's jurisdiction and Samuel did not want to undermine the authority of his colleague who took a stringent view on the status of *chametz* after Passover which was held over during the holiday.[8]

A still more drastic intervention designed to affect the demand side of the marketplace is recorded at *Mishneh Keritot* 1:7:

> It once happened in Jerusalem that the price of a pair of doves (the sacrificial requirement for a woman who gave birth to allow her to partake of sacrificial meat) rose to a golden *dinar*. Said R. Shimon b. Gamliel, "by this Sanctuary, I shall not go to sleep tonight before they cost but a [silver] *dinar*!" Then he entered the *Beit Din* and taught: If a woman had five certain births or five certain issues she need not bring but one offering, and may then partake of sacrificial flesh, and she is not bound to bring the other [offerings]. Thereupon the price of a pair of birds stood at a quarter of a [silver] *dinar* each.

[8]*Pesachim* 30a.

What R. Shimon b. Gamliel did, according to R. Solomon b. Isaac (*Rashi*, Troyes, 1040–1105), was to temporarily change the law. Relying on the principle: "For it is time to act for God, they have voided Your Torah" (Psalms 119:126), R. Shimon b. Gamliel believed that the very high price of birds would lead women to neglect their sacrificial requirements and go on to eat holy meat (*kodishim*) in a state of impurity.[9]

A less drastic interpretation of R. Shimon b. Gamliel's action is offered by *Tosafot*. In their view, R. Shimon b. Gamliel did not abolish entirely the law that each birth or even doubtful birth requires a separate sacrifice in the form of a pair of doves. What R. Shimon b. Gamliel permitted was that one pair of doves would allow the woman who had multiple births to immediately partake of *kodishim*. The remaining sacrifices would remain obligatory, but could be brought at a later time, after the price of birds had gone down.[10]

Finally, we take note of R. Hayyim Berlin's (Russia, 1737–1802) view. In his understanding, R. Shimon b. Gamliel's ruling entailed no change of law whatsoever. What the Sage did was merely to promulgate that the law of multiple sacrifices applied merely to a woman of comfortable means. As for a poor woman, even after having multiple births, a single set of birds suffices to allow her to eat *kodishim*. In the event this woman becomes wealthy, the remaining sacrifices would, however, become obligatory upon her. R. Berlin derives this leniency by observing that the multiple sacrifices rule derives from the verse: "*This law* applies whether a woman gives birth to a boy or a girl" (Leviticus 12:7). This verse appears immediately after the Torah describes the sacrificial requirements of the woman of comfortable means. It is only then (12:8) that the Torah first addresses the sacrificial requirements of the poor woman. The multiple sacrifice rule hence does not apply to a woman who was poor at the time she gave birth. R. Berlin's interpretation makes R. Shimon b. Gamliel's intervention all a matter of *eliminating ignorance* of the law, which worked to lower prices in the marketplace.[11]

---

[9]R. Solomon b. Isaac, Rashi at *Mishna Keritot* 1:7, s. v. *nikhnas*.

[10]*Tosafot*, *Bava Batra* 166a, s. v. *nikhnas*.

[11]R. Hayyim Berlin, quoted by R. Naftali Yehudah Zevi Berlin, *Harkhev Davar*, *Leviticus* 12 *ot alef*.

We now turn to the talmudic essential foodstuff ordinance. This edict set a one-sixth profit rate limit for this sector.[12]

How the ancient ordinance worked in practice is a matter of dispute. Nevertheless, the following description, we believe, represents mainstream thought on its operational significance.

1. The ordinance was not aimed at interfering with natural market forces of supply and demand. It hence did not entail price fixing; instead vendors of foodstuffs were permitted to sell at the market price.[13]

If the foodstuff ordinance allows market forces free reign, then its practical significance is merely to prohibit sellers from collusively restricting supply for the purpose of raising their profit margin above the one-sixth level. Hence, the ordinance restricts both the formation of cartels as well as restraint of trade practices by the monopoly firm in the essential foodstuff industry.

2. The foodstuff ordinance called for the appointment of market commissioners by the Jewish court (*beit din*) to monitor the regulated sector.[14] Now, if the ordinance was never intended to countermand market conditions, then the role of market officials, it appears, must merely have been to enforce the competitive norm. Without this monitoring, ignorance of market conditions could have resulted in transactions concluded in divergence from the competitive norm.

To be sure, judicial redress is often open to victims of price divergence of this sort in the form of an *ohna'ah* (price fraud) claim. But the *ohna'ah* claim is at best an ex post facto remedy. Legal technicalities often make it difficult for a complainant to legally recover losses on account of *ohna'ah*. Moreover, many instances of *ohna'ah* go undetected by the victim. Out of concern for the subsistence needs of the masses, the Sages added another layer of protection in the foodstuff sector. Price commis-

---

[12] *Bava Batra* 90a; R. Isaac b. Jacob Alfasi (Algeria, 1013–1103), *Rif*, ad loc.; Maimonides (Egypt, 1135–1204), *Yad, Mekhirah* 14:1; R. Asher b. Jehiel (Germany, 1250–1327), *Rosh, Bava Batra* 5:28; *Tur, Hoshen Mishpat* 231:27–28; *Shulkhan Arukh, Hoshen Mishpat* 231:20; *Arukh ha-Shulkhan, Hoshen Mishpat* 231:20.

[13] *Tur*, op. cit., *Shulkhan Arukh*, op. cit.; *Arukh ha-Shulkhan*, op. cit. Maimonides (op. cit.), however, identifies the foodstuff ordinance with a price-fixing obligation on the part of the Jewish court.

[14] Ibid.

sioners were assigned for the purpose of enforcing market price and preventing instances of *ohna'ah*.

3. *Labor Costs.* Another critical issue is whether an allowance for the implicit costs of the owner is included in the cost base against which the one-sixth profit rate constraint is calculated. The widely held view is that if the owner provides his labor services on a continuous basis, that is, a retailer, an allowance for the labor services is included in the base.[15] Presumably the return is limited to the competitive rate for the type of work performed.

The failure to make provision for implicit wages for the owner when his labor services are not extended on a continuous basis, that is, a wholesaler, was probably due to a conviction on the part of the framers of the ordinance that wholesalers provided no useful social service.[16]

In enacting the foodstuff ordinance, the Sages, according to R. Joshua b. Alexander ha-Kohn Falk (Poland, 1555–1614) relied on the biblical injunction: "And let your brother live with you" (Leviticus 15:36).[17] R. Falk's comment makes the edict a mandate to sellers of essential foodstuffs to forego some part of their potential profit so as to allow consumers to achieve subsistence without undue hardship.

Assessing the Laissez-Faire Argument

In this section we will evaluate from a halakhic perspective the laissez-faire approach to the pricing of pharmaceuticals.

One feature of the pharmaceutical industry is the substantial costs companies incur in research and development expenditures for new drugs. Consider that the vast majority of compounds screened for medicinal potential never even make it to human testing, let alone to the market. Moreover,

---

[15]R. Menahem b. Solomon Meiri (Perpignan, ca. 1249–1306), *Beit ha-Behirah, Bava Metziah* 40b; *Rosh, Bava Metziah* 3:16; *Tur, Hoshen Mishpat* 231, and comment of Perisha, n. 26. R. Joel Sirkes (Poland, 1561–1650), however, interpreting Maimonides's position on this matter, posits that the one-sixth profit rate is the return the owner receives for his labor services (*Bah* to *Tur*, loc. Cit., note 26).

[16]For support for this thesis, see *Arukh ha-Shulkhan*, op. cit., 231:24–25.

[17]R. Joshua ha-Kohen Falk (Poland 1555–1614), *Sefer Me'irat Einayim. Hoshen Mishpat*, 231, note 43.

drug products must pass the U.S. Food and Drug Administration's reviews for safety and efficiency before they can be sold. Without the freedom to raise prices as they please, drug companies' ability to engage in new drug development would be crippled.[18]

On the face of it, *halakhah* would find sympathy with the above argument against price regulation. Public policy discourse must consider the long term consequences of alternative courses of action. Should a particular policy offer the likely prospect of adversely impacting on certain desirable objectives, the policy alternative should be rejected. Evidencing *halakhah*'s concern for the long run in designing public policy is the following episode in the life of R. Huna, recorded at *Taanit* 20b:

> On the eve of every Sabbath [Friday] he [R. Huna] would send a messenger to the market and any vegetable that the [market] gardeners had left over he bought up and had them thrown into the river. Should he not rather have had these distributed among the poor?–[He was afraid] lest they would then at times be led to rely upon him. [In this case] let him not trouble to buy them at all?–This would lead [the gardeners] to do wrong in the future [by not providing an adequate supply].

Proceeding from the above passage is that R. Huna understood the importance of economic incentives in insuring the long-run viability of economic activity. Since he felt that the availability of an adequate supply of vegetables for the honor of the Sabbath was a desirable outcome, he took pains to craft his subsidy to this industry in a manner that would insure its long-run viability.

We take it as a given that *halakhah* would regard it as desirable to encourage the development of new drugs that alleviate suffering and promote longevity. Given the huge research and development expenditures necessary to bring forth these drugs, price regulation should apparently be rejected.

Bolstering the case for laissez faire is the consideration that *halakhah* displays a delicate sensitivity not to upset the economic incentives in the medical field. This can be seen from a point in the law dealing with

[18]"Do We Pay Too Much for Prescriptions," *Consumer Reports* 58(10) (1993): 669.

the prohibition of either demanding or offering a fee for work rendered on the Sabbath (*sekhar shabbat*).[19] Out of concern that the *sekhar shabbat* prohibition might cause a physician to hesitate in responding to a call for assistance on the Sabbath, the Sages suspended the *sekhar shabbat* interdict in connection with medical fees.[20] On similar grounds, the Sages refrained from proclaiming that physicians taking *sekhar shabbat* would see no "sign of blessing" from the fee. Such a harsh pronouncement would surely deter physicians from demanding *sekhar shabbat*, but would at the same time remove the economic incentive for them to respond to a call for assistance on *Shabbat*.[21]

What emerges from the above analysis is that *halakhah* is concerned with interfering with the physician's economic incentives even in the face of a patient's call for assistance. Interference with economic incentives in the health-related field should therefore certainly be a concern in the absence of the moral force of a patient's cry for help. Adopting a laissez-faire attitude toward the pricing of pharmaceuticals is therefore indicated.

The merits of the above argument should, however, be considered in light of Richard R. Nelson's useful distinction between basic and applied research.

Basic research refers to human activity directed toward the discovery of facts and data observed in reproducible experiments. It also refers to the discovery of theories or relationships between facts. Applied research, on the other hand, is defined as human activity directed toward the creation of new and improved practical products and processes.[22] In the drug industry, basic research takes the form of the screening of compounds for potential activity against target diseases. It includes also the conducting of animal tests and preliminary human tests.

---

[19]*Tosefta, Shabbat* 18:16; *Yad, Shabbat* 6:25; *Tur, Orah Hayyim* 306:5; *Shulkhan Arukh, Orah Hayyim 306:4; Arukh ha-Shulkhan*, Orah Hayyim 306:9.

[20]R. Hayyim Isaac Algazi (Smyrna, later 18th century), *Derekh Etz ha-Hayyim*, responsum no. 2, R. Hayyim Modai (Turkey, 1700–1724), *Hayyim L'Olam*, p. 130; R. Yehoshua Neuwirth, *Shmirat Shabbat ki-Hilkhata*, p. 164, n. 135.

[21]*Hayyim L'Olam*, loc. Cit.

[22]Richard R. Nelson, "The Simple Economics of Basic Scientific Research," *Journal of Political Economy* June 1959, vol. 67 no. 3 (1959): 299.

Since basic research entails a general foray into the unknown, only monopoly firms, with huge resources at their disposal, can be expected to undertake this investment. But, in this case only if the government imposes no restraints on the firm's pricing policy, allowing it to anticipate huge rewards on its risk taking. The other alternative is for government to finance basic research.

Once basic research has come up with some promising data or theory, the profit motive will drive the holder of the information to develop it further toward practical ends.[23]

In the United States, the lion's share of basic research in the health related area is conducted not by the drug companies but by the federal government. Historically, the federal government has footed more than half the annual bill for health-related research. Three-quarters of this federally sponsored research comes from the National Institutes of Health (NIH).

Private industry involves itself in research and development (R&D) in the drug area mostly on the applied level. It does so in several ways: first, if a compound looks promising enough, the NIH invites private companies to bid for the right to bring the drug to market. In addition, since the mid-1980s, the NIH has also negotiated formal research and development agreements with private partners. These private firms participate in NIH basic research projects in exchange for an option to negotiate an exclusive license for any commercial product that may result.[24]

Given the profit constraint *halakhah* imposes on the pharmaceutical firm, basic research in the health-related field becomes a pure public good. A pure public good is a good that is a preferred item in people's budgets, but, paradoxically, will not be produced because of the absence of the profit motive. Government taxation is the only means of insuring that the good will, in fact, be produced. This is the case in the issue at hand. Basic research is by its very nature an unfocused, general foray into the unknown, with no practical objective in mind. Moreover, society will not optimally benefit from this activity unless findings of the research are *shared*. The profit motive to engage in this activity is therefore conspicuously absent. Yet, an adequate and ongoing financial commitment

---

[23]Nelson, op. cit., pp. 302, 305.

[24]*Consumer Reports*, op. cit., p. 670.

to basic research in the health-related field will assuredly produce discoveries which will enhance the quality of life for everyone. Investment in basic research in the health-related area is hence a preferred item in everyone's budget, provided assurances are given of widespread participation, which, in turn, guarantees adequate funding at minimum individual cost. Without government taxation there is no assurance that society's preferred expenditures on basic research in the health related-area will actually take place. No coercion is involved here, as the role of government is merely to actualize a demand for a preferred item in everyone's budget.

The pure public good phenomenon finds halakhic recognition in the power it gives to the Jewish community to tax its residents to construct a town wall.[25] In respect to this levy, even majority opposition cannot legally block the project.[26]

The rationale behind the town wall levy is the presumption that all the permanent residents of the town regard security measures as a preferred item in their budgets. What the tax does therefore, is to merely eliminate the "free rider" motive in respect to an undertaking everyone desires.[27]

Given the pure public good character of basic research in the health-related area, taxation to insure the viability of this endeavor is, from the perspective of *halakhah*, a legitimate function of government.

Basic Research and *Dei Mahsoro*

Government taxation to support basic research in the health-related field proceeds also from society's duty to attend to the needs of the poor. This obligation is formulated by the Torah in the form of *dei mahsoro* (suffi-

---

[25]*Mishna, Bava Batra* 1:5; *Rif*, ad loc.; *Yad, Shekhenim* 6:1; *Rosh, Bava Batra* 1:22; *Tur, Hoshen Mishpat* 163:1; *Shulkhan Arukh, Hoshen Mishpat* 163:1; *Arukh ha-Shulkhan, Hoshen Mishpat*, 163:1.

[26]R. Moses Isserles (Poland, 1525 or 1530–1572) *Rema, Shulkhan Arukh*, op. cit., 163:1; *Arukh ha-Shulkhan*, op. cit., 163:1.

[27]For the development of this thesis, see Aaron Levine, *Free Enterprise and Jewish Law: Aspects of Jewish Business Ethics* (New York: Ktav Publishing House; Yeshiva University Press, 1980), pp. 136–147.

cient for his needs).[28] Alleviating for the poor the physical and mental anguish of sickness fits squarely into this obligation. *Halakhah* gives expenditures for this purpose the highest ranking in charity giving.[29]

Consider that basic research is the building block in developing cures and treatments for devastating diseases. A steady and adequate expenditure in this direction coupled with guarantees of free access for the poor works to significantly improve the quality of life of the poor over time.

Elsewhere, we have developed the thesis that Judaism's antipoverty obligation is a dual system, consisting of both private and public components.[30] Because basic research, as discussed earlier, takes on the character of a pure public good, reliance on voluntarism will in all likelihood not adequately finance this activity. First, without guarantees that the poor will be given free access to the fruits of basic research in the health-related area, society will not treat this expenditure as part of its charity obligation. Moreover, even if people would regard basic research in the health-related area as a charity obligation, the expenditure would rate only a low priority status. This is so because relieving misery *here and now* takes precedence over expenditures on basic research which works only to relieve the misery of the poor in *future* time periods. Another reason for neglect is that expenditures on basic research offer the prospect of producing useful findings only when the activity is conducted on a steady and large-scale basis. This may make people reluctant to contribute unless they are assured of widespread participation. Finally, reliance on voluntarism here would undoubtedly shortchange research on diseases which affect only a tiny percentage of the population.

Commitment to relieving the misery of the poor over time hence requires the public sector to act *here and now* as a proxy for future time periods. It does so by taxing society for basic research in the health-related area with the aim of assuring a steady and adequate expenditure for this purpose.

---

[28]Deuteronomy 15:8; *Ketubot* 67b; *Rif* ad loc.; *Yad, Mattenot Aniyyim* 7:3; *Rosh, Ketubot* 6:8; *Tur, Yoreh De'ah* 250:1; *Shulkhan Arukh, Yoreh De'ah* 250:1; *Arukh ha-Shulkhan, Yoreh De'ah* 250:1–3.

[29]*Shulhan Arukh*, op. cit., 249:16.

[30]Aaron Levine, *Economics and Jewish Law: Halakhic Perspectives* (Hoboken: Ktav Publishing House; Yeshiva University Press, 1987), pp. 113–133.

By insuring a steady and adequate flow of research and development, government taxation effectively shifts the risk associated with this expenditure from private industry to society at large. Under this arrangement, private industry enters the drug-development field only when profit considerations motivate it to do so. Since private industry enters the health-related field on the applied-research level, the argument that the potential for high profits must exist to insure the development of new drugs is hence considerably undermined.

Public funding of basic research carries with it a regulatory responsibility for government in the pricing of drugs. One aspect of this responsibility is to insure that the pricing policies of firms making use of government sponsored research should afford them no more than opportunity cost earnings. Another responsibility is to insure that the poor would be guaranteed free access to the drugs.

Patent Protection and the Pharmaceutical Industry

One feature of the pharmaceutical industry is that innovative drugs qualify for patent protection. Under the law, the holder of the patent is entitled to exclusive marketing rights for a seventeen-year period. At the expiration of this period, the patent holder retains exclusive use of its brand name, but competing companies are free to copy the drug and seek approval from the FDA for its sale. Drugs competing with the brand name drugs are called generic drugs.[31]

The above arrangement appears to restrict competition and therefore to contribute to higher drug prices. Economic theory, however, generally takes a favorable view toward patents. Without the prospect of monopoly protection, an inventor might despair of ever profiting from years devoted to an endless search for new products and processes. Patent law hence provides a necessary incentive to engage in innovative activity.[32] Applied to the pharmaceutical industry, patent rights are a necessary incentive to foster the development of new drugs.

Patent protection law finds its parallel in *halakhah*. R. Mosheh Sofer's (Hungary, 1762–1839) analysis of an 1820 infringement case involving

---

[31] *Consumer Reports*, op. cit., pp. 671–672.

[32] Paul A. Samuelson and William Nordhaus, *Economics*, 15th ed. (New York: McGraw-Hill, 1995), p. 155.

the *Rödelheim Mahzor* (High Holiday prayer book) bears directly on the issue of patent rights for innovative drugs.

Wolf Heidenheim, the publisher of the *mahzor*, had secured a rabbinical ban against republication by other persons for a period of twenty-five years. Shortly afterward, a publisher in Dyhernfürth proceeded to issue the *Rödelheim Mahzor*. Rabbis took opposing views, but the majority upheld Heidenheim's right to the protection of his work.

After defending Heidenheim on the basis of the rabbinical notices against republication printed in the *mahzor*, R. Sofer found an even more basic reason to restrain the publisher in Dyhernfürth. Heidenheim had not reprinted an extant edition of the *mahzor* from the public domain; rather, he had produced an improved edition of the *mahzor*, complete with revisions, annotations, and a German translation of the Hebrew text. Since the *Rödelheim Mahzor* entailed considerable innovation on the part of Heidenheim, its reissue by the firm in Dyhernfürth amounted to no less than appropriating someone else's toil and effort for the purpose of his own commercial advantage.

R. Sofer found the action of the second publisher analogous to the understanding of the talmudic dictum recorded at *Bava Batra* 21b expounded by R. Meir b. Samuel (Ramerupt, ca. 1060—ca. 1155): "Fishing nets must be kept away from a fish the full length of the fish's swim. And how much is this? Rabbah son of R. Huna [d. 322] says: a parasang."

R. Meir understands the dictum as referring to a situation where *A*, in hopes of attracting large numbers of fish to the vicinity, casts a net containing a dead fish. *B* must not cast his net in the same vicinity because interloping action of this sort is regarded as a form of robbery. Since it is *A*'s initiative which attracts the swarms of fish, *B*'s interloping action effectively appropriates *A*'s toil and effort for the purpose of his own commercial advantage.[33] Likewise, R. Sofer posits, the publisher in Dyhernfürth must be prevented from reaping commercial advantage from the reissuing of the Rödelheim Mahzor. The second publisher's action amounts to appropriation of Heidenheim's toil and effort for his own commercial gain.

Basing himself on the fisherman case, R. Sofer issued a ban against publishers to reprint the Rödelheim prayer book for a period of twenty-five years. The rationale for the twenty-five years was that it would take

---

[33]R. Meir b. Samuel, quoted in *Tosafot, Kiddushin* 59a, s. v. *ani*.

Heidenheim this amount of time, entailing multiple printings, to recoup his investment at a fair return.[34]

What follows from R. Sofer's ruling is that a discoverer of a new drug would be entitled to a monopoly privilege over a period of time so that he could recoup his investment at a fair return. Copying and commercializing his discovery before such time amounts to expropriating someone else's toil and effort for commercial gain. Secular society's patent-rights approach to protecting innovative drugs is hence very much consonant with *halakhah*.

We should note, however, that making medicine available to someone in need, as discussed earlier, is a *mitzvah* activity. As such, the provider is entitled only to opportunity cost earnings. One implication of this is that the discoverer of a new drug is not automatically entitled to an exclusive privilege to market it. To illustrate: Machliss discovers a breakthrough drug effective in the treatment of advanced stages of lung cancer. The government sets a $3 per pill price, which amounts to the cost of the recommended daily dosage. The price is geared to afford Machliss opportunity cost earnings. It is based on the assumption that Machliss will sell out his entire annual full capacity production of one million pills. But, at $3 per pill, annual market demand will exceed one hundred million pills. Machliss has no interest in devoting his time, effort, and resources to expand his capacity. Nonetheless, he has no objection to making his trade secret available to others, provided they agree to a production quota and a royalty fee. Machliss's demands are unreasonable and therefore must be rejected. At once, it is society's duty to make the cancer drug as widely available as possible. Moreover, Machliss is entitled to earn from his *mitzvah* activity no more than opportunity cost earnings. Accordingly, *hassagat gevul* law works only to protect Machliss's opportunity cost earnings, but not to guarantee him earnings above this level.

We take note that the commercial value of a new drug depends on such factors as the number of people who stand to benefit from its discovery, the income distribution among the impacted group, and the cost of producing the drug. The opportunity cost earnings of the manufac-

---

[34]R. Mosheh Sofer, *Responsa Hatam Sofer, Hoshen Mishpat* 79; see also *Responsa Hoshen Mishpat* 41 and 6:57.

turer of the drug, on the other hand, are determined by the minimum payments necessary to induce the resources involved to put out their work effort. These two values can and do diverge. Divergence between these two values is especially likely when the government assumes the function of sponsoring basic research and the pharmaceutical firms are hence not involved in a high-risk effort.

Developing a drug and bringing it to market, as discussed earlier, are *mitzvah* activities. As such, the firm involved is entitled to only opportunity cost earnings. The above consideration argues for some amount of flexibility in formulating patent rights as they apply to the health-related field. Specifically, if the commercial value of the drug is assessed to be very large relative to the opportunity cost of the manufacturer, conferring less than a seventeen-year patent may be in order.

Halakhic Guideposts and Drug Pricing

The guideposts *halakhah* calls for in the structuring of the pharmaceutical industry foster lower drug prices. We offer the following two case studies, involving the drugs Ergamisol and Clorazil, to illustrate this point.

Ergamasol

Approximately thirty years ago, Johnson & Johnson introduced Levamisole, a drug used to deworm sheep. Under the sponsorship of the National Cancer Institute, and with free pills provided by Johnson & Johnson, Dr. Charles Moertel of the Mayo Comprehensive Cancer Center tested Levamisole in combination with a staple chemotherapy drug called 5-fluorouracil as a treatment for cancer. The combination proved effective in patients with advanced (Stage C) colon cancer. It reduced recurrence of the disease by 40 percent and cut deaths by a third.

Based on Dr. Moertel's research, the (FDA) quickly approved Levamisole for human use. In 1990, the Janssen division of Johnson & Johnson introduced the drug under the brand Ergamisol. At the same time, the animal version was licensed for manufacture by American Cyanamid Co. A tremendous price differential existed between Ergamisol and the older, veterinary version of the drug. The sheep medicine sold for pennies a pill, whereas the human medicine sold for five to six dollars per tablet. Ergamisol cost $1,250 to $1,500 for a year's supply. The cost for treating sheep was as low as $14.95 per year.

The price discrepancy caused quite a stir. At the annual meetings of the American Society for Clinical Oncology in May 1992, Dr. Moertel blasted Johnson & Johnson for its unconscionable pricing of the drug. In August 1992, a consumer filed suit against Janssen. He claimed that he was forced to pay "an outrageous, unconscionable, and extortionate price for a life-saving drug" that is sold at a fraction of the cost for the purpose of treating sheep.[35]

From the standpoint of *halakhah*, the basic issue here is that the government sponsored the research that proved Levamisole effective in treating human colon cancer. As such, it was unconscionable for the government to give Janssen carte blanche in its pricing policy. Instead, it should have imposed cost-plus pricing on it. If, in fact, as Johnson & Johnson claimed, the company engaged in costly research over decades to determine if Levamisole could be used to treat humans, then these costs would legitimately be taken into account in arriving at a price.

The neglect of the government to set and enforce guideposts for the pricing of Ergamisol does not mean that the purchaser of this drug is without recourse against Johnson & Johnson. Given that the difference between Ergamisol and Levamisole is essentially *in name only*, the greater than one-sixth difference in price between the two drugs should allow the purchases of Ergamisol to void the sale and get his money back. Ordinarily, an enormous difference in price between the subject and the comparison good signals that the transaction was concluded on price terms that exceed reasonable misjudgment. Accordingly, the only plausible interpretation is that the underlying intention of the parties involved was not to trade the article at hand but rather just to use that article as a vehicle to effect a voluntary gift transfer. Given that Johnson & Johnson withheld the information that Levamisole is a colon cancer drug, plaintiff's *ohna'ah* (price fraud) claim should remain intact, notwithstanding the enormous difference in price between Ergamisol and Levamisole. Far from signalling an intent to make a voluntary transfer to Johnson & Johnson, the overcharge reflects the successful duping conduct of the seller. Plaintiff's *ohna'ah* claim hence remains intact.[35a]

---

[35]Philip Kotler and Gary Armstrong, *Principles of Marketing*, 6th ed. (Englewood Cliffs, NJ: Prentice-Hall, 1994), p. 388.

[35a]For discussion of the law of *ohna'ah* see *infra* notes 39–49 and accompanying text.

Clozaril

In 1990, Sandoz Pharmaceuticals Corp. got FDA approval to market its drug Clozaril, used to treat schizophrenia. The company's initial pricing of the drug made its annual cost to a user come to $8,944. One feature of the marketing of this drug was a *mandatory* and expensive blood-monitoring system designed to detect a side effect that could otherwise be fatal to as many as 2 percent of patients. Without its proprietary system, Sandoz claimed, some patients would die and the drug would inevitably be pulled from the market.

The blood monitoring was the more expensive part of the package and because of it, critics claimed, few would be able to afford the drug. Medicaid officials, the Veteran Administration, and others, mounted an unsuccessful campaign to force Sandoz to uncouple the drug from the blood-testing program. The VA, for instance, claimed it could do the blood work for $1.86.[36]

With the aim of facilitating analysis of the above case from a halakhic standpoint, let's assume that the basic research for Clozaril was financed by society as a whole. Within this framework, Sandoz is entitled to no more than cost plus pricing for its drug. Moreover, with the aim of reducing costs, it would be the duty of government to investigate the feasibility of uncoupling the drug from the blood-testing program. Finally, the government would require Sandoz to make its drug available to the poor free of charge. If the incidence of schizophrenia is mainly or even disproportionately on the poor, the latter requirement would assuredly make Clozaril unprofitable. In this instance, Sandoz would qualify for a government subsidy. The rationale for this subsidy is that to relieve the misery of the poor is both an individual and a societal obligation. If neither the profit motive nor voluntarism offers any prospect of relieving a particular form of misery, then, it is the duty of government to tax society for this purpose.

Unregulated Competition between Brand-Name and Generic Drugs

Another factor contributing toward the high price of prescription drugs is weak competition between brand name and generic drugs.

[36]N. Craig Smith and John A. Quelch, *Ethics in Marketing* (Homewood, IL: Irwin, 1993), pp. 441–445.

Under current conditions, patent law confers a monopoly position on a brand-name drug for seventeen years. Once a drug loses its exclusive patent rights, competition begins in earnest as manufacturers produce generic versions of the original. Because they don't have to shoulder the costs of research and development or marketing, generic companies can sell compounds far more cheaply than the brand-name equivalents. When a product goes off patent, the first generic on the market generally costs at least 30 percent less than the brand-name version. As more generic competitors enter the market, the price drops still further.

Patent law allows drug companies to trademark the specific shape and color of their pills. A generic drug may therefore not look the same as its branded equivalent, but the FDA requires that the active ingredient must be identical with the brand-name equivalent. It also requires generics to be formulated so that they are absorbed into the body at essentially the same rate.[37]

Calan and Verapamil

Since a generic drug is, with few exceptions, *therapeutically interchangeable* with its brand-name counterpart, the difference in price between these drugs is a matter of moral concern for *halakhah*. Providing a case in point is the price difference between brand-name Calan and its generic counterpart, verapamil. Calan, a calcium medication for high blood pressure, costs $45 per one hundred 80–milligram tablets. With no loss in therapeutic value, generic verapamil costs $7 for the same supply.[38]

Calan's pricing policy may be in violation of *ohna'ah* (price fraud). The law of *ohna'ah* prohibits a vendor (buyer) from knowingly transacting at a price above (below) what the item at hand is available elsewhere.[39] What is objectionable here is to prey on the opposing party's ignorance of market conditions in a commercial transaction.[40] A transaction in-

---

[37]"Do We Pay Too Much for Prescription Drugs," op. cit., p. 675.

[38]Ibid.

[39]*Baraita, Bava Metziah* 51a; *Rif* ad. loc.; *Yad, Mekhirah* 12:1; *Rosh, Bava Metziah* 4:17; *Tur, Hoshen Mishpat* 227:1; *Shulkhan Arukh, Hoshen Mishpat* 227:1; *Arukh ha-Shulkhan, Hoshen Mishpat* 227:1.

[40]For the development of this thesis, see Levine, *Free Enterprise and Jewish Law*, op. cit., pp. 105–109.

volving *ohna'ah* is regarded as a form of theft.[41] Depending on how widely the price of the subject transaction departs from the competitive norm, the injured party may have recourse to void or adjust the transaction.

Provided the price discrepancy is assessed to be within the margin of error,[42] the plaintiff's right to void the transaction is recognized when the difference between the sale price and the competitive norm is more than one-sixth.[43] When the differential is exactly one-sixth, neither of the parties may subsequently void the transaction on account the price discrepancy. The plaintiff is, however, entitled to full restitution of the *ohna'ah* involved.[44] Finally, third-degree *ohna'ah* occurs when the sale price differs from the market price by less than one-sixth. Here, the transaction not only remains binding, but, in addition, the complainant has no legal claim to the price differential.[45] In the latter instance, however, the plaintiff's claim would be denied only when the transaction involved a product which is nonstandardized in nature. Should the case involve a homogeneous product, the plaintiff's claim for the differential is honored.[46]

In evaluating the merit of the *ohna'ah* claim against Calan, the differential costs Calan and verapamil operate under must be considered. Calan's costs of production included substantial outlays on applied research and clinical trials. These outlays can only be recovered over a large number of years. Verapamil, on the other hand, brings its product to the market by simply reproducing Calan's product under a different name, shape, and color. The obvious difference in cost between the competing medications

---

[41]*Bava Metziah* 61a; *Tur*, op. cit., 227:1; R. Joshua b. Alexander ha-Kohen Falk (Poland, 1555–1614), *Sema, Shulkhan Arukh, Hoshen Mishpat* 227, n. 1; *Arukh ha-Shulkhan*, op. cit., 227:1.

[42]*Bava Batra* 78a and *Rashi* ad loc., s. v. *bikhdei*; *Rif*, ad loc.; *Yad*, op. cit. 27:5; *Rosh, Bava Batra* 5:7; *Tur*, op. cit., 220:5; *Shulkhan Arukh*, op. cit., 220:8; *Arukh ha-Shulkhan*, op. cit., 220:7.

[43]*Bava Metziah* 50b; *Rif*, ad. loc., *Yad*, op. cit. 12:4; *Rosh, Bava Metziah* 4:15; *Tur*, op. cit. 227:6; *Shulkhan Arukh*, op. cit., 227:4; *Arukh ha-Shulkhan*, op. cit, 227:3.

[44]*Bava Metziah* 50b; *Rif*, ad loc., *Yad*, op. cit, 12:2; *Rosh*, op. cit, 4:15; *Tur*, op. cit., 227:3; *Shulkhan Arukh*, op. cit., 227:2, *Arukh ha-Shulkhan*, loc. cit.

[45]*Bava Metziah* 50b; *Rif*, ad loc.; *Yad*, op. cit., 12:3; *Tur*, op. cit, 227:4; *Shulkhan Arukh*, op. cit., 227:3; *Arukh ha-Shulkhan*, loc. cit.

[46]*Arukh ha-Shulkhan*, op. cit., 227:7.

makes the exemption to the prohibition of *ohna'ah* called *noss'e be-emunah* (selling on trust)[47] apparently applicable here.

Noss'e be-emunah obtains when the vendor divulges to a prospective buyer both his cost price and his proposed profit margin. Should the buyer agree to these terms and consummate the transaction with a *kinyan*, a subsequent finding that the cost price involved *ohna'ah* does not allow the plaintiff to modify the original transaction in any manner. Agreeing to allow the vendor a specified profit margin demonstrates on the part of the buyer a lack of concern with the objective value of the commodity. Because realization of the agreed-upon profit rate required the sale to be concluded at the stipulated price, subsequent claims against *ohna'ah* are denied.[48]

Noss'e be-emunah is, however, of no help here in validating Calan's pricing policy. Consider that Calan enjoyed a seventeen-year *monopoly* before verapamil arrived on the competitive scene. Presumably, this time period gave Calan ample opportunity to recoup the differential costs it incurred in bringing its drug to market. Accordingly, when verapamil enters the competitive scene, Calan competes on an equal cost basis. Moreover, even under the unlikely event that Calan's cost differential persists beyond the expiration of its patent rights, consumers know neither Calan's cost price nor its profit margin. Stretching the *noss'e be-emunah* exemption to its limits can say no more than that consumers are willing to afford the seller a reasonable profit on the basis of his known cost differential. But, in the present state of affairs, consumers certainly don't regard the profit of drug companies as reasonable. In this regard we need only take note of the 1993 report of the Congressional Office of Technological Assessment. This report concluded that during the 1980s pharmaceutical companies, on average, earned roughly 15 to 30 percent *more* profit each year than they needed to attract adequate investment capital.[49]

---

[47]*Bava Metziah* 51b; *Rif*, ad loc.; *Yad*, op. cit, 13:5; *Rosh*, op cit., 4:17; *Tur*, op. cit., 227:37; *Shulkhan Arukh*, op. cit., 227:27; *Arukh ha-Shulkhan*, op. cit., 227:28.

[48]*Yad*, loc. cit. For a variant view of what constitutes selling on trust, see R. Israel Krems (ca. 1375), *Haggahot Asheri, Bava Metziah* 4:17.

[49]*Pharmaceutical R & D: Costs, Risks and Rewards* (Washington, DC: U.S. Congress, Office of Technology Assessment, 1993), p. 2.

The price differential a brand name drug maintains over its generic counterpart violates *ohna'ah* in a blatant manner when the brand name company itself produces and sells the generic drug. Here, the price differential amounts to a deceptive selling practice.

The Doctor's Duty to Minimize the Patient's Cost for Prescription Drugs

Irrespective of the issue of whether the brand-name drug has a right to charge more than its generic counterpart, it should be the duty of the doctor to minimize the prescription cost for his patient. It is clearly a professional responsibility of a doctor to serve the best interests of his patient. Prescribing a brand-name drug when a lower-priced generic equivalent is available amounts to ill-suited advice. Proffering ill-suited advice violates: "Do not place a stumbling block before the blind" (Leviticus 19:14).[50]

Moreover, let's consider the possibility that the doctor may be liable here to make good on the patient's loss. The case at hand is analogous to the instance where a professional moneychanger errs in his judgment that a particular coin will circulate. If the moneychanger took a fee for his services, he is liable to make good on the client's loss.[51]

Some authorities understand the moneychanger case broadly, referring even to circumstances in which the advisee feels free to ignore the moneychanger's advice.[52] Others understand the case narrowly, as referring only to circumstances where the advisee, for all intents and purposes, feels compelled to accept the moneychanger's judgement.[53] This would be the case, for instance, when the advisee was a vendor who received cash payment for his merchandise and the moneychanger is called upon to resolve a dispute between the buyer and the seller as to whether the currency paid will circulate. Should the advisee be free to ignore the judgment of the

[50]Torat Kohanim, *Leviticus 19:14*; *Yad*, *Rotzeah* 12:14.

[51]*Tur*, op. cit., 306:10; *Shulkhan Arukh*, op. cit, 306:6; *Arukh ha-Shulkhan*, op. cit., 306:13.

[52]Rabbenu Yoel quoted by R. Israel of Krems, *Haggahot Asheri*, *Bava Kamma* 9:16; R. Jonathan Eybeschuetz (Prague, 1695–1764), *Tummim*, *Shulkhan Arukh*, op. cit., 146, note 19; R. Mosheh Sofer, *Novelae Bava Batra* 30b.

[53]Rabbenu Efraim quoted in *Haggahot Asheri*, op. cit.

moneychanger, no liability obtains for the latter in the event that he made an erroneous judgment. In the case at hand, the patient is not really free to ignore the doctor's prescription. Prescription always follows diagnosis. Given the patient's investment in obtaining the doctor's diagnosis, following through with filling the prescription is rational, if not compelling. Since the indicated medication cannot be obtained without a prescription, the patient effectively has no option other than filling the prescription.

We take note that all disputants agree that communication on the part of the advisee that he relies on the judgment of the moneychanger makes the latter liable in the event of error.[54] Receiving payment for his opinion makes it as if the advisee enunciated to the moneychanger that he is relying on his opinion in the matter. Since the damage resulted directly from relying on the expert's advice, the expert's action is a form of *garmi*.[55]

What the aforementioned has indicated is that a case can be made to hold a doctor liable for a patient's loss resulting from prescribing a brand-name drug when an equivalent generic drug is available. The case is strongest when the doctor reinforces his brand name prescription with an explicit instruction to the pharmacist to dispense the prescription as written (D.A.W.). This instruction makes it illegal for the pharmacist to substitute a generic equivalent for the prescribed brand name drug.

Generic Substitution Legislation and *Halakhah*

Since the mid-1970s, state legislation has allowed pharmacists to dispense lower-priced generics in place of the prescribed brand-name drugs. Of the statutes in effect in 1980, more than three-fourths provided for permissive, rather than mandatory, substitution. In any case, explicit instruction by the physician not to substitute requires the pharmacist to dispense the prescription as given.[56]

---

[54]R. Shabbetai b. Meir ha-Kohen (Poland, 1621–1662), *Sifrei Kohen*, *Shulkhan Arukh*, op. cit., 129, note 7; *Arukh ha-Shulkhan*, op. cit., 306:13.

[55]*Arukh ha-Shulkhan*, loc. cit.

[56]James J. Wheaton, "Generic Competition and Pharmaceutical Innovation: The Drug Price Competition and Patent Term Restoration Act of 1984," *Catholic University Law Review* 35 (Winter 1986): 437–447.

By allowing pharmacists, in the absence of a physician override, to dispense brand-name prescriptions in generic form, the law effectively gives notice to the physician that his inattention to the appropriateness of a generic substitution could result in harm to his patient. The law hence places some measure of burden on the doctor to *educate himself* in respect to the generic substitution question. Since prescribing a brand-name drug when a cheaper, equivalent generic is available makes the doctor guilty, as discussed earlier, of proffering his patient ill-suited advice, the new legislation is in the right direction as far as *halakhah* is concerned. It does not, however, go far enough. What is indicated is that, in the absence of a physician override, pharmacists should be required, rather than just permitted, to make the substitution.

In respect to the physician override, statutes differ in respect to how it becomes operative. In some states, the override becomes effective when the physician signs the prescription on a line labeled "Do Not Substitute" or "Dispense As Written" (DAW). In other states, the override becomes effective only if the doctor *writes out* such an instruction. The rate of drug substitution varies significantly depending on whether the statute requires the doctor to write out the instruction or allows him merely to sign the DAW line. Wheaton suggests that this difference is due to inadvertent error. If the physician needs only to choose between signing two lines, he may inadvertently sign the DAW line, even though he has no strong preference for the brand-name drug.[57]

Proceeding as a corollary from Wheaton's supposition is that physicians do not regard it as their responsibility to save patients money by prescribing generic drugs when possible. Since *halakhah* requires the doctor to educate himself in respect to the possibility of generic substitution, *halakhah* would take a definite stance in respect to the override issue. Legislative reform in the form of making the override operative only if the doctor *writes out* the instruction is therefore indicated.

Generic Substitution Legislation and *Ohna'ah*

The generic substitution legislation does not, of course, address the *ohna'ah* issue. Recall that the essence of the *ohna'ah* interdict for the seller

[57]Wheaton, op. cit., p. 445.

is a prohibition to exploit the ignorance of his opposite number. Given that for the overwhelming majority of prescription holders the brand-name drug and its generic counterpart are *therapeutically equivalent*, the brand-name company must price its drug using the price of the generic as its reference point.

While the law allows pharmacists to dispense prescriptions generically in the absence of an override, only about 15 percent of prescriptions with a brand name are filled with a generic product.[58] The unwillingness of pharmacists to dispense prescriptions in generic form results, therefore, in a proliferation of instances of *ohna'ah*. With the aim of minimizing these instances, *halakhah* would welcome implementation of ideas which would encourage pharmacists to dispense prescriptions in generic form.

One approach to remedying the situation is through education. Pharmacists don't dispense prescriptions in generic form because they fear that, in the event consumers are harmed by the substitution, they will be held liable. This concern is reinforced in advertising by brand-name pharmaceutical manufacturers, but, as Wheaton points out, is unfounded. First, liability insurance for pharmacists is accessible and premiums for pharmacist's insurance are low. Second, many state substitution laws contain provisions stipulating that drug product substitution is not evidence of negligence. It is only negligence when the substitution product does not have FDA approval.[59]

In his treatment of the generic substitution issue, Wheaton advocates certain legislative changes, with the aim of encouraging pharmacists to dispense prescriptions in generic form.

First, drug manufacturers should be permitted to state in advertising or labeling that a product has received FDA approval. With proper disclaimers to avoid the appearance that the FDA is acting as a guarantor of quality, such legislation would enhance the acceptability of generic drugs.

Second, medical reimbursement programs, both public and private, can affect the incidence of generic drug use by tailoring their maximum reimbursements for drug costs to the prices of generic products. In state Medicaid and Medicare programs this form of cost control is imposed by

---

[58]Wheaton, op. cit., p. 446, note 56.

[59]Ibid., p. 447.

the Maximum Allowable Cost (MAC) program, which is in place in twenty-six states. Under the MAC program, the government establishes maximum allowable cost levels for multisource equivalent drugs at the lowest price at which the drug is "widely and consistently available."

The benefits of programs such as MAC extend, however, beyond the savings gained in the treatment of Medicaid and Medicare recipients. Because a MAC level is established at the "widely available" price, the price of competing drugs should fall for all consumers, and not just for Medicaid and Medicare beneficiaries.[60]

Improving the Informational Channels in the Pharmaceutical Industry

Recall that in connection with the talmudic foodstuff ordinance, the Sages called for the appointment of commissioners to monitor the foodstuff sector. It was the job of these commissioners to insure that individual sellers would not exploit consumer ignorance regarding market conditions and overcharge them. These commissioners hence enforced market price and prevented instances of *ohna'ah*.

What can be generalized from the above is that it would be of particular concern for the Sages to eliminate distortions in the information channels in those industries dealing with the subsistence needs of the masses. Cracking down on the misleading promotional activities of the pharmaceutical companies and promoting better knowledge of price differences among drugs is consistent with the above concern. Let us first turn to the misleading promotion issue.

Misleading Promotional Activities

In the current commercial environment, the promotional policies of brand-name companies have the effect of distorting physicians' prescribing choices. Objectionable practices of brand-name companies include: (1) the reward system companies set up for doctors to use their products; (2) brand-name company sponsorship of Continuing Medical Education (CME); and (3) company sponsorship of journal supplements.

---

[60]Ibid., pp. 475–478.

Rewards for Doctors

The most objectionable marketing tactic of pharmaceutical companies entails the offering of "rewards" to doctors who prescribe large amounts of a company drug. A case in point is the marketing technique Wyeth Ayerst used in connection with its blood-pressure drug Inderal. After Inderal's patent expired, Wyeth Ayerst had to compete with generic imitations of its successful drug. To succeed in the tougher market, the company offered frequent-flyer miles on American Airlines to physicians who prescribed the drug. Doctors who wrote fifty prescriptions would receive a free round trip ticket to any destination in the continental United States.

Another practice is for sales representatives of drug companies to provide doctors with "reminders" of their product. These reminders take the form of note pads, pens, rulers, and other useful "freebies" engraved both with the logo of the company and with the product's name. Similarly, drug companies provide doctors with free informational lunches to acquaint them with their product line.[61]

Some view the latter practices very innocently. First, these practices help physicians make more informed prescribing decisions. Moreover, minor gift-giving ensures that new pharmaceutical companies have a direct and effective means of promoting unfamiliar products. To be sure, these costs may be shifted to the health consumer. But, arguably, these costs are no greater than those physicians would shift if they were required to survey the literature for new drug information. Moreover, prohibiting these practices runs the risk that doctors might neglect the responsibility to make informed prescription decisions, resulting in an even greater health cost to the patient.[62]

Sponsorship of CME

CME is designed to force physicians to stay abreast of new medical technologies. Many state licensing boards require practicing physicians to

---

[61]S. H. Fisher, "The Economic Wisdom of Regulating Pharmaceutical Freebies," *Duke Law Review* (February 1991): 209–213, 238–239; "Pushing Drugs to Doctors," *Consumer Reports* (February 1992): 87–90.

[62]Fisher, op. cit., pp. 238–239.

complete a specific number of credits each year. Sponsorship of CME by drug companies runs the risk that the company's interest in promoting its product will outweigh its concern for educating doctors objectively about new medical developments.[63]

Sponsorship of Journal Supplements

Doctors consistently name medical journals as one of their main sources of unbiased information. Especially valued are peer-reviewed journals. Drug companies have found an effective way to use these journals' credibility for their own purposes by subsidizing the publication of "supplements." Piggy-backed onto regular issues of the journal, supplements use the same sober-looking design and typography as the regular articles. Frequently, the supplements are based on symposia sponsored by the same companies that pay for the publication. Exacerbating the above problem is that many journals actively market their willingness to publish supplements.[64]

Drug Company Marketing Practices and *Halakhah*

The various marketing practices described above would be regarded by *halakhah* as unethical conduct. Most blatant is the practice of directly rewarding physicians for prescribing a drug. Such conduct biases the physician to prescribe the drug in favor of competing drugs. How an offer of favor works to taint objectivity can be seen by the standard *halakhah* sets for the judicial code of ethics. Jewish law safeguards the integrity of the judicial decision-making process by means of both preventive measures and corrective action. Preventive measures take the form of prohibiting the judge of a lawsuit from submitting to any influence that might taint his integrity and calling for him to disqualify himself on the basis of bias.

By force of the verse "*You shall not distort justice*" (Deuteronomy 16:19), the judge of a lawsuit is forbidden to accept a payment to acquit the guilty or to condemn the innocent. What constitutes a corrupting payment is considerably broadened by force of the verse "*You shall take no gift*" (Exodus 23:8). Exegetical interpretation of this verse prohibits the judge from

[63]"Pushing Drugs to Doctors," op. cit., pp. 90–92.
[64]Ibid., pp. 93–94.

accepting payment from one of the opposing litigants even with the instruction to acquit the innocent or to condemn the guilty.[65] Rava's (d. 352) rationalization of the latter point of stringency is very telling: "What is the reason for [the prohibition against taking] a gift? Because as soon as a man receives a gift from another he becomes like his own person, and no man sees himself in the wrong. What [is the meaning of] shohad? *She-hu had*—'he is one with you.'"[66]

Fully recognizing that bias may be created by means other than the acceptance of money, Jewish law prohibits the judge from submitting to even a bribe of words (*shohad devarim*).[67] Illustrating *shohad devarim* is the following talmudic incident: "Amemar was once engaged in the trial of an action, when a bird flew down upon his head and a man approached and removed it. 'What is your business here?' [Amemar asked him.] 'I have a lawsuit,' the other replied. 'I' came the reply, 'am disqualified from acting as your judge.'"[68]

The stringency of *shohad devarim* applies even to words of greeting. Accordingly, in the event A did not make it a practice to anticipate judge *B*'s greeting with his own greeting, initiating this practice just prior to the time his lawsuit will come up in *B*'s docket amounts to *shohad devarim*. Since *B* is regarded as being biased toward A on account of A's newfound friendliness toward him, *B* is disqualified from serving as judge in his lawsuit.[69]

A close friendship or enmity with one of the litigants similarly disqualifies an individual from serving as judge in his lawsuit.[70]

---

[65]*Ketubot* 105a; *Yad, Sanhedrin* 23:1; *Tur, Hoshen Mishpat* 9:1; *Shulkhan Arukh, Hoshen Mishpat* 9:1; *Arukh ha-Shulkhan, Hoshen Mishpat* 9:1.

[66]*Ketubot* 105b.

[67]*Ketubot* 105b, *Yad*, op. cit., 9:4; *Shulkhan Arukh*, op. cit., 9:1; *Arukh ha-Shulkhan*, op. cit., 9:1.

[68]*Ketubot* 105b.

[69]R. Joshua ha-Kohen Falk (Poland, 1555–1614), *Sema, Shulkhan Arukh*, op. cit., 9, n. 4; *Arukh ha-Shulkhan*, loc. cit.

[70]*Sanhedrin* 29a; *Rif*, ad loc., *Yad*, op. cit., 23:6; *Rosh, Sanhedrin* 3:23; *Tur*, op. cit., 7:8, 10; *Shulkhan Arukh*, op. cit., 7:7; *Arukh ha-Shulkhan*, op cit., 7:9–10.

Judicial disqualification proceeds as a definite matter, according to majority opinion, only when the judge is either a *close* friend or a presumed enemy of one of the litigants. Here, the judge must, as a matter of strict law, remove himself from the case. Should he preside over the case, his verdict would be ren-

Judicial verdicts rendered under the influence of *shohad* are null and void.[71] Since the *shohad* payment is regarded as a forbidden receipt, the judge is legally bound to return the illicit fee. Though the Jewish court will not force the judge to return the *shohad* unless the claimant demands repayment,[72] he is, nevertheless, ethically bound to make restitution even in the absence of a petition by the claimant.[73]

The judicial code of conduct does not only apply to the individual who adjudicates a formal litigation. Residents of a community, according to R. Moses Isserles (Poland, 1525 or 1530–1572), must cast their votes in a referendum in accordance with what they perceive the public's interest to be.[74] Noting this requirement, R. Moses Sofer (Hungary, 1762–1839) invalidated a communal election for the position of rabbi when it was discovered that some of the members of the community had accepted gifts to cast their ballots for a particular candidate.[75] What follows from the principle is that the judicial code of conduct is imposed, on anyone who is called upon to make judgments in matters pertaining to the public interest and welfare.

Guideposts for the judicial code of conduct have much relevancy for the issue at hand. Since a patient relies on the medical judgment of his doctor, the doctor's professional role assumes a quasi-judicial character. A drug company's offer of a reward for prescribing their drug works only to distort a doctor's objectivity in serving the best interests of his patients. While the distorting influence is obvious when the gift consists of ex-

---

dered null and void. An association of a more superficial nature with one of the litigants requires the judge only as a matter of propriety to remove himself from the case. Should he preside over the case, his verdict would here not be rendered void. Maimonides, according to the interpretation of R. Joel Sirkes (*Bah, Tur* op. cit., 7:11) equates the superficial and close relationship cases. In both instances, the judge must remove himself from the case only as a matter of propriety, as opposed to strict law. In both instances, presiding over the case does not render the verdict null and void, despite the impropriety committed.

[71]*Bah, Tur*, op. cit., 9, n. 9.

[72]*Yad*, op. cit., 23:1; *Tur*, op. cit., 9:2; *Shulkhan Arukh*, op. cit., 9:1; *Arukh ha-Shulkhan*, op. cit., 9:1.

[73]*Arukh ha-Shulkhan*, loc. cit.

[74]*Rema, Shulkhan Arukh, Hoshen Mispat* 163:1.

[75]R. Moses Sofer, *Responsa Hatam Sofer, Hoshen Mishpat* 160.

pensive excursions, this conduct should be objectionable even when it takes on the form of reminders and informational lunches. Maintaining objectivity requires that a doctor obtain his information regarding drugs from the medical literature and from peer recommendations.

Drug company sponsorship of CME entails the creation of a false impression when it fails to disclose up front its relationship with the lecturers of the seminars. Creating a false impression violates the *geneivat da'at* interdict.[76] Disclosure of the relationship between the lecturer and the drug companies is, however, insufficient. Since the lecturer is paid an honorarium by the drug company, his presentation will inevitably be skewed in favor of the sponsor's product.

With the aim of promoting objectivity in the presentation of medical information, *Consumer Reports* proposes that the medical profession itself should assume the responsibility to adequately fund CME.[77] Shifting the sponsorship of CME from the pharmaceutical companies to the medical profession itself is, as indicated above, in line with the halakhic approach in this matter.

Similarly, a drug company violates *geneivat da'at* law when it creates the impression that the journal supplement it sponsors is part of the medical journal it is attached to. To correct this false impression, *Consumer Reports* calls for journal editors to design their single-sponsor supplements to distinguish them clearly from regular edition matter. This can be achieved by means of prominently displayed notices, different typography, and different page layout.[78] *Consumer Reports* proposal here is once again consonant with the halakhic approach in this matter.

Promoting Better Price Information

In his analysis of approaches to bring down the cost of prescription drugs, Murray Weidenbaum makes two suggestions relating to improving price information in the marketplace.

---

[76]Samuel, *Hullin* 94a; *Rif*, ad loc.; *Yad, Mekhirah* 18:1; *Rosh, Hullin* 7:18; *Tur*, op. cit., 228:5–7; *Shulkhan Arukh*, op. cit., 228:6; *Arukh ha-Shulkhan*, op. cit., 228:3.

[77]"Pushing Drugs to Doctors," op. cit., p. 94.

[78]Ibid.

Currently, many states prohibit the advertising of prescription drug prices. These prohibitions make it difficult for consumers to shop for the best price. Such restrictions should be repealed.

At the federal level, the FDA should reconsider its requirement that a "brief summary" accompany any ad mentioning both a health condition and a drug treatment. The "brief summary" is actually a lengthy statement listing side effects and contraindications. Such information is essential for physicians, but incomprehensible to the average patient. More importantly, the "brief summary" requirement works to discourage advertising by making it needlessly cumbersome and expensive.[79]

Repeal of the "brief summary" requirement for direct advertising will undoubtedly result in increased advertising outlays by prescription drug companies. Increased advertising, Rubin asserts, can be expected to bring about a better matching between patients and drugs. His assertion follows from the following considerations:

1. Advertising makes consumers aware that a treatment exists for some conditions. Upjohn's Rogaine, a treatment for some conditions of baldness, provides a case in point.
2. Advertising makes the public become aware that certain symptoms they experience may be indicative of a medical problem. Thirst, for instance, may be indicative of a diabetic condition. A consumer who does not realize that symptoms indicate a disease will not consult a physician.
3. Advertising makes consumers aware of new treatments.
4. Advertising can make consumers aware of the side effects of medication. Consumers who do not know that symptoms they are experiencing are side effects, and would not ask a physician about them, may learn from ads that there are alternatives without these side effects. Consumers who have ceased treatment because of side effects, and are thus not seeing a physician, may begin treatment again if they learn of the therapies that do not impose the same side effects.

[79]Murray Weidenbaum, "Are Drug Prices Too High?" *The Public Interest* (Summer 1993): 84–89.

Direct-to-consumer advertising will also lead to price reductions for pharmaceuticals. First, advertising can inform consumers of generic equivalency. Moreover, increased competition brought about by increased advertising can lead manufacturers to reduce prices for drugs. If one ad can simultaneously list the use of a drug, the price, and the name, then price competition among retail pharmacies can be increased. As of now, an ad cannot provide all of this information without including the "brief summary."[80]

Rabbinic tradition, as outlined earlier, has always been concerned with improving the information channels of the marketplace in respect to essential commodities. Weidenbaum's proposals are hence consonant with halakhic attitudes here.

Halakhah and the Canadian System of Regulating the Price of Prescription Drugs

In this section we will describe Canada's system of regulating the price of prescription drugs. It will be seen that this system conforms essentially with *halakhah*'s program for price regulation of pharmaceuticals.

In 1987, Canada established the Patented Medicine Prices Review Board (PMPRB). The function of this government agency was to set guideposts for the pricing of pharmaceuticals on the manufacturer's level. At its inception, the PMPRB was given the power to require pharmaceutical companies to disclose confidential information regarding drug prices. This allowed the PMPRB to effectively evaluate and establish a factory-gate price for each patented drug in order to allow the drug companies a fair return on their investment.

The PMPRB was also given the power to pull patents of companies that refused to bring their drug pricing into compliance with the PMPRB's guidelines.

Included in the 1987 law was a provision which gave seven years of market exclusivity to drug-patent holders against production in Canada and ten years of market exclusivity against importation.

[80]Paul H. Rubin, "The FDA's Prescription for Consumer Ignorance," *Consumer's Research Magazine* (June 1991): 17–19.

In 1993, new legislation introduced various changes in the law. One change lengthened the market exclusivity period for drug patent holders to twenty years from the prior seven- to ten-year period. While the PMPRB retained most of its original power, it no longer was given the power to abrogate patents. But, its remedial powers were increased in other areas. For instance, new remedies were added for cases of excessive prices, and new sanctions were created for failure to comply with the PMPRB's price-setting guidelines and failure to comply with PMPRB's regulation on providing information.[81]

As can be seen from the previous discussion, the Canadian system conforms essentially to the program *halakhah* would call for. Several areas of divergence can, however, be identified.

One area of concern is the treatment of basic research. From the standpoint of *halakhah*, government should vastly increase its role in financing basic research in the health-related field. Within the framework of a price review board, expanded government involvement in basic research effectively shifts the associated risks from private industry to society at large and hence fosters lower drug prices. An expanded role for government here also makes possible the introduction of a flexible patent system in respect to the length of time the patent holder is protected. This, too, works to lower drug prices.

In the Canadian model, the PMPRB has no jurisdiction over the prices set by pharmacies at the retail level.[82] In sharp contrast, the law of *ohna'ah* regulates the price structure of the marketplace in the halakhic model.

Another concern of *halakhah* is to foster lower drug prices by improving the information channels of the marketplace. One aspect of this approach is to set up a legal environment which encourages advertising. Another element of this approach, as described above, is to craft generic substitution legislation which would place the burden on doctors to educate themselves in respect to the appropriateness of prescribing generic instead of brand-name drugs.

[81]Michael B. Moore, "Open Wide (Your Pocket book That Is!)—A Call for the Establishment in the United States of a Prescription Drug Price Regulatory Agency," *Southwestern Journal of Law and Trade in the Americas* 1 (1994): 162–166.

[82]Ibid., p. 163, note 78.

Finally, the halakhic model calls for making medication available to the poor without charge. Implementation of this objective may very well imply that certain drugs qualify for a government subsidy.

THE FIRM'S RESPONSIBILITY NOT TO VIOLATE THE PRIVACY RIGHTS OF ITS CUSTOMERS

In this section we will address the issue of the responsibility of the firm not to violate the privacy rights of its customers. Specifically, we will examine several case studies in the consumer database industry.

AT&T's Specialty Directory

In 1989, AT&T published a specialty 800 number directory entitled "Gifts, Catalogues, and Celebrations." To decide what households were to receive the special directory, the company searched its electronic phone records for frequent callers of each 800 number category. AT&T was thus able to promise advertisers that the special directory would reach consumers with a guaranteed appetite for gift and catalogue phone services.

AT&T's project was attacked by the Chicago Association of Direct Marketing as an "invasion of privacy." AT&T responded that its special directory posed no threat to privacy. Quite to the contrary, the directory would save money and time for those using it. A company spokesperson compared searching for frequent 800 number callers to other ways that AT&T analyzed customers' calling patterns for marketing purposes. For instance, the company might offer discounts to volume long-distance callers, or a special deal on calls to a particular foreign country.

In the current state of affairs, laws on phone record privacy are weak and sometimes contradictory. A few states, including California, generally forbid disclosing phone records without a customer's consent. But the federal law that protects the confidentiality of phone conversations suggests that it's legal for phone companies to divulge their records.

In 1979, the Supreme Court of the United States in *Smith versus Maryland* held that "it is too much to believe that telephone subscribers . . . harbor any general expectations that the numbers they dial will remain secret." In that particular case, the court ruled that a suspected robber "voluntarily conveyed numerical information to the telephone company" and thus "assumed the risk that the information would be divulged"—in this case to the police without a warrant.[83]

AT&T's Special Directory and *Halakhah*

From the standpoint of *halakhah*, AT&T's publication of a special directory presents several concerns.

One concern is the privacy issue. In this regard a sharp contrast can be drawn between secular law and *halakhah*. In secular law, as mentioned earlier, a communication is not automatically confidential. It becomes so only when it is judged that the parties involved reasonably expected their communication to be confidential. In *halakhah*, however, the communication of any personal or proprietary information is *automatically* confidential unless permission to disclose it is explicitly given.

The above principle is explicated at *Yoma* 4b: "Where is it derived that [if] one relates something to one's fellow [the latter is commanded] 'thou shall not tell'? For it is said, and the Lord spoke to him from the tent of meeting, *saying*" (Leviticus 1:1).

The Hebrew word for *saying*, which appears in the text, is vocalized *laimor*. Exegetically, the four letters of the word, that is, *lamed, alef, mem,* and *resh*, can be arranged to read as two words: *lo emor*, "do not say." Taken together, the two readings of the word impart the message that had God not explicitly instructed Moses to disclose what He had told him to the Jewish people, Moses would not be permitted to do so, notwithstanding that he had no instruction either explicit or implicit *not* to disclose what he had been told.

Beyond violation of the above direction, A's disclosure of private information regarding B to C violates for A the prohibition against talebearing (Leviticus 19:16), even if the information involved is not derogatory.[84]

In *Smith v. Maryland*, Justices Marshall and Brennan issued a dissenting opinion:

---

[83]Michael W. Miller, "As Phone Technology Swiftly Advances, Fears Grow They'll Have Your Number," *Wall Street Journal*, Friday, Dec. 13, 1991, B1.

[84]*Yad, De'ot* 7:2 and R. Joseph Caro, *Kesef Mishnah* at *Yad*, loc. cit.

> Privacy is not a discrete commodity, possessed absolutely or not at all. Those who disclose certain facts to a bank or phone company for a limited business purpose need not assume that this information will be released to other persons for other purposes.[85]

Proceeding from the *laimor–lo emor* principle is that *halakhah* would be in agreement with the dissenting opinion of the court in *Smith*. Given that a confidentiality rule is operative between parties of a personal conversation, the confidentiality rule should also restrict the release of personal data to third parties. Specifically, if A gives information to *B* for a limited business purpose, *B* may not, in turn, release this information to other persons for other purposes.

Another general principle in Jewish privacy protection law emerges from an analysis of Rabbenu Gershom b. Judah Me'Or ha-Golah's (France, ca. 960–1040) edict[86] against reading another person's mail without permission. Standing at the basis of this edict, is the admonition: "You shall not go as a tale bearer among your people" (Leviticus 19:16). What the verse prohibits is the bearing of someone's private information, whether it is for self-consumption or for the purpose of revealing it to someone else.[87]

Let's now apply the above rules to evaluate the ethics of AT&T's project.

Becoming an AT&T customer entitles a subscriber (*A*) to conduct private conversations using the company's switching and electronic equipment. Recall that the interdict against tale-bearing includes the prohibition to uncover confidential information for self-consumption. Now, since *A* does not give the company *explicit* permission to examine and/or make use of his phone records, such permission extends only to what must be done for billing purposes. Developing and analyzing the information to obtain *more detailed personal information* on A is prohibited.

Now, if AT&T wants to offer frequent long distance callers a discount, analyzing its phone records to determine which customers fit into that category does not entail the *uncovering* of data beyond what it uses for billing

[85]*Smith* v. *Maryland*, 442 U.S. 735, 748 (1979). (Marshall, J., dissenting.)

[86]See R. Moses b. Naphtali Hirsch Rivkes, *Be'er ha-Golah, Shulkhan Arukh, Yoreh De'ah* 334, note 123.

[87]R. Jacob Hagiz, *Responsa Halakhot Ketannot* 1:276.

purposes. Specifically, determining which customers should be offered a discount does not necessitate an identification of the *actual* people customers call. The customer's privacy is therefore not violated here. But, compilation of a special directory for gifts, catalogues, and celebrations entails an *analysis* of phone records that connect customers to 800 number firms dealing in the above categories. Success of the venture is predicated upon AT&T's ability to convince advertisers that the phone customers that will be sent the specialty directory will make frequent use of it. AT&T's special directory project hence violates the privacy of its customers.

In defense of the policy, one could argue that the project results in a benefit for the customers who are selected to receive the special directory. Legitimacy should therefore be given to the project on the basis that it is self-evident that the targeted group give their *implicit* approval of the project in advance. This principle is referred to in the talmudic literature as the *anan sahadi* (literally *we* are witnesses [in the matter]) principle.

Illustrating the *anan sahadi* principle is the following scenario in connection with the *mitzvah* of restoring lost property (*hashavat avedah*): Suppose two animals, one belonging to *A* and the other to *B* are in danger of drowning. *A* is on the scene but *B* is not. *A* is willing to rescue *B*'s animal at the expense of losing his own, less valuable animal, but demands compensation for his loss. In the absence of *B*, a group of three can act on *B*'s behalf and agree to *A*'s stipulation. *A*'s stipulation is binding on *B* even if the sum demanded equals the replacement cost of the animal. The sentimental attachment *B* has for his animal creates a presumption that he will end up with a net advantage even if he pays the rescuer the replacement cost of the animal.[88]

The *anan sahadi* principle finds ready application to the case at hand. Requiring AT&T to seek permission from its customers before undertaking the special directory projects adds significantly to the cost of the project. We take it as a given that these incremental costs make the project less attractive compared to alternative investments for the company. AT&T hence finds itself in a position to make a judgment for its customers whether the contemplated project is in their best interest. Since the customers who receive the special directory benefit

---

[88]*Tosafot, Bava Metziah* 31b.

from the company's project, it can be presumed that they approve of the project and waive their privacy rights in the matter.

Before the *anan sahadi* principle can be invoked here it must, however, be recognized that compilation of the special directory requires the company to sift through the phone records of *all* its customers; both those who will receive the directory and those who will not. Conferring a benefit to one group of customers cannot be legitimized if it is at the expense of violating the privacy of another group of customers.

The above objection can, however, be dismissed. Violation of the privacy of the nonrecipients of the directory does not obtain here. Sifting through the phone records is accomplished by means of computer. Violation of customer privacy hence does not become an issue until the computer comes up with some list or file which the company has access to. For customers who are not selected, no file or record is maintained. The privacy of these people is hence not violated. To be sure, a company file is produced and maintained in respect to the customers who will be receiving the special directory. Privacy invasion becomes an issue in respect to this group. But, since receipt of the special directory is a clear-cut benefit for the selected group, these people presumably waive their privacy rights in this matter.

We should note that *anan sahadi* works only to legitimize the *launching* of AT&T's special directory project. Should a targeted phone subscriber refuse the special directory, it would be within his rights to insist that his name should be removed from any file the company keeps in respect to the project.

In the final analysis, the application of the *anan sahadi* principle to the case at hand is problematic. This is so because any judgment that AT&T's project results in a benefit for those selected for the special directory hinges on the status of privacy-invasion law in the United States. In the current state of affairs, the information AT&T develops regarding its customers, such as a list of frequent 800 number callers, is not subject to any government regulation in respect to disclosure to third parties or required security measures against unauthorized use of the information.[89] Currently, AT&T's internal ethical code forbids the com-

[89]"As Phone Technology Swiftly Advances," op. cit.

pany from disclosing customer information to third parties.[90] Presumably, the company installs an adequate security system to safeguard against unauthorized use of customer information. Since it is only AT&T's official policy and procedures which safeguard the confidentiality of information it develops regarding its customers, arrival of the specialty directory at the doorstep of some customers may very well be an unwelcome event. For these customers, the directory is, of course, beneficial, but it brings with it the anxiety that their lifestyle is in the *process* of becoming a matter of public knowledge.

Exploiting Customer Assets for Commercial Gain

Another problem AT&T's project raises is that production of the directory may entail exploiting the assets of its customers for commercial gain. Given the prohibition to uncover confidential information, AT&T's authority to examine phone records extends only to what its billing requirements necessitate. The information AT&T develops regarding the affinity of its customers for gifts, catalogues, and celebrations clearly goes beyond this need. This information is hence the property of its customers. Commercializing this information by producing a special directory amounts to exploiting the assets of its customers for commercial gain. The analogue of the above case is R. Yose's dictum, recorded at *Mishna Bava Metziah* 3:2: "[If] one rents a cow from another [*B*] and lends it to someone else [C], and it dies naturally, [A] must swear that it died naturally, and [C] must pay [A]. Said R. Yose: 'How does that person do business with another person's cow? Rather, the cow should be returned to the owner.'"

In view of the first opinion expressed, when the animal dies, the renter becomes exempt from paying, and acquires the animal. Since the renter is not liable for accidents, he takes the oath merely to placate the owner. Therefore, the borrower—who is responsible for accidents—must pay the renter.[91] R. Yose, however, regards the renter who lends out the deposit as an agent of the owner. Therefore, the payment for the cow should be given to the owner, not the renter.[92]

---

[90]Mary Gardener Jones, "Privacy: A Significant Marketing Issue for the 1990's," *Journal of Public Policy and Marketing* 10(1) (Spring 1991): 140.

[91]*Bava Metziah* 35b and *Rashi* ad loc., s. v. *v'hashoel.*

[92]*Rosh, Bava Metziah* 3:5.

Talmudic codifiers for R. Yose's line.[93] Accordingly, a Jewish court will order *A* to turn over to *B* the payment for the care received from C. In legal parlance a judicial ruling of this sort is called a disgorgement order. Doing business with someone else's asset will generate for the violator a disgorgement requirement. The circumstances needed to make the disgorgement requirement operative is a matter of dispute.

The majority position in this matter is to call for disgorgement whenever A makes commercial use of *B*'s property while having no right to make use of it. The circumstance that *B* suffers no loss thereby is not a saving factor according to this school of thought.

Exemplifying this point of view are the following two rulings of R. Solomon b. Abraham Adret (Spain, ca. 1235–1310):

A rents *B*'s field to C without having any authority to do so. Given that the property in question has not been up for rental, *B* suffers no loss thereby. Nonetheless, it would be unconscionable for *A* to keep the rent, as this would amount to doing business with the property of another. R. Adret, however, hedges on a definitive ruling regarding the disposition of the rent *B* received. It might be appropriate, he points out, to return the rent to C on the grounds that *B* suffers no loss.[94] In another application of R. Yose's dictum, R. Adret ruled that if A builds up *B*'s ruin and rents it to C, A must surrender the rent to *B*. Since the ruin is not suitable for rental without A's improvements, this too is a case where *A*'s commercialization of *B*'s property entails no loss for *B*.[95]

A minority interpretation of R. Yose understands disgorgement to obtain only when the following conditions are met: (1) the defendant's commercialization of plaintiff's property was unauthorized; and (2) the plaintiff suffers a loss in conjunction with the unauthorized use of his property.[96]

R. Yose's dictum finds ready application in the case at hand. Since the information AT&T develops regarding the affinity of its customers

---

[93] *Rif, Bava Metziah* 35b; *Yad, Sekhirut*, 1:6; *Rosh, Bava Metziah* 3:5; *Tur*, op. cit., 307:5; *Shulkhan Arukh*, op. cit., 307:5; *Arukh ha-Shulkhan*, op. cit., 307:5.

[94] R. Solomon b. Abraham Adret, *Rashba, Bava Kamma* 21a.

[95] *Rashba*, quoted by R. Joseph Habib (early 15th century), *Nimmukei Yosef, Bava Metziah* 8b.

[96] R. Ephriam b. Aaron Navon (Constantinople, 1677–1735), *Mahaneh Efrayim, Sekhirut, siman* 19.

for gifts, catalogues, and celebrations is the property right of its customers, the production of a special directory amounts to exploiting the assets of its customers for commercial gain. Consider also that the production of a special directory entails for the targeted group, as discussed earlier, an invasion of privacy. The call for disgorgement should therefore obtain even according to the minority opinion's understanding of R. Yose.

One could argue, however, that disgorgement does not obtain for the case at hand. Consider that for any firm other than the telephone company, ascertaining which households frequently call 800 numbers is either impossible or prohibitively expensive to obtain. What imparts value to AT&T's special directory is the company's ability to assemble data regarding the phone habits of a *huge* number of people. Companies are willing to place ads in the special directory *only* because AT&T will send the directory to a huge targeted group. Now, since it is *AT&T* that imparts value to otherwise worthless information, the production of a special directory cannot be said to exploit the assets of its customers for commercial purposes.

Recall, however, that R. Adret applied R. Yose's dictum to the instance where *A* builds up *B*'s ruin and rents it to C. What can be generalized from this application is that disgorgement applies even when the unauthorized user first enhances the market value of someone's asset before making commercial use of it. A distinction between the two cases can, however, be made. A ruin has commercial value, if only for speculative reasons alone. Building up the ruin does not therefore create value ex nihilo, but merely enhances existing value. In contrast, the type and frequency of 800 numbers an individual calls, as an isolated piece of information, has absolutely no market value. Since it is AT&T's work which creates value *ex nihilo*, the special directory cannot be characterized as exploiting the assets of its customers for commercial gain.

The Consumer Database Industry

Jewish privacy law puts to question the legitimacy of firms whose business it is to collect information about consumers from public and private sources and to produce a database from this information which they sell to direct marketing companies. To illustrate: some states allow their motor vehicle bureaus to sell driver license information. These files contain information regarding motorists' height, weight, and use of "corrective lenses." Consumer database firms buy this information. By selecting out the tall people and those whose weight is disproportionate to their height, these firms produce useful databases for marketers of weight-loss programs and manufacturers of clothing for overweight and tall people.

There can be no doubt that the typical consumer objects to allowing a third party access to information he gives a firm while transacting with it. In a 1991 *Time* magazine survey, 93 percent of those polled felt that companies that sell information regarding their customers should be legally required to ask permission from their customers before doing so. Invoking the *anan sahadi* principle as a means of justifying the practice of third-party design of databases hence has no validity.

Self-Regulation versus Government Regulation

Currently, American law protects customer records against disclosure to third parties only on a selective basis. In this regard, the Fair Credit Reporting Act, passed in 1970, allows consumers to correct errors in their credit reports, and a 1982 law limits disclosure to third parties. Under the Electronic Fund Transfer Act of 1980, banks must notify individuals when disclosing records to third parties.[97] Cable and video rental companies and public libraries may not disclose choices individuals make or other personal information without consent. Finally, the 1986 Electronic Communications Privacy Act prohibits telephone, telegraph, and other communications services from releasing the contents of messages they transmit.[98]

Recognition that disclosure of customer records to third parties violates their customers' privacy has led some firms to introduce internal codes which prohibit the practice. AT&T's and Chase Manhattan's codes, for instance, contain a flat prohibition on the disclosure of customer records to third parties. Warner Amex's code, on the other hand, states that it will disclose information about its subscribers only in ag-

---

[97]Ellen R. Foxman and Paula Kilcoyne, "Information Technology, Marketing Practice, and Consumer Privacy; Ethical Issues," *Journal of Public Policy and Marketing* 12(1) (Spring 1993): 106.

[98]Ibid., p. 112.

gregate form. The guidelines of the Direct Mailing Association (DMA), the association of firms dealing in direct mailing, contains a strong statement regarding its members' responsibility for the security of personal data and the need to take strict measures to guard against unauthorized use and access, alteration, or dissemination, both generally and by its employees specifically.[99]

From the standpoint of *halakhah*, reliance on the self-regulation of firms to insure the privacy of their customers is not an adequate approach. The inadequacy of relying on voluntarism here follows from several considerations.

One concern is that the focus of self-regulation efforts described above is on exhorting firms to safeguard the confidentiality of personal data in their possession. No guideposts are, however, offered in respect to the more fundamental issue of what kind of information a company is allowed to compile and maintain regarding its customers. *Halakhah*, as will be recalled, addresses the latter issue. It imposes a duty on the firm to guard itself against intruding on the privacy of its customers. Record-keeping beyond what is necessary for billing purposes clearly violates this duty.

Another concern is that *halakhah* recognizes that self-regulation is unreliable when the profit motive biases an individual to violate the standard involved. A case in point is *halakhah*'s call for the appointment of public inspectors to ensure the honesty of commercial weights and measures.[100] Why voluntary self-enforcement is not relied upon to insure the integrity of commercial weights and measures is explained by R. Jehiel Michel Epstein (Belorussia, 1829–1908) as stemming from the unconscious, distorting impact the profit motive exerts on vendors. R. Epstein uses this rationale to explain Maimonides's ruling[101] that in matters of *kashrut* one may only patronize a vendor who is known to be reliable.[102]

The potential the profit motive has to bias firms to violate *halakhah*'s privacy standard is particularly acute. Consider that much of the infor-

---

[99]"Privacy: A Significant Marketing Issue for the 1990's," op. cit., p. 140.

[100]Rami b. Hamma, reporting in the name of R. Yizhak, *Bava Batra* 89a; *Rif*, ad loc.; *Yad, Geneivah* 8:20; *Rosh, Bava Batra* 5:22; *Tur*, op. cit., 231:2 *Shulkhan Arukh*, op. cit, 231:2; *Arukh ha-Shulkhan*, op. cit., 231:3.

[101]*Yad, Ma'akholot Asurot* 1:15.

[102]*Arukh ha-Shulkhan, Yoreh De'ah* 119:4.

mation a firm assembles regarding its customer (A) is typically not threatening to that person. But, culling bits of information regarding A from each of the wide variety of firms he transacts with might reveal much regarding his personality and spending habits. Would not employers and insurance companies eagerly welcome the opportunity to glance at the dossiers of prospective employees and subscribers describing their health-related purchases, reading habits, leisure industry expenditures, political affiliations, and charitable contributions? The opportunity for abuse here cannot be overstated. Now, if a company regards disclosure of information regarding its customers as innocuous and this information is valuable to a third party, industry ethical codes will not prove much of a deterrent against disclosure. Within the climate of voluntarism, rampant violation of the consumer's privacy can therefore be expected.

Halakhah and Government Regulation Against Invasion of Privacy

Rather than relying on self-regulation, *halakhah* would recommend government legislation to protect the privacy of consumers. This legislation would prohibit firms from compiling and maintaining files on its customers beyond what is necessary for billing purposes. The legislation would also prohibit firms from making customer information available to third parties. Appropriate penalties for violating these codes of conduct should also be part of this legislation.

5

Balancing the Scales: *Halakhah*, the Firm, and Information Asymmetries*

Jonas Prager

It's discouraging to think how many people are shocked by honesty and how few by deceit.

—*Noël Coward,* Blithe Spirit

Rarely do counterparties in a market transaction approach each other on a level playing field. In normal circumstances, the prospective employee knows far better his own qualifications, aptitudes, and motivations than does the potential employer. Similarly, the seller's awareness of merchandise quality typically exceeds that of the prospective buyer. The economics literature analyzes this general issue under the heading of *asymmetric information*, examining the interplay between the parties as one side seeks to overcome its disadvantage while the other maneu-

*I benefited immeasurably from discussions with and comments from William J. Baumol, Michael Broyde, Israel Kirzner, Simcha Krauss, Mordecai Lando, Aaron Levine, Nachum Rakover, Michael Rosensweig, Allan Schulman, Ed Steinberg, and Jerry Todres. They, of course, cannot be held responsible for the final product. Assistance from the C. V. Starr Center for Applied Economics is also gratefully acknowledged.

vers to preserve the status quo. Although the Torah's all-embracing involvement with Jewish life led *halakhah* naturally enough to grapple with commercial relationships that were characterized by information asymmetries, this essay is primarily conceptual, seeking to unearth the essence of the classical halakhic outlook as most fully expressed in the Talmud. Hence, it avoids surveying halakhic developments through the centuries as well as the history of Jewish commercial life as reflected in responsa and Talmudic commentaries. Further, it focuses solely on the firm as the seller vis-à-vis the buyer, but it does so using categories employed in contemporary economic theory.

The argument of this essay can be summarized simply. On the one hand, *halakhah* emphasized moral authority to establish a level playing field. Thus, caveat emptor is anathema to the Jewish tradition, but so is caveat venditor, for trust arising from the parties' personal integrity should be the hallmark of commercial transactions. But, on the other hand, the Torah recognized human fallibility, and so provided for a variety of enforcement and redress mechanisms to confront those who succumbed to temptation. Some, such as compensation in instances of misrepresentation, were incorporated into the civil code while others, such as inspection of weights and measures, were placed in the hands of the local authorities. And a noninterventionist approach was sanctioned when the free interplay of market participants would insure fair transactions.

The next section presents a nontechnical overview of the asymmetric-information issue in the seller–buyer context. An analysis of the classical Jewish approach follows.

I. ASYMMETRIC INFORMATION, THE FIRM, AND THE MARKET ECONOMY

It will prove useful to distinguish between *search goods, experience goods, credence goods*, and *pure credence goods*. Nelson defines search goods as products whose quality can be evaluated prior to purchase.[1] A symphonic recording is a search good because the potential buyer can listen to it prior to purchase and so discern performance quality and recording flaws.

[1] 312, see also Stiglitz.

An experience good, as its name implies, must first be experienced before judging quality, and includes products as diverse as frozen *cholent*, which needs to be baked and tasted, and a car service, whose reliability needs to be evaluated over time. The credence good, defined by Darby and Karni as one that is "expensive to judge even after purchase"[2] encompasses such items as 93–octane gasoline or automotive repair services, and hence requires the purchaser to accept seller assurances, at least to some degree. That credibility requirement is significantly extended for a pure credence good, since such goods and services are virtually immune from evaluation. Perhaps the best examples of credence goods come from the professions, where confidence is virtually everything, either because no objective standard can be defined or because the final product results from the interaction of the service provider and the purchaser. Among the former category are such services as buyer-passive medical procedures (e.g., surgery) and litigation, while the latter encompass such services as psychotherapy and education. Abstracting from sheer incompetence, it is frequently impossible to evaluate the performance of a surgeon or criminal trial lawyer, since the practice of both surgery and litigation is as much of an art as a science. Moreover, each case is unique and hence idiosyncratic. Hence, whether the surgeon should have performed a lumpectomy instead of a partial mastectomy or whether an alternative legal strategy would have led to an exoneration are valid questions whose answers are often open to differing opinions among highly qualified authorities.[3]

This lack of standards is compounded by an inability to assign responsibility for adverse outcomes in those instances where the buyer is an active participant in the process. Was the student's poor performance

---

[2]P. 69. This relativistic definition invites complications. "Expensive to judge" depends on the importance of the good to the buyer as well as the purchaser's financial ability.

[3]Should men over 50 take a test for prostate-specific antigen (PSA)? Dr. Paul Nutting of the University of Colorado states: "I'm going to turn 50 next year, and there's no way in hell that I'll get a PSA." Dr. William Catalona of Washington University "has his PSA level measured every month." Kolata, p. C12.

Cosmetics, claimed by the manufacturers to be beneficial to the skin, or lotions that inhibit hair loss are examples of *pure credence goods*.

due to the professor's garbled lectures or the student's lack of diligence? Was the patient's poor response to the psychotherapist a result of the therapist's inadequate technical skills or the patient's deep-rooted dysfunctions that require still more fifty-minute hours?

Firms recognize that consumers face ever more perplexing decisions as they move from search to experience to credence to pure credence goods. And as product evaluation becomes more complex and expensive, firms experience increasingly powerful incentives to deflate product quality. Indeed, in an environment populated by profit-motivated enterprises, dishonest firms are dissuaded from taking advantage of ill-informed purchasers only if honesty is truly the most-profitable policy.[4] In the many instances where maintaining integrity is costly, a variety of economic, social, and legal mechanisms serve to even out the imbalance engendered by asymmetric information. These confidence-building institutions weaken if not eliminate firms' incentives to adulterate service quality.

Although consumers acquiring search products can rely on their own sampling to ensure that firms maintain product integrity, the presence of a competitive marketplace, with other sellers who provide alternative options, stimulates and strengthens seller credibility. A competitive market also reduces the credibility issue for experience goods, although here durability and hence frequency of repurchase plays a role. Relying on the integrity of the beautician is more sensible than trusting the appliance salesperson. The former is dependent on repeat business, and will lose her customers in short order if she repeatedly provides poor-quality service. In contrast, the appliance retailer need be less concerned with repeat customers and hence his credibility, given the durability of the typical refrigerator, washing machine, and oven. The odious reputation of used-car dealers may well be deserved!

Firm-initiated quality signaling and buyer-initiated monitoring mechanisms have emerged in the United States and elsewhere to deal with asymmetric information issues arising for many kinds of experience goods and a fortiori for credence goods. Perhaps foremost among the credibility-enhancing quality signals undertaken by the firm is repu-

[4]Firms maintaining product integrity may be driven into bankruptcy by firms whose costs are lower because they adulterate their output. An analogy may be found in Prager, pp. 310–311, "Pollution Pays: A Hard-Nosed Business View."

tation (see Baumol, Shapiro, and Stiglitz). A sterling reputation earned over time convinces buyers that their concerns about misrepresentation are groundless.[5] Warranties and guaranties (Akerlof, Stiglitz), conspicuous expenditures (Klein and Leffler), advertising (Klein and Leffler, Rogerson), and especially high prices (Rogerson, Shapiro, Wilson, Wolinsky) also emit signals, albeit for different reasons. Warranties not only remove some of the buyer's risk, but also attest to the firm's confidence in its product. Apparently wasteful expenditures on fancy offices and showrooms and on personality endorsements can be recouped only over a long period, and so assure buyers of the firm's intent to stay the course. High prices represent a bribe paid by consumers to sellers to preserve quality. All these quality signals are meant to demonstrate that the firm stands to lose more by cheating than through honesty. For although the deceiving firm might gain in the short run, it faces long-term losses as buyers discover the true nature of its behavior.[6]

Unfortunately, history does not testify to the integrity of brand-name producers; Beech-Nut and General Motors are merely two recent examples of companies convicted of product deceit. Moreover, quality signals are only indications, not inviolate assurances. After all, they offer no guarantee that the warranty will be valid when needed. Nor can the consumer be certain that the firm will opt for a policy of smaller but more enduring profits rather than the high-profit quick kill. In addition, since it is often impossible to distinguish honest errors from intentional ones, the unscrupulous firm can remain alive until a pattern of misrepresenting behavior becomes evident.

---

[5]A variation of the reputation argument is the brand name, which is seen by Klein and Leffler and Akerlof as a means of identifying the deceiver. Unlabeled products cannot lead to retribution, whereas brand-name items that are misrepresented can be traced back to the producer, who suffers the penalty. This, of course, deters brand-name producers from misrepresenting in the first place (Akerlof, p. 21, Klein and Leffler, p. 617). Akerlof also mentions vendor chains and licensing as variations of brand names and product guarantees.

[6]As Tirole notes, this presumes that buyers believe that once quality deteriorates, it never returns to its former level. The conclusion falls, however, if they believed otherwise (pp. 122–123). Tirole (p. 111) also notes that price signals can be confusing. High prices need not signal high quality.

In contrast to seller-initiated signaling, monitoring requires buyers or their representatives to actively protect their own interests. Monitoring encompasses verification by the purchaser, quality assurance testing by vendors and/or by third parties, government imposition and regulation of standards, and media exposés.

Although the costs of product evaluation often outweigh its benefits, that is not always the case. Certainly when the stakes are sufficiently high relative to the costs, buyers expend energy and funds on verifying quality.[7] This is best exemplified by the normal responsibilities of purchasing and quality-control departments of larger firms, which are charged with procurement specification, verification of supplier capability, and then continuously monitoring the quality of purchased products.[8]

Purchasers may rely on trade organizations, not-for-profit organizations, and for-profit firms to monitor quality. Although trade organizations might be suspected of bias if not of outright collusion with the suppliers whom they represent, their concern with industry reputation over the long run should temper conflicts of interest. In the United States, the not-for-profit Better Business Bureaus monitor quality in various ways, including accepting and reporting complaints received about individual firms. Another not-for-profit, Consumers Union, actually tests products, enabling potential consumers to become informed about experience and some credence goods at minimal cost. Consumer advocate groups are less test-oriented, but also alert consumer consciousness to product quality deficiencies. The contribution of advocacy groups may lie more in the realm of prevention; the potential expose stimulates vendor integrity.

Profit-motivated evaluation firms will emerge when a market arises for unbiased product evaluations. Thus, the Good Housekeeping Seal of Approval is sought by consumer goods producers, the Underwriters Laboratory symbol by manufacturers of electrical equipment, and Standard and Poor's and Moody's security ratings by stock and bond issuers.

---

[7]Klein and Leffler assume this possibility away (p. 620), limiting the applicability of their conclusions. Similarly, Darby and Klein's credence goods may turn out for some purchasers to be search goods. Assuring quality is especially important in interfirm purchasing.

[8]See Leenders and Fearon, Chapter 4. Taking a used car to a vehicle inspection service would be an example from the consumer sector.

The government may weigh in to protect buyer interests, although it need not, nor has it always been so. That the seller must not misrepresent is a relatively recent concept in the United States, and it is not universal. Prosser notes that the change in judicial attitude from *caveat emptor* to *caveat venditor* occurred in the United States as late as the 1930s.[9] Virtually every type of misrepresentation nowadays violates some statute or has some redress via the legal system. Criminal and civil penalties for fraud, breach of contract, and violations of product liability law may be viewed primarily as deterrents. By imposing penalties upon sellers for acts of omission and commission, the law is clearly signaling their

[9]"Earlier decisions laid great stress upon the plaintiff's 'duty' to protect himself and distrust his antagonist, and held that he was not entitled to rely even upon positive assertions of fact made by one with whom he was dealing at arm's length. It was assumed that any one may be expected to overreach another in a bargain if he can, and that only a fool will expect common honesty. . . . The recognition of a new standard of business ethics, demanding that statements of fact be at least honestly and carefully made, and in many cases that they be warranted to be true, has led to an almost complete shift in this point of view" (Keeton, pp. 751–752). The sole exception seems to be "puffing," the exaggeration by sales personnel. "The law recognizes the fact that men will naturally overstate the value and qualities of the articles which they have to sell. All men know this, and a buyer has no right to rely upon such statements" (p. 757).

Over six decades ago, Yale Law professor Walton H. Hamilton recognized the legal imbalance resulting from the asymmetry between buyer and seller. Hamilton opens his historical survey, "The Ancient Maxim Caveat Emptor," by contrasting legal rule and market fact. "The large [oil] corporation uses the resources of an intricate technology [and] employs instruments of precision to establish the minimum standard of quality which vendibility makes necessary. . . . The consumer has only the amateur's acquaintance with oils. . . . Only if his personality is corporate, or he associates himself with like buyers is he able to oppose science with science, match technique with technique, and share in the terms of the bargain. . . . [In general,] the buyer's inability to judge the quality of the ware is in striking contrast to the general legal presumption of his competence" (pp. 1134–1135). In a marvelous footnote, *ad locum*, Hamilton writes: "The head of a large department store once remarked to me: 'God created the masses of mankind to be exploited. I exploit them; I do His will.'"

obligation to act with integrity in the first place.[10] In addition, vendor responsibility is enforced by specific statutes such as the Fastener Quality Assurance Act of 1990, which not only makes fastener manufacturers responsible for testing and certifying the fasteners they produce, but also requires that their products be traceable.[11] The Food and Drug Administration's certification procedures mandate that medications must be proven effective and safe before they may be marketed, while the principles of the Securities and Exchange Act (1934) as interpreted and enforced by the Securities and Exchange Commission foster the integrity of the securities issuance process.

Of course, neither laws nor regulations are fail-safe, and they must often be supplemented by private initiative. Product liability, breach of contract, and civil fraud suits are initiated by adversely affected parties, but litigation is expensive and will be pursued only if the potential financial gain outweighs its costs. Criminal penalties for fraud surely deter some but not every person with larceny in his or her heart.[12] The effectiveness of government regulatory agencies depends on the resources devoted to monitoring, not to speak of the agencies' commitment to and efficiency in achieving their goals.

---

[10]The legal remedies available to the deceived purchaser are broad indeed, as may be seen by reading the entry for fraud (which also includes misrepresentation) in the annually updated *Words and Phrases* (St. Paul, MN: West Publishing Co., 1992). A more detailed summary of the legalities may be found in Keeton, Chapter 18, "Misrepresentation and Nondisclosure," and Calamari and Perillo, pp. 405–424, on bilateral contracts and warranties.

[11]The background of this act is most interesting. It came in the wake of a scandal about rivets in the manufacture of aircraft. The very nature of the product and the market makes fasteners highly susceptible to quality deception: the product is durable, it constitutes a small portion of the final product, and it is normally not identifiable. Extensive testing for such a financially insignificant part is not cost-efficient, while any resulting damage caused by poor quality rivets, if discovered, is unlikely to be traced to the manufacturer.

[12]My favorite fraud: A company selling a sure-fire cockroach killer was convicted of mail fraud, since those sending $2 to the company received in return two small blocks of wood and the instruction, "Place roach on one piece of wood. Bang roach with second piece."

Overall watchdog functions are performed by the media, but differently by trade and nontrade publications and broadcasts. Significant information is conveyed by a trade magazine ranking an automobile or computer as best in class, especially when accompanied by its underlying rationale. But concerns about objectivity cannot be fully dismissed as long as the top-rated companies are also advertisers. General print and broadcast journalism, backed by the integrity of independent reporters, is less subject to bias, although advertisers are not without influence. On the other hand, errors of omission may surface too often, since emphasizing the negative captures the public's interest more than accentuating the positive.[13]

In summary, then, the extensive use of quality signals and external monitoring enables firms to maintain consumer confidence in a broad range of both experience and credence goods. Whether induced by the firms themselves or by external agents, firms aim to convince purchasers that honesty is the most profitable policy.[14]

Quality signaling extends to pure credence goods as well, although in this case innate trust plays a far stronger role.[15] Professional organizations, especially through the implementation of minimum professional standards and codes of ethics, lead the campaign to overcome the consequences of correctly perceived asymmetric information.[16] Clearly, the buyer's information deficiency would be more acute in the absence of minimum standards attested to by professional licensing. Indeed, that license standard setting and enforcement are lodged in the hands of the professionals seems eminently justified; only

[13]CBS News's "Shame on You" segment investigates and responds to consumer complaints of exploitation. But its very title demonstrates its one-sidedness.

[14]See Ireland for some experiences with product quality issues in the United Kingdom.

[15]See Matthews, which I came across after writing this paper, for a number of similar points.

[16]It should be understood that the firm is identical with the professional practitioner in these illustrations.

they, not laypersons, are technically competent to set the standards.[17] Thus, nongovernment medical specialty boards testify to the quality of board-certified specialists, while educational standard setting lies in the hands of the American Medical Association, which accredits medical schools. State imprimatur is not even needed, although the state often serves to enforce the decisions of professional organizations.[18] It may enhance confidence by appearing to be neutral.

The professional code of ethics is a second institution designed to instill purchaser confidence and combat information asymmetries by setting behavioral standards for members of the professions. The best known is surely the Hippocratic Oath, which requires physician fealty to the patient's best interest.[19] The patient is asked to believe that each physician will provide her with the best possible medical care, the code having been internalized in the psyche of the professional.

Religion is a fascinating trust-instilling institution. The halo that surrounds religious practitioners has as a beneficial side effect confidence in their ethical economic behavior. Belief in the reliability of the authorities leads Catholics to accept such pure credence goods as holy water, which of course is physically indistinguishable from unblessed water, and Jews and Moslems to trust the certification of the supervisory authority that meat declared to be kosher or halal is indeed so. Truly religious people are not expected to succumb to self-interest, and especially not to monetary temptations.[20] Professionals can attain credibility insofar as secular codes of ethics secure for them an identical mantle of sanctity.

---

[17]A contrasting view that professional standards are cartel-like arrangements to limit the number of practitioners and so raise practitioner income may be found in Kessel.

[18]The state may refuse to license potential practitioners who have not completed the course of study prescribed by the professional organization.

[19]Similar codes of ethics abound in other professions, from optometry to lawyering.

[20]This is not meant to suggest that misrepresentation is alien to the religious arena or that the religious never stray from the straight and narrow. Rather, consumer skepticism tends to be relegated to the background in instances where the religious authorities have provided their imprimatur or where individuals perceived as truly religious have vouched for the product.

Although generally useful, professional licensing and education standards are far from comprehensive solutions. These broad-based institutions by their nature set floors. They do not help consumers choose among equally minimally-competent practitioners, and they testify more to the past than the current competence of professionals.[21] Codes of ethics also are deficient as instillers of confidence. First, the codes often demonstrate a cavalier attitude toward clients. Prohibitions against competition are practitioner- not client-serving,[22] although such provisions have become less prevalent subsequent to a U.S. Supreme Court decision to apply antitrust law to professional services.[23] Second, enforcement is notably lax; professionals who violate the codes are rarely penalized by their colleagues charged with administering them.

How then do high-quality professionals overcome client qualms predicated on asymmetric information? Clearly, reputation plays a major, perhaps overwhelming role. While not to be ignored, reputation based on results is not conclusive, for the lack of standards blurs the meaning of performance. To be sure, the surgeon whose fatality record is high or the consistently losing attorney is hardly likely to attract hordes of clients. Yet, outcome-based reputation by itself is likely to mislead unless other characteristics—such as the difficulty of the task at hand—are considered.[24] Moreover, reputation based on peripheral characteristics

---

[21]Only recently has the practice of continuing education become common among physicians. The predominant convention seems to lie closer to that of professional engineers. Although the Accreditation Board of Engineers and Technology (ABET) requires continuing education of its members, Mundel notes that there "are unfortunately many exceptions." He does not even venture the percentage that attend such courses, but remarks that organizational sanction is rare (pp. 14–15).

[22]Fundamental Canon 7 of the ABET's code of ethics states that "Engineers . . . shall not compete unfairly with others." This provision is amplified by such statements as "Engineers shall not accept employment from clients who already have Engineers for the same work not yet completed. . . ." Again, "Engineers shall not undertake nor agree to perform any engineering services on a free basis (with exceptions for nonprofit organizations)." ABET also includes provisions on acceptable and unacceptable types of advertising; see Mundel, pp. 28–37.

[23]*Goldfarb v. Virginia State Bar* 421 U.S. 258 (1972).

[24]The high-risk obstetrician, who takes on complicated pregnancies and deliveries, will have a lower healthy delivery success rate than her regular obstetri-

such as bedside manner rather than technical competence may not only be deceptive but actually hazardous.

The lack of objective standards may well explain the absence of either for-profit or not-for-profit third-party evaluators in this pure credence area. An organization that ranks professionals in the absence of agreed-upon quality criteria opens itself to legal action without the satisfaction gained from providing users with meaningful information. This stands in sharp contrast to their presence in fields where objective evaluation is possible but is costly, as mentioned in connection with experience and credence goods. It may also explain advertising outlays among providers of pure credence goods. The constant repetition may so familiarize the consumer with the product that confidence is instilled subliminally.[25]

Lacking quality information from objective parties, buyers turn to recommendations by other professionals, proxies such as hospital affiliation, location and perhaps fees,[26] and secondary qualities. Each of these methods is by itself inadequate, and even in combination they are no more than gross screening devices. Nevertheless, consumers do the best they can and trust that their choice is correct.[27]

The hierarchy of buyer experiences and seller reactions in the face of asymmetric information can be summed up as follows:

---

cian counterpart. Ginsburg and Moy note that databases on physician profiles and performance already exist and are being refined, which will reduce but will not eliminate the dimensions of the problem.

[25]Professional service advertising by physicians and attorneys is a recent phenomenon in the United States, again because of a Supreme Court decision that overturned professional ethics standards that prohibited advertising.

[26]Adam Smith noted in his classic *Wealth of Nations* (p. 105) that "We trust our health to the physician; our fortune and sometimes our life and reputation to the lawyer and attorney. Such confidence could not safely be reposed in people of very mean or low condition. Their reward must be such, therefore, as may give them that rank in society which so important a trust requires [which] necessarily enhance[s] the price of their labour."

[27]This may account for the expression common at least in New York Jewish circles: "He's a big doctor," implying the patient's intense confidence in his specialist. Obviously, all can't be the best. It may well be that such rationalization is a necessary adjunct to the healing process in a pure credence environment.

- Search goods are relegated to the intelligence of the buyers and the market mechanism.
- Experience goods when inexpensive are treated similarly.
- Expensive experience goods and credence goods engender responses by both sellers and buyers. Sellers attempt to signal quality by developing a reputation for integrity and by demonstrating in a variety of ways their concerns with customers' continued patronage. Buyers rely on assorted monitoring mechanisms: buyer verification, quality assurance testing, government regulation, and media exposés.
- Pure credence goods providers radiate trust, but also pay attention to such confidence-building institutions as professional standards and codes of ethics. Reputation, too, plays a crucial role.

None of these methods is fail-safe. Misrepresentation is always possible, so that skepticism is a useful attitude for buyers to adopt, and firms are aware of residual consumer caution. Nevertheless, one would be hard-pressed to deny that transactions are plentiful in all of the four categories. Apparently, the confidence-instilling institutions have succeeded in their objective.

Would an economy operated according to halakhic standards function differently?

II. *HALAKHAH* IN A WORLD OF ASYMMETRIC INFORMATION

The Torah expects each Jew to live his or her life according to its high standards of personal integrity. Indeed, an individual's intrinsic trustworthiness (*ne'emanut*) is not only an expectation but a fundamental presumption of Jewish law.[28] The Torah's attitude that honesty is un-

[28]Note, however, that the Talmud records several exceptions to the presumption of integrity. Thus, the testimony of thieves and those engaged in occupations that are likely to involve thievery such as perennial gamblers, usurer, tax collectors, and shepherds is not acceptable in a court of law (see B.T., *Sanhedrin* 24b–25b). The B.T. debates the extent to which a conflict of interest may color judgement and cancel the presumption of trustworthiness (*Bekhorot* 35a–35b).

equivocally the best policy, because it is the only ethical option, stands in sharp contrast to the pragmatic view underlying the previous section.[29] Asymmetric information is a non-issue for the buyer and seller who conduct their lives according to the Torah's model.

Yet, the Torah recognizes the selfish impulse that inspires much of human action.[30] Its laws seek to channel these drives in an ethical direction by fashioning appropriate behavioral incentives and regulations. The temptation faced typically by sellers and less often by buyers who possess information that their counterparty does not share may underlie the Torah's fashioning the incentive and regulatory structures that are analyzed in this section of the paper.

A fascinating rhetorical question of Rava appears in the Babylonian Talmud (B.T., henceforth) tractate of *Bava Metziah* (61b):

> Why did the Divine Law mention the exodus from Egypt in connection with interest, fringes [Hebrew: *tzitzit*], and weights? The Holy One, blessed be He, declared: "It is I who distinguished in Egypt between the first-born and one who was not a firstborn; even so, it is I who will exact vengeance from him who ascribes his money to a Gentile and lends it to an Israelite on interest, or who steeps his weights in salt, or who [attaches to his garments threads

[29]It also contrasts sharply with the efficiency approach that is the hallmark of the economics of the law literature. Posner, a leading theorist of the efficiency approach, writes (p. 111): "The question of liability for non-disclosure should turn on which of the parties to the transaction, seller or consumer, can produce, convey, or obtain the pertinent information at lower cost."

Biblical and talmudic sources promoting honesty are numerous, among them being "Do what is right and good" (*Devarim* 6, 18) and "Justice, justice shall you pursue" (*Devarim* 16, 20). R. Yosi b. R. Yehuda adduces an individual obligation to honor verbal commitments from the biblical verse concerning honest measures in *Yayikra* 19,36. (See B.T., *Bava Metziah*: 49a). Maimonides (Egypt, 1135–1204) formulates it quite bluntly: "It is prohibited to deceive people in business. . . . " (*Yad*, Laws of Sales 18:1). See Levine, Ch. 1, and Tamari, Ch. 3 for expanded comments on Jewish ethics and economics.

[30]I have always thought that the appropriate translation of *Bereishit* 8:21 is: "the nature of Man is self-centered even from his youth."

dyed with] vegetable blue [i.e., indigo] and maintains that it is real blue [i.e., *tekheilet*, the Torah-sanctioned dye]."[31]

Each of these three cases—usurious lending, switching dyes, and using inaccurate weights—is an instance of asymmetric information and yet each is unique. In all three, one party intentionally commits an injustice upon a counterparty predicated upon the other's ignorance. Indeed, Rava indicates quite forcefully that G-d's transcendent awareness invokes heavenly retribution, since the temporal authorities cannot impose penalties nor can the aggrieved party be compensated as long as the unlawful acts remain concealed.

But even more illuminating than the commonality of these cases are their differences. The usury case consists of a Torah commandment transgression, the lender intentionally, the borrower, who equally violates the law,[32] innocently. No monetary loss is involved, the presumption being that the borrower willingly contracted to pay the interest. The *tzitzit* case apparently involves a credence good, with the price differential between the indigo dye and the halakhically sanctioned *tekheilet* setting the stage for fraud. The buyer remains unaware of suffering not only a monetary loss, but also of his failure to perform a commandment to its fullest extent.[33] Finally, from the buyer's perspective, the misrepresentation explicit in dishonest weights leads solely to a monetary loss.

---

[31]B.T., Traditional Press edition. Immersing weights in salts distorts the true weight. See the dispute between Rashbam and the *Tosafot* on whether immersion adds or diminishes weight in B.T., *Bava Batra* 89b, s. v. *le-tomein* and *shelo yatmin*, respectively. See R. Hirsch on *Shemot* 22:24, and Tamari (pp. 179–183) on Jews' obligations to lend to fellow Jews in contrast to gentiles.

[32]B.T., *Bava Metziah*, 75b. A Jew may pay interest to a gentile but not to a Jew. In the case in point, the borrower is paying interest to a Jew under the misapprehension that the latter is merely the gentile's agent.

[33]Rabbenu Asher ben Yechiel (Germany, 1250–1327) is most explicit in viewing the case as one of a deceitful seller. *Rashi*, s.v. *kala ilan* and Tosafot, s. v. *shehtoleh* are more ambiguous, since the case might refer to individuals who wish to appear pious without bearing the cost of the authentic dye.

Before moving on to the incentive structure and the mechanisms *halakhah* set forth to confront the miscreants in all three instances, it will be useful to explore the *tzitzit* case somewhat more intensively.

The conflict between authentically dyed and indigo-dyed *tzitzit* is played out in B.T., tractate *Menahot* (42b–43a), where the Talmud details two procedures for authenticating *tekheilet*.[34] The Talmudic analysis at first suggests—and apparently does not reject—the statement that a purchaser may trust any seller of dyes. Since the dye is testable, the seller will not risk exposure of his deception. However, the Talmud proceeds to address the ritual purity of *tekheilet*, a concern that extends beyond chemical testing. In essence, although the technical character of the dye makes it a search or credence good,[35] *tekheilet* is certainly a credence (and perhaps a pure credence) good insofar as the manufacturing process's conformity to ritual law.

In short, Rava's three cases of asymmetric information deal with instances where naive buyers or borrowers may never become aware of a seller's or lender's deceitful behavior. In the *tzitzit* and weights episodes, verification of the product may be possible but is either troublesome or impractical.[36] Ascertaining the integrity of the process may be virtually impossible in the usury case or the ritual aspect of *tzitzit*.[37] In each instance, the seller's advantage was countered by halakhic measures more

[34]"R. Isaac the son of R. Judah used to test it thus: He used to mix together liquid alum, juice of fenugreek, and urine of a forty-day old child, and soak [the blue thread] overnight until the morning; if the colour faded it is invalid. . . . R. Adda stated the following test in the name of R. Avira: One should take of piece of hard leavened dough of barley meal and bake it with the blue thread inside; if the colour improved, it is valid, but if it deteriorated, it is invalid." The Talmud concludes that the initial positive is conclusive as is a negative followed by a positive. B.T., *Menahot* 42b–43a.

[35]It is not clear to me whether the tested *tekheilet* sample remains usable. Moreover, the Talmud does not indicate the volume or quantity required, nor whether the testing ingredients were easily and inexpensively available. The more expensive is the testing process, the less likely is the individual purchaser to authenticate the purchase, and the more it becomes a credence good.

[36]One would not expect customers to bring along their own weights and measures. Nor would the seller be likely to use them.

[37]See *Rashi*, B.T., *Menahot* (43a), s.v. *Mai ein la*.

tangible than the Torah's admonition to honest dealing spelled out so powerfully by Rava.

The unethical seller's ability and hence incentive to defraud apparently induced classical Judaism to impose a variety of monitoring and redress mechanisms, although it did not disregard the normal functioning of the market. The fraudulent weights case provides the clearest example of monitoring. The Talmud, cognizant of deceiving merchants (*rama'im*), rules that Jewish courts are obliged to appoint inspectors of weights and measures. Indeed, it emphasizes the importance of this function by linking the institution to a Torah verse.[38]

The Talmud's attitude to countering deception in the area of dyed fringes is less clear-cut. On the one hand, the Talmud cites a source indicating that dyes be purchased only from an "expert," for only an expert can be trusted to attest to the ritual propriety of the dye.[39] On the

---

[38]B.T., *Bava Batra* 89a. Neither the *Sefer Ha-Hinukh* (commandment 602) nor Maimonides in his *Sefer Ha-Mitzvot* (Positive commandment 208) counts the appointment of inspectors as a Torah obligation.

Rashbam (Rabbi Shimon b. Meir, Ramerupt, 1080–1174) (s.v. *Agardamin*) states that the inspectors have investigative and punitive powers, including imposing corporal penalties. Presumably, inspection by non-Jewish authorities serves equally well under the rule of *dina demalkhuta dina* ("the rule of the kingship reigns") since the result—honest weights and measures—conforms to the Torah's desires.

[39]B.T., *Menahot, op. cit.* "Expert" here means religiously reliable. The unamended text of *Tosafot* (43a, s.v. *Mai*) indicates that the expert need not be technically adept in distinguishing *tekheilet* from indigo. Accordingly, purchasing from the expert resolves only the pure credence aspect of the problem. Other textual variants noted *ad locum* suggest that the expert is also technically competent.

Parenthetically, trust plays an especially crucial role in the supervision of *kashrut* when the supervisory agency is paid by the product provider. On the one hand, the supervisor's reputation substitutes for that of the less reliable provider. On the other hand, fee-based supervision raises conflict-of-interest questions since the supervisor's income depends on the continued relationship with the provider. This is analogous to security-rating agencies, which retain market confidence only because allegations of lack of integrity would be so devastating to the firm that it would not even contemplate dishonesty. But it also raises a concern that competition in *kashrut* supervision might turn out to be "competition in laxity," to use a term coined in another context by Arthur F. Burns, former Chairman of the Federal Reserve Board of Governors.

other hand, a few lines further on, the Talmud notes that "R. Mani was most particular" in that he bought only from an expert, "whereupon a certain old man said to him, Those who long preceded you acted so, and they were successful in their business." The elder's words suggest that buying from an expert is praiseworthy and wise, but that one could legitimately purchase from a nonexpert. Indeed, the very next line states:

> Our Rabbis taught: If a man bought a garment furnished with tzitzith from an Israelite in the market, the presumption is [that it is valid] [viz., ritually acceptable]; if he bought it from a gentile, who was a merchant, it is valid, but if he was a private individual, it is invalid.

Rashi (R. Solomon b. Isaac, Troyes, 1040–1105), explaining the propriety of purchasing from a gentile trader and a fortiori from a fellow Jew, introduces a quality signal, reputation, which presumably applies both to the merchant of the fringes and to the dyes.[40] One might also distinguish between the consequences of being detected, which are significantly higher for the merchant, who depends upon repeat business, than for the occasional seller.[41]

In any event, monitoring is far less stringent in the *tzitzit* case in that the Talmud does not require supervisors of dyes for fringes. Perhaps the Talmudic masters believed that buyers would be more circumspect when Torah commandments are involved. They would seek out expert sellers of this (pure) credence good, so that eventually the market would be populated only by experts. Perhaps, too, the integrity of a standard such as weights and measures is so crucial to the smooth functioning of the market that intervention by the courts is necessary to suppress even the

---

[40]43a, s.v. *Min ha-oved kokhavim.* Maimonides requires purchasing the raw dye from an expert but permits purchasing dyed *tzitzit* from either a Jew or a gentile merchant. (See *Yad*, Laws of *Tzitzit*, 2:4 and 7.) Although this distinction corresponds to the text of the Talmud, presuming that the later comments do not reverse the Talmud's earlier thoughts, it is not evident why one can trust the merchant of the finished product, but must question the integrity of the nonexpert seller of the raw material.

[41]B.T., *Avoda Zara* 39a states openly that a reputed seller of *tekheilet* maintains a presumption of integrity unless proven otherwise, emphasizing either reputation or long-term business concerns.

suspicion of a corrupt standard. Indeed, falsifying weights and measures is considered an especially egregious violation of trust.[42] On the other hand, dishonest *tzitzit* merchants infringe only upon the purchasers; there are no societal repercussions.

Penalties, too, serve as disincentives. The ability of inspectors of weights and measures to penalize malefactors reduces sellers' incentives to use inaccurate scales.[43] The defrauded purchaser in all cases of short-weighting and undisclosed quality defects has the right either to be made whole or to cancel the purchase.[44] Moreover, the transactions are not subject to a statute of limitations.[45] In the usury case, the courts would support the borrower's demand for return of the interest, even though the interest component was a voluntarily arrangement between the parties.

In one sense, however, the penalty mechanism in all three paradigms is weak. At best, the seller is forced to compensate the buyer for the

[42]"R. Levi said: The punishment for [false] measures is more rigorous than that for [marrying] forbidden relatives. . . . [In the latter,] repentance is possible, but [in the former,] repentance is impossible." B.T., *Bava Batra* 88b. Note, too, that the Torah uses the strong pejorative, "abomination," which is typically reserved for major transgressions, in discussing violators of weight and measure integrity (*Devarim* 25:16). The practice is so reprehensible that even owning corrupt weights and measures is forbidden (see BT, *Bava Metziah*, 60b, *Bava Batra* 89b).

[43]The vast literature on the economics of crime concludes that the effectiveness of deterrence hinges on both the probability of being discovered and the penalty imposed. See Prager, pp. 17–21 for a simple overview. A 1996 symposium written for the nonspecialist may be found in *The Journal of Economic Perspectives*.

[44]Talmudic commentators debate the precise interpretation and applicability of Rava's statement (B.T., *Bava Batra* 90a, *Kiddushin* 42a): "One may withdraw [from any transaction in which] anything [had been sold] by measure, weight, or number, even [if the overcharge was] less than [the legal limit] of overcharge." See Warhaftig (pp. 341–346) for a summary of the views.

[45]This stands in contrast to overpricing cases (*ohna'ah*) where, depending on the degree of overpricing, the buyer either has no recourse or may simply be compensated by a refund. Moreover, claims of overpricing are subject to a time limit. See Warhaftig, pp. 340–341.

latter's loss. This remedy removes the seller's illicit gains but entails no out-of-pocket penalties. Misrepresentation in the *tekheilet* instance and short-weighting are not treated by classical Judaism as theft, which mandates fines,[46] and thereby fails to strengthen the deterrent impact against deceptive practices.

The Sages' reluctance to impose the more severe penalties that lie within the Torah's framework needs further explanation if deterrence is the presumed objective. Perhaps monitoring measures in conjunction with the moral condemnations were considered adequate deterrents. Moreover, some general deterrents also coexisted. The seller's loss of reputation upon discovery would be especially damaging in a premodern society, where most business transactions occurred in local markets among people who had maintained long-standing social as well as commercial relationships.[47] The loss of credibility of one suspected and certainly convicted of fraud is another powerful general deterrent.[48] The latter would imply a shift in the burden of proof in civil actions, which normally favors the seller, to the buyer.[49]

---

[46]Although the Talmud (B.T., *Bava Metziah* 61b) views short-weighting as theft and Maimonides codifies dishonest gain through false weights and measures in his "Laws of Theft," (viz., *Geneiva),* he specifies there that the statutory penalty payment imposed on the robber of double the principal (*keifel*) does not apply to short-weighting. Maimonides's motive for distinguishing between the penalties for outright theft and for weights and measure abuses is far from obvious. (See Maimonides, *Yad*, Laws of Theft, 1:3 and 7:2.) A possible resolution might be found in his *Guide of the Perplexed*, Part 3, Chapter 41 (p. 196), where Maimonides lists four characteristics determining the severity of Torah penalties: "The greatness of the sin," "The frequency of the crime," "The amount of the temptation," and "The facility of doing the thing secretly, and unseen and unnoticed." On the last, he adds: "From such acts we are deterred only by the fear of a great and terrible punishment."

It may well be that although misrepresentation should, according to this criterion of Maimonides, lead to severe penalties, the actual incidence of deception was presumed sufficiently infrequent to warrant a lesser penalty.

[47]Rabbi Michael Rosensweig, in conversation.

[48]That is clear in the case of the usurer; see note 28.

[49]The general halakhic practice is that the burden of the proof is on he who wishes to change the status quo. Thus, the purchaser who claims that the merchandise did not meet contract specifications would have to prove his case. Pro-

In summary, then, classical Judaic law grappled with firms that might consider deceptive practices by:

- Emphasizing the moral aspects of integrity in transactions and the immorality of deceptive behavior, which plays an especially crucial role in pure credence goods;
- Relying to some extent on the consumer's caution and on competition, especially in search and experience goods markets;
- Depending on the reputation of the firms or their desire to remain in business and on experts for credence goods;
- Monitoring by appointed officials; and
- Imposing penalties that were designed to eliminate the gains from deception.

Furthermore, the Jewish court's general authority to implement measures as societal circumstances warranted provided an open-ended mechanism for dealing with abuses. Essentially, all of the monitoring measures outlined in the first section of this paper could be employed by Jewish authorities to restrain firms from acting in their best economic if not ethical interests. And so, the question raised at the end of the last section—Would an economy operated according to halakhic standards function differently?—can be answered on the pragmatic level as "Not really." It is the underlying moral standard that distinguishes the halakhic perspective toward firm behavior from the pure economic or economic-legal attitude. "Do the right thing, not the expedient one" is the message Judaism broadcasts to the firm's decision makers.

fessor Michael Broyde (in an oral conversation) claims that a seller whose reputation was tarnished becomes a *hashud* ("suspect") and would lose credibility to the point that the courts would accept the buyer's claim in such cases. (See the *hashud* entry in *Ha-Entziklopedia Ha-Talmudit*.) Broyde further argues that the deceitful seller might be prohibited from serving as a witness, a prohibition that has a strong social opprobrium attached.

REFERENCES

Akerlof, George A., "The Market for 'Lemons': Quality Uncertainty and the Market Mechanism," *Quarterly Journal of Economics* 84 (August 1970): 488–500.

Baumol, William J., and Blackman, Sue Anne Batey, "(Almost) Perfect Competition (Contestability) and Business Ethics," in *Perfect Markets and Easy Virtue: Business Ethics and the Invisible Hand* (Cambridge, MA: Blackwell, 1991), pp. 1–23.

Bester, Helmut, "Bargaining versus Price Competition in Markets with Quality Uncertainty," *American Economic Review* 83(1) (March 1993): 278–288.

Bowles, Samuel, and Gintis, Herbert, "The Revenge of Homo Economicus: Contested Exchange and the Revival of Political Economy," *Journal of Economic Perspectives* 7(1) (Winter 1993): 83–102.

Calamari, John D., and Perillo, Joseph M., *The Law of Contracts* (St. Paul, MN: West, 1977).

Darby, Michael R., and Karni, Edi, "Free Competition and the Optimal Amount of Fraud," *Journal of Law and Economics,* 16(1) (April 1973): 67–88.

Ginsburg, Paul B., and Moy, Ernest, "Physician Licensure and the Quality of Care," *Regulation* (Fall 1992): 32–39.

Ha-entziklopedia Ha-Talmudit (Jerusalem: The Talmudic Encyclopedia Publishing, various dates).

Hamilton, Walton H., "The Ancient Maxim Caveat Emptor," *Yale Law Journal,* June 40(8) (1931): 1133–1187.

Hebrew–English Edition of the Babylonian Talmud, various tractates (New York: Tradition Press, 1983).

Hirsch, Samson R., *The Pentateuch* (Isaac Levy: London, 1960).

Ireland, Norman, "Information Asymmetries and Product-Quality Regulation," in *The Regulatory Challenge* (Oxford: Oxford Univ. Press, 1995), ed. Matthew Bishop and J. Kay, and C. Mayer, pp. 191–209.

Journal of Economic Perspectives, 10(1) (Winter 1996): 3–67.

Keeton, W. Page, et al., *Prosser and Keeton on The Law of Torts* (St. Paul, MN: West, 1984).

Kessel, Reuben A., "Price Discrimination in Medicine," *Journal of Law and Economics* I (October 1958): 20–53.

Klein, Benjamin, and Leffler, Keith B., "The Role of Market Forces in Assuring Contractual Performance," *Journal of Political Economy* 89(4) (1981): 615–641.

Kolata, Gina, "Whether Positive or Negative, Result of Prostate Cancer Test Can Create a Maze of Questions," *New York Times*, June 23, 1993.

Leenders, Michiel R., and Fearon, Harold E., *Purchasing and Materials Management* (Homewood, IL: Irwin, 1993).

Levine, Aaron, *Economics and Jewish Law: Halakhic Perspectives* (New York: Yeshiva University Press, 1987).

Maimonides, *The Guide to the Perplexed* (Friedlander edition: New York: Hebrew Publishing, n.d.).

——— *Sefer Ha-Mitzvot.*

——— *Yad Ha-Hazaka.*

Matthews, R. C. O., "The Economics of Professional Ethics: Should the Professions Be More Like Business," *The Economic Journal* 101 (July 1991): 737–750.

Monks, Joseph G., *Operations Management: Theory and Problems* (New York: McGraw-Hill, 1987).

Mundel, August B., *Ethics in Quality* (New York: Marcel Dekker, 1991).

Nelson, Phillip, "Information and Consumer Behavior," *Journal of Political Economy* 78(2) p. 198 (March/April 1970): 311–329.

Posner, Richard A., *The Economic Analysis of the Law* (Boston: Little, Brown, 1992).

Prager, Jonas, *Applied Microeconomics: An Intermediate Text* (Homewood, IL: Irwin, 1993).

Rakover, Nahum, *Commerce in Jewish Law* (Jerusalem: Library of Jewish Law, 1987) [Hebrew].

Rogerson, William P., "Price Advertising and the Deterioration of Product Quality," *Review of Economic Studies* 55 (1988): 215–229.

Sefer Ha-Hinukh.

Shapiro, Carl, "Premiums for High Quality Products as Returns to Reputations," *Quarterly Journal of Economics* 98(4) (November 1983): 659–679.

Smith, Adam, *An Inquiry into the Nature and Causes of the Wealth of Nations* (New York: Modern Library, 1937).

Stiglitz, Joseph E., "Equilibrium in Product Markets with Imperfect Competition," *American Economic Review* 69(2) (May 1979): 339–345.

Tamari, Meir, "*With All Your Possessions*": *Jewish Ethics and Economic Life* (New York: Free Press, 1987).
Tirole, Jean, *The Theory of Industrial Organization* (Cambridge, MA: MIT Press, 1988).
Vonderembse, Mark A., and White, Gregory P., *Operations Management: Concepts, Methods, and Strategies* (New York: West, 1991).
Warhaftig, Itamar, "*Haganat Ha-Tzarkham Le-or Ha-Halakhah* [*Halakhah* and Consumer Rights"], *Tehumin* 3 (1982): 334–370.
Williamson, Oliver E., *Economic Organization: Firms, Markets and Policy Control* (New York: New York University Press, 1986).
——— *Markets and Hierarchies: Analysis and Antitrust Implications* (New York: Free Press, 1975).
Wilson, Charles A., "Equilibrium and Adverse Selection," *American Economic Review* 69(2) (May 1979): 313–317.
Wolinsky, Asher, "Prices as Signals of Product Quality," *Review of Economic Studies* 50 (1983): 647–658.

6

Responsibility of the Firm to the Environment

Yehoshua Liebermann

I. INTRODUCTION

Modern business firms have a relatively short history, as pointed out by F. H. Knight.[1] Nonetheless, it is not exaggerating to state that their impact on the social setup of the twentieth-century world has been not less than tremendous. Observing the economic and technological development since the 1920s it might be a bit difficult to believe that one of the most dominant forces behind these processes is the simple organizational invention of the modern firm. According to Coase, the main feature of a business firm is its ability to supersede the price mechanism.[2]

Unfortunately, the bright side of business activity is not the only face of firms. Almost inevitably, business operations are quite frequently associated with some negative outcomes. For example, Galbraith contends that

[1]F. H. Knight, *The Ethics of Competition* (The University of Chicago Press, Chicago 1976 [reissue of 1935 ed.], Harper & Bros./George Allen & Unwin, 1935).

[2]R. H. Coase, "The Nature of the Firm," *Economica* New Series (4) (1937) 386–405.

gigantic business organizations cannot tolerate significant deviations from their planned course of activity since any such deviations may cause severe financial damages. As a result huge firms attempt to dominate, and in a sense even dictate, consumers' reactions to their offers, a behavior termed by Galbraith *demand management*.[3] Illegal business espionage, bribery, exploitation, and public corruption supply additional illustrations of potential adverse outcomes of businesses' struggle of existence.

Sometimes, however, the negative outcomes of routine business activity may assume a less dramatic form—although not necessarily a less negative nature. A typical illustration of such an outcome is environmental pollution. More generally, businesses (especially manufacturing ones) are frequently tempted to ignore their effects on the environment while promoting their own interests. Economists often identify this disparity of interests as a form of conflict between private and social cost.[4] In particular, a polluting firm is minimizing its own (private) waste-removal costs at the expense of neighboring residential areas that incur a (social) cost of minimizing unwarranted pollution effects. Although every individual in the pollution-threatened area is spending money from his own *private* pocket to evade pollution damages, these costs are still regarded as *social* since no individual can either represent or negotiate for the community as a whole. On the other hand, the community as a public in general is unable to negotiate directly with the polluting manufacturer, due to possibly prohibitive transaction costs[5] associated with such a process. In the language of *halakhah*, such a situation is described by the phrase: "A pot of partners is neither cool nor warm."

The above illustration reflects a practically inevitable conflict between the desire for economic progress that can be materialized through the operation of business firms and the aspiration for reaching higher levels of social welfare (in the positive sense of this term) shared by individuals who comprise one or another type of human community. Put more directly, the question is: How can motives of capitalistic firms for profits

[3]J. K. Galbraith, *The Affluent Society* (New York: Houghton Mifflin, 1958.

[4]Coase, op. cit.

[5]Transactions costs are those costs that must be incurred in order to facilitate transactions. Typical examples of transaction-cost categories are search costs, bargaining costs, and exchange costs.

be reconciled with the striving of those individuals comprising capitalistic societies for a high standard of living?

In the present paper this very same question is dealt with from a Jewish law perspective. The discussion is organized in several sections. Section II reviews the preliminary issue of overall social equilibrium. Section III outlines the concept of efficiency and examines it vis-à-vis the system of private property rights. In Section IV the notion of externalities is presented along with Coase's well-known theorem. Some legal approaches to resolving the business firm–environment conflict are explored in Section V. Then, in Section VI, corresponding economic approaches are identified. Next, a halakhic framework for treating environmental conflicts is developed in Section VII. Finally, some concluding remarks are included in Section VIII.

II. OVERALL SOCIAL EQUILIBRIUM

Typical economists are rather anxious about the term equilibrium. In equilibrium, conflicting forces meet each other at levels of action that render satisfaction to all parties involved. In a stable equilibrium no party has an incentive to change its position.

In economics terminology such a situation is known as *Pareto optimum*.[6] From an economic point of view, equilibrium can be reached at various levels of economic activity; examples are an individual, a business firm, an industry, and the overall economy. Equilibrium is reached when each such entity reaches (or approximately reaches) its goal, subject to a set of constraints. Goals can be set in an attempt to maximize individual utility, profits, national income, and the like. Constraints are the result of scarcity in such resources as budget, time, energy, and so on.

Regardless of the unit selected for examination, traditional economics used to focus on the direct parties involved in each transaction under examination. Nonetheless, quite often the actions of direct parties may have certain (intended or unintended) effects on other parties which are formally unrelated to the transaction. Sometimes these effects bear

---

[6]After the name of the 19th-century Italian economist Vilfredo Pareto, the initiator of these ideas.

a certain form of conflict between the direct parties on the one hand and the indirect parties on the other hand. Such conflicts reflect a disparity from equilibrium, since the indirect parties would like to change their present position into an improved setup. As is well-known, one of the central features of a Paretian equilibrium is the desire of the parties involved to avoid a change in their given corresponding positions.

Some illustrations might be helpful in clarifying these abstract statements and definitions. They are related to the halakhic concept of *ravha le-hai u-pesieda le-hai* (gain to one and loss to another) that reflects a deviation from a given situation (i.e., equilibrium) that results in a positive outcome to one party accompanied by a negative outcome to the other. Such a change violates the Pareto optimum because only changes that are expected to improve the position of some parties without worsening the position of *any* other party are considered as complying with Pareto optimality rules.

A startling illustration of such a conflict is associated with the history of Italian Jewry in the 16th century. More specifically, at this time the church opened a large-scale persecution campaign against the Jews in Ancona whereby some "righteous and pious" Jews were burned alive by an order of the Pope. Since Ancona's economy was dependent at least partially on trade with the coastal cities of western Turkey, an attempted retaliation measure was initiated by a group of Jewish activists in that area. Accordingly, they called upon various rabbis and community leaders in Italy to issue an agreement (*haskamah*) aimed at blocking Turkish trade, controlled by oriental Jewish merchants, with Ancona. Obviously, the desired agreement represents a gain (*ravha*) to the Jewish community of Ancona at the expense of its counterparts in Turkey. Quite as expected, not all Turkish Jewish merchants were pleased with the agreement and some (or even many) of them refused to comply with it, a disparity that brought the conflict to be discussed in several contemporary responsa, as those of R. Joseph b. David Ibn Lev of Turkey (1505–1580, *Mahari Ibn Lev*, Part A, 115) and R. Moses b. Joseph di Trani (Spain, 1500–1580; *Mabit*, Part A, 237).

Regardless of the legal outcomes of the conflict, the disparity itself reflects a social disequilibrium in the fullest sense of the term. Indeed, the described disparity involves economic dimensions, but they are by no means its exclusive feature. As a matter of fact this type of conflict involves all aspects of life, as one may expect when vital interests of two communities come to a confronting collision.

A less dramatic illustration pertains to a planned detour of a local route in Rehovot, Eretz Israel, at the beginning of this century. The change was initiated in order to enhance the welfare of community residents as a whole. However, some individuals objected to the plan, claiming it is going to inflict upon them certain (unspecified) negative effects. Presumably, such adverse effects can be comprised of noise, dust, traffic hazards, and so on. This conflict as well was brought to the decision of a Torah giant, this time Rabbi Abraham Isaac Kook (Israel, 1865–1935), then chief Ashkenazic rabbi of Eretz Israel. Again, for our purpose the decision is less important than the conflict itself, a conflict that represents the concept of social disequilibrium from a much more practical angle.

To summarize, it can be said that economic equilibrium is a private case of social equilibrium. In relative terms, economic equilibrium covers a narrow scope as compared to overall social equilibrium. Whereas economic equilibrium traditionally is made up by direct parties within the framework of a conventional marketplace, social equilibrium encompasses direct as well as all potential indirect parties, whether in the immediate arena of the traditional market place or in any other form of social interaction.

III. EFFICIENCY AND PRIVATE PROPERTY RIGHTS

One of the main threats to the peaceful existence of a social equilibrium is the potential conflict between efficiency and private property rights.[7] In order to guarantee the clarity of the following discussion it will be worthwhile to devote attention to the definition of both terms.

Efficiency is a rather specific economic term. It is defined in two alternative ways. On the one hand, efficiency is reached when a given set of resources is utilized in a way that maximizes output. On the other hand,

[7]Aaron Levine, *Free Enterprise and Jewish Law: Aspects of Jewish Business Ethics* (New York: Ktav Publishing House; Yeshiva University Press, 1980).

efficiency is obtained when a given output is produced by a minimum amount of resources. Apparently, *property rights* is basically a legal term that outlines the boundaries of what one may or may not do in an attempt to take a claim over property and in using it.[8]

Understandably, efficient operations of one party may conflict directly or indirectly with property rights of another party. Referring again to halakhic sources, straightforward examples can be found in the context of business competition laws. As shown by Liebermann, there are numerous cases where a new incoming competitor is accused by a veteran business of violating the latter's rights in that marketplace. In extreme cases the newcomer's activity might be so intensive that it completely cuts off the veteran's livelihood (*ka- pasakta le-hayuti*). Yet, many authorities (notably, R. Isaac ha-Levi Ibn Migash, Spain, 1077–1141) tend to support the new competitor's actions, for he is more efficient, that is, he is able to supply the same product or service by incurring lower costs. This advantage enables him in turn to offer his merchandise or services for a lower price per unit thereby contributing to consumers' welfare. The fact that the veteran competitor may need to quit the market does not harm overall social equilibrium. On the contrary, by Pareto optimality rules, preventing more efficient competitors from penetrating the market constitutes by itself a social disequilibrium. Nonetheless, other *gedolim* (as Nahmanides, Spain, 1194–1270) tend to support veteran competitors' property rights in the market place vis-à-vis the efficiency-based inroads made by new business rivals.[9]

It is an interesting question whether efficiency considerations may dominate more concrete property rights as well. After all, property rights that affect operations in a given market place may sound a bit abstract and not fully clear-cut. (This is presumably one of the reasons why so many halakhic disputes were documented in the responsa literature around this issue.) The answer to this question is positive. As demonstrated by Liebermann, the halakhic concept of *kofin al midat Sodom* is based on the rational of efficiency. More explicitly, under certain cir-

---

[8]For a discussion of the efficiency concept within the specific context of Jewish law, see Levine (1980), pp. 157–182.

[9]Yehoshua Liebermann, "The Coase Theorem in Jewish Law," *Journal of Legal Studies* 10(2) (June 1981), pp. 293–303.

cumstances the rule of *kofin* grants to one party the right to make a compulsory use of another party's physical property because of efficiency considerations.[10]

As indicated earlier, the justification for permitting efficiency considerations to override property rights derives from the notion of social equilibrium. The potential conflict between both principles is due to the fact that, during the intermediate stages that take place until a new and improved social equilibrium is reached, some parties may feel harmed by that process. Their call for protection is not only natural but also at least temporarily real. Economic adjustment processes might be slow, let alone the corresponding social processes. In the meantime they involve pain and suffering of human beings. These real-life features are the source of difficult and sometimes bitter conflicts that in theoretical textbooks are resolved smoothly by simply shifting a curve up or down.

IV. EXTERNALITIES AND COASE'S THEOREM

Property rights may be defined at different levels of legal clarity. Holding an official title to a physical piece of property is probably the clearest form of a property right. In the previous section a brief discussion of property rights to operate in a given marketplace was presented. This type of right is more difficult both to define and to protect. Externalities are associated with an even less clear type of property rights.

Externalities are basically side effects generated by a given party unintentionally through his regular economic activity and that may have either a positive or negative influence on other relevant parties.[11] Following the common tendency in the literature (and in real life), we will focus on negative externalities only.

Air pollution and water pollution are classical examples of such externalities. They are generated by industrial plants which emit waste, chemicals, and smoke into the air or into water resources without taking into account the potential damages associated with their waste-removal practices. Indeed, the main purpose of every business is to manu-

---

[10]Ibid.

[11]Levine (1980), op. cit.

facture, sell, and make a profit, but producing waste is an inevitable by-product of the manufacturing process. Externalities are thus a source of conflict, because the products manufactured are of a positive nature while the side effects are of a negative nature. The problem is that both elements are parts of one package deal.

As a matter of fact the problem is more deeply rooted. As phrased by Coase, the conflict embedded in externalities amounts actually to a confrontation between private and social cost. In particular, as long as the manufacturer pursues the practice of removing waste freely into the air or into the water, he minimizes his own (private) cost of waste removal. At the same time such a business inflicts (social) costs on neighboring residents who may attempt to avoid negative pollution effects by taking such measures as installing air-conditioning units or air purifiers, or going on vacation more often. In other words, private cost is minimized in this instance at the expense of social costs.[12]

Obviously, such a conflict might be handled in a different way. For example, the manufacturer may be convinced or coerced to reduce air or water pollution by using improved raw materials, increasing quality control, or setting up filters at his own cost. These alternatives will increase his private waste-handling costs and reduce those of society's.

Each alternative ends up with some pattern of cost sharing. Naturally, the business itself does not have any incentive to increase its own costs. In this context it will be merely naive to expect a demonstration of social responsibility on the part of the business. To the business, a preferable practice is to impose the costs on society. Clearly enough, society has exactly an opposing interest. How can the conflicting interests be reconciled?

Before attempting to answer this question it might be interesting to stop momentarily and ask, Why does such a conflict arise at all? Who granted permission to the polluting business to begin with this practice? An accepted answer attributes polluting behavior to unclear legal definitions of property rights over air, water reservoirs, and unrelated features. To whom do they belong? To the manufacturer? To society (of which the manufacturer is also a member)? The answer is vague, because

[12]R. H. Coase, "The Problem of Social Cost," *Journal of Law and Economics* (3) (1960), pp. 1–44.

property rights over water, air, and so on are not always clearly defined. This situation invites free polluting behavior on the part of businesses as long as it is not restricted by some factor.

What factors can restrict businesses' polluting behavior? From a pure economic standpoint the answer is apparently straightforward: the market. The exact forms of possible market-oriented solutions will be reviewed in Section VI. However, it should be noted at this point that market solutions are not always applicable. This limitation is especially relevant in the presence of transactions costs. A typical case where the operation of the market is restricted by transaction costs takes place when a single polluting business faces a large community harmed by its pollution. In this instance, a real bargaining process might prove economically prohibitive.

An alternative route to reducing pollution is the legal system. Some possible legal approaches to the problem will be outlined in the next section. Nonetheless, in his celebrated article that marked a breakthrough in economic and legal thinking on externalities, Coase pointed out that under almost all circumstances legal decisions are bound to give way to real-life economic considerations. According to Coase, economic incentives may lead to a final outcome (equilibrium) different than that suggested by the legal system.[13]

Being central to the present discussion, Coase's approach, known as the *Coase theorem*, needs some more elaboration. Its point of outset is based on a critical view of the legally accepted criteria that are traditionally used to settle disputes over property rights. A case analyzed by Coase illustrates clearly some of these criteria. The case concerns a dispute documented in England toward the end of the 19th century. A cardiologist who introduced advanced diagnostic equipment into his clinic sued a nearby textile manufacturer claiming that the noise and vibrations associated with the textile-producing process prevented him from peacefully using the sensitive equipment. The manufacturer's defense claim was that he was in the area first.

In discussing the case the court acknowledged the defense claim as a valid criterion. Nevertheless, it decided the case in favor of the doctor since the area was gradually becoming a peaceful residential neighbor-

[13]Ibid.

hood, which is more suitable to the operation of a silent clinic than a noisy industrial plant. Coase argued that both criteria are as relevant as the color of the judge's eyes. Since any decision will impose some cost on one of the parties (or on both), it is preferable from an economic standpoint to let the parties negotiate and reach an equilibrium that will optimize their positions. For example, if the industrialist's operation per unit of time is worth $1,000 while the doctor suffers a nuisance that can be compensated for by an amount of $100, the industrialist may find it worthwhile to compensate the doctor directly and stay at his place. This outcome may take place even after a court ruling in favor of the doctor.[14]

The power of Coase's theorem can be evaluated more closely in light of its splitting into three inter-related principles. This has been performed by Liebermann in his article on the Coase theorem in Jewish law. The split form of the theorem includes the following components:

1. The Reciprocity Principle.

When a certain business activity of *A* harms *B*, it is wrong to view only *A* as harming *B*. Independent of initial positions, the damage is always of a reciprocal nature since, if *A* is ordered to stop his activity, *A* is harmed. In Coase's words: "The real question that has to be decided is: should *A* be allowed to harm *B* or should *B* be allowed to harm *A*? The problem is to avoid the more serious harm."*

2. The Trading Principle.

Harmful effects of business activities, or the legal rights to such effects, can be traded in the market by the concerned parties. Trading will take place as long as it leads to a *net* increase in the value of production (i.e., an increase in the value of production less than negotiation costs).

3. The Independence Principle.

If negotiation costs are sufficiently low to permit trading to take place, the resulting equilibrium will be unaffected by contrary judicial decisions.

---

[14]Ibid.

*Coase, op. cit., p. 1.

To illustrate, suppose that A is given the *legal* power to generate harmful effects while running his business activity. Suppose further that this activity contributes $\$x$ to his annual income, whereas its prevention will contribute $\$y$ to *B*'s annual income. If $y > x$ and the negotiation costs are smaller than the differential $(y - x)$, it will pay *B* to buy from A the legal right to the harmful effects. This transaction will bring both parties to a new equilibrium in terms of income distribution without a change in their resource allocation.[15]

As can be understood from these three principles, Coase's theorem was not only a novelty to traditional economics but was contrary to traditional legal thinking as expressed in several (though not all) legal cases cited by Coase. These cases, as well as traditional economics, viewed social cost as a problem of "all or none," disregarding its reciprocal nature and the possibility of trading harmful business effects in the marketplace.

It is these special features that made the Coase theorem a key tool in analyzing social responsibility of businesses, especially in environmental contexts.[16]

V. LEGAL APPROACHES TO RESOLVING THE CONFLICT

Although Coase's theorem challenged accepted legal thinking on treating harmful business effects (i.e. negative externalities) it did not completely replace the legal approach to the problem. As a matter of fact, a specific court may take explicit account of certain economic considerations along Coasian theory lines, yet it is still likely to rule the case according to the guidance provided by a given legal doctrine. Presumably, this "bias" might be due to tradition, to professional chauvinism, or to such more realistic factors as the presence of transaction costs that threaten to reduce the chance of reaching a solution by a reasonable bargaining process. However, it should be recalled that the court itself does not have an incentive to promote an inefficient settlement. On the

[15]This statement means that both A and *B* continue to do exactly what they did prior to the legal decision, but their *joint* income is now distributed between them in different proportions.

[16]Liebermann, op. cit.

contrary, the court will try to reach a solution that not only does justice to the parties involved but also complies with efficiency considerations.

In legal terminology, harmful business effects, or negative externalities, or "public bads" are treated within the framework of nuisance law. From this legal perspective it might be useful to follow the presentation of Polinsky, who in his turn follows the conceptual approach suggested by Calabresi and Melamed by which legal reconciliation of conflicting interests in nuisance cases involves a two-stage process. Since Polinsky's discussion is clear and succinct it will be beneficial to cite his own wording:

> First, an *entitlement* must be chosen—that is, a determination must be made regarding who is entitled to prevail. The injurer can be granted the right to engage in the activity that causes harm, or the victim can be granted the right to be free from harm. Then, a decision must be made about how to protect the entitlement. One possibility is to grant the holder of the entitlement an *injunction*. If the victim holds the entitlement, protecting it by an injunction means that he can prohibit the injurer from causing harm. Thus, the injurer can cause damage only if he "buys off" the victim. Similarly, if the injurer holds the entitlement, protecting it by an injunction means that the victim must buy off the injurer if he wants damages reduced. An alternative method of protecting entitlements is to give the holder of the entitlement an amount of money—*damages*—that some governmental body, such as a court, determines. If the victim has the entitlement, he has the right to be compensated, but he cannot prohibit the injurer from causing harm as he could under an injunctive remedy. Analogously, if the injurer holds the entitlement, protecting it by a damage remedy would mean that the victim could restrict the injurer's activity but would have to compensate the injurer for the injurer's "damages" (for example, forgone profits). This last combination—entitling the injurer to damages—is very unconventional, but it has been used. Thus, there are four possible solutions, corresponding to who is given the entitlement and how it is protected.[17]

It might be interesting to add another insight to these distinctions. This insight is stressed by Cooter and Ulen in a remark to the well-known case of *Boomer v. Atla Cement*. It distinguishes between two types of damages: temporary and permanent. In particular: "*Temporary* damages

[17]A. M. Polinsky, *An Introduction to Law and Economics*, 2nd ed. (Little, Brown & Company, Boston, 1989), pp. 15–16.

are a compensatory payment for past harms inflicted. They are to be distinguished from *permanent* damages, which attempt to compensate the plaintiff for all past and all reasonably anticipated future harms."[18]

Subjecting the main two legal doctrines (i.e., injunction versus damages) to an efficiency criterion it is possible to examine them from a wider angle. In Polinsky's words:

> Although either remedy could therefore be more efficient in the abstract, it may be apparent in particular circumstances that one remedy is likely to be better than the other. For example, suppose that a court is confident that its estimate of the victim's damages is close to the truth, but believes that its estimate of the injurer's benefits is inaccurate. Then an entitlement to the victim protected by an injunctive remedy generally would be preferred because this would be likely to lead to an outcome close to the efficient solution. Alternatively, suppose that a court has poor information both about the victim's damages and the injurer's benefits, but is confident that the efficiency loss from too little activity by the injurer is small relative to the entitlement efficiency loss from excessive activity. Then an entitlement to the victim protected by an injunctive remedy would be desirable because this would guarantee that the final outcome will not be too bad. Thus, the efficiency analysis of nuisance law may be helpful even when there is some uncertainty about which and remedy to choose.[19]

A more comprehensive paradigm based on this analysis is presented in Section VII.

VI. ECONOMIC APPROACHES TO RESOLVING THE CONFLICT

It has already been mentioned several times throughout the discussion that the magic remedy recommended by economists to settle conflicts involving social responsibility of businesses is the market. However, it was also mentioned that market-oriented solutions are dependent on free functioning of the market. In other words, pure market settlements of

---

[18]R. Cooter and T. Ulen, *Law and Economics* (New York: Harper Collins, 1988), p. 171 n. 20.

[19]Polinsky, op. cit., pp. 24–25.

the conflict are possible only in the absence of transaction costs. In this case, economists would expect the parties to enter a bargaining process which will lead to a certain formula of cost sharing. As claimed by Coase, such a pattern will take place even when a legal decision was already made, since "natural" market forces and profit motives are stronger than "artificial" legal rules. In extreme cases a court decision in favor of a given party might be totally reversed by the opposing party through an attractive property rights buy-out offer.

In less extreme cases it is expected that each party will make some concessions as compared to its original position as formulated in legal terms. Along the bargaining process the parties keep evaluating suggested solutions by weighing their marginal utilities against marginal costs until an equilibrium position is obtained. A market framework thus guarantees an optimal amount of social responsibility on the part of business firms.[20]

Unfortunately perhaps, real-world situations often are not free of transactions costs. These costs create the need for legal intervention in conflicts that should be resolved otherwise by the invisible hand of the market. The question though is whether there are economic solutions to resolve such conflicts under the presence of significant transactions costs.

Basically, the answer to this question is positive. As long as the transaction costs to each party are lower than the expected gains from selling or buying (fully or partially) property rights to a source of conflict, bargaining will be attempted with a chance to reach an agreed-upon equilibrium. Nevertheless, economic theory suggests solutions even to conflicts characterized by prohibitive transaction costs. This is done within the framework of welfare theory formulated first by Pigou.[21]

The basic principle of welfare theory in the present context is that of internalization. Whereas externalities constitute a gain to one party (e.g. a business) at the expense of another party (e.g. society), internalization is intended to cancel this "unjustified" gain. The concept of internalization is based on a hypothetical structure whereby both parties are merged into a single entity. For example, suppose that a manufacturing plant that

---

[20]Coase, op. cit.

[21]A. C. Pigou, *The Economics of Welfare* (New York: Macmillan, 1981).

pollutes a river is also using it as a source of drinking water. In this instance the polluting business will very carefully calculate the amount of pollution it emits or alternatively will take measures to purify the polluted water. An economic welfare theoretic analysis assumes that all relevant property rights are owned by a single party who is bound to make an optional use of them.

Once the internalization principle is applied a simulated sub-equilibrium can be constructed by using either one or two tools: compensation awarded to the injured party or a fine imposed on the injuring party.[22] Both tools do not change the amount of harmful effects. They only attempt to financially make up for them in a certain way. Put in more professional phrasing, neither compensation nor fine will change resource allocations. The only effect of either tool is exclusively on income distribution.[23]

The theoretical internalization solution is indeed difficult to apply. It demands as a prerequisite answers to a set of such serious questions as: Who is authorized to set the monetary values of a compensation or of a fine? In what way can these magnitudes be determined? Who guarantees that all relevant variables were accounted for by the estimates? Who has the power to enforce the decisions? Practically, these questions can not be responded to by the marketplace by itself. Thus we again face a market failure situation that necessitates the operation of alternative reconcilement routes, mainly legal ones.

VII. *NIZKEI SHEKHEINIM* AS A HALAKHIC FRAMEWORK AND A MODEL FOR TREATING ENVIRONMENTAL CONFLICTS

Studying the discipline labeled by Liebermann "economics of *Halakhah*,"[24] one may adopt either one of two main approaches. The first of these is to stress the unique features of economic issues treated by *halakhah* as *shemitah*, *yovel*, or the absolute prohibition of usury. Alter-

---

[22]Y. U. Ng, *Welfare Economics* (New York: Macmillan, 1979).

[23]See footnote 4.

[24]Liebermann, op. cit.

natively, it is possible to seek accepted economic principles, insights, and ideas that are hidden in halakhic discussions and make them explicit. In a sense the second approach is a "me too" strategy that bears a potential risk of degrading *halakhah* writings into partial and fragmented economic texts. Having dealt quite extensively with *halakhah*–economics links, I feel uncomfortable when exposed to a "me too" research in the field, since sometimes it seems to imply that halakhic figures require sources in order to be acknowledged.

Yet, the case of business social responsibility within the context of environmental protection is a completely different story. It is not a fragmented piece of economic theory or analysis that can be found here and there upon examining the *halakhot* of *nizkei shekheinim*. In face of the observation that in modern economic literature the issue of social responsibility and environmental protection does not emerge extensively before the 1960s, it is particularly striking to find a fully developed framework for treating these issues in sources as early as the *Mishneh*. As a matter of fact, a whole chapter in the tractate of *Bava Batra* is devoted to environmental protection. Later writings document still further dimensions and principles based on a socioeconomic perspective. It is the purpose of the present section to construct a halakhic model from the various sources available, of which only a few will be presented as a representative sample.

The chapter of *Lo Yahpor* (one should not dig . . .) in *Bava Batra* is actually a systematic collection of environmental protection regulations aimed at restricting activities motivated by private economic incentives that tend to disregard social responsibility considerations. Examples include: a requirement of minimum distance between planted trees and city limits (to prevent insects, allergies, etc.), a requirement of minimum height between a stove in a lower story and the floor of a flat in an upper story (to avoid excessive heat), and a requirement to locate tanneries only to the east of residential areas (to avoid bad smells).

To illustrate the economic meaning of such regulations it is worthwhile to cite a few excerpts from a previous work by Liebermann, starting with a quoted Mishneh paragraph:

> If a man desires to open a shop in a courtyard his neighbor may prevent him on the ground that he will not be able to sleep through the noise of people coming and going. A man, however, may make articles in the courtyard to

take out and sell in the market, and his neighbor cannot prevent him on the ground that he cannot sleep from the noise of the hammer or of the millstones or of the children.[25]

Let us ignore for the moment the concluding words of the Mishneh, "or of the children." The question now arises why neighbors can object to a storekeeper running a store in their courtyard, yet cannot object to a manufacturer producing goods there?

One possible distinction, suggested by several scholars, is the different nature of the harmful effects caused by the two types of business. In the case of a store, the harmful effect is the large number of people entering the courtyard and bothering its permanent residents. In the case of a manufacturer it does not bother the permanent residents that much.

R. Moshe Sofer (Germany, 1762–1839), in his Response of *Hatam Sofer, Hoshen Mishpat*, 92,[26] refuses to accept this line of reasoning. He argues that the store and the manufacturing facility should be distinguished from each other by their economic characteristics. To him the crucial consideration is the relative costs to the parties. The permanent residents of a courtyard can object to the store since the storekeeper can run his business in the street almost as easily (i.e., incurring very low costs). For a manufacturer, however, it would be impossible (i.e., prohibitively costly) to move his equipment and operate on the street.

Another illustration opens also with a Mishneh paragraph:

A fixed threshing-floor must be kept fifty cubits from a town. A man should not fix a threshing-floor on his own estate unless there is a clear space all round of fifty cubits. He must keep it away from the plantation of his neighbor and his ploughed fallow a sufficient distance to prevent damage being caused.[27]

A threshing floor must be kept away from the town or from individual neighbors because the flying chaff can hurt people and dry out plants. As stated in the main code of Jewish law, *Shulkhan Arukh* (written by R. Joseph Caro, Spain, 1488–1575), individual neighbors or the townspeople

---

[25]*Bava Batra* Ch. II, Mishneh 3.

[26]R. Joseph Caro (Spain, 1488–1575), *Shulkhan Arukh, Hoshen Mishpat* 92.

[27]*Bava Batra* Ch. II, Mishneh 8.

can prevent the owner of a threshing floor from operating his business even if in the past he ran it without any objection on their part. The basis for this ruling is a distinction between damages to person and damages to property. In the first case—which according to Jewish law includes the four categories of smoke, bad smell, dust, and vibrations—the lack of protest in the past is not a sufficient justification for keeping a harmful business running if an objection to it arises now. However, most authorities on Jewish law agree that one instance where the courts will rule against a claim for damages is when the injured party sold his legal right to the harmful effects to the owner of the harmful business. Then the transaction is final and the injured party cannot reverse his decision.[28]

A straightforward implication of this ruling, though not explicitly mentioned in the code, is that the injured party may reestablish his legal right to the harmful effects by repurchasing it from the owner of the harmful business. There can be little doubt that this ruling views harmful effects of business activity as an economic good that can be traded in the market.

Trading harmful business effects in the market is not always realistic. Its actual realization depends on the costs of negotiation. In Jewish law, negotiation (or transaction) costs are considered in the context of the monetary compensation that the town residents may have to pay to the threshing-floor owner for removing his business. More specifically, the above-cited *Mishneh* and the ruling based on it assume that the threshing-floor operator wants to start a new business adjacent to an existing town. But what happens in a case where a threshing floor had been operating at a location *before* a town was established next to it?

An answer to this problem is given by R. Moshe Isserles (*Rema*, Poland, 1525 or 1530–1572) in his comments on the code of *Shulkhan Arukh*. He rules that in such cases the threshing-floor operator has to move his business out of the fifty-cubit limit, and a full monetary compensation will be paid to him by the people of the town.[29] R. Yehoshua b. Alexander ha-Kohen Falk (*S'ma*, Poland, 1555–1614), also one of the code commentators, emphasizes the order of the two acts. The operator has to remove his plant first, and only then will he be compensated by

[28]*Shulkhan Arukh*, op. cit., 155:34–36.

[29]R. Moshe Isserles (Poland, 1525 or 1530–1572), *Rema, Hoshen Mishpat* 155:22.

the town residents. The reason for this order is the negotiation cost to the people of the town. R. Falk claims that if the owner is compensated first he will never remove his plant because no town resident will be willing to bear the responsibility of negotiating removal conditions with him.[30] In other words, there will be no negotiations since the negotiation cost to an individual resident exceeds the gain to him from removing the harmful threshing floor. It is therefore necessary to eliminate negotiation costs by a law order and thus reduce net social cost to the parties involved.[31]

Both illustrations not only demonstrate the public-economics understanding of the *Mishneh* Sages in particular and of *halakhah* authorities in general but also pave the way for constructing the overall business–society relationships model mentioned earlier. The remainder of the present section is devoted to this task.[32] For this purpose let us first classify all the possible solutions to environmental conflicts into five groups (which were already presented partially and in a different form in Section V). The classification follows in its general line the comparable paradigm set by Mickelmann and later by Calabresi and Melamed.[33]

1. Property rule against the polluter and in favor of the injured party.
2. Property rule against the injured party and in favor of the polluter.
3. Liability rule against the polluter and in favor of the injured party.
4. Liability rule against the injured party and in favor of the polluter.
5. Inalienability rule.

This classification scheme needs some words of clarification. Property rules is an economic term standing for the legal term of "injunction," while liability rules is the economic translation of the legal term "damages." A property rule can be applied in favor of each party. Assuming the injured party is the plaintiff and the polluter is the defendant, an

---

[30]R. Joshua b. Alexander ha-Kohen Falk (Poland, 1555–1614), *S'ma*, op. cit., note 11.

[31]Liebermann, op. cit.

[32]The discussion draws to some extent on Ilani (1982).

[33]G. Calabresi and A. D. Melamed, "Property Rules, Liability Rules, and Inalienability: One View of the Cathedral," *Harvard Law Review* 85 (April 1972). See also C. Mickelman, "Pollution as a Tort: A Non-Accidental Perspective on Calabresi's Costs," *Yale Law Journal* 80 (1971): 1089–1128.

application of a property rule against the defendant means an injunction against his (existing or planned) activity. A property ruling in favor of the defendant means clearing the way for continuing the polluter's operations along with blocking the way of any counteractions by the injured party. Alternatively, applying a liability rule will allow the defendant's activity (or the plaintiff's counteraction) only if damages are paid by the relevant party to its counterpart. As already mentioned, property rules affect resource allocation while liability rules affect only income distribution. Finally, the inalienability rule states that the property rights in question cannot be transferred by their owners under any condition, even if both parties are interested in the transaction.

It is interesting to discover that all these possibilities are discussed by halakhic authors and in a quite systematic approach. We turn now to an examination of a small though representative sample of rulings that fit the outlined paradigm, following some brief introductory comments.

From an economic viewpoint, the application of either rule should be based on efficiency criteria. In particular, for each conflict the optimal solution is the one that minimizes joint private and social cost caused by operating or prohibiting the nuisance. While the rules are all based on the joint-cost minimization criterion, we expect the various rules to be applied under different joint-cost conditions. Specifically:

1. A property rule against a polluter will be applied when we know that the costs of reducing or preventing the nuisance effects to the polluter are smaller than the corresponding costs to the injured party. Under such a condition one may consider buying the property rights of the nuisance from the injured party.
2. A property rule against an injured party will be applied when we know that it is less costly to him to live along with the nuisance than the cost of reducing or preventing it is to the polluter. In other words, to apply the property rule we have to identify the *least* cost-avoiding party, and to direct the rule against him.
3. A liability rule against a polluter will be applied when we do not know clearly which side is the least cost-avoiding party. The damages paid in this instance are intended not only to compensate the injured party but also to test whether the operation of the nuisance is efficient indeed, since it has the potential of both, covering cost of operation (including normal profit and payment of damages inflicted).

4. A liability rule against an injured party will be applied when one party (typically an individual) enjoys clear-cut property rights to a nuisance while the nuisance effects to the injured party (typically part of the public) are more costly than the cost of removing the nuisance to the polluter. In this instance, the liability payments are intended to compensate the polluter for his property rights. Such instances are quite rare.
5. An inalienability rule will be applied when any transfer of property rights to a nuisance among the relevant parties will cause an externality to part of society whose members (or future generations' members) cannot be identified and/or compensated.

Understandably, the economic criteria do not play an exclusive role in deciding actual social responsibility cases by courts. Other considerations (such as primacy, social welfare, and security) are quite frequently involved in halakhic treatment of business–society conflicts.

To construct the halakhic "model" of resolving environmental conflicts, the five-rule classification will be used as a conceptual framework. It will be shown that different rules were applied in light of economic considerations blended with halakhic concepts. The way each rule has been applied will be demonstrated by exhibiting a representative relevant case or cases. References to other cases are made in corresponding footnotes.

1. *Property rule against the polluter*

The halakhic reasoning underlying the application of a property rule against the polluter emerges from a unique perspective that views the polluter as an invader (*gazlan*) who makes direct use of the injured party without first obtaining the latter's permission. Referring to a resident who plants a tree next to his neighbor's water shaft Nahmanides says: "It is not a tort case but rather a *gezeilah* case."[34]

Yet, not always is a polluter (in the wide sense of the term) considered as an invader. His halakhic status depends significantly on relative-

[34] Nahmanides (Spain, 13th century). Commentary (*Hidushim*) *Bava Batra*, 26. Z. Ilani, *Efficiency Criteria in Dealing with Ecological Nuisances According to Halachic Literature as Compared to Modern Economic Theories*. Master's Thesis, Department of Economics, Bar-Ilan University, 1982.

cost criteria. In this context we are able to distinguish among three versions of this rule.

1a. *Property rule against the polluter when the relative cost of nuisance removal is not excessively high*

When the relative cost to the polluter of reducing or removing a nuisance is unreasonable, the property rule is not operated against the polluter. For example, R. Solomon b. Abraham Adret (*Rashba*, Spain, ca. 1235–ca. 1310) Responsa, Vol. II, 45 rules that the requirement to remove a smoke nuisance refers only to industrial smoke emission and does not include light smoke pollution that is being emitted by households' kitchens or any other ordinary housekeeping activity. Restricting normal household uses of fire means imposing an excessive, and perhaps prohibitive, cost on small polluters whose daily life cannot practically be conducted without causing what must be defined a socially acceptable level of pollution.[35] R. Adret's responsa, as interpreted by R. Moshe Sofer, which was cited above (pp. 17–18) serves as another example of the same relative restriction.

1b. *Property rule against the polluter when the relative cost of nuisance removal is low*

When the relative cost relationships are reversed, one may expect to observe corresponding reversed rulings. As a matter of fact, R. Joseph b. David Ibn Lev exactly follows this prediction.[36] His ruling pertains to an injunction sought by Levi, resident in an upper story in a certain building, against Reuben, who operates a business of wool dying on the ground floor of that same building where he lives as well. The production process involved the use of urine in which the wool was soaked. Levi complains that he cannot stand the smell that is diffused in the air when the wool is being tumbled in the urine. For his defense Reuben claims that this type of a production process is a common practice in that city whose economy depends fully on this industry.

---

[35]R. Solomon b. Abraham Adret (Spain, ca. 1235–ca. 1310).

[36]R. Joseph b. David Ibn Lev (1505–1580), *Responsa Mahari Ibn Lev*, Part III, 33.

R. Ibn Lev issued the injunction requested. Explaining his position he states that the nuisance to Levi is highly significant and there is no justification to request him to move to another home. On the other hand, the production process of wool dying is indeed an accepted practice, but most manufacturers place the urine vessels outdoors instead of within their homes. The economic interpretation that can be attributed to the ruling is quite straightforward: R. Ibn Lev applied the property rule against the least-cost avoider.

1c. *Applying a property rule against the polluter under any condition*

Efficiency tests are not always applied to nuisance cases. Nahmanides takes an extreme position on this issue by claiming that a polluter must always remove a nuisance which he is responsible for regardless of costs. Furthermore, the removal process should be carried out as soon as possible so as to prevent any unnecessary costs to the injured party.[37] Since Nahmanides also advocates the least-cost avoider principle, it has to be said that according to Nahmanides the absolute property rule will be applied only when the injured party acquires an indisputable title to the property rights in question. In this instance, overall economic considerations support the legal protection to property rights since otherwise individuals' private costs of protecting property rights are likely to distort resources allocation.

2. *Operating a property rule against the injured party*

Illustrations of this treatment category have already been mentioned above. For example, the interpretation suggested by R. Moshe Sofer to the *Mishneh* of running a shop in a courtyard. He applied his interpretation to a conflict between three brothers who inherited a two-story house from their father, two of them receiving the upper level of the house and the third its lower level. The conflict arose when one of the brothers in the upper level wanted to open a bar. The brother on the first floor objected, claiming that the bar would generate disturbing traffic in the front

---

[37]Nahmanides, *Hiddushim, Bava Batra* 26a. Z. Ilani, *Efficiency Criteria in Dealing with Ecological Nuisances According to Halachic Literature as Compared to Modern Economic Theories*. Master's Thesis, Department of Economics, Bar-Ilan University, 1982.

yard of the house, which belonged equally to all three brothers. R. Moshe Sofer's position emphasized the nature of the product sold by bars. Liquor is not just a beverage but a social and psychological service. People do not drink on the street, but in bars where there is an opportunity to socialize and "to relax their fears." R. Moshe Sofer concludes that making the brother run his business on the street would be prohibitively costly since he would not be able to sell his product there. (And, as it implicitly seems, making him rent another place for the bar would be prohibitively costly to him as well.) As R. Moshe Sofer puts it, if the legal right to object to such business activities were granted, then "nobody would ever be able to make his living."[38]

Another example relates to the same type of conflict handled by R. Ibn Lev in Section VII, subsection 1b above. Interestingly enough, other *halakhah* authorities issued reversed rulings, supporting Reuben's (i.e., the manufacturer's) position. The basis for this different position is quite unanimous, and emphasizes the public interest which stems from the fact that wool dying is a dominant industry in this locality and that the livelihood of many families depends on it.[39]

A typical case was ruled in this spirit by a contemporary authority, Rabbi E. Valdenburg (*Tzitz Eliezer*). It was issued as a response to an injunction sought by residents of a condominium against a doctor operating a clinic in their building. Rabbi Valdenburg rejected the suit in face of an apparently straightforward opposing *halakhah* formulated in *Shulkhan Arukh*. Reconciling the obvious contradiction he offers a surprising line of reasoning. Healing a patient amounts to returning to him a loss (his health). Since returning a loss is an obligation imposed on every Jew, the neighbors are requested to contribute their part to preserving patients' health. They can (and must) do so by withdrawing their objection to the operation of the clinic. Evidently, the ruling is motivated by a tendency to attribute a higher weight to social costs (to be incurred in case doctors are not permitted to operate clinics in residential buildings)

---

[38]R. Moshe Sofer (Germany, 1762–1839), *Responsa Hatam Sofer, Hoshen Mishpat* 92.

[39]*Responsa Maharshack* II, 98. See also *Responsa Shemesh Tzedaka* (R. S. Morforgo), *Hoshen Mishpat* 34:11.

as opposed to private costs (incurred by the residents due to the ongoing operation of such clinics).[40]

3. *Operating a liability rule against a polluter*

A liability rule allows the continuing operation of a nuisance, but demands that the operator make a compensation to the injured party. The amount of compensation may vary with the extent of the harmful effects caused by the nuisance. A typical halakhic case can be found in responsa *Nofet Tzufim* written by an 18th century authority, R. Petahia Mordecai Berdugo (Morocco, 1764–1820). The specific responsum was written as a reaction to a petition submitted by residents living next to a *Talmud Torah* nursery facility. In the petition an injunction was requested against the facility whose students were accused of messing up the joint toilet room, thereby causing a nuisance of excessive bad smell. R. Berdugo denied the petition, stating that since *Talmud Torah* is a *mitzvah* of public interest, the facility cannot be evacuated. Nevertheless, the management of the place was pronounced responsible for any damages generated by the children and respectively was requested to compensate the neighbors for any harmful effect produced.[41]

4. *Operating a liability rule against the injured party*

In order to avoid redundancy, the reader is referred to the above discussion of the threshing-floor *Mishneh*. It supplies a detailed documentation of this instance, including the handling of economic versus legal considerations.

5. *Liability rules under social and religious constraints*

As maintained by Coase, liability rules are not absolute but lend themselves to potential bargaining procedures. In these instances economic motivation overrides legal paradigms.[42] Nonetheless, as Levine points

---

[40]R. Eliezer Judah Valdenburg, *Responsa Tzitz Eliezer* part X, clause 25, Chapter 30.

[41]R. Petahia Mordecai Berdugo (Morocco, 1764–1820), *Responsa Nofet Tzuphim, Hoshen Mishpat* 191.

[42]Coase, op. cit.

out, from a halakhic perspective social religious considerations may sometimes gain priority over other motives in order to prevent situations whereby narrow bargaining interests produce results that conflict with desired public goals. Some illustrations are offered by the author.[43]

6. *Operating an inalienability rule*

Under this rule some property rights to nuisance are determined to be untradable. In *Shulkhan Arukh*, four such representative types of nuisances are enumerated: smoke, bad smell, noise, and wall vibrations.[44] According to a number of halakhic authorities the transfer of property rights to these harmful effects from an injured party to a polluter can always be reversed by a plea of the injured party. Consequently, courts are directed to return property rights to their original holder even in cases where the polluter operated the nuisance over prolonged periods of time.[45]

Maimonides (Egypt, 1135–1204) offers a line of reasoning to support this approach. It says that the voluntary consent of the injured party to be exposed to these nuisance categories is limited to past actions only, and does not cover future planned operations. In other words, even if a contract has been signed between the parties it can be declared not binding.[46] R. Solomon b. Abraham ha-Kohen (*Maharshakh*; Ottoman empire, 16th century) explains that the original contract was signed in light of an erroneous evaluation made by the injured party. As the signer now recognizes his mistake, he may claim his violated property rights.[47]

VIII. CONCLUDING REMARKS

The main thrust of the previous sections was a focus on actual negative externalities that take the form of either bodily harm or property dam-

---

[43]Levine (1980), op. cit., pp. 68–69.

[44]*Shulkhan Arukh.*, *Hoshen Mishpat* 156.

[45]Nahmanides, R. Yom Tov b. Abraham Ishbili (Spain, ca. 1270–1342, *Ritva*), and R. Meir Abulafia (Spain, 1170?–1244; *Yad Ramah*) on *Bava Batra* 23b.

[46]Maimonides (Egypt, 1135–1204), *Nizkei Shekhenim* 11:4.

[47]*Responsa Maharshakh* part II, 183.

age. This category of externalities was analyzed by means of the halakhic "model" developed. Nevertheless, there exists another category of negative externalities that consist of *potential* negative effects. Such externalities are imposed when a property owner is unable to use his property in a way he likes to, because of operations of a neighbor in his own property. In his pioneering book on economics and Jewish law, Levine postulates that as long as the party imposing the potential harm on a neighboring party is making a significant normal use of his property, it is commonly agreed by *halakhah* that his action cannot be restrained.[48] In case the defendant's activity does not represent a major normal use of his property halakhic authorities differ whether such an action can be restrained. However, if the plaintiff is able to prove that by imposing the potential harm some benefit to the defendant is being derived *presently* from the plaintiff's property, then an injunction can be issued now to avoid future damages.

[48]Levine (1980), op. cit., pp. 63–64.

7

Ethical Investment: The Responsibility of Ownership in Jewish Law

D. B. Bressler

It has been said that ethical investment is an idea whose time has come.[1] Frequently known as socially responsible investment (SRI), the movement seeks to make capital unavailable for socially repugnant business opportunities, including such "sinful" activities as the consumption of tobacco and liquor, gambling, weapons production, polluting the environment, and discrimination. It also seeks to use investment as a means of encouraging positive goals such as community development, employee relations, and product quality.

Support for the ethical investment agenda comes from an increasing number of shareholder resolutions seeking to implement policies consistent with the SRI thesis, victories achieved by minority stockholders,

[1]For a comprehensive discussion of the goals and achievements of the ethical investment movement, see Peter D. Kinder, Steven D. Lydenberg, and Amy L. Domini, *Investing for Good* (New York: Harper, 1993); John C. Harrington, *Investing with Your Conscience* (New York: John Wiley, 1992); Amy L. Domini and Peter D. Kinder, *Ethical Investing* (Reading Maar: Addiam Wesley, 1984).

increasing numbers of mutual funds with "socially responsible" objectives, significant amounts of pension fund money invested in companies that follow ethically correct goals, and the aggregate amount of capital invested that way. Statistical demonstrations of the consistency of ethical investment and positive profits, albeit not necessarily profit maximization, are being increasingly used to buttress the contentions of the ethical investment agenda.

As such, the movement flies in the face of much of the traditional economic analysis of "positive economics," most notably represented by Milton Friedman.[2] In his characteristic way of expressing economic absolutes, Friedman has summarized the traditional view: "A corporate executive's responsibility is to make as much money for the stockholders as possible, as long as he operates within the rules of the game. When an executive decides to take action for reasons of social responsibility, he is taking money from someone else—from the stockholders, in the form of lower dividends; from the employees in the form of lower wages; or the customer in the form of higher prices."[3] Needless to say, Friedman's contentions have been disputed by adherents to the SRI thesis.[4]

As the movement has developed momentum, attempts have been made to identify the earliest forerunners of the ethical investment approach. It is, indeed, notable that the germ of the approach can be traced to the 17th-century Quakers, who refused to profit from the war and slave-trading industries that were major sources of income at the time. Nonetheless, except for isolated instances, as with the Pioneer Fund, founded in 1928, which barred alcohol and tobacco products from its portfolio, no movement toward socially responsible investment could be detected until the late 1960s.

Building upon the successes of Ralph Nader's *Campaign* GM and the socially responsible resolutions introduced at the General Motors annual meeting, numerous shareholder resolutions have been subsequently filed

---

[2]Milton Friedman, *Capitalism and Freedom* (Chicago: University of Chicago Press, 1962) and "The Social Responsibility of Business Is to Increase Its Profits," *New York Times Magazine*, September 13, 1970.

[3]Milton Friedman as quoted in Harrington, op. cit., p. 3.

[4]See, for example, Christopher D. Stone, "*Where the Law Ends*" (New York: Harper, 1975), pp. 80–87.

involving topics such as the condemnation of investment in South Africa, environmental pollution, nuclear power, and expansion of military weapons. The first modern socially responsible fund, the Pax World Fund, appeared in 1971. The largest of the socially screened funds is the Calvert Social Investment Fund, with more than $1 billion in assets. Presently, there are more than one hundred such funds in the Unired States, Canada, Britain, and in other areas of the world. In addition, such prominent pension funds as the Teachers Insurance and Annuity Association College Retirement Equity Fund (TIAA-CREF) and the California Public Employees Retirement System have insisted that their considerable funds be invested only in what their managers deem to be socially responsible ventures. It is noteworthy that despite such restrictions, their earnings have been outstanding, although it has not been demonstrated that earnings would not otherwise have been greater.

Jewish law (*halakhah*) has recognized aspects of ethical investment from its earliest formulation. Thus, a Jew is enjoined from producing or selling non-Kosher food, whether as a sole proprietor or as a partner in an enterprise. Nor may a Jew be a partner in business transactions taking place on the Sabbath, even if his partner is not Jewish. Similarly, a Jew is proscribed from engaging in business activities that may help others violate ethical, moral, or religious codes. A Jew is not permitted to own all or part of a company that unnecessarily destroys trees, pollutes water or air, collects usury, produces or sells offensive weapons, or engages in deceitful and misleading practices.

What is, however, a relatively simple matter for a sole proprietorship or partnership becomes problematic in the context of complex business organizations. With giant corporations and the concomitant separation of ownership and management, can things be the same? Even within large partnerships, there are those who are only "limited" partners. A stockholder may be considered an "owner" on paper, but for all practical purposes have no power whatsoever. He cannot issue orders, implement his objectives, or utilize company assets. Moreover, his vote invariably is meaningless and his liability limited. If he holds shares in a mutual fund, he has title to a very small portion of a company which itself owns shares in a variety of other companies and whose ownership claim is itself defuse. Thus, although the value of a corporate investor's holdings may be enormous, he is bereft of any of the usual rights, privileges, and authority of ownership.

In light of this amorphous ownership right, what are the obligations, restrictions, and limitations of a stockholder? Does Jewish law permit him to purchase shares in a company whose activities are morally questionable or even repugnant? Does the fact that he will have no effect on company behavior regardless of what he does play any role in determining his obligations? Is a mutual fund like any other corporate entity? Does a shareholder have to be concerned with the secondary, tertiary, or indirect effects of company actions? What if company actions are unknown or uncertain but suspected to be unethical? Are the individual's needs for subsistence or the needs of society for the maintenance of efficient and orderly markets relevant to the legal determinants of Jewish law? Are shareholders ethically or legally responsible to join in support of shareholder resolutions seeking to steer the corporation on a more socially acceptable course?

The activities of companies which could be problematic fall within the following categories:

1. Business improprieties with respect to workers, consumers, suppliers, competitors, government, and community.
2. Production which harms the environment and thus endangers physical well-being through such things as air and water pollution, contamination, disease, destruction of forests and ozone, waste materials, hazardous chemicals, and nuclear power.
3. Products which harm people directly, such as cigarettes, alcohol, guns, and military weapons.
4. Business activity which is morally or spiritually repugnant such as the gambling industry, vulgar and indecent advertising, prohibited food, and lewd clothing.
5. Discrimination and inequitable treatment of groups or individuals.

In the event that there is an ethical obligation to abstain from investing in the types of business described above, what about a firm that does business with one of those companies? What about a firm that leases or rents space or provides supplies to such companies?

The issues we have raised can only be dealt with after considering how Jewish law defines and views ownership; the extent of one's responsibility for the acts of others; limitations on aiding, abetting, and/or assisting moral misconduct; business ethics; and the individual's obligations to society and the environment.

OWNERSHIP IN JEWISH LAW WITH SPECIFIC REFERENCE TO THE CORPORATION

Just as modern technology and science have brought with them new and complex halakhic issues that have challenged the most creative and erudite of experts in Jewish law, so have changes and innovations in the economy and business organization opened new and difficult vistas in the application of Jewish law. What electricity is to the *halakhic* application of physics, and heart transplants are to the *halakhic* application of biology, the corporation is to the *halakhic* analysis of economics and business.

A corporation is qualitatively different from other forms of business organizations in that it is a legally constructed entity which is independent of the people who own it. It is unlike a partnership which is nothing more or less than the sum of the constituent interests and where each partner owns a proportionate share of the totality. Individuals who put up capital for a corporation, on the other hand, are not legal owners of the ventures created and run by the corporation. Each merely owns shares in the corporate entity which, in turn, owns the ventures.

Moreover, corporations carry with them the legally sanctioned concept of limited liability; that is, shareholders are not legally liable for any claims that go beyond the capital invested. The corporation thus has a life, identity, and liability of its own independent of any of its shareholders. Of course, there are numerous "family corporations" where one or more related persons own 100 percent of all shares. In such cases, the distinction between the corporate entity and the persons who are shareholders is paper-thin. The shareholders (one or several) do, indeed, control all policies, actions, and distribution of income of the corporation. The corporate form of organization is primarily used in such contexts to reap the benefits of limited liability. More typically and in all intermediate, large, and multinational corporations, any one shareholder owns only a minute portion of the total stock of the corporation. Salaried managers and officers hired by a corporate board run the corporation and make all vital decisions. The officers, managers, and directors themselves do not typically own more than a negligible portion of the total stock.

Hence the result is separation of management and control from ownership. The *halakhic* issue is thus joined. The entire talmudic and *Shulkhan*

Arukh literature refers to ownership as either that of a single proprietor or a partnership of varying size. It was not necessary to explicitly address a system of organization that did not exist in practice. The challenge for contemporary experts in Jewish law is to use the principles directed to simple one- or two-dimensional business organizations and to extend them not only to multiple ownership, but to the case where legal ownership is not associated with control.

We must therefore be precise about the *halakhic* definition of ownership. This is crucial for many issues in Jewish law, such as *ribit*, *chametz*, and *Shabbat*. If a shareholder is considered a bona fide owner, then when the corporation collects interest, owns *chametz* on *Pesach*, or runs its production on *Shabbat*, it is as if the individual does those things. On the other hand, if the shareholder, because of his inability to control or influence decisions, is not construed as possessing ownership rights, then such corporate activities are not to be associated with him. Responsa literature on the corporation has almost exclusively centered on these issues. This discussion must now be extended to the issues that are connected to ethical investment.

Various approaches have been taken to the determination of the essence of ownership. Is ownership the ability to transfer title to others, or is it the ability to use resources of the company as desired? Perhaps the key factor is the power to make company decisions. Alternatively, it can be argued that ownership is associated with receipt of profits or with the liability for debts. For the case of a single proprietorship or partnership, these considerations are mostly academic because all of the above features are collectively present. The corporate case is, however, qualitatively different because ownership status for the typical shareholder depends upon which of the above definitions is used.

We will therefore outline different views of corporate ownership and then discuss the implications for ethical investment decisions.

VIEWS OF CORPORATE OWNERSHIP

1. R. Joseph b. David Ibn Lev *(Mahari Halevy; 1505–1580)*. Shareholders (common or preferred) do not possess ownership rights because they have no power to use, consume, or transfer the assets of the corporation.[5] The same cannot, however, be said for a corporate director or

executive, even if he owns only a negligible amount of stock. By inference, such an executive would be deemed to have an ownership stake. Extending this reasoning, limited partners, even without any corporate entity, would have the same status as corporate shareholders primarily because they have no legal right to utilize partnership assets. Limited partnership would thus not confer ownership.

1b. R. Henokh Dov Padwa (*Heshev ha-Efod*). Essentially the same view as R. Joseph Ibn Lev.[6]

2. R. Shaul Weingart (*Yad Shaul*). Shareholders do not possess ownership status because they are not personally liable for company debts.[7] Following this line of thought, it can be inferred that even directors and executives with some stock ownership would not be considered to have ownership status. Again, pursuing this mode of reasoning, limited partners would also not be considered as having ownership status since they bear no personal liability. General partners who incur personal liability would, on the other hand, be accorded ownership status in Jewish law.

3. R. Moshe Sternbuch (*Mo'adim Uz'manim*). The concept of a corporation existing as a separate entity distinct from the persons who own its stock is not recognized in Jewish Law.[8] Consequently, the purchase of corporate stock does not confer ownership. Instead, stockholders become virtual creditors of the company. It is, however, recognized that shareholders could advance capital on condition they become direct owners of the business enterprise with no personal liability (*shibbud haguf*). Only in that case would a shareholder have ownership status. In practice, however, corporate stock is bought and sold in accordance with a legal fiction that is only secularly recognized. Invariably then, no ownership status can be assigned to shareholders unless they are part of management.

---

[5]R. Joseph b. David Ibn Lev (1505–1580), *Mahari Halevy*, vol. 2, no. 124. For a detailed discussion of this view, see R. Isaac Jacob Wiesz (b. 1902), *Minhat Yitzhak*, vol. 3, no. 1 and R. Solomon Ganzfried (Hungary, 1804–1886), *She'arim Metzuyanim Be-Halakhah* 114:28.

[6]R. Henokh Dov Padwa, *Heshev ha-Efod*, no. 62. See *Minhat Yitzhak*, vol. 7, no. 26 for a detailed discussion of this view.

[7]R. Shaul Weingart, *Yad Shaul*, pp. 35–50. See *Minhat Yitzhak*, vol. 3, no. 1.

[8]R. Moshe Sternbuch, *Mo'adim Uz'manim*, vol. 3, no. 269, no. 1.

Notwithstanding all that has been said, a stockholder would be required to sell his stock in companies dealing in *chametz* before *Pesach* because we must take account of other views that stockholders do possess ownership status.

In *Teshuvot V'hanhagot*, the same author expresses the view that a shareholder whose holdings become public knowledge will have the same obligations as a full-fledged owner.[9] This is not essentially because of a genuine ownership status but because of *marit ayyin*, that is appearance sake. Since the shareholder is perceived to be an owner, he must assume ownership obligations. How to measure public perception is left unexplained. One possible standard could be ownership of 5 percent of the total shares since at that level the Securities and Exchange Commission (SEC) requires public disclosure.

Following the general line of R. Sternbuch's reasoning, a limited partner would be very different from a corporate shareholder because the concept of a partner who does not accept all the usual partnership obligations is certainly recognized in Jewish law.[10] Therefore, a limited partner would presumably possess ownership status even without any decision-making power; this is in contradistinction to a corporate shareholder.

4. R. Moshe Feinstein (*Iggerot Moshe*). A private or family corporation whose shareholders control company policy is like any other partnership. Shareholders are to be accorded ownership status.[11] On the other hand, shareholders in large public corporations who have no control over company policy or decisions are not to be considered to have ownership status.[12] Corporate directors or executives, or shareholders who own large blocks of shares, are considered partners who have ownership status. Those who control substantial proxies would, by this reasoning, also be given the same status as would mutual fund managers. This line of reasoning also leads to the conclusion that limited partners in a company would not be considered owners.

---

[9] R. Moshe Sternbuch, *Teshuvot V'hanhagot*, no. 421.

[10] On this point see latter portion of discussion in *Mo'adim Uz'manim*, op. cit.

[11] R. Moses Feinstein, *Iggerot Moshe, Orah Hayyim*, vol. 1, no. 90.

[12] *Iggerot Moshe, Even ha-Ezer*, vol. 1, no. 7.

5. R. Isaac Jacob Wiesz (*Minhat Yitzhak*; b. 1902). A corporate shareholder is considered to have ownership status if and only if he has the right to vote and be heard in regard to business policy, even if this right can be exercised only annually at a shareholders meeting.[13] Thus, common shareholders who usually have voting rights are deemed to be owners even if their voting power is negligible. Preferred shareholders or owners of common stock carrying no vote are not to be considered to have ownership status. Following this line of reasoning, limited partners who do not have voting rights would also not be accorded ownership status.

5b. R. Shelomo Kluger (*Ha-Elef Lekha Shelomo*; Poland, 1785–1869): Those shareholders who have no vote or voice in business policy are not deemed to be owners.[14] R. Solomon Ganzfried (Hungary, 1804–1886) notes that this view appears to agree with that of R. Wiesz.[15] An examination of the text reveals a very terse one-paragraph response to the question about the status of corporations in Jewish law. As such, it is difficult to be certain about the context of both the question and the response.

6. R. Menashe Klein (*Mishneh Halakhot*). A corporation is nothing more than a partnership of all shareholders.[16] Each shareholder has ownership status proportionate to his holdings in the company. The fact that shareholders have limited liability does not dilute their ownership standing. Presumably, a limited partner would have the same ownership status.

6b. R. Shelomo Gantzfried (*Kitzur Shulkhan Arukh*; Hungary, 1804–1886). A Jew is enjoined from owning bank stock because each shareholder is an owner.[17] Thus even if the majority of stock is owned by non-Jews, when the bank collects interest, it is as if each shareholder is receiving a proportionate share of forbidden interest.

6c. R. Jacob Isaiah Bloi (*B'rit Yehudah*; Israel, b. 1929). A corporate shareholder is an owner in all respects.[18] One should therefore avoid the

[13]*Minhat Yitzhak*, vol. 3, no. 1 and vol. 7, no. 26.

[14]R. Shelomo Kluger, *Ha'elef Lekha Shelomo*, no. 238.

[15]*She'arim Metzuyanim be-Halakhah* 114:28.

[16]R. Menashe Klein, *Mishneh Halakhot*, vol. 6, no. 277.

[17]R. Solomon Ganzfried, *Kitzur Shulkhan Arukh* 62:25.

[18]R. Jacob Isaiah Bloi, *B'rit Yehudah* 2:59,n.

purchase of stock in corporations whose policies and practices are not in accord with Jewish law.

Summary

Our survey has shown significant diversity of views in regard to the ownership status of corporate shareholders. Shareholder responsibility for corporate actions that are counter to Jewish law depends, at least in part, on whether the shareholder has ownership standing. According to the views of R. Feinstein, R. Ibn Lev, and R. Padwa, only corporate directors and executives bear responsibility. R. Wiesz would assign responsibility to any shareholder with voting rights. R. Sternbuch would only assign ownership responsibility to a limited partner but not to a corporate shareholder. At one end of the spectrum we find R. Weingart, who assigns no owner responsibility to a shareholder. At the other extreme, we encounter R. Klein and others who believe that a corporate shareholder is totally responsible for company actions.

In an attempt to present an overall perspective of these different views, scan the range of views and derive a consensus view, the following table has been constructed. Each row concisely represents one of the views presented above. The columns refer to different categories of investors. All table entries are given by

R = responsible for company actions
NR = not responsible for company actions.

Table 7–1

	Corporate Voting Shareholders	Corporate Nonvoting Shareholders	Limited Partner	Corporate Director/ Executive
Iggerot Moshe, Mahari Halevy, Hesher ha-Efod	NR	NR	NR	R
Yad Shaul	NR	NR	NR	NR
Mo'adim Uz'manim	NR	NR	R	R

(continued)

Table 7–1 (*continued*)

Minhat Yitzhak	R	NR	NR	R
Mishneh Halakhot	R	R	R	R
Consensus*	NR	NR	NR	R

*In deriving the consensus view on each question, the only works that were considered were those which both represented primary sources and where textual conclusions were outgrowths of a comprehensive analysis of all the ramifications of the pertinent issues. Thus the discussion of *Ha-Lef Lecha Shlomo* and *Kitzur Shulkhan Arukh* were brief, cryptic, sometimes ambiguous and hardly decisive, while *Brit Yehuda* is essentially of the views of the others.

We are led to the conclusion that while a diversity of views exist concerning corporate shareholder responsibility, the consensus is that only corporate directors and executives bear ownership accountability. This would mean that according to Jewish law only such shareholders would, because of their ownership status, have the legal obligation to examine ethical questions before investing. Our task is, however, far from complete, because we have to examine responsibility that may arise from other sources.

LIFNEI IVER—ABETTING MORAL MISCONDUCT

A cardinal principle of Jewish law is mutual responsibility for the acts of others, that is, *arvut.*[19] This implies that a Jew may not remain silent when another member of the community commits a sinful act. Corrective speech and action should follow.[20] This injunction can, however, go only as far as one's influence prevails.[21] Additionally, a Jew is enjoined, regardless of the extent of his influence, from actually abetting a morally reprehensible act. This injunction is described scripturally as, "Before a blind person, do not place a stumbling block."[22] This is taken, in its figu-

[19]*Sanhedrin* 27b, *Shevuot* 39a.

[20]Leviticus 19:17, "Rebuke thy neighbor." See, for example, R. Samson Raphael Hirsch's (Germany, 1808–1888) commentary.

[21]*Sanhedrin* 27b.

[22]*Leviticus* 19:14.

rative sense, to refer to moral and spiritual obstacles that are created by the act of aiding someone to violate Jewish law.[23]

This injunction is ably described by R. Samson Raphael Hirsch (Germany, 1808–1888): "Our care and consideration must be exercised for the benefit of our neighbor to prevent him coming to any material or moral harm through our means."[24] Even in the event that the other person seems totally aware and cognizant of his actions, he is considered morally blind to the true and long-term consequences of his actions.[25]

Our earlier discussion of ownership led us to the conclusion that the consensus view of Jewish Law would not assign ownership responsibility to shareholders with the exception of those who are corporate directors or executives, but accepting this lack of ownership responsibility only settles matters with regard to *chametz*, *ribit*, and *Shabbat*. These cases are relatively straightforward. A lack of Jewish ownership removes any problems in those domains.

The lack of ownership does not, however, give us closure with regard to ethical investment. Even absent ownership status, shareholders may be considered to be abetting unethical acts. If corporate policy promotes or allows improprieties, or environmental damage, or production of harmful products, have shareholders violated Jewish law?

To adequately deal with such questions, we must turn to the structures that emerge from the *lifnei iver* doctrine. We therefore compile the principles associated with that rule and examine the applicability of each to the corporate setting.

PRINCIPLE OF *LIFNEI IVER* (ABETTING MORAL MISCONDUCT)

1. *Unfeasibility Principle.*

The biblical injunction against abetting sinful activity is only applicable where the commission of the misdeed would not have been pos-

[23] *Avoda Zara* 6b, 15b, 55b, *Pesachim* 22b, *Moed Katan* 17a, *Kiddushin* 32a.

[24] R. Samson Raphael Hirsch, *Leviticus* 19:14.

[25] R. Aaron ha-Levi (Barcelona, 13th century), *Sefer ha-Hinukh*, *mitzvah* 232.

sible without that aid.[26] Note, however, that if the only other way to commit the sin is through the help of another Jew, *lifnei iver* does apply.[27] (The issue of whether there remains a rabbinic stricture even absent the biblical injunction will be discussed in the next section.)

Application. The usual corporate situation would therefore not qualify for the biblical injunction against abetting sinful activity because company policies could not be expected to be affected by any individual stockholder. Thus, whatever may be ethically objectionable within company policy will be independent of the action of any individual stockholder. The purchase or sale of stock, the expression of a point of view, the assignment of proxies, discarding them, and attendance or absence at the annual stockholder meeting will all make no difference if the shareholder is the typical small holder of stock.

However, if the shareholder is a very large (albeit minority) investor, or someone who controls the share of many stockholders like a mutual fund manager, his objections may carry weight and deter management from implementing morally objectionable policies and actions. Under such circumstances, assigning his proxies to management would constitute an act of abetting sinful activity because management needs his support to successfully implement their policies. Needless to say, the executive or corporate director who is Jewish and who is influential in setting corporate policy certainly transgresses by allowing reprehensible policies to go forth without objection.

2. *Probability Principle.*

Lifnei iver applies only if it is probable that a sinful act will occur. In the event of a 50 percent chance that no objectionable act will take place, the stricture against abetting such acts will not apply.[28]

An illustration of this principle is found in the writings of R. Tzvi Pesach Frank (Israel, 1873–1960), who was asked by an observant

---

[26]*Avoda Zara* 6b.

[27]R. Judah Rosanes (Turkey, 1657–1727), *Mishneh L'melekh, Malveh* 4:2

[28]R. Zevi Pesach Frank (Israel, 1873–1960), *Har Tzvi, Orah Hayyim*, vol. 1, no.125; *Iggerot Moshe, Orah Hayyim*, vol. 2, no. 62. See also R. Yom-Tov b. Abraham Ishbili (Spain, ca. 1270–1342), *Ritva, Avoda Zara* 63; R. David b. Samuel Segal (Berlin, 18th century), *Taz, Yoreh De'ah* 151:1; R. Moshe Sofer (Germany, 1762–1839), *Responsa Hatam Sofer, Yoreh De'ah* 19.

Moshav in Israel whether it would be permissible to accept the loan of an agricultural machine from the government in a case where the machines were distributed in pairs to adjoining settlements. The acceptance of the machine would result in the adjoining nonobservant *Moshav* utilizing the machine on *Shabbat*. R. Frank ruled that if there would be a fifty-fifty chance that desecration of *Shabbat* would take place, the *lifnei iver* stricture would not apply. Since in that particular case it is customary and expected that the nonobservant *Moshav* would use its machinery on *Shabbat, lifnei iver* applies.[29]

R. Moshe Feinstein also uses the probability principle to permit a jobber to give merchandise on consignment to a Jew who may sell that merchandise on *Shabbat* and for a wholesaler to sell merchandise outright to someone who may do business on *Shabbat*. In each case, it is uncertain what will be done with the merchandise considering that stocks of inventories are usually accumulated. Consequently, the doctrine of *lifnei iver* was ruled not to apply.[30]

Application. On the basis of the above decisions, there should be no concern about investing in a company that may engage in business practices antithetical to Jewish Law, as long as there is not a preponderance of expectation that this will occur.

3. *Universality Principle.*

Despite the fact that Jewish Law pertains to Jews only, it would violate the *lifnei iver* doctrine to enable any person to perform an act proscribed by Noahide precepts.[31] Moreover, the doctrine of *lifnei iver* would include abetting someone to violate a rabbinic injunction.[32] The legal basis for both of these extensions is similar. Abetting sin of any kind, regardless of nature or source, is proscribed.

4. *Directness Principle.*

Actions which enable someone who is not Jewish, and hence not bound by *lifnei iver*, to abet someone else in a sinful act are not enjoined because they are too indirect.[33]

---

[29] *Har Tzvi*, op. cit.

[30] *Iggerot Moshe*, op. cit.

[31] R. Solomon Zalman Auerbach, *Minhat Shelomo* 35:3.

[32] *Har Tzvi*, op. cit.

[33] *Avoda Zara* 21a; See also R. Ya'akov Kanevski, *Kehilat Ya'akov*, no. 4.

Application. Jewish Law does not preclude investing in a company that does nothing improper but does sell raw materials to a company that pollutes the environment or conducts itself in some other improper manner.

5. *Counterbalancing Principle.*

The stricture against abetting moral misconduct doesn't apply if, in the process of aiding someone to do some improper deed, the person is simultaneously deterred from a more profound sin. R. Solomon Zalman Auerbach utilizes this principle to permit serving food to someone who will not pronounce a blessing if in the process the person will be precluded from anger and hatred.[34]

Application. The *lifnei iver* dictum does not pertain to investment in a company that intends to alter its production process so as not to produce carcinogens but instead to unleash a chemical which produces mild respiratory discomfort.

Summary

On the basis of our analysis of the principles of the doctrine of *lifnei iver*, we may conclude that its restrictions against abetting a morally unacceptable act would pose problems for investors in companies engaged in unethical behavior only if the following conditions prevail:

a. Shareholders with very large blocks of stock who have some leverage to influence or pressure management are required by Jewish Law to do what they can to rectify policies and actions that involve business improprieties or harm to individuals or to society. This will frequently apply to mutual fund or pension fund managers, but also in certain circumstances to large individual investors.

b. Shareholders who ordinarily can have no effect on corporate policy as individuals may be able to influence corporate policy, directions, and actions by joining a shareholder movement to present resolutions at the annual corporate meeting. If there is such an incipient movement, an investor wishing to be in accord with Jewish law is obligated to partici-

---

[34]*Minhat Shelomo*, no. 35; See also R. Abraham Isaiah Karelitz (Israel, 1878–1953), *Hazon Ish, Shevu'ot* 12:9; *Iggerot Moshe, Yoreh De'ah*, vol. 1, no. 72, and *Orah Hayyim*, vol. 2, no. 67.

pate or divest himself of company holdings. Failure to do so is tantamount to supporting the status quo power of unethical management.

c. Executives or directors who are part of a management team and frequently help each other through their distinct and special expertise and insights are obligated to use their strategic positions to eliminate improper and harmful business practices.

d. The obligations noted above do not apply to the typical individual investor who has no power to influence corporate policy and has no stockholder movement to join. Moreover, even in the case of large holders of stock, these obligations would only pertain where it was likely—not simply possible—that the company would engage in unethical practices. Similarly, the injunction against abetting misconduct would not pertain to a company that does nothing improper except to sell raw materials or other products to companies who engage in business improprieties or discriminatory practices. Finally, if the power of a large shareholder is insufficient to totally eliminate all misdeeds but is sufficient to manipulate the company into exchanging a morally offensive act for one which is less harmful, appropriate action should be taken.

e. These guidelines for shareholder obligations only relate to restrictions inherent in *lifnei iver* or abetting sinful activity. As we shall see in the next section, there is yet another class of moral obligations which we must pursue.

ASSISTING MORAL MISCONDUCT—*MESAYA L'YIDAY OV'REI AVEIRA*

We have in the previous section indicated that the biblical injunction against abetting sinful acts only applies where the commission of the misdeed would not have been possible without the aid. A rabbinic injunction, however, exists against providing assistance to someone in the commission of moral misconduct even if that act could have been implemented without the help.[35] This is especially significant in the context

[35]*Tosafot* (*Shabbat* 3a); R. Nissim b. Reuben Gerondi (1310?-1372?), *Ran*, and R. Asher b. Jehiel (Germany, 1250–1327), *Rosh* (outset of *Avoda Zara*); R. Shabbetai b. Meir ha-Kohen, *Shakh*, *Yoreh De'ah*, 151:6. There is some dis-

of a corporate situation where the actions of an individual investor—even if helpful—can hardly be described as essential.

The conditions under which the rabbinic injunction of assisting moral misconduct apply are diffuse, complex, and sometimes overlap those for *lifnei iver*. They are culled from an analysis of talmudic source material and integrated with decisions found in responsa literature. Although in some respects, they mirror *lifnei iver*, these principles are generally more extensive and restrictive.

PRINCIPLES OF *MESAYA L'YIDAY OV'REI AVEIRA* (ASSISTING MORAL MISCONDUCT)

1. *Feasibility Principle.*

Assisting someone in the commission of a misdeed where it is feasible to accomplish the objective even without the assistance violates the rabbinic prohibition of *mesaya*, that is, assisting moral misconduct. The purview of this principle is, however, the subject of significant dispute and is the subject of the next principle.

2. *Exclusionary Clause.*

The *Shakh* (R. Shabbetai b. Meir ha-Kohen, Poland, 1621–1662) holds that the rabbinical injunction of *mesaya* applies only to moral misconduct by a Jew. Moreover, the dictum does not apply to a Jewish apostate (*mumar*).[36]

This can be understood philosophically in accordance with the explanations of R. Judah Loew b. Betzalel (*Maharal;* d. 1609) and R. Moses Alshekh (*Alshekh*; Israel, d. ca. 1593) that responsibility for the deeds of others arises out of the fact that the Jewish nation is like one person with different body parts.[37] Hence, a person who has removed himself

---

pute whether R. Mordecai b. Hillel, *Mordechai,* holds that there is no such Rabbinical injunction. On this point, see R. Moses Isserles (Poland, 1525 or 1530–1572), *Rama, Yoreh De'ah* 151:1, and *Shakh,* op. cit.

[36]*Shakh,* op. cit.

[37]R. Judah Loew b. Betzalel (Prague, d. 1609), *Maharal* (*Netivot Olam, Netiv ha-Torah,* Chapter 2); R. Moses Alshikh (16th century), *Alshikh, Deuteronomy* 29:9.

from commitment to Jewish practices or someone not Jewish is not covered by this injunction. The view of R. Eliezer Judah Waldenberg (*Tzitz Eliezer*; Israel) is in accord with the conclusion of the *Shakh*.[38] R. Jehezkel Landau (*Dagul me-Revavah*; Poland, 1713–1793) extends the exclusionary clause of the *Shakh* to include not only an apostate but also someone who generally subscribes to Jewish law but on a particular occasion intentionally performs a certain misdeed.[39] R. Abraham Abele Gombiner (*Magen Abraham*; Poland, 1637–1683), on the other hand, holds that the dictum against assisting moral misconduct does apply to aiding an apostate and apparently even to helping any human in the commission of a deed which is counter to the Noahide laws.[40]

The view of R. Moses Isserles (*Rema*; Poland, 1525 or 1530–1572), as expounded by R. Aaron Kotler (1892–1962), contrary to that of the *Shakh*, applies the dictum of *mesaya* to all cases.[41] This leads R. Kotler to the conclusion that Jewish law would preclude renting a store to an apostate who will desecrate *Shabbat* in that store, whereas according to the *Shakh*, such a rental would be permitted.[42] R. Elijah b. Solomon (*Gera*; Vilna, 1720–1797), as expounded by R. Kotler, takes the more stringent view that *mesaya* applies to assisting misconduct of a Jew, non-Jew, apostate, or intentional violator.[43] In light of this opinion, it would, concludes R. Kotler, be extremely difficult to be lenient in this matter.[44] R. Israel Meir ha-Kohen Kagan (*Mishneh Berurah*; Radin, 1838–1933) also apparently subscribes to the view of the *Gera*.[45] R. Feinstein reaches an essentially similar conclusion without explicitly mentioning *Gera*.[46] Moreover, R. Kotler concludes his discussion with a plea to avoid any semblance of assisting anyone performing a moral misdeed.[47]

Application. According to the *Shakh*, shareholder investment—even in substantial amounts—in a company that engages in business improprieties

---

[38]R. Eliezer Judah Waldenberg, *Tzitz Eliezer*, vol. 20, no. 20.
[39]R. Jehezkel Landau (18th century), *Dagul Me-Revavah, Yoreh De'ah* 151.
[40]R. Abraham Abele Gombiner, *Magen Abraham, Orah Hayyim* 347:4.
[41]R. Aaron Kotler (1892–1962), *Mishnat Rebbe Aaron, Teshuvot*, vol. 1, no. 3.
[42]Ibid.
[43]R. Elijah b. Solomon (Vilna, 1720–1797), *Gera, Yoreh De'ah* 151:8.
[44]*Mishnat Rebbe Aaron*, op. cit.
[45]R. Israel Meir ha-Kohen Kagan (Radin, 1838–1933), *Mishneh Berurah* 347:7.
[46]*Iggerot Moshe, Yoreh De'ah* vol. 1, no. 72.
[47]*Mishnat Rebbe Aaron*, op. cit.

or endangers people or the environment would not violate *mesaya* if the company is run by non-Jews or Jewish apostates. A problem would, however, arise with substantial investment in companies with Jewish management that are not apostates but misconduct themselves in business. R. Landau would find even this circumstance not a problem. Nonetheless, if Jewish management mistakenly misconduct themselves or are ignorant of Jewish law, it would violate the *mesaya* doctrine to invest substantially and in that way assist management in their continued moral misconduct. While this set of circumstances could occur anywhere, it is most probable to encounter this situation with Israeli corporations controlled by Jewish management who in large part are ignorant of Jewish law.

Following the views of the *Gera*, endorsed by R. Kagan, R. Kotler, and R. Feinstein, we would extend the *mesaya* injunction to non-Jewish or apostate ownership. It is, however, necessary to stress that such problems in Jewish law would arise with new issues or new capitalization of corporations or limited partnerships and not with the repurchase of stock or a limited stake in a partnership. In the latter cases, management gains nothing and is not in any way assisted by a simple change in ownership identity.

The problem of *mesaya* would, however, also appear if shareholders assign proxies to a management team that misconducts itself or with mutual fund managers (or others) whose purchase of stock could be substantial enough to wield influence and to assist or deter management in pursuit of questionable goals and misconduct.

In a similar vein, if there is a shareholder movement attempting to pass resolutions at the annual company meeting that would prevent management from implementing some business impropriety or harmful practice, it would be incumbent upon shareholders to support such proposals. To do otherwise would be tantamount to assisting company misconduct. Finally, those governed by Jewish law are constrained from joining a management team or a board of directors of a corporation, or from becoming a general partner in a company that engages in business improprieties or harmful conduct.

3. *Probability Principle.*

The *mesaya* dictum applies only if it is probable that moral misconduct will occur. In the event that such probability is no greater than 50 percent, the injunction does not apply.[48]

[48]*Iggerot Moshe, Orah Hayyim*, vol. 2, no. 62; *Minhat Yitzhak*, vol. 3, no. 29.

Application. To invest significantly in a new issue of a company or for a mutual fund manager to purchase large blocks of stock in a company that may engage in business improprieties or harmful activities does not violate *mesaya* where there is no greater than a 50 percent chance that the improper conduct will occur.

4. *Association Principle.*
Even if no action is done to actively assist moral misconduct, mere association, in a formal way, with a sinner is considered to violate the *mesaya* doctrine.[49] Thus, membership in an organization, institution, or group whose actions are repugnant violates Jewish Law, provided that such membership is public knowledge.

This principle is used by R. Feinstein to prohibit membership in a charitable institution performing acts of kindness and charity because the organization desecrated *Shabbat*. By being numbered as one of the members of the institution, he is considered to be a supporter of acts which violate Jewish law.[50] Being publicly associated with an enterprise conducting itself improperly could also violate the doctrine of *marit ayin*, that is, appearance of performing a sinful act.[51]

Application. Any ownership of corporate stock equal to or in excess of 5 percent is required by SEC regulations to be publicly disclosed. As such, it appears that such a shareholder would be considered to be a *mesaya* if the company is involved in business improprieties or harmful conduct. This would apply even if the shareholder has no power or influence over company policy or action.

5. *Severe Income Loss.*
In cases where the potential for significant loss of income exists, the lenient ruling of the *Shakh* mentioned in Principle 2 may be followed. This would mean that the *mesaya* injunction would not pertain when assisting an apostate.[52] It is on this basis that R. Feinstein permits

[49] *Iggerot Moshe, Orah Hayyim*, vol. 2, no. 61.

[50] Ibid.

[51] *Iggerot Moshe, Orah Hayyim*, vol. 2, no. 64, and vol. 4, no. 54; *Minhat Yitzhak*, vol. 1, no. 72, and vol. 3, no. 1.

[52] *Iggerot Moshe, Yoreh De'ah*, vol. 1, no. 72, and *Orah Hayyim*, vol. 2, no. 67.

the rental of a catering hall for weddings on days proscribed by Jewish law.[53]

Application. A Jewish member of a McDonald's management team that produces a cholesterol-laden non-nutritious hamburger need not resign his position if he stands to have a substantial income loss thereby and the company is not violating any legal statute or regulation. This assumes that their policies will be unaffected by whatever he does as an individual.

6. *Orderly Market Principle.*

Where a consumer market would be disrupted—especially in case of necessities—if assistance were not provided to someone not committed to Jewish Law, the injunction against *mesaya* may be waived. This leniency applies only to cases where there is no certainty of sinful activity.[54]

Application. A shareholder in a company producing necessities may assign proxies to management even if there is some probability that they may pollute or practice other business improprieties. This assumes that management has enough votes to prevail in any event and that the assignment of proxies only helps to strengthen their hand.

7. *Diversion Principle.*

In the event that assistance is provided to help accomplish something permissible but it is expected that the resource given will also be diverted for an improper use, *mesaya* does not apply.[55] On this basis, R. Feinstein and R. Ovadiah Yosef (*Yabi'ah Omer*) permit the rental of an apartment to someone who desecrates *Shabbat* even where it is expected that he will ignite the fuel burner by turning on hot water.[56]

Application. A shareholder or fund manager may invest substantial sums into new issues of stock of a company that has no production need to

---

[53]*Iggerot Moshe, Yoreh De'ah*, vol. 1, no. 72.

[54]*Iggerot Moshe, Orah Hayyim*, vol. 2, no. 62.

[55]*Iggerot Moshe, Orah Hayyim*, vol. 2, no. 66, and *Yoreh De'ah*, vol. 1, no. 72; *Yabiah Omer*, vol. 2; *Orah Hayyim*, no. 15.

[56]*Iggerot Moshe, Orah Hayyim*, vol. 2, no. 66; *Yabiah Omer*, op. cit.

pollute but where management does so on certain occasions because of some opportunity for monetary gain.

8. *Counterbalancing Principle.*

As in the case of *lifnei iver*, *mesaya* does not apply if, by assisting someone in the commission of an impropriety, some more serious sinful act will be avoided.

Application. It would be permissible to assign proxies to management who intend to implement new production processes that will maintain a certain amount of air pollution if in the process an older production process which resulted in both air and water pollution will be abandoned.

9. *Proximity Principle.*

The *mesaya* doctrine applies only where there is some proximity between the assistance given and the commission of the morally improper act.[57]

Application. Purchase of shares of a new corporate issue is permissible where the company plans to initially use the funds in a morally acceptable manner even if it is uncertain how the company will use the funds in the future.

Summary

Our analysis of the *mesaya* doctrine suggests that its restrictions against assisting moral misconduct, even where the actions could be accomplished without the help, would pose problems for investors in companies engaged in business improprieties or harmful activities in the following cases:

a. The purchase of shares of a new issue or new capitalization of a corporation or limited partnership where the company engages in busi-

[57]R. Samuel Ehrenfeld (1835–1883), *Teshuvot Hatan Sofer, Yoreh De'ah*, no. 83; R. Naphtali Zevi Judah Berlin (Russia, 1817–1893), *Responsa Meishiv Davar*, vol. 2, no. 3; R. Shalom Mordecai Shvadron (Galicia, 1835–1911), *Responsa Maharsham*, vol. 2, no. 93; R. Nisson Ben-Tzion b. Menakhem Shmuskovich, *Responsa Binyan Tzion*, no. 15.

ness improprieties, endangers or harms people or the environment, discriminates, or otherwise participates in morally reprehensible behavior is enjoined. This would apply even with the purchase of an insignificant amount of shares and even where the shareholder has no illusion of influencing or affecting decision-makers. The mere purchase of such shares assists the company (unlike the repurchase of shares owned by others).

b. The restrictions in Jewish law against assisting management in morally repugnant activities applies whether or not management and the board of directors are Jewish. Jewish law is, of course, directed to those who are Jewish, but portions of it also apply universally to all humankind. This refers to the entire civil realm, including theft, deceit, misrepresentation, prompt and fair payment of workers and suppliers, equitable and decent treatment of consumers and employees, conforming to government regulations, and vigilance in the avoidance of harm to all humankind and animals.[58] Polluting water and air, or harming others through faulty and destructive products is enjoined either as a form of theft or as damaging society's resources. It is also proscribed because such action ultimately harms humans and animals. All of the actions stated above are thus included in the Noahide codes of law.

c. The repurchase of shares of stock held by others generally does not assist management because no new capital is thereby provided. Nor can individual demand for a company's stock inflate the price except in the case of a very large purchase, as when a mutual fund places a large order. The latter type of purchaser, therefore, does have to be concerned about the moral rectitude of the company.

d. The assignment of proxies to management is enjoined if the company is engaged in business improprieties or activities harmful to others or to the environment.

e. In the same vein, it is incumbent upon shareholders to support resolutions attempting to prevent management from immoral or harmful behavior. Failure to do so would have the effect of assisting management in the implementation of morally repugnant policies and actions and be included in *mesaya*. This would apply even if there is little or no expectation that the shareholder resolution will succeed.

---

[58]Nahmanides (Spain, ca.1195–ca.1270), *Ramban, Bereishit* 34:13; *Teshuvot ha-Rama* No. 10; *Teshuvot Hatam Sofer*, vol. 6, no. 141, *Tzitz Eliezer*, vol. 16, no. 55.

f. Becoming a member of a management team or of the board of directors of a company that commits unethical acts would certainly be proscribed by the *mesaya* principle even if the person, as an individual, can have little effect on policies.

g. The above restrictions do not, however, apply unless there is at least a probability greater then 50 percent that moral misconduct on the part of the company will occur. The injunctions are also not pertinent if investing in the company will aid a socially redeeming cause that will more than balance any harmful effects. Similarly, the strictures are inapplicable unless the expected immoral conduct is imminent.

h. Even in the event that investing in a company will do nothing to assist the objectionable policies and goals, as when existing stock is purchased and the stockholder will have no influence, he will be enjoined from such purchases if he attracts public notice. A benchmark figure of 5 percent may be employed, since that will trigger the SEC requirement for public disclosure.[59]

CONCLUSION

Having presented a detailed analysis of the concepts of *ba'alut* (ownership), *lifnei iver* (abetting moral misconduct), and *mesaya* (assisting moral misconduct), we are able to address the issue of ethical investment from the perspective of Jewish law. As we have demonstrated, the determination of what Jewish law demands is much more complex than what others have implied.[60] Below we present the conclusions that we have developed. While variations of views are evident, an overall pattern of what Jewish law requires does emerge.

1. Business improprieties with respect to employees, consumers, or competitors, production which harms the environment or the well-being of individuals, and discrimination of any kind is proscribed in Jewish law. This applies to both Jew and non-Jew. As such, corporate manag-

---

[59]I am indebted to Dr. Aaron Levine for first suggesting to me the significance of SEC disclosure regulations.

[60]See, for example, Meir Tamari, *The Challenge of Wealth* (Northvale, NJ: Jason Aronson, 1955), p. 95.

ers and directors must pay heed to the moral and ethical consequences of their policies and actions. This applies even to an executive who is but one member of a larger team. Even if he is a minor cog in the management machine, his participation would violate *mesaya*.

2. Shareholders who are deemed to be genuine "owners" of a corporation are accountable for the moral and ethical consequences of corporate policies and actions. Therefore, owners or partners of closed or family corporations, or general partners of a company bear full responsibility for such corporate behavior.

3. Shareholders who are not managers or directors retain partial ownership status according to R. Klein and others. They are therefore, regardless of how small their interest, responsible for all the moral consequences of the corporation. Presumably, it would not then be permissible to acquire any shares of a corporation that engages in business improprieties or harms the environment or the physical and spiritual well-being of anyone. This same stricture would apply to limited partners of any business enterprise.

R. Wiesz would, however, hold that only stockholders with voting rights would be considered genuine owners and hence morally responsible for corporate acts. Consequently, such shareholders would have to divest themselves of shares of corporations whose practices are morally reprehensible. Shareholders without voting rights and who are not part of the management team are not considered corporate owners in any practical sense.

R. Sternbuch views only limited partners, and not corporate shareholders, as genuine owners and thus responsible for corporate action.

R. Feinstein, among others, expresses the consensus view that only corporate managers or directors are responsible for corporate action. Individuals owning stock in companies with ethically indefensible policies and practices have no ownership responsibility.

4. Even if a shareholder is not considered an owner of the company, he will violate *lifnei iver*, that is, he will be abetting moral misconduct, if he is a large stockholder with power to influence corporate policies and actions. Such a stockholder, mutual fund, or pension fund manager would not be permitted to acquire shares of a company whose actions are morally repugnant.

5. Small shareholders, ostensibly with no leverage to influence corporate policies or actions, may yet be subject to the restrictions of *lifnei*

iver in the event there are shareholder resolutions to limit the power of management. A stockholder who through such resolutions could influence corporate policy would be morally bound, by the doctrine of *lifnei iver,* to join the insurgents. In the event that even by supporting the resolutions, he cannot realistically influence policy through the support of the resolution, his failure to support the resolutions would violate the *mesaya* doctrine.

6. Unlike shares of stock already held by other stockholders, the purchase of newly issued shares or capitalizations, even in small doses, is considered "assisting" management in their objectives even if the shares would have been sold in any event. Consequently, such purchases of newly issued stock of a corporation that engages in behavior that is morally objectionable would be prohibited because of the doctrine of *mesaya*, (assisting moral misconduct).

7. Assignment of proxies to management who are responsible for and perpetuate ethically reprehensible conduct is tantamount to assisting moral misconduct. As such it is violative of *mesaya* and enjoined by Jewish law.

8. A shareholder with holdings of existing stock too small to influence company policy would still be violative of *mesaya* or *marit ayin* if his ownership percentage was large enough to attract public notice. One measure of this is the point where the SEC rules require public disclosure—that is, at 5 percent.

9. Shareholders who do not fall into any of the above categories do not have to be concerned about the ethical implications of their investments. This would apply to a shareholder with relatively small amounts of already issued stock who is not a member of management, does not assign his proxies to management, and has no opportunity to participate in shareholder resolutions.

10. Most corporate investors do, indeed, fit into the description given in the preceding paragraph. Thus, they need not apparently be concerned with the ethical behavior of the company. Nonetheless, there are a sufficient number of pertinent instances described above to make ethical investing a realistic requirement in Jewish law under proper circumstances.

11. Moreover, there appears to be significant sentiment in the relevant literature to go beyond strict requirements and to voluntarily factor ethical considerations into investment decisions even when they are

not strictly mandated. This view is most cogently and passionately expressed by R. Aaron Kotler, who concludes his discussion with a plea to not necessarily be content with the letter of the law, but instead to have as a goal that no person is, even in a negligible way, an accessory to improper behavior.[61]

[61]*Mishnat Rebbe Aaron*, op. cit., p. 9.

8

The Corporate Veil and *Halakhah*: A Still Shrouded Concept

*Michael J. Broyde and Steven H. Resnicoff**

PART I. INTRODUCTION

Corporations are ubiquitous in the American marketplace. They account for a large percentage of the national economy, and both consumers and businesses enter into transactions with corporations on a daily basis. There are various kinds of corporations, and people form them or invest in them for disparate reasons. Despite the significance of corporations, relatively few publications have discussed their halakhic ramifications. None has provided a detailed description of corporate governance or has comprehensively dealt with the many different scenarios that diverse types of corporations present. By contrast, this chapter identifies the relevant aspects of American corporate law and then explores its halakhic

*The authors would like to thank Michael S. Berger, J. David Bleich, David R. Blumenthal, William J. Carney, Eli Clark, Eliezar Eisenberg, Moshe Heinemann, Aaron Levine, Aaron Small, Mark Weber, and John Witte, Jr., for their gracious and generous advice and assistance.

consequences.[1] Indeed, how Jewish law (*halakhah*) characterizes a corporation—and whether it considers a Jewish shareholder to be responsible for corporate actions, an owner of the corporate assets, or a party to corporate lawsuits—plays an important part in resolving countless halakhic questions and a decisive role in some.[2]

Secular law and secular commercial models affect Jewish Law on at least two levels. On one level, secular commercial institutions may create or involve "facts" that directly resonate in principles indigenous to Jewish Law. For example, *halakhah* often recognizes the Jewish Law validity of commercial customs and such customs may be based on prin-

[1]It seems likely that the Jewish law analysis employed in this chapter would apply to corporations in many countries, at least those with Western-style economies. Nevertheless, because this analysis involves the interaction between Jewish law and secular legal theory and reality, it is appropriate to limit the scope of this English piece to the secular system with which the authors are most familiar. One commentator rejects the suggestion, apparently made to him, that, in light of existing governmental regulation, corporations should be regarded as if they were owned by the government and not by the shareholders. *See* R. Menashe Klein, *Mishneh Halakhot* 6:277 (exaggerating the power of shareholders by comparing the corporation in the hands of its shareholders to clay in the hands of a sculptor). This rejection seems generally appropriate in democratic countries, where government restriction is relatively mild. Prior to the implementation of economic reforms, however, government regulation in Communist block countries was so pervasive as to provide some support for the notion of a corporation as a government-owned entity. *See*, for example, Andrei A. Baev, "The Transformation of the Role of the State in Monitoring Large Firms in Russia: From the State's Supervision to the State's Fiduciary Duties," *Transnational Law* 8:247 (1995).

[2]For example, *halakhah* requires that Jews pay their debts. If a corporation becomes insolvent, must a Jewish shareholder use his personal resources to satisfy an unpaid corporate debt? *Halakhah* requires the giving of charity. If a corporation makes charitable contributions, has a Jewish shareholder fulfilled her personal obligation? If a banking corporation exacts interest when it lends money to Jewish borrowers, has its Jewish shareholder disobeyed *halakhah* and must she return the interest that the corporation collected? If a corporation owns *hametz* on Passover, has its Jewish shareholder committed a transgression? May a Jewish consumer purchase *hametz* that was owned during Passover by a corporation with Jewish shareholders? All of these questions, and many others, are addressed at some length in the book we are preparing for publication.

ciples of secular corporate law. Similarly, Jewish law involves presumptions regarding people's intentions and expectations. These presumptions may be shaped by corporate realities. On another level, Jewish law contains a doctrine, "the law of the land is the law" (*dina de'malkhuta dina*), which validates, for purposes of Jewish law itself, certain secular laws. In fact, *dina de'malkhuta dina* arguably provides a prism through which Jewish law perceives various commercial activities.[3] Consequently, in order to

---

[3]Consequently, if Jewish law authorities misunderstand secular law, they may reach incorrect conclusions about *halakhah*. For example, under Jewish law, certain unsecured debts not paid before the sabbatical year (according to some authorities, before the beginning of the sabbatical year and according to others, before the end of the sabbatical year), cannot thereafter be enforced under Jewish law. Assume *A* owes *B* $1,000 and, prior to the sabbatical year, *A* gives *B* a $1,000 check that is dated prior to the sabbatical year. For some reason *B* does not deposit the check until after the sabbatical year. The question arises as to whether *B* can deposit the check now. At least one prominent Jewish law authority states that when *A* gives *B* the check, *A* "pays" the underlying debt with the check, and, therefore, *B* is permitted to deposit the check even after the sabbatical year. This authority explains that the reason why the giving of the check is deemed to be payment of the underlying debt is that: (1) secular law forbids a person from stopping payment on his check; (2) there is a Jewish law principle (which will be discussed in detail later, in Part V of this chapter) that makes this secular law religiously valid; and (3) the check is considered as if it were a cash payment. R. Moshe Feinstein (New York, 1895–1986), *Iggerot Moshe, Hoshen Mishpat* 2:15.

Actually, however, secular law does not necessarily forbid someone from stopping payment on a check. Although it may be unlawful to fraudulently issue a check with the intention of stopping payment, one may stop payment if unanticipated circumstances develop after a check is issued. In addition, even if payment on a check is not stopped, there may be no money in the drawer's account. It could be that the drawer was mistaken about his or her balance when the check was issued. Alternatively, the drawer could have known that there was no balance but mistakenly believed that money would soon be deposited into the account. Another possibility is that the drawer made no mistake and there was sufficient money in the account at the time the check was issued. Meanwhile, however, other checks (perhaps issued by a co-drawer on the account) were presented and paid, thereby depleting the account. Or maybe another of *A*'s creditors obtained a judgment and garnished the balance of *A*'s account, before *B* could present the check. Indeed, secular law recognizes these scenarios and specifically provides that, unless the parties agree otherwise, when

effectively evaluate alternative Jewish law theories regarding corporations, it is crucial to identify and examine the facts and circumstances of secular corporate law.

Part II describes the principal types of American corporations—and analogous commercial vehicles—and explains the primary secular purposes for, as well as the principal secular ramifications of, employing such forms. Part III assesses the various Jewish law theories.

PART II. THE AMERICAN CORPORATION AND ANALOGOUS COMMERCIAL CONSTRUCTS

Under secular American law, when individuals join together, pursuant to an oral or written agreement, to pursue a commercial venture on an unincorporated basis, they are usually recognized as a general partnership. The partners of a general partnership are deemed to be authorized agents for each other in connection with the conduct of partnership business.[4] Consequently, the partners of a general partnership are jointly and severally liable for partnership debts. Thus, if collection efforts by partnership creditors exhaust partnership assets, the creditors may col-

---

B takes an ordinary check from *A*, the underlying debt from *B* to *A* is not discharged. Instead, the taking of the check merely suspends the underlying obligation until and unless the check is in fact paid or dishonored. If the check is paid, the underlying debt is at that time discharged. If the check is dishonored, then the underlying debt is no longer suspended, but may be enforced. *See* Uniform Commercial Code § 3–310(b). It is quite possible that this Jewish Law authority was not apprised of these details of secular law. Had he been aware of them, he may have reached a different conclusion. *See also* Michael Broyde, *The Pursuit of Justice and Jewish Law* (Yeshiva University Press: New York, 1996), pp. 115–122.

[4]In light of the large, transcontinental partnerships—particularly professional partnerships of lawyers and accountants—where many, or most, partners have not even met one another, the appropriateness of this theoretical perspective and the doctrine of unlimited liability should be rethought. See, for example, Steven H. Resnicoff, The Unlimited Personal Liability of Partners: Bankruptcy Implications for Professional Partners, published in 67th Annual Meeting of the National Conference of Bankruptcy Judges, Orlando, Florida, October 17–20: Educational Program (1993).

lect any deficiency from individual partners. The risk of unlimited personal liability is a severe disincentive for participating in a partnership. In addition, a partnership's existence is precarious. It typically terminates automatically, for example, if any of the partners dies. Moreover, general partnership interests are not easily sold, partly because of the financial risk incurred upon becoming a partner. The corporate form is often used to avoid these problems. Although initially corporations were, at least for the most part, created by special act of a ruler, such as an emperor or pope,[5] corporations may now be easily formed by compliance with applicable state or federal law.[6]

Understanding what a secular corporation is and how American law characterizes it serves two purposes. First, it facilitates a comparison between this secular view and the halakhic perspective. Second, and more central to the thrust of this chapter, the secular characterization may influence *halakhah* itself, because, as will be more fully explained below, certain specific halakhic doctrines give legal effect to secular law and secular commercial practice.

A few facts are essential to an appreciation of the modern corporation. There is a basic, although increasingly blurred, distinction between corporations that are formed "for-profit" (known as "business corporations") and corporations that are "not-for-profit" or "nonprofit."[7] The

---

[5]For descriptions of the historical development of corporations, see, for example, Philip I. Blumberg, *The Multinational Challenge to Corporation Law* (Oxford, 1993); Gerald Carl Henderson, "The Position of Foreign Corporations in American Constitutional Law," in *Harvard Studies in Jurisprudence*, vol. 2 (1918).

[6]The first state to adopt a flexible, general corporation law was New York, which did so in 1811. By the 1850s, such state laws were common. See Jonathan R. Macey, *Corporation Practice Guide* (Aspen Law and Business), paragraph 1101. Corporations, such as federal banks, may be created pursuant to federal law. See, for example, *McCulloch* v. *Maryland*, 17 U.S. (4 Wheat.) 316, 409–12 (1819) (federal creation of Second Bank of the United States was constitutional).

[7]There has been an enormous increase in the extent of commercial activities conducted by nonprofit corporations. See, for example, *The Role of Foundations Today and the Effect of the Tax Reform Act of 1969 Upon Foundations*, U.S. Congress, Senate, Subcommittee on Foundations (1973); Evelyn Alicia Lewis, "When Entrepreneurs of Commercial Nonprofits Divorce: Is It Anybody's Business? A Perspective on Individual Property Rights in Nonprofits," North Carolina Law Review 73:1761 (1995).

essential difference between these two categories is that a business corporation has shareholders who are entitled to receive distributions of and from the corporation's net profits, while a nonprofit corporation does not have shareholders (although it may have voting or nonvoting "members") and, in most cases, is forbidden from distributing its net profits.

A business corporation is permitted to provide for the issuance of different classes of stock and different series of stock in each class. The types of stock usually vary as to their voting rights (some, in fact, may have no voting rights at all) and as to their economic rights. For example, some stock, such as "preferred stock," may be entitled to a specified annual return even if the company shows no profit, while "common stock" is typically entitled to dividends only if there is a net or an operating surplus. On the other hand, upon a corporation's dissolution, the return to preferred stock may be specifically capped, while common stockholders are entitled to the entire residual value of the corporation once corporate debts are paid. In addition, certain stock may be convertible, under specified circumstances and according to a particular schedule, from one form into another. Stock may be acquired from the corporation, when it "issues" stock, or may be purchased from a previous owner of the stock. State and federal laws regulate the transfer and sale of stock.

Incorporation offers several principal advantages. First, shareholders or members are not ordinarily personally liable for a corporation's financial obligations.[8] This insulation from personal liability is often referred to as the "corporate veil." The corporate veil provides an incentive to start businesses or participate as members in nonprofits. Similarly, confidence as to the limited extent of personal risk encourages investors to buy stock even when they realize that they do not have the time, expertise, or interest necessary to monitor a business' operations. Consequently, limited liability, which is often a chief reason for incorporation, affords prospective shareholders more attractive business and investment

[8]As to general business corporations, see, for example, Henn and Alexander, *Laws of Corporations and other Business Enterprises* § 73 (1983), at 130; Macey, *Corporation Practice Guide* (Aspen Law and Business), paragraph 1114. As to nonprofit corporations, see, for example, Revised Model Nonprofit Corporation Act § 6.12; California Nonprofit Corp. Law, Cal. Corp. Code §§ 5350, 7350; New Jersey Nonprofit Corporation Act, *N.J. Stat. Ann.* 15A:5–25.

opportunities, while facilitating the raising of capital through the issuance of stock.[9]

Second, a corporation enjoys perpetual existence. Neither the death of officers, directors, shareholders or members,[10] nor the transfer of ownership interests from one shareholder to another, terminates the corporation's legal authority to continue its business.

Third, the corporation's stock serves as a relatively liquid investment vehicle. In many instances, public trading in stock provides investors with some degree of assurance regarding a stock's value.

Fourth, as a general rule, a corporation is centrally managed.[11] Not only does a shareholder have the right to refrain from personally participating in the corporation's decision-making processes, but even if he or she should want to influence the corporation's decisions, there are many restrictions on the right and ability to do so. Indeed, the dichotomy between control and beneficial ownership is a central feature of corporate law[12]—and one which, as discussed below, may be of central importance in the way in which Jewish Law treats a corporation.

There is no authoritative typology of business corporations. Instead, assorted labels are utilized to refer to corporations that pursue specific activities, possess certain characteristics, or qualify for particular tax treatment. For purposes of this chapter, it is useful to identify only a few of these labels:

---

[9]See, for example, Demerios G. Kaouris, "Note, Is Delaware Still a Haven for Incorporation?" *Delaware J.Corp.L.* 20:965 (1995); Michael J. Phillips, "Reappraising the Real Entity Theory of the Corporation," Fla. St. U.L.Rev. 21: 1061, 1083 (1994); Frederich G. Kempin, *Historical Introduction to Anglo-American Law in a Nutshell*, (West Publishers: 3d ed. 1990) pp. 278–279.

[10]By contrast, partnerships come to an end when one of the partners dies. See Uniform Partnership Act, § 31(4) (partner's death dissolves the partnership).

[11]The "Kintner Regulations" provide that, in order for a business organization to be treated as a corporation for tax purposes, it must possess three of these four characteristics: (1) limited liability, (2) continuity of "life", (3) free transferability of interests, and (4) centralized management. See Treasury Regulation § 301.7701-2(a) (1995).

[12]See, for example, Adolph A. Berle and Gardiner C. Means, *The Modern Corporation and Private Property* (New York: Macmillan 1932); (corporations are controlled by their managers and not by the "shareholders," their owners).

1. Public corporations

For purposes of this article, "public corporation" is used in its modern sense to refer to a corporation whose shares are publicly traded—and this is the way in which this chapter employs the term. A public corporation usually has thousands of different shareholders who live throughout the world. Typically, no single individual or institutional shareholder owns an absolute majority of the shares of a public corporation.

2. Close corporations

The term *close corporation* usually refers to corporations with relatively few shareholders, who are either personally involved in the operation of the corporate business or who are related to those who are, and whose stock is not traded publicly and is subject to significant transfer restrictions. A number of states have specific statutory provisions dealing with *close corporations*. These statutes usually state that they apply: (a) to any corporation with no more than a specified, low number of shareholders and whose shares are subject to transfer restrictions, have not been publicly offered, and are not listed on a securities exchange; (b) to any corporation that elects to be designated as a "close corporation"; (c) to any corporation that so elects and also meets the statute's definitional criteria of a "close corporation"; and (d) to any corporation that initially elects to be designated as a "close corporation" as well as to pre-existing corporations who choose to be considered a "close corporation" prospectively so long as these pre-existing corporations satisfy certain statutory criteria. Many corporations that possess the characteristics of a close corporation nonetheless do not elect to be so designated and, therefore, are treated by law as general business corporations. Nonetheless, irrespective of the label applied to a corporation by state law, this chapter will refer to it as a "close corporation" so long as it bears the typical characteristics of close corporations. The mere fact that a corporation is, or qualifies to be, a close corporation does not mean that the corporation is a financially small enterprise; close corporations may have enormous assets.

Close corporations are almost always formed by small numbers of individuals who are actively and importantly involved in the businesses the corporations will pursue. Indeed, in many instances, the expertise, experience, or contacts of these persons are central to a close corporation's success. Such people may choose a corporate format primarily to enjoy limited personal liability. As a consequence, these key individuals—or their close family members—may be the sole shareholders of the close corporation and may establish very restrictive conditions on the transferability of their shares. Thus, close corporations are profoundly different from public corporations in that: (1) their stock is not a highly liquid investment vehicle; and (2) there may, in fact, be no meaningful separation of control from beneficial ownership. As will be discussed in more detail later, these distinctions between close corporations and public corporations could be of substantial halakhic significance.

3. *Professional corporations*

Many states have enacted special statutes to enable professionals to incorporate and, thereby, enjoy some or all of the advantages of limited liability for corporate debts. Nonetheless, whether—and, if so, to what extent—particular types of professionals are protected is limited by a number of factors.[13] Individual statutes may either expressly exclude certain professions or provide that, even if members of these professions incorporate, they nonetheless remain liable for certain categories of liability, such as those arising from their own malpractice, the malpractice of other professionals who are shareholders and/or the malpractice of any other professionals under their supervision. Similar restrictions may arise as a result of ethical opinions or other rules promulgated by the state bodies that regulate individual professions.

Ownership of stock in professional corporations is virtually always limited to the professionals who work for the corporation or who have worked for the corporation. Typically, the stock cannot be transferred to third parties, even if such persons happen to hold the same type of professional license. Consequently, just as with close corporation stock, stock in professional corporations is not a liquid form of investment.

Whether or not there is a meaningful dichotomy between control and beneficial ownership in a particular professional corporation depends on

[13]Sherri J. Conrad, "Protecting Personal Assets: Does the Professional Corporation Shield Lawyers From Vicarious Liability?" *No. 1 Legal Malpractice Rep.* 5:3 (1996).

other specific facts about the professional corporation. If there are few shareholders, then one might expect that there is no great split between control and beneficial ownership. If, however, the professional corporation is a major law firm with hundreds of shareholders, it may be structured in a way in which the voices of very few shareholders are heard.

4. Analogous structures

Two common business forms bear similarity to corporations: *limited partnerships* and *limited liability companies*. These organizations, like corporations, are created in accordance with specific state statutes that confer limited liability to limited partners and to owners of interests in limited liability companies.

American law characterizes a corporation as a discrete entity.[14] Courts almost always treat corporations as distinct entities. Legislatures frequently define the word "person" to include corporations and, when legislatures are silent, courts routinely construe the statutory, and sometimes even the constitutional,[15] term "person" to include corporations. The entity theory is consistent with the principal corporate characteristics: limited liability,[16] perpetual existence, and the easy transferability

---

[14]Although a modern subcategory of the aggregate theory has received considerable support among legal academics, see, for example, Michael J. Phillips, "Reappraising the Real Entity Theory of the Corporation," Florida State U.L.Rev. 21:1061, nn. 1–2 (1994) (theory that a corporation is a nexus of individual contracts among the various participants in the corporation), the entity theory continues to be espoused by many social philosophers. Moreover, courts, lawyers, and legislatures, for the most part, continue to characterize and treat corporations consistent with the entity theory.

[15]After a number of opinions apparently based on aggregate theory, the Supreme Court, in *Southern Railway Co.* v. *Greene*, 216 US 400 (1910), clearly adopted the entity theory with respect to the "privileges and immunities" clause of the Fourteenth Amendment of the United States Constitution, declaring "[t]hat a corporation is a person, within the meaning of the Fourteenth Amendment, is no longer open to discussion."

[16]The concept of limited liability emanates easily from the entity theory. See, for example, Michael J. Phillips, "Reappraising the Real Entity Theory of the Corporation," Florida. State U.L.Rev. 21:1061, 1083 (1994). The text only states

of shares. Similarly, consonant with this characterization, corporations hold property in their own name, they are entitled to sue in their own name[17] (and should be sued in their own name),[18] they are entitled to assert federal diversity jurisdiction, they are (usually), taxed separately from their shareholders;[19] they may be convicted of civil or criminal offenses, and, although a person cannot enter into a contract with himself, corporations may contract with their own shareholders. By contrast, shareholders are not deemed to own a divided or undivided interest in particular pieces of corporate assets, they cannot individually exercise control or dominion over corporate assets, they cannot bring suit in their names against corporate creditors, they cannot bind the corporation to any undertaking, they cannot be disqualified as an "interested executor" of an estate against which their corporation asserts a claim.[20] Twentieth-century statutory developments also apparently indicate acceptance of the entity theory by, among other things, providing that directors can make decisions based on factors other than the immediate interests of the stockholders, and by substantially depriving shareholders of as an ability to meaningfully participate in corporate governance.[21]

---

that the entity theory is *consistent* with the doctrine of limited liability, because it would be possible to espouse the entity theory while supporting unlimited shareholder liability. Indeed, the entity theory seems historically to have preceded universal acceptance of the doctrine limiting the liability of individual shareholders.

[17]Fletcher Cyc. Corp. § 25, n. 4.

[18]See, for example, *Goulding* v. *Ag-Re-Co, Inc.*, 233 Ill.App.3d 867, 599 N.E.2d 1094 (1992).

[19]An important exception applies to corporations qualified under Subchapter "S" of the Internal Revenue Code, which are are not taxed as separate entities. Instead, the shareholders of a "Subchapter 'S' corporation" are treated as if the corporation's tax-year profit had been received directly by them in their individual capacities. *I.R.C.* § 1366.

[20]For more on the various issues discussed in this paragraph, see Fletcher Cyc. Corp. § 25–30.

[21]In fact, however, secular law does not really seem to regard shareholders as the "owners" (*ba'alim*) of a corporation, as the term *ba'alim* is used in Jewish law. The English "owner" is ambiguous and is often used with imprecision. For example, title to property is sometimes held in the name of one person (referred to as its "owner of record" or its "legal owner"), while the benefits of the prop-

PART III. EVALUATING HALAKHIC PERSPECTIVES OF CORPORATIONS

This part examines how corporations should be treated as a matter of Jewish law by critically examining the principal approaches. The five chief theories are: (1) the "*halakhic* entity" approach; (2) the "*halakhic* partnership" approach; (3) the "*halakhic* creditor" approach; (4) the "purchaser of entitlements" approach; and (5) the "relationship" approach. Part A will consider the first two approaches together, because they represent some of the clearest contrasts.

Part A. The *Halakhic* Entity and *Halakhic* Partnership Approaches

1. Introduction

Under Jewish law, who is the owner of the property that secular law considers to be owned by a corporation (*i.e.*, "the corporate assets")? Before answering, it should be noted that the question implicitly assumes that *someone* does own these assets. After all, it is counterintuitive to assume that this property is ownerless. Such an assumption would yield the unsettling consequence that anyone—even someone with no connection at all with the corporation—would be entitled to come along and take the property for herself. All of the Jewish law authorities that address this question adopt the position that the property has an owner.

The most obvious answer to this question would be that, just as secular law recognizes the corporation as the owner of the corporate assets, so does Jewish law. Indeed, this is the conclusion reached by the authorities who adopt the *halakhic* entity approach. Because the shareholders are not the owners of the property, many Jewish Law problems, such as those involving dough on Passover and lending on interest, would be

erty are supposed to inure to someone else (referred to as its beneficial or equitable owner). By referring to shareholders as a corporation's owners, secular commentators and courts seem to mean no more than that the corporation is supposed to operate solely to benefit its shareholders. While this assertion—that the corporation should advance the shareholders' interests—if true, would still be of Jewish law significance, it might fall far short of the halakhic concept of ownership (*ba'alut*) germane to particular Jewish law questions.

avoided. Similarly, because the *halakhic* entity approach assumes that the corporation is a separate entity, any actions by corporate directors, officers or employees would not be ascribed to the shareholders, thus avoiding other potential problems.[22] According to this approach, the shareholders, by virtue of their owning shares, would presumably be perceived as owning certain rights with respect to the corporation, the independent *halakhic* entity.[23]

Nevertheless, other commentators believe that, as a general rule, under Jewish Law only human beings can own or acquire property.[24] According to this opinion, if a corporation were regarded as an artificial legal entity separate and apart from its shareholders,[25] neither the corporation nor its shareholders would own the property. Many of these

---

[22]See, generally Part II of this chapter, as well as Part III:A:2, generally.

[23]This assumes that the shareholders are not perceived as the "owners" of the corporation. One of the principles of Jewish law is that if a person owns a slave, then he automatically owns all of the slave's property. See, for example, *Shulkhan Arukh* (R. Joseph Caro, Safed, 1488–1575), *Yoreh Deah* 367:22, and *Hoshen Mishpat* 127:1; B.T., *Pesahim* 88b. Therefore, even if a corporation were recognized under Jewish law as a separate entity, if shareholders owned the entity, they might be perceived as owning the corporation's property. The possibility of a halakhic problem if shareholders are regarded as owners of the corporate entity does not seem to have been raised by any of the authorities who have addressed this issue. See, for example, R. Moshe Sternbuch , *Moadim U'Zemanim* 3:269, n. 1 ("If the acquisition [of shares] occurred according to the conceptualization of the non-Jews, a Jewish shareholder would certainly not violate the prohibition against keeping *hametz* on Passover because all he would own are shares of stock").

[24]"In Jewish law, corporations and organization lack capacity to hold property as 'legal persons.' Property must be held by individuals, otherwise it is ownerless." See R. J. David Bleich, *Contemporary Halakhic Problems*, p. 388. See also R. Menashe Klein, *Mishnah Halakhot* 6:277, pp. 169–170 (only human beings may acquire property); R. Moshe Sternbuch (Israel, contemporary), *Moadim Uzmanim* 3:269, n. 1 (the existence of a company does not prevent the shareholders from being the owners of the corporate property); R. Yitzhak Wasserman, "Interest from Loans to Banks," Noam 3:195–203 (5720).

[25]The corporation would also be considered separate and apart from the other human beings representing various corporate constituencies.

authorities resolve this dilemma by declaring that under Jewish Law a corporation is a partnership.[26]

According to the *halakhic* partnership perspective, all—or some[27]—of the shareholders are partners and, as such, own a percentage interest in all of the corporate assets. Consequently, Jewish shareholders could be found liable for violating Jewish Law if the corporation owns dough on Passover, operates on the Shabbat and on other Jewish holidays, charges interest for loans, and so on. According to the *halakhic* entity approach, which provides that shareholders do not own the corporate assets, these Jewish Law problems would not arise.

2. The Analytical Basis of the *Halakhic* Entity Approach

Of critical importance to those who support the *halakhic* entity approach is the argument that corporations are qualitatively different from partnerships, such that corporate shareholders should not be deemed the owners of the corporation's property. Parts II and III of this chapter reveal that some of these differences depend on the type of corporation considered (particularly as to whether the organization being considered is a public corporation or a close corporation). Nevertheless, before introducing the analyses of individuals proponents of the *halakhic* entity position, the basic differences between partnerships and public corporations should be summarized:

1. In a Jewish partnership, the partners are agents for each other. In a public corporation, the shareholders are not agents for each other.
2. In a Jewish partnership, at least one of the partners has the authority to operate the business. In a corporation, none of the shareholders, as shareholders, is authorized to act on behalf of the corporation. They cannot bind the corporation, gain access to or use

[26]See, for example, R. Solomon b. Joseph Hirsch Ganzfried (Hungary, 1804–1886), *Kitzur Shulkhan Arukh* 65:28; R. Menashe Klein, *Mishnah Halakhot* 6:277. See also R. Moshe Sternbuch, *Moadim Uzmanim* 3:269 (a partnership unless all or most of the shareholders are non-Jews).

[27]See, Part III:B below for a discussion as to whether a shareholder's rights or status under Jewish law depends on whether he or she possesses voting or nonvoting shares.

its assets, or assert the corporation's rights against third parties. Secular law provides that the corporation is a separate legal entity that owns its own property. It also invests authority for running the corporation in the board of directors. In fact, the shareholders have extremely limited control, legally and practically, directly and indirectly, over a public corporation's short-term and long-term operations. Among other things, the proxy system, antitakeover legislation, and corporate constituency statutes have essentially disenfranchised shareholders, especially those with relatively small holdings.

3. Under secular law, the directors of a corporation are not agents of the shareholders. The shareholders do not have the choice of doing without a board of directors. The shareholders cannot remove individual directors whenever they want; they must follow a statutorily prescribed procedure. Even if shareholders follow the required steps, they may be unable to remove directors unless they have legally sufficient "cause." They cannot give the directors binding instructions; indeed, the directors must exercise their independent judgment and are legally entitled to reject instructions from shareholders. The directors are expected to make their decisions for the best interests of the corporation, not in accordance with the best interests of the actual, flesh-and-blood shareholders. Statutes expressly provide that directors can take into consideration the interests of other non-shareholder groups, such as employees and local communities.
4. The officers and employees of a corporation, inasmuch as they are selected and controlled (directly or indirectly) by the corporate directors, are also not the shareholders' agents. Instead, they are the agents of the corporate entity.
5. Unlike a Jewish law partnership which automatically terminates on the death of one of the partners, a corporation does not terminate upon the death of one of its shareholders. In fact, a corporation would not automatically terminate even if all of its shareholders died at once.
6. Unlike a Jewish law partnership, in which partners may be personally liable to third parties for a variety of partnership debts, corporate shareholders, as a general rule, are not personally liable for corporate debts.

When some of a corporation's shareholders, directors, officers or employees are not Jewish, an additional factor influences some authorities to conclude that a secular corporation is, under Jewish law, a new *halakhic* entity—and not a *halakhic* partnership. Jewish partnership law arguably presupposes that the partners may act as agents for each other. Jewish law, however, generally[28] provides that non-Jews cannot effectively act as agents for Jews, and vice versa.[29] Similarly, to the extent that directors, officers, or employees are gentiles, they could not be deemed under Jewish law to act on behalf of Jewish shareholders.[30]

---

[28]Some Jewish law authorities, however, rule that in deciding whether a particular act or failure to act is permissible, *halakhah* is "strict" and assumes that non-Jews *could* act as agents for Jews. See R. Yeheil Mekheil Epstein (Belorussia, 1829–1908), *Arukh HaShulkhan, Hoshen Mishpat* 188:1 (citing the views of *Rashi* and *Tosafot*). In addition, some authorities argue that even though *minhag hasohrim* and *dina de'malchuta dina* are not powerful enough to import the secular corporate entity theory into Jewish law, they may be sufficient to enable non-Jews to serve as halakhicly valid agents for Jews. See R. Yitzhak Wassermann, "Interest from Loans to Banks," *Noam* 3:195–203 (5720); R. Yitzhak Yaakov Weiss (Israel, contemporary), *Minhat Yitzhak* 3:1. As explained in our longer work, secular law does not treat shareholders as "agents" of one other. Nor does secular law treat corporate directors, officers or employees as "agents" of the flesh-and-blood shareholders. Consequently, irrespective of the possible potency of these doctrines, neither the validity of commercial custom (*minhag hasohrim*) nor the effectiveness of secular law (*dina de'malchuta dina)* in fact operates to make such non-Jews the agents of Jewish shareholders.

[29]*Shulkhan Arukh, Hoshen Mishpat* 158:1.

[30]There is a view that a non-Jewish daily worker *could* act on behalf of a Jewish employer in a manner similar to that of an agent. See, for example, R. Ephraim b. Aaron Navon (Constantinople, 1677–1735), *Mahne Ephraim, Hilkhot Shluhin V'Shutfin*, no. 11. Corporate employees might qualify as "daily workers." Nevertheless, if the people who hired these employees were not themselves agents for Jewish shareholders, the employees would probably not be considered daily workers of the Jewish shareholders. It seems unlikely that corporate directors would fall into the class of "daily workers."

R. Shaul Weingart[31] is one of the first Jewish law commentators to *expressly* advance the *halakhic* entity approach.[32] R. Weingart considers the Jewish law prohibitions against a Jew's owning hametz *during* Passover and against a Jew's benefitting *after* Passover from dough that was illegally owned by a Jew during Passover.[33] He argues that, because a corporation as a *halakhic* entity is not "Jewish," its ownership of *hametz* during Passover does not violate Jewish law, and Jewish shareholders—as well as Jewish consumers—may benefit from the *hametz* after Passover.[34]

R. Weingart supports the *halakhic* entity position in two ways. First, he attempts to portray it as reasonable by focusing on the dramatic differences between corporations and traditional partnerships. He emphasizes not only the ways in which a shareholder's rights are restricted—that is, that a shareholder has no right to eat, sell, or destroy the corporation's *hametz* or to use or even to enter the corporation's premises[35]—but also the fact that a shareholder enjoys unusual financial protection—that is, corporate creditors have no right to sue a shareholder to collect a corporate debt even though they could ordinarily sue the partners of a debtor partnership. In

[31]R. Saul Weingart, "Corporations and *Hametz*," in Yad Shaul (1954), pp. 35–49 (apparently with respect to an Austrian or German corporation).

[32]As will be discussed in Part III:D, below, earlier halakhic authorities also stressed the uniqueness of the relationship between corporations and shareholders. Nevertheless, these authorities did not explicitly recognize corporations as separate legal entities.

[33]The fact that a business is a corporation may affect the applicability of these prohibitions, irrespective of whether the corporation is considered an independent halakhic entity. This issue will be further developed in Part III:A:2, below.

[34]R. Weingart believes that it is nonetheless appropriate to conduct oneself in accordance with the other theories if doing so would not be too inconvenient. Consequently, he suggests that if it is not too difficult, Jewish shareholders should, prior to Passover, sell their shares in companies that possess *hametz*. Nonetheless, if they do not do so, he rules that they may rely on the halakhic entity theory.

[35]Of course, these shareholders—just as any other consumers—could enter corporate premises as customers.

addition, R. Weingart argues that two widespread practices can only be justified by treating corporations as *halakhic* entities. He asserts that rejection of the *halakhic* entity approach would mean that countless Jews would be violating Jewish law.[36]

The truth, however, is that the practices that bother R. Weingart, at least as he presents them, do not really seem troublesome. R. Weingart refers to: (1) ownership of "paper" of the "government bank"; and (2) ownership of governmental currency ("paper money").[37] He seems to argue that, but for the *halakhic* entity approach, one must conclude that anyone owning paper of the government bank owns a percentage of the assets of that bank and that anyone owning government currency[38] owns

---

[36]R. Weingart's last point is questionable. That rejecting the halakhic entity approach is unthinkable simply because it would mean that numerous Jews are in violation of the Jewish law is not logically persuasive. Even though it would be lamentable if many Jews were found to be transgressing religious strictures, it could be that the practices he points to are improper. The prohibition against benefitting from dough that was illegally owned by a Jew during Passover (*hametz she'avar alav ha-Pesach*) is of rabbinic origin. One halakhic principle is that any rabbinic rule that most of the community cannot conform to is intrinsically invalid. Perhaps R. Weingart's implicit argument is that one must endorse the halakhic entity theory because otherwise the entire rabbinic ban on *hametz she'avar alav ha-Pesach* would be invalidated. Nevertheless, he does not make this argument explicitly.

Alternatively, and more happily, these practices may be justified on other Jewish law grounds. Indeed, it could be that the halakhic entity approach is even unnecessary to justify stock ownership in the corporation Weingart considers. Although R. Weingart rejects the "relationship test" discussed in Part III:D of this chapter, his dismissal of that test may be unwarranted. Similarly, other approaches not addressed by R. Weingart—such as the purchaser of entitlements approach examined in Part III:C—may be correct.

[37]The transliteration of the word R. Weingart uses is "papiergelt." The German word "gelt" is used for "money."

[38]The truth is that R. Weingart is unclear in expressing his argument with respect to currency. Thus, he says that "every citizen in the country has a share of the property that belongs to the government and the paper money ("papiergelt") is itself a document attesting to his share. . . ." His reference to "every citizen" suggests that his argument is based on some political theory as to the relationship between the government and its citizens. It is possible that R. Moshe

a percentage of the government's assets. Consequently, such a person likely violates Jewish law because during Passover, the government bank and the government surely are involved in, and profit from, transactions involving *hametz*. The weakness of his argument lies in the fact that banknotes and paper currency seem to reflect debts, not ownership interests. Even if these commercial papers create or represent Jewish law liens on the debtor's assets, the liens would not apply to personality.[39] Even if the liens did apply to such dough, so long as the *hametz* is not in the lienholder's possession, there would be no Jewish law violation.[40]

R. Weingart is substantially correct in differentiating the characteristics of a corporation from that of a traditional partnership. The difficulty is that he does not adduce adequate authority for the proposition that Jewish law would therefore treat a corporation as a separate *halakhic* entity.

Others offer more convincing support for the *halakhic* entity position.[41] For example, at least one decision of the Rabbinical Court of Israel also

---

Sternbuch, *Moadim Uzmanim* 3:269, n. 1 (which argues that the right R. Weingart referred to was not transferrable), interpreted R. Weingart as making this argument. Nevertheless, it does not seem reasonable to suggest that paper currency attests to any rights based on political theory. After all, noncitizens may possess paper currency while some citizens (who, for instance, may live abroad) may not. Consequently, as stated in the text, it seems that R. Weingart's argument is based on the fact that currency represents a debt from the government to the holder of the currency based, perhaps, on the assumption that the holder could present the currency to the government and demand some payment therefor. This right would seem to be transferrable by transferring ownership of the currency to someone else. This seems to be the way in which R. Yitzhak Yaakov Weiss, *Minhat Yitzchok* 3:1, seems to have understood R. Weingart. Incidentally, it is worth noting that many, perhaps most, countries are no longer legally obligated to pay anything in exchange for their currency. In such countries, R. Weingart's argument seems to be completely undermined.

[39]See, generally, *Shulkhan Arukh, Hoshen Mishpat* 39, 40.

[40]*Shulkhan Arukh, Orah Hayyim* 440:4.

[41]As discussed in the text, the Israeli Rabbinical Court and R. Regensberg are among those who explicitly adopt this approach, and several other authorities, such as R. Isaac Aaron Ettinger (Lemberg, 1827–1891) and R. Moshe Shick (Hungary, 1807–1879; *Maharam Shick*), may have implicitly endorsed it. See Part III:A2(a) and associated text, below.

adopts the *halakhic* entity approach.[42] A cause of action had been alleged against corporate shareholders, and the court had to decide whether these shareholders or the corporation itself was the "real" defendant. Because the father of several of the shareholders had passed away, they were considered by Jewish law to be minor orphans. Jewish law provides that a court can entertain valid legal arguments on behalf of such orphans even if the orphans, or their legal representatives, fail to raise the arguments themselves.[43] The majority opinion concludes that the corporation is the real defendant and, therefore, the rule regarding orphans is irrelevant. As to corporations, the court broadly declares: "A corporation is considered a legal person according to Jewish law as well. This has Jewish law relevance to such matters as corporate work on the Sabbath, lending on interest, ownership of *hametz* during Passover, and the like, as the responsibility of these actions does not reside with the owners of the shares."[44]

The Israeli Rabbinical Court justifies the *halakhic* entity approach: (1) by demonstrating that the concept of a corporation is indigenous to Jewish law; and (2) by arguing that, even if the specific notion of a corporation were initially foreign to Jewish law, that concept can be incorporated into Jewish law through other indigenous Jewish law doctrines.

a. Corporate analogs in Jewish Law. The Israeli Rabbinical Court begins by contending that the concept of a corporation is already embodied within traditional Jewish law by the concept of the "public" (*tzibur*). The court differentiates between a partnership, which is a conglomeration of persons in which each person retains his individuality and each of whom possesses a rich and complete form of ownership in partnership property, and the public, which is a separate legal entity in which persons do not retain their individuality, in general, or their individual ownership rights, in particular.[45] The court argues that this distinction

[42] *Piskei Din Rabanayim* 10:273 at § 7 (as reported in Bar Ilan's CD-Rom *Judaica Library*, version 4.0). But see *Piskei Din Rabanayim* 6:322.

[43] *Piskei Din Rabanayim* 10:273 at § 7 (as reported in Bar Ilan's CD-Rom *Judaica Library*, version 4.0).

[44] *Ibid.*

[45] See also R. Shemaya Eliezer Dekhovsky, *Naot Desha*, at pp. 40–56; R. Moshe Ameil, *Responsa Darkei Moshe-Derekh HaKodesh* 1:5(10–11); R. Yitzhak Bari,

explains the dissimilar rules applicable to a voluntary sacrifice brought by a partnership and a voluntary sacrifice offered by the public.[46]

In addition to referring to other authorities who provide more extensive discussions of the distinction between a partnership and a community,[47] the court cites a few examples.[48] Citing R. Menachem Zemba (Poland, 1883–1943) the distinction is apparent in the rules applying to the mandatory Passover sacrifice.[49] Such an offering is not allowed to be made if its owner still has dough in his possession. When a group of people brings a Passover sacrifice together, the people in the group do not lose their individuality. Consequently, if any one of the members in the group still has *hametz*, the sacrifice may not be offered. The Talmud explains that R. Yehuda's view is that, on the day before Passover, the daily offering of the public may also not be brought if the public has *hametz*. Nonetheless, according to R. Zemba, *Tosafot*[50] states that R. Yehuda agrees that this offering of the public may be brought even if there is an individual among the public that still possesses *hametz*. The reason for this is that the public is a legal person that is considered as a whole; the fact that an individual member of the public has *hametz* is insignificant.[51]

Ha-torah V'hamedina 11–13:461; R. Menachem Zemba (Poland, 1883–1943), *Zera Avraham* 4:21–24; Hayyim David Regensberg, *Mishmeret Hayyim* (1966), at pp. 134–137.

[46]For example, when a partnership brings this sacrifice, a process known as *smikhah* is required, in which the owners of the animal press down on its head before it is slaughtered. This step is not required with respect to a communal offering.

[47]See, for example, R. Menachem Zemba, *Zera Avraham*, no. 4:21–24; R. Moshe Amiel, *Darkei Moshe-Derekh HaKodesh* 1:5 (10, 11). See also R. Hayyim David Regensberg (Israel, contemporary), *Mishmeret Hayyim*, pp. 135–137.

[48]The author of the ruling writes that he had elsewhere expounded on the qualitative distinction between *tzibur* and partnership.

[49]R. Hayyim David Regensberg makes the same argument. See R. Hayyim David Regensberg, *Mishmeret Hayyim*, at pp. 135–137.

[50]*Tosafot*, B.T., *Menahot* 78b, s.v. *oh*.

[51]R. Zemba construes the *Rambam, Mishneh Torah, Temurah*, Chapter 1:1, as disagreeing with *Tosafot*, because the *Rambam* states that members of the *tzibur* constitute a partnership with respect to public sacrifices such that, by a particular improper action or intention, an individual could disqualify the *tzibur*'s offering. Nevertheless, R. Zemba and the Israeli Rabbinical Court argue that this

The court explains that another distinction between a partnership and the public is that the public, just as a corporation, enjoys perpetual existence. The Talmud states that "the public never dies."[52] Jewish law requires that an animal may only be sacrificed while its owner is alive; no atonement may be offered for individuals who have died.[53] On the other hand, the Talmud declares that when a particular atonement[54] is effectuated for the public, this atonement functions to achieve an atonement for the sins of the Jews who participated in the exodus from Egypt—even though that entire generation of Jews has long since died. The current nation of Israel is not considered a separate public. Instead, the public is regarded as an ongoing entity that is more than—and different from—the sum of its individual parts and that endures indefinitely.[55]

R. Hayyim David Regensberg, who makes some of these same observations, also argues that this discrete concept of the public is supported by a *Mishneh* in the fifth chapter of the tractate "Vows" (*Nedarim*).[56] Jewish law generally permits a Jew, through a vow, to ban another from deriving any benefit from the first's person or property. The *Mishneh* provides that:

> [If an individual says] "I am forbidden to you," the one to whom this is said is forbidden to derive benefit from the person or property of the one who spoke . . . [If a person says] "I am forbidden to you and you are forbidden to me," both are prohibited from deriving benefit from the other. Both are permitted to derive benefit from the things that belonged to those who came up from Babylon. Both are prohibited from deriving benefit from things that belong to the particular city [in which the two people live].

---

aspect of partnership is present in every *tzibur*, but that it does not negate the overall concept of *tzibur* as a separate and distinct legal entity.

[52]In Hebrew, *ain tzibur maitim*. See B.T., *Temurah* 15b and the accompanying commentary by *Tosafot* s.v. *ka*.

[53]B.T., *Temurah* 15a.

[54]The process through which this atonement is achieved is referred to as the *egla arufa*.

[55]B.T., *Temurah* 15b. See also *Encyclopedia Talmudit* 10:435–438.

[56]B.T., *Nedarim* 46b.

The Talmud explains that the things that belonged to the people that came up from Babylon include the Temple mount, the courts of the Temple and the well on the road between Babylon and Israel.[57] R. Solomon b. Isaac (Troyes, 1040–1105; *Rashi*) explains that the reason why the two people may derive benefit from these things is that the Jews that came up from Babylon—when Babylon allowed the Jews in exile to return to Israel—"abandoned" these properties "to all Israel." The phrase "all Israel" refers to the people of Israel as a public. Because these properties are owned by the public, no person possesses any individualized ownership interest in them. When a person derives benefit from this property, he or she does not derive benefit from other Jewish individuals but, instead, only from the public. It is for this reason that the two people mentioned in the *Mishneh* may continue to benefit from the properties of those that came up from Babylon despite the vow that was taken.

R. Regensberg[58] also suggests that R. Yochanan ben Zachai endorses this view of the public as a legal entity in his dispute with Ben Buchri, reported in the fourth *Mishneh* of the first chapter of tractate *Shekalim*.[59] R. Yochanan ben Zachai rules that Jews of the priestly tribe (*Kohanim*), just as everyone else, are obligated to contribute money for the purchase of public offerings; Ben Buchri believes that *Kohanim* are under no such obligation. R. Yochanan ben Zachai explains that the *Kohanim* believed that if they contributed money to the public funds used to buy offerings, the offerings purchased would be considered, at least in part, to be offerings "brought by a *Kohain*." But if the offererings were so considered, an inconsistency would arise among biblical passages.[60] While one verse states that: "[e]very flour-offering brought by a *Kohain* must be completely burned; it shall not be eaten,"[61] other verses clearly require that *Kohanim* eat—and not burn—three types of flour offerings that are purchased with

---

[57]B.T., *Nedarim* 48a.

[58]R. Hayyim David Regensberg, *Mishmeret Hayyim*, at p. 136. See also R. Moshe Ameil, *Darkei Moshe-Derekh HaKodesh*, vol. II, at p. 308.

[59]In the Talmud, this *Mishneh* is cited in tractate *Shekalim* 3b as the third *halakhah* in the first chapter.

[60]See R. David Frankel, *Korban Ha-Eida*, on *Jerusalem Talmud, Shekalim* 3b.

[61]Leviticus 6:16.

public funds.[62] The *Kohanim* therefore argued that it was only because they were exempt from contributing to the public fund that prevented these three types of flour-offerings from being deemed to have been "brought by a *Kohain*" and, therefore, permitted the *Kohanim* to eat the offerings.

R. Regensberg suggests that the *Kohanim* erroneously believed that, in making financial contributions for public offerings and thereby participating in the offerings that were brought, Jews retained their individuality, that they acted as partners in a partnership. Consequently, they would retain their identity as *Kohanim* and the rules pertaining to the offerings of *Kohanim* would apply to their portion of the offerings, prohibiting them from eating the flour offerings. R. Yochanan ben Zachai, however, argues that the *tzibur* is not merely a conglomeration of individuals but, instead, a separate legal entity. Thus, even if the *Kohanim* contribute funds for the three flour offerings brought by the *tzibur*, the offerings are considered to be those of the *tzibur* as a whole and can be eaten.[63] R. Moses ben Maimon (Egypt, 1135–1204; *Rambam* or *Maimonides*) states that Jewish law is in accordance with R. Yochanan ben Zachai.[64]

The Jewish law concept of the public arguably applies at certain subnational levels as well. For example, the Jewish people is divided into tribes, and it is possible for a particular tribe to possess certain properties or intangible rights which are not "owned" by individual members of the tribe. Thus, the tribe of Levi is entitled to have its members receive certain contributions of food from other Jews, but no individual Levi has the right to demand any particular contribution.[65]

---

[62]These three offerings are: (1) the *Omer*, consisting of barley; (2) the two loaves of wheat bread offered on the holiday of Pentecost (*Shavuot*); and (3) the shewbread, consisting of twelve loaves of bread brought each week.

[63]Ben Buchri disagrees, but nonetheless opines that if the *Kohanim* contribute with a full heart, they may totally abandon their personal ownership of the funds they contribute, such that the offerings purchased with the funds would not at all be considered to belong to them.

[64]*Rambam, Mishneh Torah, Shekalim* 1:7.

[65]*Rambam, Mishneh Torah, Maaser* 6:15–17 (discussing when such money must be returned).

Similarly, there is a concept of the "tribe" of the poor.[66] Each local community establishes a public charity fund[67] in which money is held for the needy. The Talmud indicates that the money so collected is beneficially owned by the poor as a whole (as the tribe of the poor) and that those who collect such funds act on behalf of this community of the poor.[68] Individual indigents have no standing to litigate matters on behalf of the public charity fund or to demand that the public charity fund make particular distributions.[69] The public charity fund could be characterized as a corporation that owns money for the tribe of the poor. Four hundred years ago, in the days of R. Joseph b. Moses Tranti (1568–1639; *Maharit*), the custom was to charge interest when lending monies from a fund, the principal of which was consecrated for charity. Tranti explains this custom by stating that the poor, for whose benefit the money was held and used, are not really "owners" of the money.[70] In this same vein, R. Shimon Greenfeld (d. 1930; *Maharshag*) wrote that "I am almost ready to say that monies consecrated for the poor may be loaned on interest because they do not have 'known' owners."[71]

The holy Treasury,[72] the conceptual domain that owned and administered assets that were consecrated for use in connection with the Temple or Temple services, arguably constitutes another traditional analog to a corporation.[73] The Temple treasurer[74] participates in the

[66]In Hebrew, *shevet aniyim.*

[67]In Hebrew, a *havurat tzedakah.*

[68]See, for example, B.T., *Bava Kamma* 36b.

[69]*Rambam, Mishnah Torah, Matanot Aniyim* 8:5.

[70]R. Moshe Natan Lemberg, *Ribit B'Halva'ah Bankit, Noam* 2:241.

[71]Id. Although he states that the problem is that there are no "known" owners, it seems, in context, that he means not only that the owners are not known but that there exist no specific owners. Note that although the *Maharshag* refers to these monies as *hekdesh aniyim*, he does not mean the concept of *hekdesh* referred to earlier in this text.

[72]The holy Treasury is known as *hekdesh.*

[73]This is analogous to treatment of a bishop as a *corporation sole* in early English law. Bishops were deemed to own church property in a corporate capacity.

[74]The treasurer is known as the *gizbar.*

acquisition and sale of the properties,[75] administers them and represents the interests of the Treasury in any Jewish Law litigation.[76] The Treasury and, to the extent that he superintends the property of the Treasury, the Treasurer are exempt from many laws that govern individuals, including ritual and financial responsibilities.[77] Property that belongs to the Treasury is exempt from these rules because they are not considered property that belongs to another person as that phrase appears in the Bible.[78] Although the Talmud refers to these properties as money belonging to "the above" or "to the One who dwells above (*i.e.*, God),"[79] R. Regensberg suggests that this phrase may merely be intended to make it clear that the property does not belong to any individual.[80]

R. Regensberg states that by regarding the holy Treasury as a *halakhic* entity, one can better understand the position taken by *Tosafot* and R. Shimon ben Meir (Ramerupt, ca. 1080–1174; *Rashbam*) that the Treasury cannot acquire property by a process known as "acquisitions made by one's yard."[81] Jewish law recognizes that a normal person may acquire property in two ways, by his own act or by the act of others. Just as a person may actively pick up and acquire property with parts of his own body, such as his hand, the Sages say that, in certain circumstances, one

[75]*Hekdesh, Encyclopedia Talmudit,* 10:435–438.

[76]Aaron Kirschenbaum, "Legal Persons," in Menachem Elon, ed., *Principles of Jewish Law*, at columns (Jerusalem: Keter Publishing House, Ltd., 1975), pp. 162–163.

[77]*Hekdesh, Encyclopedia Talmudit* 10:399–431. For example, *hekdesh* was exempt from obligations to provide certain properties to the poor, to the priests, or to the members of the tribe of Levi (such as the *mitzvot* of *leket*, *shickcha*, *peah*, *terumot*, and *maasrot*), ritual rules (such as the prohibition against owning dough on Passover), and limitations on financial transactions (such as prohibitions against lending on interest and overcharging).

[78]This phrase is transliterated as *shel re'eihu*.

[79]This phrase is transliterated as *mamon govoha*.

[80]R. Hayyim David Regensberg, *Mishmeret Hayyim*, at p. 136. R. Regensberg also suggests that because the property of *hekdesh* is dedicated for particular holy purposes, individuals are not permitted to derive personal benefit from it. He indicates that the expression *mamon govoha*, which may be translated as "money pertaining to that which is lofty," is intended to describe the elevated purpose to which the property is consecrated.

[81]The Hebrew expression is *kinyan hatzer*.

may acquire property that lands in his yard. In a sense, the yard that belongs to him acts as if it were his hand and could grasp otherwise ownerless objects that come within its boundaries. R. Regensberg reasons that because the Treasury, as an artificial or legal person, but not a natural person, cannot act on its own to acquire property,[82] it cannot acquire property that lands in its yard either. Instead, the Treasury can only acquire property which someone else transfers to it. R. Regensberg thinks that R. Moses ben Nachman (Spain, 1194–1270; *Ramban* or Nahmanides), who disagrees and rules that the Treasury may acquire property through its yard, does so because this process operates even if the owner of the yard is oblivious to what is happening. Because the process does not require human thought or intention,[83] *Nahmanides* believes that it can work for an artificial legal entity even though that entity does not possess the faculty of human thought or intention.

Reminiscent of the sentiments of many secular theorists,[84] R. Regensberg argues that the notion of the public as more than merely a combination of individuals is a well-established "sociological reality."[85] Although the same argument might be used to argue that a partnership—which is also an *association* of people—might constitute a separate sociological reality, R. Regensberg contends that individuals have the choice of organizing in a way in which they maintain their individuality—as through a partnership—or in a way in which they lose their individuality and become part of a larger, different whole—as through a corporation.[86] Of course, even if one can generally distinguish between the sociological dynamics of public corporations and partnerships, it is difficult to argue that this distinction exists between close corporations and partnerships.

---

[82]Obviously, Jewish law does allow *hekdesh*, as a legal person, to act through its agents, such as *gizbar*. R. Regensberg, however, would presumably say that the ability to act through an agent is itself an innovation (a *hidush*), and, according to *Tosafot* and *Rashbam*, cannot be extended further to *kinyan hatzer*.

[83]The Hebrew expression is *daat*.

[84]See, for example, Boudewijn Bouckaert, "Corporate Personality: Myth, Fiction or Reality," 25:2 *Israel Law Review* 156 (1991), pp. 170–172; David Millon, "Theories of the Corporation," *Duke L.J.* 201 (1990), pp. 211–221.

[85]R. Hayyim David Regensberg, *Mishmeret Hayyim*, at pp. 136–137.

[86]Id.

The Israeli Rabbinical Court cites *tefisat habayit*, loosely translated as a "decedent's estate," as another example of a "legal person" whereby two or more individuals enjoy beneficial rights in property but are not considered its owners. When an individual dies with two or more heirs, the inheritance is said to be held by the decedent's estate until it is divided to the heirs. When an individual owns animals, there is a requirement that some animals be set aside and given to members of the Jewish tribe of Levi.[87] When partners own animals, no animals need be set aside. While an inheritance is owned by the decedent's estate, however, animals must be set aside. The Rabbinical Court maintains that this is because Jewish law treats the property as if it were owned by a special "legal person" rather than by the joint heirs.

Although opponents of the *halakhic* entity approach may not deny all—or even some—of the descriptions of the above Jewish law concepts, they do deny that these concepts provide a precedent for recognizing a secular corporation as a separate *halakhic* entity. None of the above examples involves a voluntary association of individuals to promote their own personal financial gain. Rather, the examples merely represent naturally existing Jewish Law institutions. The critics argue that new institutions cannot be created, certainly not by the voluntary actions of individuals intending their own personal gain.[88]

The cogency of this argument is difficult to evaluate. There are no clear-cut rules as to how exact a paradigm must exist before concluding that the concept of a corporation exists in Jewish law. Perhaps the fact that the classical *halakhic* legal persons discussed above were not voluntarily created for the purpose of operating a business is insignificant.[89] On the other hand, some of these institutions, such as the charity fund,

---

[87]The animals set aside are referred to as *maaser behaima*.

[88]R. Yitzhak Wassermann, "Interest from Loans to Banks," *Noam* 3:195–203 (5720); R. Menashe Klein, *Mishneh Halakhot* 6:277; R. Moshe Sternbuch, *Moadim Uzmanim* 3:269, n. 1; Simcha Meron, "The Creation known as a 'Corporation' in Jewish Law," *Sinai* 59:228 (5726). Cf. R. J. David Bleich, *Contemporary Halakhic Problems*, vol. 3, at p. 388.

[89]Some of them, such as *havurat tzedakah*, were voluntarily created, even if not for the purpose of conducting a business.

were, arguably, voluntarily created.[90] Others, such as the decedent's estate, were typically used for generating private profit. Moreover, although the *secular* concept of a corporation appears to have arisen in connection with *nonprofit* institutions, the concept was thereafter applied to *commercial* organizations.[91] To a large extent, the split of authority between proponents of the *halakhic* entity and *halakhic* partnership approaches seems based on whether or not the transition from nonprofit to profit organizations is perceived to be a natural one.

Opponents of the *halakhic* entity position also argue that a large number of Jewish law authorities have implicitly rejected it. They point to the substantial body of Jewish law literature discussing whether it is permissible to pay or charge interest when dealing with a banking corporation. They contend that, according to the *halakhic* entity theory, there should be no problem with interest. Nevertheless, many authorities found that there was a problem regarding interest.[92] Still others resolved the interest issue through rather complicated rationalizations.[93] According to the *halakhic* entity approach, these critics argue, the interest problem should have been a non-issue.

There are at least two partial responses to this criticism. First, there may be a historical explanation for this phenomenon, at least as to early Jewish Law literature. As explained in Parts II and III of this chapter, until relatively recently, secular law provided for a closer relationship between shareholders and their assets. Moreover, although English and early American law adopted the corporate entity theory rather early, the aggregate theory retained for quite some time considerably greater standing in Europe, where these early responsa originated. In addition, shareholders of many corporations were not entitled to limited liability. Indeed, even the early responsa that allow investing in banking corporations

[90]Critics of the halakhic entity approach, however, might argue that even a *havurat tzedakah* is not a "voluntary" endeavor, because there is a communal obligation to create such an institution.

[91]See, for example, R. Hayyim David Regensberg, *Mishmeret Hayyim*, at p. 135.

[92]See, for example, R. Tzvi Pesah Frank (Jerusalem, 1873–1960), *Har Tzvi, Yoreh Deah* 126.

[93]For a discussion of a variety of such solutions, *see* R. Yitzhak Blau (Contemporary), *Brit Yehuda* 7:25.

that charge interest because of the restricted role of corporate shareholders do not cite the principle of limited liability as a factor.

Second, a careful reading of responsa suggests that some important early authorities may have been advancing a version of the *halakhic* entity theory.[94] R. Isaac Aaron Ettinger (Lemberg, 1827–1891), for instance, rules that there is no problem in being a shareholder in a banking corporation that loans on interest.[95] Among other things, R. Ettinger refers to the end of the *Mishneh* in *Nedarim* that was quoted above. The *Mishneh* provides that if a person vows that his fellow should derive no

[94]A number of responsa that permit Jews to hold shares in corporations that lend on *ribbit* describe the attenuated relationship between Jewish shareholders and the corporation's issuance of a loan and, basically, the Jewish shareholder's lack of control over corporate conduct. They do not specifically explain why these factors are significant as a matter of Jewish law.

Although R. Moshe Shick, in *Maharam Shick, Yoreh Deah*, no. 158, writes at length, his view is also a bit unclear. It is possible that he also implies the halakhic entity theory. *Maharam Shick* discusses whether there is a problem of collecting interest for those who invest in a company that lends money on interest. R. Shick states that each bit of money contributed by Jewish and gentile investors is dedicated, *meshubad*, to the company. Although he uses the word *shutfut*, which is customarily used to mean "partnership," the responsum makes it clear that the case involves a corporation. The prohibition against lending with interest refers to the lending of "your money" (*kaspekhah*). R. Shick argues that money that is so *meshubad* is not called *kaspekhah*. On the surface, however, this contention is troubling. If a Jewish investor makes his money *meshubad* to himself and to a gentile investor, the money should be no less his money (*kaspekhah*) than if he had made it *meshubad* only to a gentile. Yet it does not seem that a Jew prevents his money from being *kaspekhah* when he makes it *meshubad* to a gentile. Realty belonging to a Jew that is *meshubad* to a gentile still belongs to the Jew. For example, if the Jew sells the property, the sale is valid. Consequently, if the property in *Maharam Shick*'s case is not considered *kaspekhah* of the Jew, there must be something more at play than a mere lien (*shibud*) in favor of a gentile. *Maharam Shick*'s words are that each bit of the money invested is *meshubad* to the company. Perhaps it is possible that what he really means is that since the money was given to the company, it no longer belongs to the individual investors. If so, to whom does it belong? Perhaps to the company as a distinct halakhic entity.

[95]R. Isaac Aaron Ettinger, *Maharyah Ha-Levi* 1:54.

benefit from him and that he shall derive no benefit from his fellow, they are both prohibited from deriving benefit from things that belong to the city in which they both live. The Talmud explains that this refers to properties such as the public square, the bathhouse, the synagogue, the ark (in which the Torah was kept), and the holy books.[96] Rashi explains that the reason for this prohibition is that these properties are deemed to be owned by the citizens of the town in partnership. The Talmud explains that the two people mentioned in the *Mishneh* could permissibly derive benefit from the property if they would first transfer their ownership of the property to the someone else, such as the political leader of the community.[97] Once they no longer owned interests in this property, they could derive benefit from the property without deriving benefit from each other. Nonetheless, in addressing this solution, Nahmanides states that transferring the ownership interests in this way is a little like a trick.[98] With respect to the case of the bank, R. Ettinger states that

> all of the loans are made in the name of the bank and if the borrower does not want to pay, the *malveh* [*i.e.*, the Jewish shareholder][99] cannot assert any complaint; only the bank can bring suit in a Jewish court or in a Gentile court. In addition, the money belongs to the bank and this is better than [the case in *Nedarim* in which one] transfers his share to the political leader of the

---

[96]B.T., *Nedarim* 48a.

[97]The political leader is known as the *Nasi*. Although the Talmud only explicitly mentions transferring these interests to the *Nasi*, Jewish law authorities make it clear that the Talmud only mentioned the *Nasi* as an example; people could confidently transfer their interests to the *Nasi* without fear that the *Nasi* would prohibit them from using his share in the community property. Jewish Law commentators indicate that a transfer to anyone else would also work. See, for example, R. Yeheil Mekheil Epstein, *Arukh HaShulkhan, Yoreh Deah* 224:7.

[98]A person who formally transfers his interest in this type of property to the community's political leader does not expect any change in his ability to utilize the property. Prior to the transfer, he was entitled to use it because of his partnership interest. After the transfer, he intends to use it based on the political leader's own partnership interest in the property. The transferor is fully confidant—and justifiably so—that the political leader of the community would ordinarily permit the transferor to use the property.

[99]Interestingly, the Jewish term *malveh* literally means "lender."

> community because that [process] involves a bit of a trick, as . . . [Nahmanides] says there, unlike our case [of the bank].[100]

The basic point this excerpt makes is that the bank, not the shareholders, owned the money that was lent. But if the bank were a partnership, then the shareholders' individualized interests in the partnership money would be problematic. By stating that the bank scenario was "better than" the solution mentioned in *Nedarim*, R. Ettinger seems implicitly to be stating that the bank was a separate legal entity and not merely a partnership. Later on R. Ettinger makes basically the same point, although he puts it a little differently, when he says that "[n]ever were any of them [the shareholders or the bank directors] made a lender or a borrower. Rather, the bank received the money [from its shareholders] and did business with it on the advice of its managers."*

Opponents of the *halakhic* entity theory may also argue that some—or all—of the individual analogies are inapt in other ways. Thus, some contend that the public was really a partnership, not a corporate body.[101] They point out that, according to the Talmud, if a legal dispute arose involving assets of the public, none of the members of the public could serve as a judge or witness in the case *because of bias.*[102] Nevertheless, the merit of this contention is dubious for two reasons. First, bias could exist even if the members of the public are not partners, or owners, of the public's property; they could be biased simply because they have a beneficial interest in the public's assets.[103] Second, the testimonial dis-

---

[100]In the case of the bank, the Jewish shareholder really does not have the power to control collection of the loan. R. Isaac Aaron Ettinger, *Maharyah Ha-Levi* I:54, at 30.

*R. Isaac Aaron Ettinger, *Maharyah Ha-Levi* I:54, at 30.

[101]At least one commentator argues that the public was treated as a partnership in the Talmud but was transformed, in post-talmudic literature, into a corporate body. See Aaron Kirschenbaum, "Legal Person," in Menachem Elon, ed., *Principles of Jewish Law*, at col. 161.

[102]Id. See also *Shulkhan Arukh, Hoshen Mishpat*, no. 37.

[103]The language of the *Rambam*, for instance, suggests that the disqualification is not based on the concept of "ownership" but because members of the public could benefit themselves from self-serving testimony. See, for example, *Rambam, Mishneh Torah, Aidut* 15:1 ("A person may not testify if his testimony will benefit him because it is as if he were to testify about himself").

qualification seems to have pertained to disputes involving property of the particular community, as to which the community members may have been considered a partnership, and not to property dedicated to the Jewish people as a whole, such as the property of those who came up from Babylon. The concept of the public that arguably embodies the notion of a corporation is that which refers to the Jewish people as a whole, on a tribe-by-tribe basis, or as to the "tribe" of the poor—not one which refers merely to the people who live in a particular geographical area.

Another argument that critics of the *halakhic* entity theory use is that corporate shareholders, if they were to act as a whole, could control the corporation's assets and, indeed, could cause the corporation to dissolve and distribute the assets. They sometimes compare corporations to cases in which one could seek release from a vow. Because this person could obtain release from the vow, it is considered, for certain purposes, as if he had already been released.[104] Proponents of the *halakhic* entity theory might respond in two ways. First, in many instances, even if the shareholders would unanimously agree, they could not *immediately* dissolve the corporation.[105] Second, they might argue that what could happen if there were unanimous agreement is irrelevant. The talmudic reference to someone's obtaining release from a vow is inapt, because such release is, as a practical matter, almost surely within the individual's ability to obtain; by contrast, the agreement of other shareholders is certainly not within this ability. Indeed, merely obtaining the names and addresses of the other shareholders and communicating with them may be prohibitively costly. Of course, as discussed below, the critics' position is far stronger as to close corporations, especially those that are governed by a sole shareholder who serves as a sole director as well.

b. The Creation of New Halakhic *Rules.* The Israeli Rabbinical Court observes that some, such as R. Wasserman, assert that if there is no halakhic precedent for the concept of a corporation, there is no way that this concept can be created through the use of traditional Jewish law rules. The court declares that the assertion is incorrect and argues that, even if there were no precedent for the halakhic entity approach, Jew-

[104]*Hafara, Encyclopedia Talmudit* 10:121, 123.

[105]See, generally, Daniel J. H. Greenwood, *Fictional Shareholders: for Women Who Are Corporate Managers Trustees, Revisited*, 69, Southern California Law Review 1021 (1996), n. 90.

ish law doctrines would allow a court to treat a corporation as a halakhic entity. The court cites four doctrines: (1) a rabbinical court may declare property ownerless (*hefker beit din hefker*); (2) conditions agreed to regarding monetary matters are valid (*kol tenai shebimamon kayam*); (3) commercial custom is binding (*minhag hasohrim*); and (4) the law of the secular government is religiously binding (*dina demalkhuta dina*).

i. A Rabbinical Court May Declare Property Ownerless *Hefker beit din hefker* authorizes a rabbinical court (*beit din*) to deprive a person of ownership of particular property. The Israeli Rabbinical Court asserts that this principle permits a rabbinical court to treat a corporation as a new *halakhic* entity. The court apparently believes that this authority enables a rabbinical court to strip shareholders of their rights as "owners" and to transfer such rights to a corporation.

Although there is considerable disagreement as to this principle's precise parameters, it is cited as a justification for promulgation of rabbinic rules affecting ownership. For example, there is a dispute as to whether the Torah recognizes the efficacy of liens. R. Aryeh Leib b. Joseph Ha'Kohen Heller (1745–1813) states that those who assert that liens are Biblically invalid do not distinguish between implicit or explicit efforts to create liens. Accordingly, they believe that even though the Torah allows a person to sell her property, it does not allow her to transfer a lien, because the Torah does not recognize "a partial transfer of ownership rights."[106] As the Israeli Rabbinical Court comments, this view perceives the creation of a lien as a type of unprecedented hybrid—a transfer of *ownership rights* that does not transfer *ownership*. Nevertheless, even those who espouse this position admit that, at least as a matter of rabbinical law, liens are effective. The Israeli Rabbinical Court argues that just a rabbinical courts can introduce into Jewish Law the concept of a voluntarily transferred lien, they can also introduce the secular concept of a corporation as a distinct entity.[107]

[106]R. Aryeh Leib b. Joseph Ha'Kohen Heller (1745–1813), *Kitzot Ha-hoshen* 39:1. Interestingly, the point made in the text might also have been phrased that the Torah does not allow a transfer of *partial* ownership rights. Nevertheless, the translation in the text is true to the original Hebrew.

[107]The Israeli Rabbinical Court asserts that a Rabbinical court has the power to invoke *hefker beit din hefker* to rule that a corporation is a distinct halakhic entity. Nevertheless, perhaps because it adduces alternative grounds for the

Opponents of the *halakhic* entity approach raise at least two objections. First, they argue that even if rabbinic authorities *could* implement the concept of a corporation into Jewish law, rabbinic authorities have not done so yet.[108] Second, critics can contend that the doctrine that allows rabbinical courts to declare property ownerless is not sufficiently robust as to permit introduction of this particular Jewish law innovation, the creation of an artificial *halakhic* entity. They contend that, although the doctrine may permit a rabbinical court to deprive someone of his or her ownership rights, it cannot function to create ownership rights for someone—or something (corporeal or incorporeal)—to which Jewish Law does not otherwise give any such rights.[109] Supporters of the *halakhic* entity approach can point out that there are authorities on both sides of the issue as to whether rabbinical courts may not only deprive one per-

---

halakhic entity theory, the court does not elaborate on the practical consequences of the *hefker beit din hefker* approach. It does not seem that *hefker beit din hefker*, if used on a case-by-case basis, would resolve all of the relevant halakhic problems. Not all of these matters would be likely to involve litigation or a *beit din*'s ruling. Moreover, even if there were such a ruling, it would likely be prospective, not retroactive. Consequently, conduct prior to the ruling, before recognition of the corporation as a separate halakhic entity, would remain problematic.

On the other hand, the court might have believed that it could invoke its power pursuant to the doctrine of *hefker beit din hefker* to promulgate a general decree that would recognize all corporations as independent halakhic entities. The difficulty with this argument, however, is that it is unclear whether a particular Israeli Rabbinical Court panel would be entitled to enact such a decree, thereby binding other Israeli Rabbinical Courts. Even if it could under *Israeli* law, it is unclear whether it could as a matter of *halakhah*. Moreover, the Israeli Rabbinical Court is not at all authorized by Jewish law to issue decrees that would be binding outside of its immediate jurisdiction—and, therefore, any such decree would not resolve halakhic issues in the United States or in other parts of the world.

108See, for example, Simcha Meron, "The Creation Known as a 'Corporation' in Jewish Law," *Sinai* 59:228 (5726).

109See, for example, R. Moshe Sternbuch, *Moadim Uzmanim* 3:269; R. Menashe Klein, *Mishneh Halakhot* 6:277; R. Yitzhak Wasserman, "Interest in Bank Loans," *Noam* 3:195 (5720).

son of ownership but also *create* ownership rights for someone else.[110] Except for the *halakhic* entity theorists themselves, no one seems to say that a rabbinical court can create ownership rights for something which, under biblical law, has no way of acquiring property.

ii. Validity of Conditions in Monetary Matters and the Importance of Commercial Custom Jewish law provides that: (1) any condition that is agreed upon with respect to monetary matters is valid under Jewish law; and (2) customs established among merchants acquire Jewish law validity,[111] provided that the practices are not otherwise prohibited by Jewish Law. [112] These two precepts are arguably interrelated; commercial customs are sometimes said to be binding because business people implicitly agree to abide by them.

The *Mishneh* pronounces the validity of commercial customs. It states:

> What is the rule concerning one who hires workers and orders them to arrive to work early or to stay late? In a location where the custom is to not to come early or stay late, the employer is not allowed to compel them [to do so] . . . All such terms are governed by local custom.[113]

The *Shulkhan Arukh* makes it clear that common commercial practices override many Jewish law default rules that would otherwise govern a transaction.[114] Moreover, these customs are valid even if the majority of the business people establishing them are not Jewish. R. Moshe Feinstein explains:

---

[110]Menachem Elon, *Principles of Jewish Law*, columns 507–515, 686–690, 913–920.

[111]Id.

[112]Doing business on the Sabbath is prohibited by Jewish law. No matter how often merchants might, regrettably, violate this rule by operating on the Sabbath, their illegal conduct could not establish a valid custom to work on the Sabbath.

[113]B.T., *Bava Metziah* 83a.

[114]*Shulkhan Arukh, Hoshen Mishpat* 331:1. See also *Jerusalem Talmud, Bava Metziah* 27b (statement of Rav Hoshea, "Custom supersedes *halakhah*"); R. Joseph Kolon, *Maharik*, no. 102; and R. Shlomo Shwadron (Israel, contemporary), *Maharashdam*, no. 108.

> It is clear that these rules which depend on custom . . . need not be customs . . . established by Torah scholars or even by Jews. Even if these customs were established by Gentiles, if the Gentiles are a majority of the inhabitants of the city, Jewish law incorporates the custom. It is as if the parties conditioned their agreement in accordance with the custom of the city.[115]

In addition, many authorities rule that such customs are valid under Jewish law even if they were established because the particular conduct in question was required by secular law.[116]

Nevertheless, just as there are authorities who dispute whether the rule allowing rabbinical courts to declare property ownerless can introduce new Jewish law concepts, authorities debate whether commercial custom can substantially alter Jewish law. There are various customs as to how to "seal a deal." In some industries, it is said that a handshake is considered binding. These customs are referred to as *situmta*. It is agreed that *situmta* can make a *kinyan*, that is, transfer title to property. This is true even though, but for the custom, the particular practice would not otherwise constitute a valid form of transferring title according to Jewish law. Thus, *situmta* can be used as a substitute for the normal procedures for achieving a *kinyan*. There is a classical controversy among *Rishonim*, talmudic commentators who lived from 600 to 1,000 years ago,

---

[115]R. Moshe Feinstein, *Iggerot Moshe, Hoshen Mishpat* 1:72. See also R. Yeheil Mekheil Epstein, *Arukh HaShulkhan, Hoshen Mishpat* 73:20. See, generally, Steven H. Resnicoff, "Bankruptcy: A Viable Jewish law Option?" *Journal of Halacha and Contemporary Society* 24:10–14 (1992).

[116]See, for example, R. Moshe Feinstein, *Iggerot Moshe, Hoshen Mishpat* 1:72; R. David Chazan, *Nidiv Lev*, no. 12; R. Eliyahu Chazan, *Nidiv Lev*, no. 13; R. Isaac Aaron Ettinger, *Maharyah Ha-Levi* 2:111; R. Avraham Dov baer Shapiro, *D'var Avraham* 1:1; R. Israel Landau (Israel, contemporary), *Beit Yisroel*, no. 172; R. Yitzhak Blau, *Piskei Choshen, Dinei Halva'ah*, ch. 2, *halakhah* 29, note 82. For example, R. Yosef Iggeret, *Divrei Yosef*, no. 21, states:

> One cannot cast doubt upon the validity of this custom on the basis that it became established through a decree of the King that required people to so act. Since people always act this way, even though they do so only because of the King's decree, we still properly say that everyone who does business without specifying otherwise does business according to the custom.

however, as to whether *situmta* is effective *to accomplish tasks that cannot normally be transacted according to Jewish law.*

R. Asher b. Jehiel (Germany, 1250–1327; *Rosh*), R. Shlomo b. Jehiel Luria (Poland, 1510–1573), and others argue that *situmta* can do more than traditional Jewish law forms of effecting a deal. For example, even though Jewish law has no native mechanism for transferring ownership of an item that does not now exist in the world, this approach argues that, if the commercial practice of a particular society included a procedure for such transfers, Jewish law in that place would incorporate the practice as valid and enforceable.[117] For instance, no basic Jewish law form of *kinyan* permits someone to sell *something* that does not yet exist or to sell to *someone* who does not yet exist.[118] Nevertheless, R. Shlomo

[117]R. Asher ben Yeheil, *Responsa of the Rosh* 13:20; *Maharam Me'Rutenberg* (R. Meir b. Baruch of Rothenburg, 1215–1293), cited in *Mordechai* (R. Mordechai b. Hillel, 1240–1298), on B.T., *Shabbat* 472; R. Shlomo Luria, *Maharshal* 36. See also R. Jacob Lorberbaum (Lisa, 1760–1832), *Netivot, Biurim on Shulkhan Arukh, Hoshen Mishpat* 201:1, who appears to agree.

[118]Jewish law distinguishes between different categories of things "that do not yet exist." Perhaps the case about which there is greatest dispute concerns a person's ability to agree to sell property that exists but that he does not possess. The origin of this controversy is found in a difference of opinion between the Sages (a term used to refer collectively to a number of Rabbis) and R. Meir regarding the case of a man who attempts to take all the legal steps necessary to marry a woman at a time before it is legally permissible for them to be wed.

"Suppose a man says to a woman, "Be wedded to me after . . . your husband dies." . . . [Then the woman's husband dies. The Sages rule:] she is not wed. R. Meir rules: she is wed. B.T., *Kiddushin* 63a. According to Jewish law, formation of a Jewish marriage requires a man to acquire "ownership" interests in his intended and the woman's agreement to transfer herself to him. Consequently, the Talmud interprets the debate between the Sages and R. Meir as founded on the basic issue as to whether a person has the power to effectuate a deal involving property not yet in existence or not yet in his possession. The Talmud applies and extends this argument to the sale of a field that the seller has not yet acquired (B.T., *Bava Metziah* 16b), to "what my trap shall ensnare" (id.), to "what I shall inherit" (id.), and to the fruit that will grow on a particular tree in the future (id., at 33b). In each of these cases, the Sages rule that the agreement is not legally effective or binding.

ben Avraham Aderet (Spain, 1235–1310; *Rashba*) states: "Great is the power of the community, which triumphs even without a *kinyan* . . . Even something which is not yet in existence can be sold to someone who does not yet exist [if community practice so provides]."[119]

If R. Aderet is correct and commercial custom can allow transactions to be accomplished that could not otherwise have been achieved under Jewish law, it is possible that the commercial custom of recognizing corporations as distinct entities that can own their own property and conduct their own business, albeit through agents, could also be introduced into Jewish law.

Critics of the *halakhic* entity theory, however, could raise at least three basic objections. First, they might try to distinguish between the relatively limited novelty of introducing into Jewish law the ability to transact business with a person, or a product, that does not *yet* exist and the arguably much greater novelty of introducing the ability to transact business with a Jewish law entity which never has and never will "exist." Thus, some authorities argue that the creation of a *halakhic* entity is like allowing property to acquire other property, something which cannot be done.[120]

Second, unless commercial custom "gives life" to a corporation and allows it to *actually acquire property*—and not merely permits *financial* matters to proceed "as if" the corporation were a separate entity—commercial custom would not avoid many of the Jewish law problems that have been identified, such as the prohibitions against charging interest and owning dough over Passover. By contrast, if rabbinic authorities could—and did—use the principle allowing them to declare property ownerless to take property from shareholders and put it into the dominion of the corporation as a *halakhic* entity, these problems would not arise. Although the principle works *directly* only as to monetary matters, here, because the shareholders would no longer own the property, the rule allowing rabbinic courts to declare property ownerless would *indirectly* affect nonmonetary Jewish law issues as well.

Third, critics argue that *Rashba* is wrong. Thus, Rabbenu Yeheil and others maintain that custom functions only as a *substitute* method by

---

[119]R. Shlomo ben Aderet, *Teshuvot Ha-Rashba* 1:546.

[120]R. Menashe Klein, *Mishneh Halakhot* 6:277.

which to transfer title and cannot be more effective under Jewish law than the forms of *kinyan* recognized by the Talmud. According to this approach, if the concept of a corporation were foreign to Jewish law, use of *situmta*, a new method of accomplishing traditional transactions, could not introduce the corporate concept into Jewish law.[121]

iii. THE LAW OF THE LAND INCORPORATED INTO JEWISH LAW

(1) *THE JEWISH LAW VALIDITY OF SECULAR LAW—AS APPLIED TO JEWS*

The Jewish law doctrine that "the law of the land is the law" provides that, in certain circumstances and for particular purposes, secular law is legally effective under Jewish law. In its opinion, the Israeli Rabbinical Court mentions this principle as another way through which secular legal concepts can be incorporated into Jewish law. A survey of the scope of the obligation to obey secular law is well beyond the scope of this chapter. However, a brief review of the relevant theories is required. There are three principal perspectives regarding "the law of the land is the law":

1. R. Joseph Caro (Safed, 1488–1575) rules that secular law is binding under Jewish law only to the extent that it directly affects the government's financial interests. Thus, secular laws imposing taxes or tolls would be valid under Jewish law.[122]
2. R. Moshe Isserles (Poland,1525 or 1530–1572) agrees that secular laws directly affecting the government's financial interests are binding, but adds that secular laws enacted for the benefit of the people of the community as a whole are also, as a general matter, effective under Jewish law.[123]
3. R. Shabtai b. Meir HaKohen (Poland, 1586–1667; *Shakh)* disagrees with R. Isserles in one respect. He believes that even if secular laws are enacted for the benefit of the community, they are not valid

---

[121]Rabbenu Yeheil is cited in *Mordekhai*, on B.T., *Shabbat* 472. A similar approach can be found in R. David ibn Zimra (Spain, 1480–1574), *Radvaz* 1:278, and is accepted as correct by R. Aryeh Leib HaKohen Heller, *Kitzot Ha-Hoshen on Shulkhan Arukh, Hoshen Mishpat* 201:1.

[122]*Shulkhan Arukh, Hoshen Mishpat* 369:6, 11.

[123]*Shulkhan Arukh, Hoshen Mishpat* 369:11. Note, R. Moses Isserles is known as the "*Rama*."

under Jewish law if they are specifically contrary to indigenous Jewish law precepts.[124]

There is substantial debate among Jewish law authorities as to which approach to follow.[125] Nevertheless, it seems that most modern authorities agree that, at least outside of the State of Israel, R. Isserles's view should be applied.[126]

---

[124]Shabtai HaKohen (*Shakh*) on *Shulkhan Arukh, Hoshen Mishpat* 73:39. Thus, for example, according to *Shakh*, secular law can require that one return lost property in a case that Jewish law permits, but does not mandate that it be returned, but cannot permit one to keep a lost object that Jewish law requires be returned.

[125]See, for example, R. Yaakov Breish (Israel, contemporary), *Helkat Yaakov* 3:160 and R. Shmuel Shilo, *Dina De'Malkhuta Dina*, at pp. 145–160, who list authorities adopting either the approach of *Shakh* or *Mehaber*.

[126]This was the approach of R. Moshe Feinstein, see R. Moshe Feinstein, *Iggerot Moshe, Hoshen Mishpat* 2:62, and R. Yosef Eliyahu Henkin, *Teshuvot Ibra* 2:176. See also R. Shmuel Shilo, *Dina De'malkhuta Dina*, at p. 157, who asserts that most Jewish law authorities adopt the *Rama*'s view and lists many of these authorities.

A contemporary authority, R. Menashe Klein, questions whether *dina de'malkhuta dina* applies in the United States. He states:

> [The applicability of the principle of] *dina de'malkhuta dina* in our times, when there is no king but rather what is called democracy needs further clarification. As I already explained the position cited in the name of *Rivash* quoting *Rashba*, one does not accept *dina de'malkhuta dina* except where the law originates with the king. But in a case where the law originates in courts, and the judges have discretion to rule as they think proper, or to invent new laws as they see proper, there is no *dina d'malkhuta dina*, as there is no law of the king. . . . This is even more true since we have here [in the United States] an institution called a "jury" where the government takes drunks from the market who have never studied law and who establish the law based on a majority vote. Indeed, even the government sometimes creates law and the Supreme Court contradicts it. Certainly in such a system there is no *dina de'malkhuta dina* according to *Rivash* and *Rashba*.

Despite R. Klein's views, it is important to note that most authorities have held that *dina de'malckuta dina* does not apply only to laws issued by a king. R. Menashe Klein, *Mishneh Halakhot* 6:277. Moreover, a number of preeminent Jewish Law authorities have specifically held that *dina de'malkhuta dina* applies within the United States and have not found any problems caused by the demo-

Of course, just as with respect to commercial custom, there is a question as to precisely what "the law of the land is law" can accomplish. Some Jewish law decisors clearly rule that when this doctrine incorporates

---

cratic form of government, the judiciary, the jury system, or the possibility of judicial review. See references to Rabbis Moshe Feinstein and Eliyahu Henkin, above.

Indeed, once one acknowledges that *dina de'malkhuta dina* applies to nonmonarchical governments, it is unclear why these other factors would, as a general matter, be problematic as a matter of Jewish law. For example, juries (and sometimes judges) perform a fact-finding role, that is a necessary element in the application of law. A Noahide system of law could surely invest juries (and judges) with this responsibility without impairing the legitimacy of *dina de'malkhuta dina*. At least as to civil law, where there is no formal notion of jury nullification, juries are not supposed to create law.

Nor is there any apparent Jewish law deficiency in the secular system for interpreting the law. Even if a king were to promulgate written laws, he would undoubtedly delegate the daily responsibility of judging cases to others, and such judges would have to interpret the law. An argument might be made that in the American system, a jury is sometimes required not only to find facts but to make decisions regarding "mixed questions of law and fact." Although a comprehensive analysis of the jury function is beyond the scope of this work, the question of jury interpretation is also not significant as a matter of Jewish law. A secular system must delegate the interpretative function to someone and it is not fatal under Jewish law even if the secular system were to delegate some aspect of this function to juries. Although R. Klein obviously questions the jurors' ability to make any reasonable decisions, he has not demonstrated that this criticism is significant under Jewish law.

In any event, even if there were some irregularity in the secular procedure for applying the law, and even if this would deny Jewish law validity to the *outcome* of a secular case, it would not prevent *dina de'malkhuta dina* from rendering the substantive rules of secular law valid as a matter of Jewish law. For example, disputes between Jews, even when *dina de'malkhuta dina* applies, are supposed to be litigated in Jewish courts who would decide the dispute in accordance with secular law rules. In such instances, the Jewish courts themselves would serve as the fact-finders.

Judges are also required to determine whether legislative acts are consistent with legally superseding documents—such as treaties, constitutions, or even certain other legislative acts. There seems to be no reason why a secular legal system division of power between legislative and judicial branches should impair *dina de'malkhuta dina*.

secular law into Jewish law, the secular law so incorporated can accomplish things that would have been hitherto impossible under Jewish law.[127]

For example, there is a Jewish law dispute as to the validity of a secular will. A will purports to transfer assets from the deceased's estate after his death. Conventional Jewish law rules would not allow this transfer. Once a person dies, her property automatically transfers to her Jewish law heirs. Thus, the problem with a secular will is not just that no traditional method of transfer would work. The problem is that, according to Jewish law, there is no decedent's estate to transfer funds from; as a matter of Jewish law, all of the decedent's possessions are automatically and immediately transferred to the Jewish law heirs upon the decedent's death. Consequently, for the beneficiaries under the will to take possession of the affected property would, under Jewish law, be tantamount to taking property that was owned by others, namely, the Jewish law heirs, and would be prohibited as a form of theft. Nevertheless, there is a plethora of preeminent authorities who rule that this is not theft.[128] Although not all of these explicitly declare that "the law of the land is law" can accomplish more than an ordinary Jewish Law procedure, this proposition is at least implicit in their rulings.[129] On the other hand, the authorities who disagree either explicitly or implicitly maintain that secular law cannot transfer property in a case where a traditional Jewish law procedure would be ineffective.

---

[127]See R. Aryeh Leib HaKohen Heller, *Kitzot Ha-Hoshen*, and R. Jacob Lorberbaum, *Netivot* on *Shulkhan Arukh, Hoshen Mishpat* 201:1.

[128]See, for example, R. Moshe Feinstein, *Iggerot Moshe, Even ha-Ezer* 1:104, 105; R. Shlomo Shwadron, *Maharsham* 224; R. Yaakov Ettlinger, *Binyan Tziyon*, at p. 24; R. Ezekiel Ledvalla, *Sefer Ikkarei ha-Dat, Orah Hayyim* 21; and R. Aaron Parchi, *Perah Mateh Aharon* 1:60. R. Isaac Herzog also maintains that these wills are at least post fact valid. See R. Isaac Herzog, *Techukah le-Yisrael al pi ha-Torah*, vol. 2, ch. 5 (1989).

[129]*Situmta* is the talmudic term for a secular convention for the transfer of title that is incorporated into Jewish Law by common commercial practice. For more on *situmta*, see *Shulkhan Arukh, Hoshen Mishpat* 201 and R. Aryeh Leib HaKohen Heller, *Kitzot Ha-Hoshen* and R. Jacob Lorberbaum, *Netivot*, who discuss whether this is a biblical or Rabbinic form of acquisition. See also Menachem Elon, *Principles of Jewish Law*, at columns 916–920.

(2) THE JEWISH LAW VALIDITY OF SECULAR LAW—AS APPLIED TO NON-JEWS

Before leaving this subject regarding the significance of secular law under Jewish law it is important to note that the three principal approaches to "the law of the land is the law" described above dealt with the Jewish law validity of secular law as it applies directly to Jews. But Jewish law also takes a position as to the validity of secular law in transactions between non-Jews.

Jewish law provides that non-Jews are bound to observe "the seven laws of Noah," referred to as the "Noahide Code." In part, the Noahide Code requires non-Jews to establish a system of commercial laws. According to most Jewish law authorities, such laws may differ from the rules governing transactions that are only between Jews.[130] Moreover, the majority view is that, in a country governed by non-Jews, the secular law consequences of transactions among non-Jews is valid and can generally be relied upon by Jews.[131] For example, assume that *A* and *B* are not Jewish, and that *A* sells *B* a widget in a transaction that would not be effective under Jewish Law,[132] but is effective under secular law. C, a

[130]See, for example, R. Moshe Feinstein, *Iggerot Moshe, Hoshen Mishpat* 2:62. See also Michael Broyde, *The Pursuit of Justice*, pp. 83–99, and Nahum Rakover, "Jewish Law and the Noahide Obligation to Preserve Social Order," 12 *Cardozo L.R.* 1073, 1098–1118, and App. I and II (1991) for a discussion of this issue.

[131]Secular rules enacted pursuant to the Noahide Code *may* be enforceable by a Jewish litigant against another Jewish litigant, but only if the latter has no substantial connection to Jewish Law and would not wish to be governed by Jewish law. Thus, R. Sternbuch, in *Teshuvot ve-Hanhagot*, vol. 1, no. 795 (revised edition), suggests the possibility that a litigant who does not generally observe Jewish law and who would not adhere to Jewish financial law when it would be to his detriment *may* not be entitled to insist on Jewish law's rules when they would inure to his benefit. In some areas of law, an apostate has the same status as a gentile. R. Sternbuch states that it is not clear whether this rule applies to commercial transactions in which it would operate to the apostate's detriment. For more on this, see Yehudah Amihai, "A Gentile Who Summons a Jew to *Beit Din*," *Tehumin* 12:259–265 (1991). Thus, even authorities who would not ordinarily apply *dina de'malkhuta dina* to enforce secular law against religiously observant Jews enforce secular law against nonobservant Jews.

[132]For example, the sale might be void or voidable as violative of the Jewish law prohibition against price gouging. See, for example, R. Aaron Levine, *Free Enterprise and Jewish Law*, pp. 99–110.

Jew, can rely on secular law to establish that *B* owns the widget and, by purchasing it from *B*, C becomes its owner under Jewish law. Consequently, it seems likely that, as between non-Jews, secular law's view of a corporation as a distinct legal entity might well be effective as a matter of Jewish law.[133] Indeed, one of the Jewish law authorities that vigorously rejects the *halakhic* entity theory as applied to Jewish shareholders seems implicitly to acknowledge that it would apply to transactions among non-Jews.[134] Nonetheless, it is possible that some opponents of the *halakhic* entity approach would argue that some parameters apply even as to the types of laws that can be created pursuant to the Noahide Code. Creating a theoretical entity—breathing life into it—and allowing it to acquire and own property could, according to these critics, be beyond the pale.

IV. Creation of "New" Rules—Ownership and Limited Liability

Virtually all of the Jewish law issues that arise in connection with the characterization of a corporation involve, at least in part, two questions: (1) is a Jewish shareholder an owner of the corporate asset, and (2) does the secular doctrine of limited liability apply to immunize Jewish shareholders from being personally liable for corporate debts.

As discussed, the *halakhic* entity and *halakhic* partnership approaches inevitably conflict as to the ownership issue. The *halakhic* partnership proponents—as well as proponents of the other positions considered below—deny that any apt analog to the corporation exists in the Talmud. They also deny that any of the above-mentioned doctrines has the power to create this new *halakhic* entity.

Nevertheless, even critics of the *halakhic* entity approach have relatively little difficulty in concluding that corporate shareholders are en-

---

[133]An example illustrates the significance of this issue. Assume that corporation A's shareholders are not Jewish. Assume further that Corporation A's director is, under applicable secular corporate law, authorized to sell certain corporate property. Nevertheless, shareholders holding 54 percent of the corporate stock have contacted the director and told him that they do not want him to sell the property. May a Jew purchase the property and, under Jewish law, acquire ownership thereby? If secular corporation law is valid as an exercise of Noahide law, the answer is yes.

[134]R. Moshe Sternbuch, *Moadim Uzmanim* 3:269.

titled to the benefit of limited liability, at least as to voluntary creditors (*i.e.*, those, such as suppliers or purchasers, who voluntarily transacted business with the corporation). *Halakhic* partnership theorists usually state that the partners, inter se, cannot demand from each other that they personally pay the business debts because it is *as if* the partners had agreed to the limited liability rule as a condition when they formed the partnership. As to third-party creditors, some authorities specifically state that limited liability is justified—either because any condition agreed to regarding monetary matters is valid or because commercial custom is binding—pointing out that people in the business world realize that corporate shareholders are not going to be personally liable and it is on the basis of this understanding that they do business with corporations.[135] Although a particular plaintiff may in fact not have known the law of limited liability, he or she could and should have found out about it beforehand. Consequently, he is bound as if she had known the custom and had agreed to it.[136] Others argue that because a corporation is a creation of secular law, a person's financial rights when dealing with a corporation are limited to those set forth by the law.[137] Still others just seem to assume that the limited liability rule would be valid under Jewish law without even discussing why.[138]

The failure by some authorities to articulate precisely which Jewish Law doctrine justifies the limited-liability rule is problematic for two

[135]R. Menashe Klein, *Mishneh Halakhot* 6:277; R. Moshe Sternbuch, *Moadim Uzmanim* 3:269, n. 1; R. Ezra Batzri (Israel, contemporary), *Dinei Mamanot*, vol. 3, p. 315.

[136]Id. See also R. Moshe Feinstein, *Iggerot Moshe, Hoshen Mishpat* 1:72.

[137]R Yitzhak Blau, *Brit Yehuda* 7:25–26; R. Yitzhak Blau, *Pitkhei Hoshen, Shutfut* 1:76.

[138]See, for example, R.Yitzhak Yaakov Weiss (Jerusalem, contemporary), *Minhat Yitzhak* 3:1; R. Moshe Sternbuch, *Moadim Uzmanim* 3:269; Shaul Weingart, "Corporations and *Chametz*," in Yad Shaul (written in 1938, and published in 1954). Many authorities disagree as to whether the limited liability principle avoids the prohibition against the charging or paying of interest in loans involving corporations in which Jews own stock. Virtually all of the authorities at least implicitly assume that there *is* such limited-liability. The debate focuses only on the *effect* of limited liability on the prohibition against charging or paying interest.

reasons. First, depending on which doctrine is used, it is possible that the rule would not apply to all possible claims. Consider, for instance, claims asserted by nonconsensual creditors, such as those that assert tort claims against the corporation.[139] If one believes that the limited-liability rule is effective because it is as if those doing business with a corporation agree to the rule (either because all conditions agreed to regarding monetary matters are effective or because commercial custom is binding), then shareholders might not be entitled under Jewish law to limited liability against tort claims asserted by people, such as a pedestrian struck by the corporation's vehicle, who never agreed to do any business with the corporation. On the other hand, if one believes that the limited-liability rule is effective under Jewish law because rabbinical courts can declare property ownerless or "the law of the land is law," the rule *might* operate as to tort claims as well.[140]

Of course, if an individual shareholder personally committed the tort, he may not enjoy limited liability even as a matter of secular law.[141] Consequently, the only torts at issue are those based on the actions of third persons (such as vicarious liability for the actions of agents or employees), or based on injuries caused by the shareholder's property. Although a comprehensive analysis of Jewish tort law is beyond the purview of this paper, internal Jewish law rules—unlike secular laws—do not generally impose vicarious liability on principals for the tortious acts of their agents, whether the tortious conduct is purposeful or merely

---

[139]Of course, even some tort victims, such as those who assert claims for injuries arising out of product defects, might be considered to have "voluntarily" entered into transactions with the corporation.

[140]*But see* R. Moshe Feinstein, *Iggerot Moshe, Hoshen Mishpat* 2:62 (suggesting that *dina de'malkhuta dina* does not apply to damages caused by one's animals, as well as to certain other types of laws).

[141]See, for example, *Van Dam Egg Co.* v. *Allendale Farms, Inc.*, 199 N.J.Super. 452, 489 A.2d 1209 (1985) (sole shareholder and president of corporation could be personally liable for inducing supplier to deliver on credit by purposefully misrepresenting corporation's ability to pay for the goods). See, generally, Fletcher Cyc. Corp. § 11.35 (1996 Cum. Supp.) (describes rules regarding personal liability of corporate officers, directors, and agents for torts they committed or in which they participated).

negligent.[142] Consequently, the only way shareholders *could* be vicariously liable as a matter of Jewish law is because secular tort law is somehow incorporated into Jewish Law. In such cases, it would seem likely that Jewish law would assimilate the secular limited-liability rule as well.[143] Thus, as a practical matter, the difference between justifying the limited-liability rule by the rules that all conditions agreed to regarding monetary matters are valid, or that commercial custom is binding, on the one hand, or by justifying it by the rules that a rabbinical court may declare property to be ownerless or "the law of the land is the law," on the other, would involve cases in which the corporation's property caused injury, such as when a brick from the corporation's building falls on someone or a farming company's bull gores someone.[144]

[142]Where the act to be performed by a purported agent would violate Jewish Law, the primary explanation for the fact that the principal is not liable is a talmudic dictum to the effect that if the Master's words (the words of the Almighty) contradict a pupil's words (the words of a mere mortal), the Master's words should be heeded. See B.T., *Kiddushin* 42b. See also R. Yeheil Mekheil Epstein, *Arukh HaShulkhan, Hoshen Mishpat* 182:9–13. Consequently, no purported agent is deemed to be acting for the "pupil," the supposed principal, in violation of Jewish law. Instead, the purported agent is deemed to be acting for himself. Because of this logic, the agency is valid where the agent did not realize that the action violated Jewish law or where the agent was forced to comply with the principal's directions. See, generally, Israel Herbert Levinthal, "The Jewish Law of Agency," in Edward M. Gershfield, ed., *Studies in Jewish Jurisprudence* (New York: Hermon Press, 1971), pp. 51–58. Similarly, Jewish law provides that if an agent acts negligently, the principal is not responsible because he can assert "I only appointed you to act for my benefit and not for my harm." See, for example, *Shulkhan Arukh, Hoshen Mishpat* 182:3; R. Yeheil Mekheil Epstein, *Arukh HaShulkhan, Hoshen Mishpat* 182:17. See, generally, Steven F. Friedell, "Some Observations on the Talmudic Law of Torts," *Rutgers L.J.* 15:897 (1984); Hayyim S. Hefetz, "Vicarious Liability in Jewish Law," *Dine Israel* 6:49 (1975).

[143]Of course, it is theoretically possible to justify incorporation of vicarious tort liability on a basis that would not necessarily warrant incorporation of the limited-liability rule.

[144]Perhaps a more interesting question would involve the seepage of a corporation's property, such as toxic wastes, onto adjacent land or into adjacent water supplies.

Second, which doctrine is used to justify the limited-liability rule may also affect the Jewish law rule as to consensual creditors in cases in which secular law pierces the corporate veil. If the limited-liability rule is based on "the law of the land is the law," one might suppose that wherever secular law imposes personal liability, *halakhah* would impose personal liability. On the other hand, if limited liability is based on the validity of consensual conditions or upon commercial custom, it is as if the shareholders and each consensual creditor agreed to the limited liability rule. What precisely constitutes commercial custom, however, requires a careful sociological analysis of people's expectations. As explained in Part II, above, the rules for piercing the corporate veil are unclear and the holdings are inconsistent. Even assuming that "specified" circumstances are satisfied, courts retain substantial discretion as to whether or not to pierce the corporate veil. It *may* be that the commercial custom, which involves the expectations of the people who do business, is that corporate shareholders will enjoy limited liability. The unlikely possibility that a secular court could pierce the corporate veil in a particular case might not meaningfully affect such expectations.[145]

Interestingly, an Israeli Rabbinical Court initially expressed doubt as to the limited-liability process even as to voluntary creditors.[146] Possibly assuming that a corporation is a *halakhic* partnership, not a *halakhic* entity, this court described the rule by saying that shareholders give corporate creditors a lien in the assets of the corporation—which serves as collateral—without assuming any personal liability for the debt.[147] The

[145]Of course, adding another level of analysis, one might argue that the reasons why a court pierces the corporate veil may be relevant. Creditors' expectations may depend on the fact that they are dealing with a "corporation." If a court pierces the corporate veil because the corporation did not conduct itself as a "corporation," the creditors' expectations were arguably based on a misunderstanding of the reality and, therefore, should not be used to limit their ability to recover from the shareholders personally.

[146]*Piskei Din HaRabanayim* 3:354.

[147]Id. The court's position as to the halakhic entity approach is unclear. Had the court adopted the halakhic entity rule, it might have explained that the corporation became "personally" liable for its debts, and that the right to sue it and collect from its property was not at all in the nature of collateral (a *mashkhon*) for the debts of the shareholders. Indeed, according to the halakhic entity

court stated that, according to at least one interpretation of Rabbenu Asher's commentary, this type of transaction would be invalid according to fundamental Jewish law rules. Those rules, according to Rabbenu Asher (*Rosh*), provide that a person's property can only serve as a "guarantor" that the person will pay his or her debt. If the person, however, is not obligated to pay a debt, then there is nothing to guarantee, and nothing can be collected from the guarantor.

Rabbenu Asher's view is expressed in connection with the following talmudic discussion: "*Rava* states in the name of R. Nahman: "When a man proposes to a woman stating 'Marry me with this *mana* [*i.e.*, a specified sum of money]' and he leaves her collateral instead of the *mana*, they are not married, as she has neither the money nor the collateral."[148]

Under Jewish Law, merely by *saying* "Marry me with this *mana*," a man does not legally obligate himself to transfer a *mana* to the woman to whom he is speaking.

Rabbenu Asher comments on this passage, stating:

> This ruling is correct because a person is only allowed to place a lien on his property for money that he owes to another; something for which he is not obligated [such as paying a *mana* to the woman mentioned in this passage] cannot give rise to a valid lien on his property . . . [and the attempted betrothal is legally ineffective].[149]

The Israeli Rabbinical Court did not suggest that R. Asher's position would require finding the corporate shareholders to be personally liable. On the contrary, it assumed that the corporate shareholders would not

---

approach, the shareholders, as shareholders, are simply not part of any transaction between the corporation and corporate creditors. However, even if the court were inclined to support the halakhic entity rule, it might have thought the concept of personal liability—that, according to the *Rosh* was a sine qua non to create a lien on property—was simply inapplicable to a *halakhic* entity, that is, that it was meaningless to talk about the personal liability of a corporation. But cf. R. Ezra Batzri, *Dinei Mamonot*, vol. 3, p. 316 (argues that this Israeli Rabbinical Court apparently did not believe that the corporate entity theory was part of indigenous Jewish law).

148 B.T., *Kiddushin* 8a-8b.

149 R. Asher ben Yeheil, B.T., *Kiddushin* 1:10.

be personally liable. It considered ruling that the corporate creditors could not even collect from the corporation itself, because, if the shareholders were not personally liable, the "lien" on the assets placed "in" the corporation would not be valid. Nevertheless, the court concluded that even Rabbenu Asher would agree that the "lien" on the corporation's assets would be valid because of commercial custom or "the law of the land is the law."

Thus, those authorities that support the *halakhic* partnership approach apparently must, if they want to rule in accordance with Asher, acknowledge that these doctrines can incorporate new rules into *halakhah*, even rules that would otherwise be inconsistent with *halakhah*.[150] But, once *halakhic* partnership theorists acknowledge that these doctrines can introduce new rules into Jewish law, including rules that would otherwise be directly inconsistent with Jewish law, it becomes easier for *halakhic* entity supporters to argue that these doctrines could similarly incorporate the corporate entity theory into Jewish law.

Halakhic partnership supporters could respond in several ways. First, they could rely on the approach of Nahmanides and R. Aderet who categorically disagree with R. Asher, explaining that that there are technical reasons why advancing collateral for a "debt" that is not actually owed fails to effect a valid betrothal. Generally, however, they believe that one may create asset-based liability without incurring personal obligation.[151] Many, if not most, Jewish law authorities appear to accept the approach of Nahmanides and R. Aderet.[152] Second, they could argue that Rosh

[150]As discussed above, *Shakh* would apparently not agree that *dina de'malkhuta dina* could introduce a commercial rule inconsistent with *halakhah*. Perhaps, *Shakh* would not impose the same limits on the principle of *minhag hasohrim*. Alternatively, *Shakh* may disagree with *Rosh* and construe the talmudic passage in accordance with the views of *Ramban* and *Rashba*.

[151]Commenting on B.T., *Kiddushin* 8a.

[152]*Shulkhan Arukh Even Ha-Ezer* 29:6, and the comments of R. Moshe Breish (Israel, contemporary), *Helkat Mehohek*; R. Shmuel M-Purdah, Beit Shmuel and R. David b. Shmuel HaLevi (Poland, 1586–1667), *Taz* ad loc. This is also endorsed by Beit Yosef, commenting on *Tur* (R. Jacob b. Asher, Toledo, 1270–1340) *Even Ha'ezer* 29. R. Aryeh Leib HaKohen Heller, *Avnei Meluim* seems to accept this approach, too. See commentary on *Shulkhan Arukh, Even Ha-Ezer* 29:10d.

himself was only referring to a situation in which the owner of the collateral had not done anything to become financially obligated in any way. *Halakhic* partnership advocates might be able to differentiate that case from a situation in which corporate shareholders, through the corporation, incurred some "obligation" by, for example, acquiring property sold by a corporate creditor. The corporate transaction could arguably be perceived as the creation of an actual personal liability coupled with the corporate creditor's agreement that the shareholders need not personally pay for the liability. Of course, they could also, once again, attempt to distinguish the *halakhic* entity theory as being an allegedly more radical innovation, more fundamentally inconsistent with Jewish law than the limited-liability rule. Nevertheless, if one assumes that the limited-liability rule is, according to the Rabbenu Asher, inconsistent with traditional Jewish law, it is difficult to find a principled basis on which to distinguish incorporation of the limited liability rule from incorporation of the *halakhic* entity approach. Asserting that one rule is more radical than the other proves neither the assertion nor that any such asserted discrepancy is significant under Jewish law.

B. The *Halakhic* Creditor Approach

Not all Jewish Law authorities characterize the corporation as either a *halakhic* entity or a *halakhic* partnership. Some authorities characterize the relationship between Jewish shareholders—or some types of Jewish shareholders—and the corporation as that of a creditor to a borrower. For instance, R. Moshe Sternbuch believes that Jewish law, even after considering the various doctrines described above, does not recognize a corporation as a *halakhic* entity. R. Sternbuch argues that if Jews constitute the essential part of a corporation's shareholders,[153] the corporation could be characterized under Jewish law as a partnership subject to certain conditions, such as limited liability, agreed to by the partners.[154] He

[153]R. Sternbuch does not clarify whether the essential part of the shareholders is based on the percentage of investors who are Jewish or on the percentage of shares owned by Jews. Nor does he provide guidance as to how to approach this question when there are different classes of shares.

[154]The validity of the limited-liability condition against third parties is discussed in the text associated with Part III:A:2:b:iv, above.

contends that Jewish law could "force" the transaction to be construed in this manner even though the shareholders really intended only to become stockholders in a secular corporate entity.[155]

R. Sternbuch implies that the shareholders have not really agreed to the conditions he specifies but that Jewish law somehow *forces* them to be treated as if they had. He much more clearly implies that there is some difference between the rights and duties of shareholders under secular law and the rights and duties of Jewish law partners, even assuming the partners had agreed to the various "conditions" he describes.[156] This implication renders his version of the *halakhic* partnership theory somewhat troublesome.

If, however, non-Jews constitute the essential part of the investors, R. Sternbuch argues that the non-Jewish shareholders have the right to be shareholders of a corporate entity and that Jewish law cannot make them be partners in a partnership.[157] Consequently, R. Sternbuch states that if a Jew tries to purchase stock in such a corporation, the money he

---

[155]It is unclear whether R. Sternbuch would contend that Jewish law would infer such agreement if some of the Jewish shareholders were not religiously observant and would not ordinarily desire to be bound by Jewish law.

[156]R. Sternbuch does not identify what these differences are. He states: "If a company of Gentiles or of a majority of Gentiles issues stock, they [the Gentiles] intend to act only in accordance with the secular law, to create an entity whose name is "company" and who will be the sole owner as we explained before and it is not possible to force them [the Gentiles] to other transfers even if there is not much of a practical difference." R. Moshe Sternbuch, *Moadim Uzmanim* 3:269, n. 1.

[157]R. Weiss argues that R. Sternbuch is inconsistent. R. Weiss reasons that if Jewish law would treat a corporation as a partnership if the shareholders are all Jews, then it would treat it that way even if most of the shareholders are not Jews. See R. Yitzhak Yaakov Weiss, *Minhat Yitzhak* 3:1. One might question R. Sternbuch's approach from the opposite direction as well. If non-Jewish investors are entitled to be treated as corporate shareholders when they constitute the essential part of the shareholders, exactly why do these non-Jews lack this right, according to R. Sternbuch, when they do not constitute the essential part of the shareholders? Moreover, R. Sternbuch is not explicit as to how the rule applies when there is a shift such that Jews or non-Jews initially constituted the essential part of the body of shareholders but no longer do so.

pays constitutes a loan to the "managers of the corporation."[158] According to R. Sternbuch, if the enterprise succeeds, it is proper under Jewish law for the Jewish shareholder/lender to take the profits that are distributed to him by the corporate managers. On the other hand, if the corporation fails and the Jewish shareholder/lender has not recovered the principal of the "loan" that he made, then, according to Jewish law, the shareholder/lender would really be able to collect the unpaid principal from the corporate managers.[159]

There are several noteworthy aspects of this approach. First, it is interesting that even though neither the Jewish shareholder nor the corporate managers intend for there to be a loan, R. Sternbuch states that Jewish law would treat it as a loan. It is unclear who R. Sternbuch means when he refers to the corporate managers. Perhaps he means the people who received the Jewish investor's payment for the stock.[160] These managers thought they were acting on behalf of the corporate entity. However, according to R. Sternbuch, they were not acting on behalf of the corporate entity because Jewish law does not recognize that any such corporate entity exists. Consequently, if these managers were not acting on behalf of the corporate entity, they must be deemed to have acted for themselves. By taking a Jewish investor's money without giving anything in exchange, the corporate managers are deemed under *halakhah* to have borrowed the money.[161]

---

[158]R. Sternbuch refers to the corporation's *menahalim*.

[159]R. Moshe Sternbuch, *Moadim Uzmanim* 3:269, n. 1. Interestingly, although most authorities agree that corporate shareholders would have limited liability for corporate debts, R. Sternbuch's analysis results in corporate *managers* being *personally* liable for debts they never thought they were incurring.

[160]This "seems" to be the case because it allows for the explanation set forth in the text. R. Sternbuch himself provides no indication as to who he means when he uses the word "*menahalim*."

[161]*Taz*, in his commentary to *Shulkhan Arukh*, *Yoreh Deah* 150, makes a similar argument. *Taz* deals with a case in which A, *B*, and C are Jews. A, thinking that *B* is his agent, gives money to *B* so that *B* can deliver the money to C, thereby consummating a loan from A to C pursuant to which C has agreed to pay interest (*ribit*). In fact, however, Jewish Law does not allow *B* to serve as A's agent for the purpose of consummating the loan from A to C, because such a loan, since it involves *ribit*, would violate Jewish Law. Consequently, *Taz* says that

If the corporate managers are Jews, then, according to R. Sternbuch, if the company fails, it seems that they face possible personal liability, enforceable in a Rabbinic court, to repay the amount that was paid to them by the Jewish investors.[162] If the corporation succeeds and the Jewish investors are paid more than their principal, it is possible that the transaction would violate a Rabbinic rule against collecting interest.[163]

Second, R. Sternbuch's explanation seems to presuppose that the Jewish shareholders bought their stock from the corporation. It is unclear what R. Sternbuch's position would be in the very common case in which a Jewish investor purchased shares from an existing shareholder. Consider, for instance, a Jewish investor who purchases shares from a non-Jewish shareholder. The non-Jewish shareholder was not considered a creditor of the corporate managers, and they had no personal liability to him. Indeed, according to R. Sternbuch, it seems that, as far as non-Jews are concerned, the corporation is a secular legal entity and a non-Jewish shareholder has certain rights, as a shareholder, against the corporation.[164] When a Jewish investor purchases the non-Jew's shares, none of the purchase money goes to the corporation or to the corporate

---

when *A* handed the money to *B*, *A*, under Jewish Law, made a loan to *B*, even though neither *A* nor *B* intended such a loan. Since Jewish Law prevents *B* from having taken the money as *A*'s agent, *B* must be treated as if he took the money for himself.

[162]Note: if the limited-liability rule applied, there are Jewish law authorities who would argue that there would be no prohibition regarding the charging of interest on loans. However, if, as R. Sternbuch suggests, it is a loan from the Jewish investor to the corporate *managers* and if, as R. Sternbuch continues to suggest, the corporate managers would not be entitled to limited liability, the question of charging interest is certainly relevant.

[163]Rabbinic rules regarding the charging and paying of interest are too complex to consider in depth in this chapter. See, generally, Yeheil Grunhaus, "The Laws of Usury and Their Significance in Our Times," *Journal of Halacha and Contemporary Society* 21:48–59 (1982).

[164]Assume, for instance, that a predominant portion of the shareholders are non-Jewish. Even R. Sternbuch seems to assume that in such a situation the non-Jews, as to themselves, have the ability to create a corporate entity. This seems implicitly to be based on the rules regarding Noahide laws. See text associated with Part III:A:2:b:iii, above.

managers. Consequently, neither the corporation nor the corporate managers could be found to have directly borrowed money from the Jewish investor. Even assuming the Jewish investor could acquire the rights previously held by the non-Jewish shareholder, the Jewish investor would not be deemed to have loaned money to anyone, because the non-Jewish shareholder had not loaned money to anyone. This seems to leave two possibilities. One is that the Jewish investor actually acquires his predecessor's status as a corporate shareholder and, in this scenario, R. Sternbuch would approve the *halakhic* entity theory.[165] Yet this occurrence is common, and R. Sternbuch provides no explicit basis for believing that he would approve the *halakhic* entity theory at all! The other possibility is that the Jewish investor could not acquire the non-Jewish shareholder's rights and the attempted purchase of shares would be ineffective. Consequently, the money paid to the non-Jewish shareholder would constitute a loan from the Jewish investor to the non-Jewish shareholder who received it. Thus, the Jewish investor would, unbeknownst to himself, have no claim against the corporation but would have a claim as a creditor against the shareholder from whom he had attempted to buy the shares. Similarly, the non-Jewish shareholder, unbeknownst to himself, would owe money to the Jewish investor and would really still own the corporate stock under Jewish law.

Another creditor-oriented approach is advanced by R. Yitzhak Yaakov Weiss. Interestingly, R. Weiss believes that the corporation is a *halakhic* partnership with respect to Jewish shareholders who own voting shares, even if as a practical matter such shareholders have no meaningful ability to influence corporate conduct. As a result, any Jew with voting shares would be deemed to own a percentage of the corporate assets. If the assets consisted of dough, then the Jewish shareholder, according to R. Weiss, would face the prohibition of owning dough on Passover.

On the other hand, R. Weiss rules that a Jew who owns only nonvoting shares—even if the shares are of common stock—is not a partner

---

[165]Approval of the halakhic entity theory in this context could be a result of construing the Noahide laws as capable of creating rights and relationships that could not exist under Jewish law—and capable of transferring such rights and relationships to Jewish purchasers.

but, rather, a lender.[166] R. Weiss interprets the position of certain other Jewish law authorities as concluding that whenever a Jewish investor owns shares in a secular corporation, the Jewish investor is merely making a loan and not becoming a partner.[167] R. Weiss says that he made a kind of a compromise (*k'ayn hechrah*) between those who say that a secular corporation is never a partnership and those that say it is always a partnership.[168]

Critics of R. Weiss's position argue that the distinction between voting and nonvoting shares is not defensible.[169] The distinction seems to be based on form, not substance, because a nonvoting shareholder with a large investment in a corporation might in fact have a much greater ability to influence a corporation's conduct than a voting shareholder who owns very few shares. Another difficulty with R. Weiss's approach is that he fails to explain, when there is a loan, To whom is the loan made? Would he, for instance, agree with R. Sternbuch and rule that the loan is made to the corporate managers? Or would R. Weiss believe that the loan is made to the partnership consisting of the shareholders holding voting stock? As was evident when discussing R. Sternbuch's position, there could be Jewish law consequences arising from such a loan and, therefore, it is important to know to whom it is made.

Part III:A, above, explained that a responsum of R. Ettinger with respect to the charging of interest could be interpreted as supporting the

---

[166]R. Yitzhak Yaakov Weiss, *Minhat Yitzhak* 7:26 and 3:1. We query how R. Weiss would characterize the status of a person who owns voting stock but who, because of a control share acquisition statutes, described in our longer work, is not entitled to vote such shares for a number of years.

[167]R. Weiss says that this is the view of Rabbis Ettinger (citing his *Responsum* 2:124), Moshe Shick (*Maharam Shick*), and Hanoh Dov Padua (*Kheishev Ha-Ephod*). See R. Yitzhak Yaakov Weiss, *Minhat Yitzhak* 7:26.

[168]Interestingly, R. Weiss seems to cite R. Ettinger as one of those who thinks that a corporation is never a partnership. Although R. Ettinger does not discuss whether the Jewish shareholders in the cases before him had any voting rights, it seems that R. Weiss assumes that they did. Otherwise, R. Weiss could have argued that it was possible R. Ettinger could have agreed with him.

[169]See, for example, R. Moshe Sternbuch, *Moadim U'zemanim* 3:269; Israeli Rabbinical Court, *Piskei Din Rabanayim* 10:273; Hanoh Dov Padua, *Kheishev Ha-ephod* 2:52.

halakhic entity analysis. Citing a different responsum of R. Ettinger, R. Weiss contends that R. Ettinger follows the creditor approach.[170] Nevertheless, a close reading of that responsum does not provide any specific support for R. Weiss's interpretation. Although R. Ettinger states that Jewish shareholders do not own corporate property, he does not say that the Jewish shareholders loaned any money to anyone.

R. Ettinger considers the case of a corporation, some of whose shareholders are Jewish, that had a large supply of beer (a form of *hametz*) that it had owned throughout Passover. Specifically, he ponders whether the corporation's Jewish shareholders are allowed to derive benefit from this beer. He answers that the reason that the Sages prohibited such products was to penalize Jews who failed to fulfill their responsibility to destroy *hametz* prior to Passover. He reasons that, inasmuch as Jewish shareholders have no right to use, sell, or destroy the corporation's property, they had no *halakhic* obligation to destroy the beer in question prior to Passover. Therefore, he writes that the penalty enacted by the Sages would not apply. In addition, he argues that the Jewish shareholders were not obligated to sell their stock prior to Passover. He acknowledges that the value of the beer was linked to the financial interests of the shareholders (in *halakhic* terms, that the shareholders are *aharoi* for the beer), that if the beer had been destroyed the shareholders would suffer a loss. Nevertheless, he states that the Jewish shareholders did not own the beer itself (the *guf hahametz*)—because, as he explains, they had no right to consume, sell or destroy it—and they had no right, as shareholders, to *enter or use the corporation's premises*. As a result, he declares the case is "*like*" that of a Jew who is *aharoi* for *hametz* of a non-Jew that is in the possession of the non-Jew, in which case the *hametz* is not prohibited after Passover.

It is possible to construe this responsum in the same way that his responsum regarding the charging of interest was interpreted in Part III:A, above, that is, that the corporation is considered as if it were a separate *halakhic* entity that owned the *hametz*.[171] Alternatively, it is *possible* to

[170]See R. Yitzhak Yaakov Weiss, *Minhat Yitzhak* 7:26, citing R. Isaac Aaron Ettinger, *Maharyah Ha-Levi* 2:124.

[171]According to this interpretation, when Ettinger says the case is "like" that of a Jew who is *achroi* for the *dough* of a gentile in the possession of the non-Jew,

construe it: (1) as supposing that the Jewish shareholder merely purchased a right to a portion of the corporation's profits, and as similar to the view discussed in Part III:C, below, or (2) as evaluating the overall relationship of the Jewish shareholder to the dough, and as similar to some of the views described in Part III:D, below.[172] Nowhere in the responsum does the *Maharyah Ha-Levi* state that the Jewish investors *loaned* money to anyone. If he thought that Jewish investors had loaned their money, it would have been necessary for him to explain to whom the loan was made and to describe the consequences if the "borrowers" were Jews.

Of course, the *halakhic* creditor approach shares the problem mentioned above in connection with R. Sternbuch's *halakhic* partnership analysis. A Jewish investors does not seem to be lending money to corporate managers. He does not perceive himself as a lender, but as an investor. A Jewish investor who purchases corporate shares from a non-Jewish shareholder surely does not perceive himself as lending money to the non-Jewish shareholder. To say that this is what is happening is to push—with both hands—a square peg into a round whole.

C. The Purchaser of Entitlements Approach

R. Moshe Feinstein discusses the Jewish law status of corporations in a number of scattered responsa. In several, he briefly indicates that a corporation is not a new type of entity and refers to it as a partnership. Nevertheless, it seems *possible* that in at least some of these responsa he is referring to close corporations.[173] On the other hand, in another

---

what does he mean by the word "like"? He might mean that it is similar to that case because, although the corporation is not a "gentile," it is a Jewish law entity and it is not a Jew.

[172]According to this approach, when R. Ettinger says that the case is "like" that of a Jew who is financially responsible for the dough of a non-Jew that is in the possession of the non-Jew, he is *comparing* the two situations qualitatively and not equating them.

[173]This "possibility" is not equally true with respect to all of his responsa. In one case, R. Moshe Feinstein, *Iggerot Moshe, Hoshen Mishpat* 2:15, for example, he states that corporations are not "a new creation by itself" as was suggested in the *Darkhei Teshuva* 160:15. But *Darkhei Teshuva* seems to be dealing with large corporations and not small, close corporations.

responsum he specifically discusses the widespread practice of purchasing stock in public companies that do business on the Sabbath. He states that:

> [T]he simple reason that this practice is permissible under Jewish law is that someone who purchases shares of a company but does not really have a meaningful say in the company's business should not be considered even as a pro rata owner. Nor does such a purchaser of shares want to be an owner of the business or to purchase any of the business. Instead, he wants to purchase part of the profits and losses that the business will have according to the shares that he buys. [In fact] it seems more reasonable to say that he does not make any Jewish law acquisition, but only acquires [rights to the profits and losses] according to the laws of the land. That, according to the condition on which he made his purchase, a shareholder can vote to elect the president [of the corporation] is . . . [devoid of any practical significance], because, in fact, they [presumably meaning those who control the corporation] keep for themselves more than a majority of the shares so that the purchaser cannot effectively influence [the corporation's conduct].[174] Nor does this purchaser desire to influence [the corporation's conduct] and does not intend to acquire such a right . . . But it certainly is prohibited for one to acquire so much stock that his opinion will be considered [by those who control the corporation] even in non-Jewish factories or businesses . . . [unless] one makes the type of conditional agreement required when a Jew enters into a partnership with a non-Jew as set forth in *Shulhan Arukh, Orah Hayyim*, no. 345.[175]

Thus, R. Feinstein believes that individual investors who are not involved in a corporation's operations, who do not own a sufficiently large percentage of shares as to enable them in fact to control the corporation's business, and who have no intention of obtaining such control seem to acquire no more than an interest in the corporation's profits. Pursuant to ordinary Jewish law rules, the acquisition of rights in future profits and losses might be difficult or impossible to accomplish because such prof-

[174]R. Feinstein is referring to a public company; it is unlikely that the original investors retain an actual majority of stock. Because of the proxy system and the diffusion of stock ownership among countless people who do not know each other and who, in many cases, have relatively minor holdings, much less than an absolute majority of stock is required to control the corporation.

[175]R. Moshe Feinstein, *Iggerot Moshe, Even Ha-Ezer* 1:7.

its and losses are "things" that "do not exist."[176] This seems to be the reason why R. Feinstein suggests that the acquisition is pursuant to the principle of "the law of the land is the law." Thus, unlike R. Weiss, R. Feinstein does not look to the *formal* distinction between voting and non-voting stock, but to the *substantive* distinction between shareholders who can or intend to influence the corporation's conduct and those who merely want to purchase a part of the corporation's profits and losses.

Neither R. Ettinger's responsum cited by R. Weiss, and discussed above in Part III:B, nor the responsa of R. Shlomo Kluger (R. Solomon b. Judah Aaron of Brody, 1785–1869, *MaHaRShaK*), R. Azreil Hildesheimer, or R. David Zvi Hoffman (Germany, 1843–1921), discussed below in Part III:D, are necessarily inconsistent with R. Feinstein's approach. They emphasize that Jewish shareholders do not own the corporate property directly and that all they have is a right to the corporate profits. Although they do not explain the Jewish Law process or processes through which these shareholders acquired the right to corporate profits, they could theoretically agree that the right was purchased through "the law of the land is the law."[177]

There are, however, several difficulties and ambiguities with respect to R. Feinstein's approach. R. Feinstein mentions two relevant factors—the investor's intent to purchase a right to influence corporate conduct, and the investor's ability to do so. First, it is uncertain whether both of these factors are necessary before there is a problem requiring "the type of conditional agreement . . . required when a Jew enters into a partnership with a non-Jew, as set forth in *Shulkhan Arukh, Orah Hayyim*, no. 345"[178] or whether either factor would be sufficient. For example, assume an investor purchased stock with the intent to try to influence corporate conduct—perhaps by way of rallying other shareholders and trying to add shareholder resolutions to the proxy materials distributed by management—but, in fact, the shareholder was unsuccessful in these

[176]*Shulkhan Arukh, Hoshen Mishpat* 209:1–3

[177]But see R. Yitzhak Yaakov Weiss, *Minhat Yitzhak* 7:126, who states that, according to R. Ettinger, the Jewish shareholders made a *loan*. R. Weiss does not say to whom the loan was made and whether such a loan would raise questions regarding the charging or collection of interest.

[178]R. Moshe Feinstein, *Iggerot Moshe, Even Ha-Ezer* 1:7.

efforts. Given that the shareholder owned some stock and tried to change corporate conduct, would he be considered a "partner" in the corporation or must he actually obtain enough "power" to impact corporate governance?

Incidentally, assuming that possession of a certain measure of corporate influence is required before someone is regarded as an "owner" of corporate assets, how much power is enough? R. Weiss seems to say a single share of voting stock is sufficient. R. Feinstein clearly disagrees and says that ownership of a small number of shares is insufficiently significant. Instead, he says that the problem of ownership arises when one acquires "so much stock that his opinion will be considered [by those who control the corporation]."[179] But what does it mean for an opinion to be "considered"? What if a minority shareholder attends stockholder meetings and even sits on the board of directors—but is always outvoted. Is the mere fact that the minority shareholder voices his view significant?

Not only is it unclear whether meaningful "power" is absolutely necessary, but, assuming someone has real voting power, it is uncertain whether such power is sufficient to make the shareholder an "owner." Assume, for instance, a particular shareholder has a sufficiently large holding that she could affect corporate governance but she simply has no interest in doing so.[180] Would R. Feinstein rule that this person is an "owner" of the corporate assets?

---

[179]Id.

[180]R. Lintz reports views expressed by Rabbis David and Reuven Feinstein, sons of R. Moshe Feinstein. R. Lintz does not assert that Rabbis David and Reuven Feinstein are explaining their father's perspective. It is interesting to note that Rabbis David and Reuven Feinstein may disagree about the very factors discussed in the accompanying text. While R. David Feinstein seems to suggest that some threshold amount of potential control is enough to cause someone to be an "owner," R. Reuven Feinstein seems to argue that potential control may be insufficient if the shareholder has no interest in exercising it.

> When asked . . . [about whether a partner or corporate shareholder violates the prohibition against dealing in non-kosher foods if the partnership or corporation deals in such foods], . . . R. David Feinstein posited that the determining factor is whether or not the investor is involved in the running of the business. He made no distinction between the various investment structures such as partnerships, limited partnerships, or corporate stock. According to . . . [R. David] Feinstein, if an in-

Another problem with R. Feinstein's approach is that, assuming the corporation is not a *halakhic* entity and not all of the shareholders are owners of the corporate property, when investors purchase corporate stock from the corporation, from *whom* are they acquiring a right to a share of the corporation's profits and losses? Moreover, precisely who *does* own the corporate property? If there are certain shareholders who own a significant portion of the stock and, individually or jointly, are able to control the corporation, perhaps R. Feinstein would characterize them as the real partners in this "corporate partnership." But what if *no individual*, or group of individuals, owns a significant percentage of shares? Who would own the corporate property? If the corporate directors themselves owned some shares and also exercised control through manipulation of the proxy system, would R. Feinstein characterize the corporation as a partnership comprised of such directors? If so, however, what degree of ownership interest would each such director possess?

An additional difficulty arises because of R. Feinstein's focus on a person's intent at the time he purchases his shares. Consider a few examples. Assume that there are 100,000 shareholders, each of whom owns 1 share of the corporation's total of 100,000 shares of stock. Because none of these shareholders purchased the stock with the intent to take an active role in corporate governance, R. Feinstein would presumably con-

---

vestor owns a substantial enough amount of stock of a corporation to involve himself in the voting or management of the company, even if he is a minority shareholder, he is subject to the prohibition of trading in non-kosher products. He added that the same criteria apply to determining whether a stockholder may retain his ownership of a company which owns *chametz* on *Pesach* [footnote omitted] . . .

. . . R. Reuven Feinstein added that in his view the intention of the stockholder is a determining factor in the question. If, for instance, a shareholder with only one share intends to get involved in dictating policy of the company by speaking at shareholder meetings or contacting other shareholders, then even that limited amount of ownership would be prohibited. On the other hand, if a person's intention is just to profit from short-term market moves, then even a large block purchase would be permissible . . . [R. Reuven] Feinstein said it was questionable whether a small percentage of a company which is intended to be held for a long time (for example, for a retirement plan) is permissible.

See George Lintz, "May a Jew Purchase Stock in McDonald's? (and Related Questions)," *Journal of Halacha and Contemporary Society*, 24:69 (1992).

sider them merely as purchasers of entitlements from the corporation and not as partners who owned any interest in the corporate property. But what if a new person, A, decided that this corporation was undervalued and wanted to obtain control of it? A then purchases the shares of stock owned by 50,001 of the corporate shareholders and, with this majority interest, is able to elect the corporate directors and direct corporate conduct. According to R. Feinstein, is A an owner of the corporate assets? But from whom could A have acquired an interest in the corporate property? A merely purchased shares from the existing shareholders and, according to R. Feinstein's approach, those existing shareholders did not own interests in the corporate property.

Changing the hypothetical a little, assume that A had originally purchased from the corporation 50,001 of the corporation's 100,000 shares of stock with the intention of being actively involved in running the corporation, such that R. Feinstein would deem A to be a partner with an ownership interest in the corporate property. Assume, however, that A dies and that his stock is inherited by many different people, none of whom has the intent to be active in corporate affairs or enough shares to be successful in influencing corporate affairs even if he or she wanted to. Are these inheritors nonetheless considered owners of a pro rata share of A's original ownership interest in the corporate assets because they inherited it? If not, what happens to A's ownership interest?

The difficulty posed by these last examples seems based on the traditional concept of linking ownership with the possession of "legal title." Indeed, it is the emphasis on who owns "legal title" that seems to have led some of those who reject the *halakhic* entity theory to adopt the *halakhic* partnership approach.[181] Thus, in the first case, if the 50,001 individual shareholders owning one share apiece did not own title to the corporate property, someone who simply purchases their rights does not seem to have acquired title at all; there was no one who could have transferred title to her. Similarly, in the second case, if a shareholder who does own title passes away, it would seem that the title he owned would be inherited.

---

[181]See, for example, R. Menashe Klein, *Mishneh Halakhot* 6:277. Contemporary halakhic authority R. J. David Bleich also argues that whoever possesses "legal title" to property is the property's owner. Letter from R. Bleich on file with the authors.

Maybe R. Feinstein believes that a person who acquires an amount or percentage of corporate stock acquires two things: (1) a right to share in the profits; and (2) an option, of unlimited duration, to acquire an "ownership" interest in the corporate property. No technical act would be required for the shareholder to exercise this option. She would merely have to formulate the intent to acquire the relevant ownership interest. Contemporary halakhic authority R. Moshe Heinemann suggests that this is R. Feinstein's position.[182]

This explanation is somewhat troublesome. First, R. Feinstein does not mention anything about an option. Second, neither the purchasers nor the sellers of corporate stock mention such an option when they transfer ownership of the stock. Without relevant discussion between the parties, it is difficult to discern what precisely creates the option, particularly since secular law does not recognize that the sale of stock involves such options. Third, until the new purchaser of the stock decides to exercise the ownership interests attendant to the stock, who, if anyone, enjoys these interests? For example, assume a majority shareholder—who presumably possesses ownership interests commensurate with her shareholdings—sells some of her shares to a new minority shareholder. Does the seller retain the ownership interests attendant to the shares sold until and unless the new minority shareholder exercises his option? Even if this were the case, what if the majority shareholder sells all of his stock to a number of new minority shareholders? In light of the fact that the seller no longer owns any stock, it seems impossible to say that the seller retains the applicable ownership interests. Do these interests exist in limbo until the new shareholders decide that they want to be owners? Does the right to ownership interests attach to the stock and blink on and off based on a particular stockholder's desires?

Alternatively, perhaps R. Feinstein implicitly suggests a new concept of ownership that does not require possession of legal title. Perhaps he believes that control plus beneficial interest can constitute a form of "ownership." Nonetheless, it remains unclear: (1) what the authority is for such a proposition; (2) what degree of control is required; and (3) what degree of beneficial interest is required.

---

182 See R. Moshe Heinemann's handwritten comments on an earlier version of this draft on file with the authors.

Neither of the above alternative explanations answers who, according to R. Feinstein, would be the owner of the corporate assets if no shareholder had significant control over the corporation. Nor do these alternatives grapple with the fact that, even if a particular shareholder possesses some ability to influence the corporation, secular law prescribes that the corporate directors—who may be more powerful than the shareholder—are not the shareholder's agents, but, rather, the agents of the corporate entity.

D. The Relationship Approach

The final approach to corporations reflected in Jewish law literature does not explicitly address what a corporation is, but, instead, identifies the unusually attenuated relationship between Jewish shareholders and a particular corporation and relies on the nature of this relationship in reaching specific Jewish law conclusions. Thus, some authorities argue the fact that a shareholder is not personally liable for a corporation's debt permits the corporation to pay interest on a loan from individual Jews. Similarly, others contend that the prohibition against doing business with forbidden foods poses no problem for Jewish shareholders so long as they are not personally involved in a corporation's business.[183]

The relationship approach is yet another way of understanding the responsum of R. Ettinger discussed in Part V:B, above. After examining all of the restrictions confronting shareholders, R. Ettinger states that the relationship between the shareholders and the corporation's dough is "like that" between a Jew and the dough of a non-Jew in the non-Jew's possession for which a Jew is financially responsible. Perhaps R. Ettinger is not saying that the two cases are factually identical, but merely that the extremely limited connection between the Jewish shareholder and the dough owned by the corporation is so attenuated that it should be treated under Jewish law the same way as the dough of a non-Jew in the non-Jew's possession for which a Jew has a financial interest.

---

[183]See, generally, George Linz, "May a Jew Purchase Stock in McDonalds? (and Related Questions)," *Journal of Halacha and Contemporary Society*, 24:69 (1992).

Similarly, when asked about the propriety of owning shares in a corporation that did business with dough over Passover, R. Shlomo Kluger stated:

> that the custom of people with shares in . . . corporations . . . is that they just have only a part of the profit or loss. They do not have any right to direct or manage the operations of the business [or] the sales and purchases necessary for the business . . . Therefore, . . . [a Jewish shareholder] has no obligation to sell [his shares before Passover].[184]

Thus, without naming the Jewish law doctrine he is relying on, R. Kluger uses the limited relationship between the shareholder and the corporate dough in ruling that stock ownership is not a problem with respect to Passover. Adopting this same approach, R. Hanoh Dov Padua cites the responsa of R. Ettinger and R. Kluger.[185]

R. Azriel Hildesheimer, as cited by R. David Tzvi Hoffman, permits Jewish shareholders to derive benefit after Passover from dough owned by their corporations during Passover because, in part, the shareholders did not own any part of the dough and, even if they would have asked the directors for dough in return for their shares, the directors could have refused to give any.[186] R. Hildesheimer does not explain who did own the dough during Passover. But he focuses on the shareholders' inability to demand the dough as a reason for saying that they were not responsible for it. R. Hoffman, although questioning other arguments raised by R. Hildesheimer, treats this one favorably.[187]

Thus, Rabbis Ettinger (at least in his responsum regarding the charging of interest), Kluger, Padua, Hildesheimer, and Hoffman all focus on the relationship between the Jewish shareholder and the corporation's

[184]See R. Shlomo Kluger, *Ha-alef Lekhah Shlomo, Orah Hayyim*, no. 238. It is not clear from this responsum whether shareholders had absolutely no voting rights or whether they had voting rights but, as a practical matter, these rights did not afford shareholders any meaningful ability to control the corporation's conduct.

[185]R. Hanoh Dov Padua, *Heishev Ha-Ephod* 2:52.

[186]See R. David Tzvi Hoffman, *Melamed Lehoil* 1:91.

[187]Id.

assets, but do not expressly explain either who did own such assets or which precise Jewish law doctrine formed the basis for their rulings.

R. Ezra Batzri, a contemporary redactor of Jewish law clearly familiar with secular corporation theory, writes at length about evaluating the precise relationship between Jewish shareholders and corporate property.[188] His argument echoes that of secular scholars who refer to ownership as a bundle of rights and contend that one might be the owner for certain purposes but not for other purposes.[189] Thus, R. Batzri argues that although the limited liability rule might *seem* to prevent a shareholder from being an owner of corporate property, there are a number of legal "threads" that nonetheless tie shareholders to the property. He argues that the *theoretical* ability of secular law to pierce the corporate veil and find shareholders personally liable for corporate debts is one such thread. Nonetheless, he specifically refuses to reach any conclusions as to whether the threads linking a shareholder to corporate property are, in fact, sufficiently strong so as to consider the shareholder the Jewish law owner of such property.

One might argue that, as to a public corporation, where the likelihood of piercing the corporate veil is almost nil, the theoretical possibility of this event is too slender to meaningfully connect shareholders as "owners" of the corporation. The probability of piercing the corporate shell, however, is much more likely in a close corporation.

CONCLUSIONS

Secular corporation law covers numerous categories of organizations—profit and nonprofit, public and close. The realities of corporate governance may differ greatly even from one corporation to another within a particular category. Some shareholders own voting stock, while others have only nonvoting stock. Some shareholders are personally involved in the corporation's business and others are not. Some shareholders attempt to affect corporate conduct, and others do not. Some sharehold-

[188]See R. Ezra Batzri, *Dinei Mamanot*, vol. 2, pp. 314–321.

[189]See, generally, J. E. Penner, "The 'Bundle of Rights' Picture of Property," *University of California, Los Angeles Law Review* 43:711 (1996).

ers have the ability to affect corporate decisions, even if they do not exercise this ability, while others lack even the potential to impact corporate behavior. Some corporations have primarily Jewish shareholders, and others do not.

The literature on the relation of corporate ownership to Jewish law obligations reflects five principal positions:

1. The "*halakhic* entity" approach. This view maintains that Jewish law deems a corporation to be an independent entity that owns its assets and conducts its business. According to this view, shareholders do not own title to the corporate assets and are not in violation of *halakhah* when the corporation commits a forbidden act.
2. The "*halakhic* partnership" approach. There are three versions of this view. The first contends that *halakhah* recognizes a corporation as a "partnership" (*shutfut*). The shareholders are regarded as partners who own a percentage interest of the corporate assets. A second version maintains that Jewish shareholders are partners only if the corporation has primarily Jewish shareholders. A third alternative describes Jewish shareholders as partners only if they own voting shares.
3. The "*halakhic* creditor" approach. Some authorities who espouse the second or third versions of the *halakhic* partnership theory believe that Jewish shareholders who are not partners are, instead, creditors who have loaned money to the corporation or to the corporation's managers. As creditors, such shareholders would not be responsible under *halakhah* for the corporation's conduct.
4. The "purchaser of entitlements" approach. At least one authority suggests that in many instances a Jewish shareholder is merely a purchaser of a certain share in the corporation's future profits.
5. The "relationship" approach. Some authorities do not use a single label to describe the abstract relationship between Jewish shareholders, on the one hand, and corporate assets and activities, on the other. Instead, they examine diverse aspects of the relationship and ask whether, as a whole, it constitutes ownership such as to implicate particular Jewish Law problems. Exponents of this approach consider, for example, the shareholders' ability and intention to control corporate conduct and use or sell corporate assets.

None of the Jewish Law theories of a corporation is entirely satisfying or compelling. Perhaps the reason is that these efforts, for the most part, are insufficiently sensitive to the many different types of secular corporations. Assuming, for example, that the *halakhic* entity approach were correct across the board, it would enable use of a corporate form to resolve countless Jewish law difficulties. The dilemma is that it might resolve too many problems. It would theoretically enable Boruch the Baker to form a corporation of which he is the sole shareholder, director, and officer, and to allow the corporation not only to keep dough throughout Passover but, if he hires non-Jewish bakers and salespersons, to sell *hametz* throughout Passover as well as on the Sabbath and other Jewish holidays. Although it is possible that secular law creates the opportunity of using a corporation to circumvent Jewish law, this conclusion would be as unnatural to swallow as it would be to swallow the *hametz* on Passover. While many of the arguments asserted in favor of the *halakhic* entity approach focus on notions regarding the attenuated relationship between shareholders and corporate assets, these arguments do not apply to many close corporations, where the substantive relationship is much richer and more dynamic than the formal relationship. Nevertheless, no one has yet articulated a consistent set of easily applicable principles that would distinguish between scenarios in which the *halakhic* entity approach should and should not apply.

While the *halakhic* entity approach might seem in some instances to permit what should be impermissible under Jewish law, the *halakhic* partnership approach has the opposite defect. By treating all shareholders as partners, no matter how insignificant their numbers of shares, how inactive they are in corporate affairs, and how unlike their status is to that of traditional partners, the partnership approach prohibits certain forms of conduct—particularly regarding public corporations—which do not appear as if they should be prohibited under Jewish law.

Epilogue

*Aaron Levine**

My purpose here will be to raise issues that proceed from the papers of this volume for further study.

THE NORMATIVE ROLE FOR THE MANAGER OF A BUSINESS ENTERPRISE

One fundamental issue is the position *halakhah* takes in the neoclassical-stakeholder theory debate regarding the *normative* role for the manager of a business enterprise. We offer the proposition that *halakhah* adopts elements of both viewpoints but must be described as a distinctively separate theory.

We begin our thesis with an identification of the legal relationship between the manager and the owners of capital of a firm. Bearing on this issue is a talmudic passage at *Bava Metziah* 104b, which deals with *iska*.

*My thanks to Dr. Moses Pava for his comments on an earlier draft of this paper . My gratitude to Elisha Graff for his technical assistance and meticulous work in validating the sources cited in this paper. My thanks to Tova Zitter for technical assistance.

Iska is a special type of business partnership that *halakhah* regulates.[1] The distinctive feature of *iska* is that the financier plays no operational or managerial role in the business enterprise. If the active partner (*A*) and the silent partner (*B*) have not stipulated the division of profits and losses, *halakhah* calls for profits and losses to be divided equally. The portion of the capital for which A assumes responsibility takes on the character of a loan (*milveh*), and the remaining portion takes on the character of a deposit (*pikkadon*). Commenting on the dual character of *iska*, the Talmud states:

> Now that we say that it is a semi-loan and a semi-trust, if he [the trader] wishes to drink beer therewith [i.e., for the loan part] he can do so. Rava said: [No.] It is therefore called *iska* [business] because he can say to him 'I gave it to you for trading, not for drinking beer.'"

Talmudic decisors regard Rava's position as normative.[2] Insofar as no *explicit* restriction was agreed to regarding the disposition of the *milveh* portion of the *iska*, Rava's position requires an explanation. Addressing himself to this issue, R. Solomon b. Isaac (Troyes, 1040–1105) regards the restriction to proceed from the implicit mandate *A* is operating under to manage the *iska* in a manner that maximizes *B*'s return on his investment. Because putting the *milveh* portion of the *iska* at risk in the venture effectively drives *A* to be more diligent in his management of the enterprise, *the requirement to do so* is self-evident in the agreement.[3] In a similar vein, *Tosafot* (12th-14th century school of French and German talmudic commentators) point out that the consequence of not investing the *milveh* in the venture is to expose immediately *B*'s entire capital to risk of loss, with no additional capital to draw upon if needed.

---

[1]The purpose of these regulations is to avoid violation of the rabbinic interdiction of *ribbit*, called *avak ribbit*. For a description of these regulations, see Aaron Levine, *Free Enterprise and Jewish Law: Aspects of Jewish Business Ethics* (New York: Ktav; Yeshiva University Press, 1980), pp. 165–170.

[2]Maimonides (Egypt, 1135–1204), *Yad, Sheluhin ve-Shutefin* 7:4; R. Jacob b. Asher (Germany, 1270–1343), *Tur, Yoreh De'ah* 177:42; R. Joseph Caro (Safed, 1488–1575), *Shulkhan Arukh, Yoreh De'ah* 177:30.

[3]R. Solomon b. Isaac, Rashi at *Bava Metziah* 104b, s.v. *l'hakhi*.

The implicit mandate to operate the *iska* to maximize B's gain, therefore, requires A to invest the *milveh* portion of the *iska* in the venture.[4] We should note that in respect to the *pikkadon* portion of the *iska*, a bailor-bailee (*mafkid-nifkad*) relationship exists between the financier and the active partner. A's use of the funds in a manner that departs from B's mandate constitutes misappropriation (*shelihut yad*).[5]

Proceeding from the above analysis is that the manager of an *iska* arrangement is under a *fiduciary* duty to the financier. Implicit in this duty is a mandate to maximize profits for the financier. Moreover, the manager's authority is limited to the pursuit of profits. This can be seen from a point in the law of charity as it pertains to *iska* profits: Suppose it is the widespread custom for business partners to devote 10 percent of their *iska* profits to charity. Here, the active partner, according to R. Moses Isserles, has no right to take it upon himself to donate 10 percent of the *iska* profits to charity. Instead, the financier is entitled to receive his full pretithing share of the profits and be given the opportunity to allocate his charity funds in a manner of his own choosing.[6]

Proceeding clearly from R. Isserles's ruling is that even when a business entity operates under an implicit mandate to donate a specific percentage of its profits to charity, the *disposition* of the charity funds is a matter of individual shareholder prerogative and does not fall under the purview of the business entity. How much more so does this judgment hold when the business entity operates without any understanding that a portion of its profits shall be devoted to charity?

Does the above conceptualization of the role of the manager extend from *iska* to the modern business entity? Recall that the salient feature of *iska* is that the financier is a silent partner and has no say in the running of the business. The modern business entity that most resembles *iska* is the *limited partnership*. This arrangement consists of general and limited partners. The general partners manage the business and are personally liable for its debts. The limited partners contribute capital and share in profits and losses, *but take no part in the running of the business*

[4]Tosafot, *Bava Metziah* 104b, s. v. *d'lo*.

[5]R. Moses Isserles (Poland, 1525 or 1530–1572), *Rama, Shulkhan Arukh, Yoreh De'ah* 177:5.

[6]*Rama*, op.cit., 177:22.

and incur no liability with respect to partnership obligations beyond their contributions to capital.

Given that *halakhah* severely circumscribes the discretion of the manager when the investor *agrees in advance to have no say* in the operation of the business enterprise, the same mandate should hold for the manager when the investors retain ultimate control in the decision-making of the business. In the modern scene, owners retain control when the business assumes the form of a single proprietorship, a partnership, or a closely held corporation. The halakhic conceptualization of the role of a manager of an *iska* should therefore apply equally to the manager within the above organizational structures.

The above thesis of limited discretion for the manager requires further clarification. Suppose the manager encounters a business opportunity which his mandate does not explicitly cover. Does the manager enjoy discretion to decide what is in the best interest of the owner? Bearing on this issue is the following ruling by the seventeenth-century decisor R. Joseph Trani (Venice, 1568–1639):

> Reuben consigned merchandise to Shimon, with the instruction to convey it to Egypt and sell it there. Reuben gave Shimon total discretion to decide on price and terms of sale. The agreement also set compensation for Shimon for a period of six months for his toil and effort. At the conclusion of the six-month period, Shimon was unsuccessful in finding customers for the merchandise. Seeing that the merchandise began to deteriorate, Shimon took it upon himself to sell it to a vizier on credit. The vizier resided outside Egypt. Subsequent to making this deal, Shimon agreed to sell his note on the vizier to Levi at a one-third discount. In turn, Levi committed himself to collect the debt from the vizier and within three months to make good to Shimon the prorated portion of the debt due him. Toward his obligation to Shimon, Levi made an immediate payment of 1,000 *girsh*.
>
> Shimon informed Reuben of his dealings. Reuben's response was "what you have done is done." Reuben also agreed to compensate Shimon for his toil and effort for the additional time he spent in Egypt.
>
> As matters turned out, Levi reneged on the deal, insisting on the return of his 1,000 *girsh*. Because Levi was a powerful individual, Shimon had no choice but to comply. To meet Levi's demand, Shimon borrowed 1,000 *girsh* from Judah. Thereupon Shimon set out to the port to book passage to the vizier and collect the debt from him. Shimon was, however, denied passage on the boat. He, then, turned to Judah for help. Judah agreed to book pas-

> sage, collect the debt from the vizier, and keep for himself 1,000 *girsh* as payment for his loan. Judah was successful in collecting the debt.

At issue here is whether Shimon is entitled to any share of the profits realized from the sale of the goods to the vizier. Since Reuben apparently acquiesced after the fact to the deal Shimon struck up with Levi, Shimon should take Levi's place in the deal as soon as the latter reneged. R. Trani ruled that Shimon is not entitled to any share of the profits. His claim consists only of compensation for toil and effort. Notwithstanding that Shimon acted in the best interest of Reuben, selling the merchandise on credit to someone who resides outside Egypt clearly exceeds Reuben's mandate. Reuben's subsequent acquiescence to the deal does not retroactively change the mandate Shimon must operate under. The matter at hand is analogous to the case recorded at *Bava Metziah* 22a. Here we are told that Mari bar Isak's sharecropper took it upon himself without authorization to honor a group of visiting rabbis with a platter of fruit. Mar Zutra refused to partake of the fruit even after Mari bar Isak joined the group and proclaimed to the sharecropper that he should have offered a better quality fruit platter to the rabbis. Rather than taking his remark as indicating genuine happiness that the sharecropper had offered the rabbis fruit, Mar Zutra felt the comment was said out of embarrassment (*kesufa*) so as not to appear miserly to the rabbis. Here too, Reuben's acquiescence to what Shimon did manifests only a desire on his part to extricate himself from the arrangement in the best possible manner. Expressing approval after the fact does not, however, change the circumstance that Shimon violated Reuben's mandate. The original arrangement therefore remains intact and Reuben hence is not required to share any of the profits with Shimon.[7]

THE RESPONSIBILITY OF THE FIRM TO ITS STAKEHOLDERS

As the agent of the owners of the business entity, the manager must carry out the responsibility of the owners to the stakeholders of the firm. In

[7]R. Joseph Trani, *Maharit, Hoshen Mishpat* 112.

this regard, *halakhah imposes* certain minimum duties on the firm vis-à-vis its stakeholders. These duties may not be abrogated by the owners of the firm. The role of the manager hence is to implement these duties whether or not they were explicitly given to him by the owners in the form of a mandate. Put a different way, the manager enjoys little discretion to determine what the firm's duty is to its various stakeholders, as halakhic principles will make this determination for him.

The following two examples illustrate the above proposition. The first concerns the disclosure obligation. Elsewhere, we have demonstrated that *halakhah* adopts the "reasonable man" standard. Applying the standard to advertising messages requires the firm to insure that its messages will not deceive the average man. It need not, however, be concerned if the message solely deludes the ignorant man.[8] For example, Coca-Cola comes up with a slogan: "Coke is it!" The company conducts a pilot test of this ad and finds that the great majority of those exposed to it understand the slogan to convey the claim that coke refreshes and tastes great. After running the ad, the company receives complaints that some people are reading into the ad that Coke is a cure for cancer (the "it" that they had long been searching for). Because the company has met the halakhic standard, it is not required to stop using the slogan "Coke is it!" so as not to deceive even the ignorant man. Here, the manager enjoys no discretion to accede to the pressure of the stakeholders who want Coca-Cola to revamp its advertising. If the manager desires to incur the expense of coming up with a new ad to satisfy the ignorant man, he may not do so without the *authorization* of the shareholders.

Severance pay provides another illustration of this principle. Suppose it is the long-standing practice of Boson Tea Company to pay out to a fired employee one month's salary for each year of employment. Given the frequency of the practice, severance pay of this amount becomes an implicit contractual item for employees of the firm.[9] Severance payment in excess of this amount would, however, requires the explicit authorization of the Boston Tea Company.

[8]Aaron Levine, *Economic Public Policy and Jewish Law* (Hoboken, NJ: Ktav Publishing House; Yeshiva University Press, 1993), pp. 67–92.

[9]R. Moshe Feinstein (New York, 1895–1986), *Iggerot Mosheh, Hoshen Mishpat* 1:75, anaf. 3.

LIFNIM MI-SHURAT HA-DIN AND MANAGERIAL DISCRETION

The proposition that the manager enjoys little discretion in determining what the firm's duties are vis-à-vis its stakeholders requires clarification in respect to the firm's duty to conduct itself *lifnim mi-shurat ha-din* (beyond the letter of the law).[10] Does the manager determine what *lifnim mi-shurat ha-din* conduct is on a case-by-case basis? Arguing for limited managerial discretion here is *Tosafot*'s formulation of this norm. In their view, this norm generally makes a claim only on an individual's time and effort but not on his financial resources. Accordingly, if the letter of the law does not require of the individual a financial outlay, *lifnim mi-shurat ha-din* conduct will generally not require it either.[11] To illustrate how this formulation operates to limit managerial discretion, let's return to the "Coke is it!" slogan. Suppose the company receives complaints that a few customers are reading into the slogan that Coke is the cure for cancer. Since the company's advertising copy satisfies the "reasonable man" standard, the manager enjoys no discretion to engage an advertising agency to come up with a new slogan that will not delude even the ignorant man. Such action requires the advance authorization of the shareholders.

A higher level of *lifnim mi-shurat ha-din* conduct,[12] exegetically derived from Proverbs 2:20, consists of waiving a damage claim against an employee who is guilty of negligence.[13] R. Joseph Hayyim b. Elijah al-Hakkam (Baghdad, 1834–1909) posits that such conduct is expected only of the ethical elite.[14] What follows is that without explicit authorization from the shareholders, the manager should enjoy no discretion to engage in this conduct.

The thrust of the above discussion should not be taken as asserting that the firm is not required to expend any resources to engage in *lifnim mi-shurat ha-din* conduct. Organizational structure cannot obviate the

---

[10]*Bava Kamma* 100a.

[11]*Tosafot, Bava Metziah* 24b, sv. *lifnim*.

[12]Ibid.

[13]*Bava Metziah* 83a.

[14]R. Joseph Hayyim b. Elijah al-Hakkam, *Ben Yehoyada, Bava Metziah* 83a.

lifnim mi-shurat ha-din obligation. An issue relating to customer service will illustrate the point: Lazarus is the owner-manager of a digital diary manufacturing company. Lazarus sells a unit of his product to Mishkin. Mishkin returns to the store after the expiration date of his warranty with the complaint that the data refuses to display on the screen. Mishkin requests that Lazarus use his expertise to retrieve his data for him.

Since the defect occurred after the warranty expired, Lazarus is under no *legal* obligation to accede to the request. But acceding to the request fulfills for Lazarus an aspect of the *mitzvah* of *hashavat avedah* (restoration of lost property).[15] To be sure, Lazarus is no more *obligated* than other experts to help Mishkin. Consider, however, that Lazarus both manufactured the unit and sold it to Mishkin. It becomes therefore a matter of *lifnim mi-shurat ha-din* conduct for Lazarus to exert himself for Mishkin and retrieve the data for him. Recall that *lifnim mi-shurat ha-din* conduct generally makes a claim only on an individual's time and effort but not on his financial resources. Accordingly, if Mishkin shows up with his request when the store is teeming with customers, Lazarus would be excused from immediately giving attention to Mishkin's problem, as doing so might result in a loss of business. To fulfill his *lifnim mi-shurat ha-din* duty, Lazarus should offer to look into Mishkin's problem within a specified period of time, say, within a week. During this interval, Lazarus should either attend to the problem during a lull in business or deal with the problem in off-business hours.

Let us now change the above scenario a bit. Suppose Lazarus removes himself from the day-to-day operation of his business and hires a manager for this purpose. Realizing that he devoted quite a chunk of time engaging in *lifnim mi-shurat ha-din* conduct, Lazarus sets out to *structure* the job of manager so as to eliminate *lifnim mi-shurat ha-din* conduct from the operation of the firm. Toward this end, Lazarus hires Kaldor and confers on him with a job with a description that is *guaranteed* to fill up his day. In respect to customer service, Lazarus instructs Kaldor that if the request is not covered by the warranty, it should be denied, albeit in a courteous fashion. Kaldor's contract calls for overtime pay if he works beyond normal business hours. Because the above arrangement makes *lifnim mi-shurat ha-din* conduct for Kaldor either a dereliction of duty or

---

[15]Deuteronomy 22:1–3.

triggers an obligation to pay him overtime, the plan effectively eliminates *lifnim mi-shurat ha-din* from the operation of the firm.

The above arrangement violates *halakhah*. The obligation to run a business vis-à-vis its stakeholders in a *lifnim mi-shurat ha-din* fashion resides squarely with the owners. It is the owners who must exert toil and effort in this regard. If the owners choose to remove themselves from the everyday operation of the business, they must designate surrogates to perform their duty for them, even if this entails an expenditure on their part. Setting up the business in a manner that eliminates the practice of *lifnim mi-shurat ha-din* is therefore unacceptable.

What follows from the above analysis is that a policy that routinely denies customer requests that fall outside the terms of their *legal* entitlement violates *lifnim mi-shurat ha-din* law. Instead, accommodations with the customer should be made when it entails no cost for the firm. If acceding to the requests entails an out-of-pocket expense, this expense may, of course, be passed on to the customer. But, the *lifnim mi-shurat ha-din* negotiation should not be converted into a *profit* opportunity for an additional service rendered. Moreover, to charge the manager with the above policy only when he or she is not busy with new business is unacceptable. Doing so makes *lifnim mi-shurat ha-din* an occasional or seasonal practice, when it should be a permanent and constant feature of business practice.

THE BUSINESS JUDGMENT RULE AND *HALAKHAH*

What emerges from the above discussion is a clear-cut difference between *halakhah* on the one hand and secular law on the other in respect to the *normative* role of the manager of a business corporation.

In secular law, the manager of a corporation is subject to the duty of due care. This, in effect, requires the manager to exercise the kind of care than an ordinarily prudent person would exercise in a similar position and under similar circumstances.

Although held to a standard of reasonable care, a manager is not liable for honest mistakes of judgment. Under this so called *business judgment rule*, a court will not hold a manager liable for the consequences of a decision, even if harm resulted to the corporation, so long as the manager made a reasonably informed decision and apparently acted in a good-faith belief at the time that the decision was in the best interests of the corporation.[16]

In sharp contrast, *halakhah* keeps the manager on a short leash. Any action not falling within his mandate must be turned back to the shareholders for approval before it can be implemented.

BUSINESS SOCIAL RESPONSIBILITY AND *HALAKHAH*

Denying the manager discretion in deciding what the duties of the firm are vis-à-vis its stakeholders does not preclude the possibility for the firm to engage in altruism. All that is needed is proper authorization from the owners of the firm. The nature of this authorization will depend upon the type of altruism involved. Two categories of altruism can be identified:

1. "Do-Good" Projects for Society at Large

In Judaism, the charity obligation is both an individual responsibility and the responsibility of society as a collective.[17] Philanthropy implemented by means of managerial discretion hence *co-opts* both individual and government prerogatives.

Moreover, given that the manager operates under a mandate to manage a business or invest capital, using the resources entrusted to him for altruistic projects amounts to diverting funds from their intended use and amounts therefore to *shelihut yad* (misappropriation).

Given the above considerations, minority shareholders should have a right to veto "do-good" projects for society at large. Authorization

---

[16]John R. Allison, Robert A. Prentice, and Rate A. Howell, *Business Law, Text and Cases*, 5th ed. (Chicago, Dryden Press, 1991), p. 685.

[17]R. Hayyim Soloveichik (Russia, 1853–1918), quoted in the name of Rabbi Joseph B. Soloveichik by Rabbi Daniel Lander, "*Be-Inyan Dei Mahsoro*," in *Kavod ha-Rav* (New York: Student Organization of Yeshiva Rabbi Isaac Elchanan Theological Seminary, 1984), pp. 202–206. For an elaboration of this thesis and its implication for public policy, see Aaron Levine, *Economics and Jewish Law* (Hoboken, NJ: Ktav Publishing House, Yeshiva University Press, 1987), pp. 127–129.

for such projects therefore requires unanimous consent of the shareholders.

Supporting the above contention is R. Solomon b. Abraham Adret's comment regarding the limits of communal legislative authority. The specifics involved the validity of a communal practice of taxing a resident on the basis of his ownership of assets located in a different town. Since the edict effectively subjects a segment of the community to "double taxation," R. Adret ruled that the provision amounted to outright robbery.[18] His ruling implies that a majority decision violates minority rights when the body making the decision has no authority to deal with the issue at hand. Similarly, a majority vote by shareholders of a business organization to commit resources of the firm to "do-good" projects for society at large violates the rights of the minority shareholders, as undertaking the project changes the goals of the organization.

2. Altruism Which Is Presented as Business Investment

Illustrating this genre of altruism is the introduction of a pension plan for the employees of the firm. If competitive pressure is not prompting this initiative, the proposed expenditure cannot be categorized as a necessary business expense. Various rationales could motivate the proposal. One possibility is that it reflects management's notion of industrial justice. Another possibility is that it represents management's belief that employee productivity will rise in response to the firm's demonstration of commitment to their future well-being. Still another possibility is that the proposal reflects elements of both convictions. Since a long-run profit motive behind the pension plan proposal is not clear-cut, it may not be implemented without the approval of the shareholders. If majority decision regards the plan as consistent with long-run profit maximization for the firm, the plan assumes the character of a business investment. Minority protestation that the expenditure in reality is a disguised form of altruism is rejected. With majority vote *defining* the investment character of the expenditure, no shareholder has the right to demand that his prorated share of the firm's resources should not be expended on the plan.

---

[18]R. Solomon b. Abraham Adret (Spain, ca. 1235–1310), *Responsa Rashba* 1:788.

Another example of the second category of altruism is the indigent patient program of a pharmaceutical company. Under this program, qualified indigent patients receive brand-name prescription drugs free of charge. Some shareholders might object to the program, regarding it as pure and simple philanthropy. Since the company was organized as a business with the aim of making profit for its shareholders, it has no right to engage in philanthropy. Other shareholders might regard the program as a prudent investment. It serves to head off government legislation to regulate the price of pharmaceuticals. Moreover, the program will generate substantial good will among consumers and hence work to increase sales. Since the business motive behind the program is debatable, management enjoys no discretion to introduce the program without shareholder approval. Again, a two-tier approval process is indicated. First, the shareholders should decide by majority vote whether they consider the project to be philanthropy or a business investment, consistent with long-run profitability for the firm. Should majority decision decide that it falls into the category of philanthropy, the item immediately moves off the firm's agenda. On the other hand, should the shareholders regard the project as an investment expenditure, majority decision will decide whether the recommendation of management should be followed.

HALAKHAH AND THE NEOCLASSICAL STAKEHOLDER THEORY DEBATE

The analysis above has identified significant differences between *halakhah* on the one hand and the neoclassical and stakeholder theories on the other hand regarding the *normative* role of the manager of a business enterprise. In stakeholder theory, the shareholders are seen as but one of many stakeholders exerting a claim on the resources and policies of the firm. The fiduciary duty the managers owe the shareholders is not seen as automatically overriding other claims made on the firm. The theory provides neither a criterion for evaluating the merit of a stakeholder's claim on the firm nor a guidepost for mediating between competing claims. All this is apparently left to the discretion of the manager.[19] In sharp contrast, in the halakhic system, the fiduciary duty

[19]See John R. Boatright, *Ethics and the Conduct of Business*, 2nd ed. (Upper Saddle River, NJ: Prentice-Hall, 1997), p. 363.

of the manager to the shareholder is overriding and translates into a profit-maximizing mandate for the manager. Moreover, the manager operates under a short leash, enjoying little discretion to use his own judgment to decide what is in the best interest of the shareholders. In respect to the profit-maximizing mandate, an affinity between *halakhah* and the neoclassical school can be seen. But *halakhah* breaks sharply with the neoclassical school in its conceptualization of the firm's duties to its stakeholders. As the shareholders' agent, the manager must carry out their duties to the firm's stakeholders. What these duties are is not a matter of managerial discretion, but rather is determined by halakhic moral principles which translate into specific duties. The responsibility of the manager is to carry out these duties whether the shareholders specifically mandated them or not.

RABBI WALTER WURZBURGER ON CORPORATE SOCIAL RESPONSIBILITY

In this volume, Rabbi Walter Wurzburger argues in favor of corporate social responsibility. Our purpose here will be to provide a critique of his thesis.

Rabbi Wurzburger's thesis begins with the premise that *halakhah* imposes a variety of both positive and negative duties on an individual when he interacts with his fellow man as a principal. These duties do not suddenly disappear within the context of the operation of a business entity. Regardless of how the business entity is organized, the manager is the agent of natural rather than artificial people—individuals who themselves are subject to moral imperatives. Being hired as a manager does not allow the individual to adopt an attitude that his function is solely to serve the best interests of his principals with no regard for the social consequences of his actions.[20]

The above proposition argues only for social responsibility in the form of *mandated* halakhic duties. In respect to these duties, shareholders cannot use organizational structure and chain of command as a mechanism to reduce or abrogate what *halakhah* requires of them as principals. In a similar vein, as the agent of the shareholders, the manager must

[20]Please turn to p.147 of this volume.

conduct himself with the stakeholders of the firm as *halakhah* requires, whether or not the specific situation at hand was covered by his mandate. To illustrate, suppose the shareholders issue a policy directive that, in the event an employee-at-will is fired, no notice should be given. Since *halakhah* requires notice,[21] the manager must disregard this directive. The rights of the employee here will be backed up by the Jewish court.

Indeed, the firm which governs itself by *halakhah* should be designated an *altruistic firm*. This is so because some of these *mandated* duties are of the type that firms would not voluntarily assume on the basis of enlightened self-interest. A case in point is the opportunity-cost approach *halakhah* takes in respect to the pricing of prescription drugs and its very protective privacy laws.[22]

But, Rabbi Wurzburger calls for business social responsibility beyond the level of halakhic mandated duties. Recall that he advocates that corporations should provide scholarships for the children of their employees and should donate funds to educational institutions.[23] Because these expenditures work to upgrade skill and increase productivity, they undoubtedly contain an investment element. But these benefits will, for the most part, be enjoyed by society at large, rather than captured by the firm making the expenditure. From the standpoint of the firm, the expenditure is certainly not an optimal investment. Given that the initiatives are neither prescribed by *halakhah* as a stakeholder duty nor do they satisfy for the manager his profit maximizing duty to the shareholders, the projects cannot be undertaken without prior shareholder approval.

CORPORATE ALTRUISM AND COERCION

Another halakhic concern in connection with corporate altruism is that this practice sets in motion a likely scenario that entails unlawful coercion. By way of illustrating this moral pitfall, let us return to Rabbi Wurzburger's proposal that the corporation provide college tuition schol-

[21]*Piskei Din shel Battei ha-Din ha-Rabbaniyim be Yisrael*, 3:281–283.

[22]Please turn to pp. 75–111 of this volume.

[23]Please turn to pp. 40–42 of this volume.

arships for the children of its employees. Suppose Roberts, the CEO of Boston Tea Company, presents this proposal to the company's board of directors. The board of directors rejects the proposal. Taking the rejection personally, Roberts threatens to resign if his proposal is not accepted. Out of fear that Boston Tea will plunge into turmoil without Roberts's leadership, the board turns around and votes in favor of the project. Roberts's conduct here is morally objectionable. Elsewhere, we have detailed the halakhic case that Roberts's action may constitute extortion and/or coercion.[24]

Rabbi Wurzburger objects to the above reasoning. Were my analysis correct, he reasons, all professional fundraising by charitable institutions should be put to question.[25] Rabbi Wurzburger confuses persuasion with coercion. Inducing an individual to cooperate by expanding that person's options constitutes persuasion and is a permissible action. Inducing someone to cooperate by reducing that person's options is, however, coercion and is prohibited.[26] Now, if the fund-raiser overcomes the initial resistance of the would-be donor by *deepening* his appreciation for the cause, the solicitation should be viewed as persuasion and hence permissible. If, on the other hand, the solicitor overcomes the initial resistance by suggesting that refusing to contribute will antagonize some of his close business associates and jeopardize future business, the solicitation should be viewed as coercion and hence prohibited. Roberts's ultimatum to the board clearly falls into the latter category.

CORPORATE ALTRUISM AND MISPLACED PRIORITIES

Another concern corporate altruism raises in *halakhah* is the issue of misplaced priorities. A firm that engages in "do-good" projects for soci-

---

[24]Aaron Levine, "Aspects of the Ideology of Capitalism and Judaism," in David Shatz, Chaim I. Waxman, and Nathan Diament, *Tikkun Olam, Social Responsibility in Jewish Thought and Law* (Northvale, NJ: Jason Aronson, 1997), pp. 83–88.

[25]Please turn to p. 43 of this volume.

[26]The distinction between persuasion and coercion made in the text is taken from Paul Heyne, *The Economic Way*, 6th ed. (New York: Macmillan, 1991), p. 367.

ety at large, while paying its workers below-industry average wages and falling behind in paying its bills, evidences skewed priorities. This can engender only cynicism by the underprivileged or mistreated parties, contaminating the moral climate of society. In response, media and insider pressure for the firm to set its own house straight before engaging in altruism for society at large is warranted. Elsewhere, we have detailed the halakhic basis for objecting to corporate altruism that entails misplaced priorities. The halakhic principle involved is called *yohara* (false piety).[27]

CORPORATE ALTRUISM AND THE PUBLICLY TRADED COMPANY

We now turn to the issue of altruistic projects sponsored by publicly traded companies. Our concern here will be altruism not mandated by *halakhah*. From the standpoint of *halakhah*, the legal relationship between the manager and shareholders of a business is determined by the mandate the former agrees to operate under. Organizational structure per se does not alter this mandate. Accordingly, for a given mandate, the manager of a publicly traded company enjoys no more discretion than his counterpart situated in a business organized differently. The judgment that altruistic projects take the manager beyond the parameters of his given mandate holds therefore for the publicly traded company as well.

Altruistic projects sponsored by publicly traded companies are today a frequently encountered phenomenon. Given the frequency of corporate altruism, the practice, according to Rabbi Wurzburger, should be viewed as enjoying the tacit consensus of the shareholders.[28]

The above argument has, however, limited applicability. Suppose shareholders launch a class action suit against management for engaging in corporate altruism projects. Here, the tacit consensus argument can be invoked to knock down the claim of misappropriation. Given the long history of the practice, corporate altruism does not dash the legiti-

---

[27]Levine "Aspects of the Ideology of Capitalism and Judaism," op. cit., pp. 288–289.

[28]Please turn to p. 42 of this volume.

mate expectations of investors. Plaintiff's claim of misappropriation is hence unproved. But, long-standing practice does not make for *clear-cut shareholder approval*. Note that the salient feature of the public corporation is *diffusion* of ownership. Changing managerial policy hence requires a considerable expenditure of time and resources in the form of marshaling sufficient support among fellow shareholders for the change. Far from signaling shareholder approval, lack of protest against corporate "do-good" projects may reflect an attitude that given the tiny percentage[29] of the firm's resources involved, the effort to overhaul the practice is not worth it. Ironically, one concern might be that such a campaign would tarnish the image of the firm, projecting it as "mean spirited." Removing "do-good" projects from the firm's agenda might leave the public in doubt as to whether the firm discharges its mandated duties to its shareholders.

Recall that *halakhah* requires a manager to operate under a clear-cut mandate. Seeking ex post approval for unauthorized action does not suffice. The survival of the corporate "do-good" phenomenon may very well provide a classical example of the operation of the talmudic *kesufa* principle referred to earlier.

In recent years, statutes in over half the states, as well as case law in the state of Delaware, have authorized directors of a public corporation to consider the interests of corporate stakeholders other than shareholders. These non-shareholder constituencies include employees, creditors, and local communities.[30] The import of this development is to give stakeholders *advance* notice that a percentage of their investment dollars may very well be used for social welfare causes which will result in less than profit maximization for their share value.

To be sure, the above development moves corporate structure in the direction of reducing shareholder dashed expectations when the public company engages in altruistic projects. But, this approach is far from optimal. To illustrate: suppose *New Haven Tea Inc.* devotes 1 percent of

---

[29]Few corporate contributions exceed 1 percent of pretax profits. (John R. Boatright, *Ethics and Conduct of Business*, 2nd ed. [Upper Saddle River, NJ: Prentice-Hall, 1997], p. 348.

[30]Eric W. Orts, "Beyond Stakeholders: Interpreting Corporate Constituency Statutes," *George Washington Law Review*, 61(1) (November 1992):16, 26–31.

its net profits to altruistic projects over a number of years and suddenly changes that percentage to 2 percent. Does not the change in policy dash the legitimate expectations of shareholders? Similarly, suppose that *New Haven Tea* sticks with the 1-percent allocation but increases its outlays for "do-good" projects for society at large and reduces its expenditures on *lifnim mi-shurat ha-din* conduct vis-à-vis its immediate stakeholders. Here, the change in policy not only dashes shareholder and especially *stakeholder* expectations, but also introduces skewed priorities and hence violates halakhah. Finally, suppose *New Haven Tea* introduces a check-off system, wherein 5 percent of employee wages are earmarked for donation to a choice of three charities, say, the Red Cross, the American Cancer Association, and United Way. Since this policy co-opts the employee's legitimate prerogative to donate to the charity of his or her choice, *halakhah* would find disfavor with it.

An approach more consistent with *halakhah* would require all public corporations to deal with the issues of altruism in their charter of incorporation. Specifically, the percentage of net profits to be devoted to corporate altruism should be specified. How these funds should be allocated between "do-good" projects for society at large and *lifnim mi-shurat ha-din* conduct toward the corporation's immediate stakeholders should be designated. Finally, the charter should provide measures to insure that neither skewed priorities nor the co-opting of employee prerogatives will be introduced.

VEILED MISCONDUCT AND MORAL EDUCATION

The asymmetric information phenomenon both equips and tempts the seller in the marketplace to engage in veiled misconduct. In this volume, Professor Jonas Prager compares the economic-legal and halakhic approaches to this problem. In the economic-legal approach, firms themselves, buyers, and third parties attempt to level the playing field with a variety of confidence-building measures, including reputational signals, purchaser monitoring, and government regulation. Would an economy operated according to halakhic standards function differently? Professor Prager's answer is "not really."[31] I disagree.

[31]Please turn to p. 143 of this volume.

My purpose here will be to extend Professor Prager's discussion of Judaism's moral preachments against veiled misconduct. I will demonstrate that these exhortations support a clear-cut advocacy of moral education. The case for public subsidization of moral education will be made.

From a Torah perspective, the root cause of veiled misconduct is the failure of the home and the school to achieve effective moral training. Judaism's primary countervailing force against veiled misconduct is *character building* in the form of effective moral training. Without vigorous public commitment to moral training, increased government deterrence efforts may, ironically, work only to spur wrongdoers to more sophisticated means of avoiding detection and/or to shift veiled misconduct to industries where government monitoring is less aggressive.

MORAL EDUCATION

The case for moral education begins with the recognition that invisible misconduct manifests a failure on the part of the perpetrator to meet the standard of *yirat shamayyim* (fear of Heaven) that the Torah expects from him. This can be seen by the Torah's selective use of the phrase "*And you shall fear your God*" in connection with its admonitions relating to interpersonal conduct.[31a] Use of this phrase is reserved for instances where the target of the admonition may convince himself that he can violate the norm without detection and hence avoid loss of social standing.[32]

Admonishing veiled misconduct with the phrase "*And you shall fear your God*"conveys the notion that overcoming a test of piety is a matter of strengthening one's *yirat shamayyim*. But, *yirat shamayyim* cannot be fos-

---

[31a]The Torah makes use of the phrase, "And you shall fear your God" in connection with the following moral imperatives: (1) the prohiition against offering ill-sited advice (Leviticus 19:14); (2) the duty to bestow honor to a talmudic scholar (Leviticus 19:32); (3) the injunction against causing someone needless mental anguish (Leviticus 25:17); (4)the interdict against charging interest (Leviticus 25:36); and (5) the prohibition against working a Hebrew bondsman oppressively (Leviticus 25:43).

[32]Kiddushin 32b, and R. Solomon b. Isaac (Troyes, 1040–1105), Rashi, s.v. *davar ha-masur la-lev*.

tered in a vacuum: "*A boor cannot be fearful of sin*" (*Avot* 2:6). To be an effective deterrent against veiled misconduct, *yirat shamayyim* must be cultivated in an individual from early childhood. The Sages assigned parents[33] and re-

[33]The father's moral-educational role proceeds most directly from the *mitzvah* of *hinnukh*. This rabbinically mandated *mitzvah* requires the father to train his children in the performance of *mitzvot* that they will be subject to when they reach adulthood (*Hagigah* 4a). Similarly, this *mitzvah* assigns the father an interventionist role whenever he observes his children engaged in wrongdoing, with the additional duty to scold them for their misconduct. Cf. R. Joseph Caro, *Shulkhan Arukh, Orah Hayyim* 343:1. The father's role of remonstrator continues, of course, even after his children reach adulthood by dint of the pentateuchal *mitzvah* of *tokhahah* (reproof; Leviticus 19:17).

The *hinnukh* a son receives in normative conduct is potentially reinforced by dint of the father's pentateuchal obligation to teach him Torah (*Kiddushin* 29a). This obligation requires the father to teach his son the entire *Torah She-biktav* (Written law; cf. *Shulkhan Arukh, Yoreh De'ah* 245:6 and comments ad loc. of *Taz*, no. 2 and *Shakh*, note 5).

For a glimpse at how the moral-educational role of the father worked itself out in practice, see R. Israel Ibn Al-Nakawa (Spain, 14th century), *Menorat ha-Maor*, ed. H. G. Enelow, vol. 4, c. 2, (New York: Bloch, 1932), p. 145.

For the mother's role as enabler in connection with the *mitzvah* of *Talmud Torah*, see *Berakhot* 17a. For the mother's obligation to transmit the experience of Sinai to her children, see R. Ahron Soloveichik, "The Fire of Sinai," in *Building Jewish Ethical Character*, ed. Joseph Kaminetsky and Murray I. Friedman (New York: Fryer Foundation, 1975), p. 12.

Authorities dispute whether the sages imposed the *mitzvah* of *hinnukh* on the mother. For opposing views, cf. R. Abraham Abele b. Hayyim ha-Levi Gombiner (Poland, ca. 1637–1683), *Magen Avraham* to *Shulkhan Arukh, Orah Hayyim* 343, no. 1, and R. Samuel b. Nathan ha-Levi Kolin (Bohemia, 1720–1806), *Mahatzit ha-Shekel* to *Shulkhan Arukh, Orah Hayyim* 343, n. 1. In any case, *halakhah* assigns a vital role to the mother as a moral educator of her children. One manifestation of this role is the mother's responsibility to scold her children for their wrongdoing. In this regard many authorities assign greater responsibility to the mother than the father; cf. R. Isaiah ha-Levi Horowitz (Poland, 1565–1630), *Shelah, Sh'ar ha-Otiot, ot Derekh Eretz*.

For a description of the vital role mothers historically assumed in the moral education of their daughters, see R. Moses b. Hanoch, *Sefer Brontshpiegel*, quoted and translated by Solomon Schimmel, "Ethical Dimensions of Traditional

ligious educational institutions the duty to impart religious instruction and training (*hinnukh*) to youth.[34] Moral education is certainly one aspect of this mission:

> R. Zeira further ruled: One should not promise a child to give him something and then not give it to him, because he will thereby teach him lying, as it is said: They have taught their tongues to speak lies . . . (Jeremiah 9:4).[35]
>
> It is necessary to be exceptionally careful with children, so as to teach them to speak the truth without swearing, in order that they should not become accustomed to continual use of oaths, in the manner of the heathens. This procedure is as much as a duty incumbent upon their parents and upon the teachers of the young . . .[36]

In the thinking of R. Isaiah ha-Levi Horowitz, training in truth telling is the centerpiece of the moral training of youth. The ideal is for the father to spare no effort in emphasizing to his child the importance of truth-telling. Toward this end, a father should magnify for his child the punishment for those who lie, and glorify for the child the reward for those who speak truthfully. If the child is caught lying, the father should admonish him harshly, instilling great trepidation in him. This approach will guarantee that the child will always follow the straight path, even when not under the supervision of the father. Because the child will feel forced always to tell the truth, he will always feel compelled to depart from evil and do good.[37]

Further insight into the connection between truth telling and the ability to resist the temptation of veiled misconduct can be gathered by the connection the Sages make between truth telling and belief in God:

He who speaks truth harbors *belief* (*emunah*) in God. [In contrast] chronic liars harbor idolatrous fancies.[38]

Jewish Education, in *Studies in Jewish Education*, vol. 1, ed. Barry Chazen (Jerusalem: Magnes Press, 1983), pp. 94–95.

[34]*Bava Batra* 21a.

[35]*Sukkah* 46b.

[36]Maimonidies, *Yad, Shevu'ot* 12:8.

[37]R. Isaiah ha-Levi Horowitz, *Shnei Lukhot ha-Berit, Shaar ha-Otiyot* 4.

[38]*Midrash Pinhas*.

R. Eleazer also said: If one dissembles his speech it is as though he had engaged in idolatry: Here it is written, And I shall seem to him as a deceiver (Genesis 27:12); and elsewhere it is said, they are vanity, and the work of deceivers.[39]

The key to understanding the connection between deceptive speech and idolatry, according to R. Judah Leow b. Bezalel (Prague, ca. 1525–1609), is that the seal of the Almighty is truth. He who possesses the attribute of truthfulness therefore *clings to the Almighty Himself*. To engage in deceptive speech amounts, however, to embracing something that has no existence at all. What idolatry and deceptive speech share is that both are vanities; that is, they are matters which have no real existence. Hence, whoever dissembles his speech is considered as though he engaged in idolatry.[40]

Judaism's standard for truth telling makes it a sin to lie even when the fabrication causes no harm or damage to others. Two varieties of harmless lies are identified; namely, the lie that brings the prevaricator some advantage or benefit, and the lie that brings the speaker no discernible benefit. Both varieties are prohibited by Torah law. The latter variety is more egregious and therefore warrants greater punishment[41] because it reflects a love of falsehood for its own sake.[42]

SELFISHNESS AND THE ABILITY TO PERCEIVE TRUTH

Hinnukh efforts directed at truth-telling face a formidable barrier in the form of man's natural inclination toward selfishness, greed, and self-

---

[39]Jeremiah 10:15 (*Sanhedrin* 92a).

[40]R. Judah Loew b. Bezalel (Prague, ca. 1525–1609), *Hiddushei Aggadot, Sanhedrin* 92a.

[41]R. Jonah b. Abraham Gerondi (Spain, ca. 1200–1264), *Sha'ari Teshuvah, sha'ar* 3:186; R. Israel Meir ha-Kohen Kagan (Radin, 1838–1933), *Sefat Tamim* 6; *Yad ha-Ketanna, De'ot* 10, note 9; R. Eliezer Judah Waldenberg, *Responsa Tzitz Eliezer* 15:12. A minority position in this matter is advanced by R. Eliezer b. Samuel of Metz (ca. 1175). In his view, a falsehood that generates no harm or damages to someone else does not violate Torah law (*Yere'im* 235). In R. Waldenberg's opinion *(Tzitz Eliezer, ad loc.)*, *Yere'im* would be in agreement that such a falsehood is nevertheless *prohibited* by dint of rabbinical decree.

[42]*Sefat Tamim*, op. cit.

aggrandizement. These tendencies distort our ability to perceive truth and to act with integrity.

Because greed blinds man's perception of truth and what constitutes integrity, successful moral training in the attribute of truth (*emet*) perforce must include training against selfish conduct.

Moral training against selfishness begins with the notion that denying one's fellow a benefit when it costs one nothing constitutes obnoxious conduct. The Sages identified such conduct with the sin of Sodom.[43] If we can only muster up lip service for the Sages' condemnation against sodomitic conduct, our moral training against selfishness stands on a weak foundation. To make advanced inroads against the attribute of greed one must both *believe* on an intellectual level and *feel* on an emotional level that sodomitic conduct is obnoxious.

It would therefore be a mistake to begin the moral training of youth with notions of generosity, while skipping, as unnecessary, condemnation against sodomitic conduct. Such an approach places the child's moral education on a shaky foundation because it takes society's *condemnation* of sodomitic conduct for granted. As a means of illustrating that society's notions against sodomitic conduct require considerable reinforcement, consider the following scenario: *A* meets his neighbor *B* at a social affair many miles from their respective homes. *A* drove to the function in his car. *B* arrived by means of a car service. The encounter is unexpected by both parties. Upon exchanging pleasantries, *A* becomes aware that *B* arrived at the affair by car service and offers him a ride home. Notwithstanding that the gesture allows *B* to save the cost of a car service on his return trip, it is unethical for *A* to request *B* to pay tolls on the drive home. Since *A* would bear the expense of tolls in any case and *B* does nothing to increase *A*'s expense, it is Sodomitic to request *B* to make this payment.

In the above scenario it has become almost common practice for the passenger (*B*) to offer to pay the tolls. In everyday practice, the driver (*A*) sometimes accepts the offer and sometimes does not. Now, if *A* re-

---

[43]Cf. Ketubot 103a. For an excellent survey and analysis of the *kofin* principle in the talmudic and responsa literature, see Dr. Shmuel Shilo, "*Kofin al Midot Sedom: Jewish Law's Concept of Abuse of Rights, Israel Law Review*," 15(1) (1980): 49–78.

ally regarded *requesting* his passenger to pay the tolls as *obnoxious*, he would never take up *B* on his offer to pay the tolls!!

MORAL TRAINING AND CONTROLLING ENVY

To be sure, it is man's inclination toward greed that distorts his perception of truth and of what constitutes integrity. But it is envy that fuels greed and hence intensifies it considerably. Effective moral training in the attribute of *emet* therefore requires training against envy.

But the Sages did not view envy as a totally evil trait. Witness the talmudic aphorism: "*kinat soferim tarbeh hokhmah* (jealousy between scholars increases wisdom)."[44] The objective is therefore not to *suppress jealousy entirely* but rather to *sublimate* it into healthy channels.

Supportive of the notion that controlling envy assumes a central role in moral training is an analysis of the socioeconomic life of the Jewish people in biblical times in the forty-year period of Wilderness (*dor hamidbar*). One feature of the economic life of that time was the *manna*, which descended from Heaven on a daily basis.

The society of *manna* was not a historical curiosity. Its diadic role for all posterity is clearly indicated by the following instruction Moses gave to Aaron ". . . take one jar and put a full *omer* of *manna* into it; place it before the Eternal for a *safekeeping* for your generations" (Exodus 16:13). In what manner did the *manna* serve as a *safekeeping*? Perhaps the answer lies in the control this society exerted over the expression of envy in the daily lives of the people. Let's investigate the role envy played in this society. We begin with the material dimension.

Notwithstanding that no one in the society of *manna* had to engage in any profession or trade to earn a livelihood, deriving sustenance from the *manna* is termed by the Torah an *affliction*: "Who fed you in the wilderness with *manna*, which your fathers know not; that he might *afflict* you . . ." (Deuteronomy, 8:16). Commenting on why deriving sustenance from the *manna* is regarded as an affliction, the Talmud, offers the following rationale:

---

[44]*Bava Batra* 22a.

> R. Ammi and R. Assi [are disputing], one said, you cannot compare one who has bread in his basket with one who has none. The other said: You cannot compare one who sees what he eats with one who does not see what he is eating. R. Joseph said: This is an allusion to [the reason] why blind people eat without becoming satisfied.[45]

The view that regards the *manna* as a form of affliction because it was of unchanging appearance requires further elucidation. Preliminarily, we take note that underlying this view is the dictum that the *manna*, with few exceptions,[46] imparted whatever food taste the consumer conjured up as he partook of it.[47] Now, since one's imagination could cause the *manna* to produce practically any food taste, the *manna*'s failure to assume the actual form of the food item experienced was a matter of frustration, generating a feeling of deprivation. Adding to this feeling of deprivation was the presumed failure of the *manna* to emit the aroma of the food item being experienced.[48] But, why was this deprivation effect necessary?

Addressing himself to this issue, R. Menahem Mendel of Rimanov (1745–1815) posits that God limited the amenities of the consumption experience of the *manna* to reduce feelings of jealousy. As long as A's consumable *manna* was *outwardly* the same as B's consumable *manna*, invidious comparisons could not be made. But, if A's *manna* took on a specific form and color and emitted an aroma, then, B, even though he could duplicate for himself A's consumption experience, would imagine that A derives greater pleasure from his consumption experience than himself. Outward differences in *manna* inevitably produce invidious comparisons.[49]

---

[45]*Yoma* 74b.

[46]One Amoraic opinion recorded at *Yoma* 75a; *Pesikta Zutrata B-ha-alotkha*. The exceptions were the taste of cucumbers, melons, leeks, onions, and garlic. The *manna* could not substitute for these foods because they were injurious to women in pregnancy.

[47]*Yoma* 75a; *Tosefta Sotah* 4:1; *Exodus Rabbah* 25:3.

[48]The *Torah Discourses of the Holy Tzaddik Reb Menachem Mendel of Rimanov* (1745–1815), translated by Dov Levine (Hoboken, NJ: Ktav Publishing House, 1996), p. 543.

[49]Ibid, pp. 543–547.

What *manna's* limitations as a real food did was to produce a *net benefit* for Jewish society. On the one hand, these limitations were felt as detracting from the potential *utility* of the consumption experience. But, at the same time, this circumstance weakened the force of envy and therefore worked to foster a level of spiritual growth, otherwise not possible.

To be sure, envy was not absent in the society of *manna*. Consider that the necessary exertion and time spent in both gathering in the *manna* as well as preparing it for consumption varied widely. Time spent and effort exerted here was inversely proportional to one's spiritual status. Everyday life in the society of *manna* was no laid-back existence. People were *graded* on a daily basis on their level of spiritual status. Invidious comparisons were surely made. Instead of playing out in the material realm, these jealousies played out in the spiritual realm.

What the above analysis points up to is that *manna* was preserved as a *safekeep* for future generations because it presented for posterity a model of how envy should be dealt with. In the material realm, concerted efforts should be made to reduce envy; but in the spiritual realm jealousy should be viewed not just as a tolerable evil but rather as a *positive good*. We must recognize that envy is a human trait and that it cannot be eliminated from human society. If envy is suppressed in one realm, it surely will seek expression elsewhere. To successfully reduce envy in the material realm, a proper incentive–disincentive system must be set up to foster competition in the spiritual realm. The exact form this competition should take will, of course, be a matter of debate. But, one thing is for certain, new directions from current attitudes and practices are needed. To cite one example: the current attitude in many circles is that testing post-high-school students in Torah study programs is in conflict with or at least detracts from the ideal of studying Torah for its own sake.[50] Injecting competitive pressures into the Torah educational enterprise at all levels should, however, provide a solid example of how jealousy can be directed into a healthy outlet.

---

[50]R. Herbert W. Bomzer, *The Kolel in America* (New York: Shengold Press, 1985), p. 24. For R. Bomzer's suggestions for improving evaluation and accountability in the Kolel, see, Bomger, op. cit., pp. 141–142.

HAKKARAT HA-TOV (GRATITUDE) AND THE MORAL PERSONALITY[51]

Another key to the moral personality is the character trait of *hakkarat ha-tov* (gratitude). In developing this point, let's examine the biblical narrative of Joseph's struggle in overcoming the wiles of Lady Potiphar, together with the Talmudic account of this incident:

> He adamantly refused. He reasoned with his master's wife. "My master does not even know what I do in the house. He has entrusted me with everything he was. No one in this house has more power than I have. He has not kept back anything at all from me, except for you, his wife. How could I do such a great wrong? It would be a sin before God!"[52]
>
> The woman grabbed him by his cloak. "Sleep with me!" she pleaded. He ran away from her, leaving his cloak in her hand, and fled outside. At that moment, his father's image appeared to him through the window and said, "Joseph, your brothers will have their names inscribed upon the stones of the *ephod* (sash of the high priest's robe) and yours amongst theirs. Is it your wish to have your name expunged from amongst theirs and be called an associate of harlots?!" Immediately his bow abode in strength. R. Johanan said in the name of R. Meir: [This means] that his passion subdued.[53]

What emerges from the above descriptions of Joseph's struggle against sin is the equation of moral turpitude with betrayal. Joseph made this equation on several levels.

On one level, proceeding from biblical narrative itself, Joseph equated succumbing to Lady Potiphar with *betraying* the trust of her husband, who was his master. Logic does not compel that a test of piety be interpreted as a test of loyalty to Potiphar. Clearly, it was Joseph's revulsion at being an ingrate that pushed this equation on him. In other words, Joseph's deep sense of *hakkarat ha-tov* (gratitude) to Potiphar *personalized* his dilemma, tearing him between lust and loyalty.

---

[51]This section draws from my work *Economic Public Policy and Jewish Law* (Hoboken, NJ: Ktav Publishing House; Yeshiva University Press, 1993), pp. 95–113.

[52]Genesis 39:8–9.

[53]Genesis 39:12 and 49:24; *Sotah* 36b.

By force of *Sotah* 36b, Joseph's moral dilemma is *personalized* on a different level as well. Recall that Joseph invokes his loyalty to God as a means of resisting Lady Potiphar's wiles (Genesis 39:9). But, in the moment of truth, this is apparently not enough to deter him from sin. What provided the extra push for Joseph was the image of his father both admonishing him against sin and reminding him of his destined greatness. In the final analysis, Joseph is deterred from sin by equating succumbing to sin with betraying both his father's moral teachings and his high hopes for him. Now, if Joseph merely gave lip service to Jacob's teachings, what influence could they have had on him once he was no longer under his father's control? What influence could these teachings have had at the moment Joseph faced the seductive powers of lust and at the same time was convinced that his father thought he was either dead or hopelessly missing? Overcoming a sin of passion by conjuring up an image of his father could only be efficacious under the assumption that Joseph cherished his father's moral teachings and harbored a deep sense of gratitude for them. Hence, for Joseph, *hakarrat ha-tov* was the link that transformed moral training into virtuous conduct.

FOSTERING *HAKKARAT HA-TOV*

The previous section has identified *hakkarat ha-tov* as a vital factor in achieving effective moral education. Its essential role is to make an individual equate failing a test of piety with letting down (betraying) his parents and/or moral educators. The challenge is therefore to put the family and school system on solid footing so that these institutions can maximize their impact on the moral climate of society.

For parents to realize their full moral educational potential, their child-rearing and moral educational roles must be fully integrated. Such integration makes moral training permeate every aspect of the life experience. In addition, it makes the gratitude parenthood compels inseparable from the gratitude their moral training elicits. This, in turn, works to *personalize* the moral dilemma. The converse of this proposition is that the more compartmentalized moral education is, the less it will elicit ethical conduct.

The self-same assertion can be made in respect to education. Specifically, to be effective, moral education must permeate the entire curriculum, and character building must comprise a central goal of the educational enterprise. Assigning moral education this role catapults it from the periphery to being an integral part of the educational process. This, in turn, fosters a bonding between students and educators, which, in turn, works to *personalize* moral action when students are faced with temptation.

GOVERNMENT SUBSIDIZATION OF THE FAMILY AND SCHOOL SYSTEM

In Jewish society, religious education is compulsory[54] and the religious education of the poor is subsidized.[55] Consider that one aspect of religious education is moral training, which is both the mission of parents and the religious educational enterprise. Part of the aid given to the poor should therefore be targeted to equip and encourage the family and the school to carry out their moral educational function.

The Cost Disease of the Service Sector

In assessing the adequacy of the level of support provided, we must consider what Baumel and Blinder call the "*cost disease of the service sector*."[56] We will begin with a brief description of this phenomenon and its relevancy to the issue at hand.

The cost disease of the service sector refers to the phenomenon that the prices of services consistently rise faster than the general inflation rate. Consider these facts: from 1948 to 1995 the consumer price index (CPI) in the United States increased at an average annual rate of about 4 percent per year compounded annually. Over this same period, the corresponding rate of increase of hospital care, education per pupil, and a visit to a physician was 8.6 percent, 7.5 percent, and 5.5 percent respectively. This disparity arises because productivity gains in manufac-

---

[54]*Bava Batra* 21a; Yad, *Talmud Torah* 1:1; *Tur*, *Yoreh De'ah* 245:1; *Shulkhan Arukh*, *Yoreh De'ah* 245:7; *Arukh ha-Shulkhan*, *Yoreh De'ah* 245:9.

[55]*Arukh ha-Shulkhan*, op. cit., 245:9, 27.

[56]William J. Baumel and Alan S. Blinder, *Economic Principles and Policies*, 7th ed. (New York: Dryden Press, 1997), pp. 316–319.

turing outpace productivity gains in the service sector. Productivity gains lag in the service sector because services by their very nature require direct contact between those who consume the service and those who provide it. Doctors, teachers, and librarians are all engaged in activities that require direct person-to-person contact. Moreover, because the quality of services will deteriorate if less time is provided per user, it is difficult to introduce labor-saving techniques in the service sector.

Notwithstanding the service sector's lagging productivity gains, the competitive marketplace will force it to raise wages at more or less the same rate as the manufacturing sector. If this were not so, the service sector would lose its labor force. Since costs are increasing faster in the service sector relative to the manufacturing sector, the profit motive will drive the service sector to cut corners in its employment of labor to maintain its profit margins. Hence, if the marketplace is left to its own devices, the quality of the output of the service sector is likely to deteriorate over time.

The cost disease of the service sector does not make deterioration of the quality of its output inevitable. To see why, we need only point out that the source of the problem is not declining productivity in the service sector, but rather, rising productivity in the manufacturing sector relative to the service sector.

Increasing productivity can never make a nation poor. We have a choice. More and better services over time can be obtained, but at some sacrifice in the rate of growth of manufacturing. Government can influence the mix of output between services and manufacturing. Many vital services, such as education and health care, are subsidized by the public sector. To ensure that the quality of these services does not erode over time, the public must be committed to increase its support level per annum above the inflation rate.[57]

The Cost Disease of Moral Training

Let us now relate the cost disease of the service sector to the moral-educational sector. At once, it must be recognized that moral training is essentially a cottage industry. Its effectiveness is predicated upon *quality*

[57]Baumel and Blinder, op. cit.

time, that is, personal contact between parents and children and between teachers and students. Without this quality time, the moral dilemma will not be personalized. Thus, moral training is subject to a cost disease.

What the cost disease of moral training implies for government subsidization of the schooling system is clear cut. If the quality time (i.e., the personal contact between teachers and students) is not to deteriorate over time, the government must be prepared to increase its support level per annum over the inflation rate. Moreover, since moral education will be effective only if it is integrated into the entire curriculum, this subsidy must increase for the entire educational program.

As far as the parental institution is concerned, it is a vital service sector that operates outside the marketplace, and this fact must be recognized. Given the economic pressures to earn a livelihood and the tantalizing rewards of the marketplace, parents must be provided with appropriate incentives to take their parenting and moral educational roles seriously. With the aim of putting the family on a sound economic footing, government subsidization of the basic needs of the family is required. Such programs as subsidized health care and generous tax deductions for dependents indexed to the CPI are indicated.

ETHICAL INVESTMENT

In this volume, R. Barry Bressler investigates the issue of ethical investment (see Chapter 7). He approaches the issue from the standpoint of technical *halakhah*. My purpose here is to add a few nuances on the technical front and propose a *hashkafic* philosophical framework for consideration.

For the purpose of contrasting the technical and *hashkafic* approaches to ethical investment, let's focus on the ethics of investing in the fictitional company, The Rawley Tobacco Company.

TECHNICAL *HALAKHAH* AND ETHICAL INVESTING

Let us begin with the technical perspective. The most basic issue here is whether *halakhah* establishes a clear-cut prohibition against smoking. Rabbis dispute this point. Those who prohibit smoking cite the overwhelming medical evidence that links smoking to various dreadful diseases. This evidence should make smoking a prohibited activity by dint of the biblical injunction: "Only take heed and watch yourself very carefully . . ." (Deuteronomy 4:9).[58] Other rabbis take the evidence as making smoking only a very imprudent activity. But, the evidence does not make for a clear-cut prohibition against smoking. This is so because smoking does not expose an individual to an immediate danger and, in addition, the habit of smoking is reversible.[59]

Suppose we adopt the viewpoint that smoking entails a clear-cut prohibition. The production and sale of cigarettes, then, becomes a menacing threat to the public's health. By dint of the injunction: "Do not stand idly by the blood of your neighbor" (*lo ta'amod al dam rei'akha*, Leviticus 19:16) we would be required to do whatever we could to extricate our fellow from the health danger of cigarette smoking. Admonishing smokers in respect to the dangers of smoking as well as lobbying the government to prohibit the production and sale of cigarettes represent appropriate actions. The extent to which *halakhah* demands that someone engage in anti-cigarette-smoking activities will, of course, depend on that person's circumstance and expected impact. Nevertheless, because we are all *theoretically* obligated to extricate our fellow from the dangers of cigarette smoking, investing in Rawley Tobacco stock is unthinkable. Such action amounts to an implicit *approval* of the company's operations and hence makes an *outright mockery* of the *lo ta'amod* obligation.

Suppose we adopt the viewpoint that *halakhah* does not adopt a clear-cut prohibition against cigarette smoking. Adopting this viewpoint does not, however, lead to the judgment that Rawley Tobacco is free of halakhic violation. Consider that Rawley Tobacco aggressively markets tobacco products internationally. Given the enormous health risk smoking entails, persuasive advertising amounts to offering the public

---

[58]Rabbinical authorities cited by Dr. Fred Rosner, "Cigarette Smoking and Jewish Law," in *Journal of Halakhah and Contemporary Society*, 4(1982): 40, 44–45.

[59]This is the position taken by Rabbis S. Z. Auerbach and Ovadiah Yosef, quoted in A. S. Abraham, *Medical Halakhah for Everyone* (Jerusalem; New York: Feldheim, 1980), p. 6. See also Rabbi J. David Bleich, *Tradition* 16(4) (Summer 1977): 121–123; 17(3) (Summer 1978): 140–142.

ill-suited advice and hence violates the *lifnei iver* interdict.[60] Moreover, Rawley Tobacco fails to inform the public of the health risks smoking entails in those countries where health warnings are not required by law. Does the above negative assessment lead to a prohibition to invest in Rawley Tobacco? Not necessarily. If Rawley Tobacco were a Jewish company, a Jew would be duty bound to reprove its policy-makers and urge them to make the indicated changes.[61] To be sure, an assessment that reproof (*tokhahah*) would be of no avail might very will free an individual of this duty.[62] But, Rawley Tobacco is not a Jewish company. As a matter of strict duty,[63] *tokhahah* does not apply to the conduct of a non-Jew.[64]

At this juncture, it is relevant to consider to what extent shareholders of a public corporation are responsible for the policies of the company. Several articles in this volume consider this issue.[65] One widely held view is that responsibility for policy applies only to shareholders whose stake in the firm is sufficiently large to force the directors to take their opinion into account. If the investor's stake in the company does not reach this level, the investor bears no moral responsibility for the sins of the firm.[66] What follows is that a nonsignificant investment in Rawley Tobacco stock should be permissible.

Another issue to consider here is whether the investor in Rawley Tobacco stock should be regarded as *assisting* the company in carrying out its prohibited policies. Abetting or assisting someone in the commis-

---

[60]Leviticus 19:14; *Torat Kohanim*, ad loc.; Maimonodies, *Yad*, *Rozeah* 12:14.

[61]Leviticus 19:17.

[62]This is the view of R. Isaac b. Jacob Alfasi (Algeria, 1013–1103, *Rif*, *Yevamot* 65b) and *Tosafot* (*Bava Batra* 60b, s.v. *mutav*). R. Moses Isserles (Poland, 1525 or 1530–1572), *Rema, Shulkhan Aruch Orah Hayyim* 608:2), however, regards the *tokhahah* duty as remaining intact even when it will not be heeded.

[63]Correcting a Noahide from sinning is commendable. *Sefer Hasidim* (Section 1124) derives this from the circumstance that God sent Jonah to Nineveh to return the Ninevitea to His path.

[64]R. Solomon b. Isaac (Rashi, Sanhedrin 75a, sv. *v'im*); R. Shabbetai b. Meir ha-Kohen, *Siftei Kohen, Shulkhan Arukh, Yoreh De'ah* 151:6; R. Naftali Zevi Yehudah Berlin (Russia, 1817–1893), *Meishiv Davar* 2:31.

[65]Please turn to pp. 175–178 of this volume.

[66]Ibid, p. 175 and p. 176.

sion of a sin violates for the facilitator the *lifnei iver* interdict.[67] The issue entails the question of investing in new equity shares as well as investing in the secondary market.

Let's first take up the issue of purchasing new equity shares. Preliminarily, note that Rawley Tobacco markets its new equity shares by eliciting the services of an underwriter, Golden. Golden guarantees a price on its securities and then sells these securities to the public. To be sure, Golden's underwriting activity makes it *temporarily* a significant shareholder of Rawley. But, consider that Golden does not make its commitment to Rawley before it has its customers in the secondary market lined up. This circumstance should remove Golden from being halakhically regarded as a significant shareholder of Rawley and hence responsible for its prohibited policies.

Two scenarios present themselves. In one scenario Golden is the only investment banker willing to underwrite Rawley's new issue. Because Rawley cannot market its new equity shares without Golden, Golden should be regarded as a facilitator of Rawley's prohibited policies and hence be in violation of *lifnei iver*.

Suppose, however, that if Golden does not underwrite Rawley, another investment banker, Bennet, would do so. This circumstance reduces the severity of the *lifnei iver* issue at hand to a Rabbinical rather than a Torah level.[68] Consider further that as a non-Jewish company Rawley Tobacco regards itself in no way bound by *halakhah*. Since American law does not regard Rawley Tobacco's policies as illegal, the company would certainly deliberately ignore *halakhah*, even if its objections were presented to the company's officers. Now, if Rawley Tobacco is presumably ready to violate Halakhah's dictates deliberately and can

---

[67]Leviticus 19:14; *Yad, Rozeah* 12:14.

[68]R. Nissim b. Abraham Gerondi (Barcelona, 1310–1375), *Ran, Avodah Zorah* 6b. *Tosafot* (*Hagigah* 13a), however, takes the view that if the sin is accessible to the violator without the aid of A, A's facilitating action is entirely permissible, even on a rabbinical level. Both views are quoted by R. Moses Isserles (*Rema, Shulkhan Arukh, Yoreh De'ah* 151:1). *Rema* rules in accordance with *Tosafot*, but recommends that pious people follow *Ran*'s stringent position.

easily obtain capital from Bennet instead of from Golden, Golden is not regarded as a facilitator even on a rabbinical level.[69]

Let's now turn to the secondary financial market. Consider that *A*'s purchase of Rawley Tobacco's shares in the secondary market does not furnish the company with any new capital. What happens is that *A* gives up his cash to *B* in exchange for *B*'s Rawley Tobacco shares. Decidedly, the transaction does not furnish the company with new capital. Given the *indirect* role an investor in the secondary market plays in enabling Rawley Tobacco to carry out its prohibited policies, the investor's action should fall under the *lifnei de-lifnei* leniency. Under this leniency, an individual is not regarded as "placing a stumbling block before a blind man" if a supervening event (*lifnei de-lifnei*) is required before the untoward outcome occurs. Providing an illustration of this leniency is the permissibility of selling incense of the type used in idol worship to a non-Jew for resale. Since the first purchaser resells the incense, and thus does not use it for idolatry, the second purchaser's use of it only constitutes *lifnei de-lifnei* from the standpoint of the original seller and thus does not entail an infraction of the law for him.[70] Clearly, an investment in Rawley Tobacco shares purchased in the secondary financial market plays only a *lifnei de-lifnei* role in enabling Rawley Tobacco to carry out its prohibited policies. The investment should therefore be permitted.

THE CONGLOMERATE AND ETHICAL INVESTMENT

Consider the following scenario: ASL is a conglomerate whose shares are publically traded. The company controls three subsidiaries. its main

[69]R. Shabbetai b. Meir ha-Kohen (Poland, 1621–1662), *Siftei Kohen, Yoreh De'ah* 151:6, and comments of R. Ezekiel b. Judah ha-Levi Landau (Prague, 1713–1793, *Dagul me-Revavah*, ad loc.) on *Siftei Kohen,* loc. cit. The proposition that *lifnei iver* on a rabbinical level is suspended when the transgressor sins deliberately is advanced by *Dagul me-Revavah* only in the instance when the transgressor is a Jew. In the relevant circumstances, when the transgressor is a non-Jew, *Siftei Kohen* may very well suspend the *lifnei iver* interdict even when the transgressor sins unwittingly.

[70]*Avodah Zarah* 14a.

businesses, carried out by two of its subsidiaries, are chewing gum and detergents. Its third subsidiary is Rawley Tobacco. ASL issues new equity shares. In its prospectus, ASL describes its investment plan to consist of the purchase of a new computer system. Here, *halakhah* should find no objection for our investment banker, Golden, to underwrite the new issue even if no other underwriter is willing to do so. An analogous case was dealt with by R. Mosheh Feinstein (New York, 1895–1986): R. Feinstein permitted a caterer to rent his hall and provide food for a wedding feast even though it was certain that social dancing would take place at the affair. The rationale behind the permissible ruling was that making an object available to an individual cannot be regarded as abetting a transgression unless the article is used primarily for prohibited purposes. Should this not be the case, subsequent use of the article by the recipient for a prohibited purpose does not brand the one who makes it available an abettor of a transgression. Accordingly, since the catering hall is primarily rented for permissible purposes, that is, the wedding ceremony and banquet, its rental should not be regarded as abetting transgressors. In R. Feinstein's view, the circumstance that the hall is rented primarily for permissible purposes is sufficient to remove the *lifnei iver* problem even in a setting where the issue is violation of this interdict on a biblical level.[71]

Let's apply the above ruling to the case at hand: Golden's purchase of ASL's new equity issue should be permissible even though it is a matter of certainty that the tobacco business will directly benefit from the new computer installation. Given that the main businesses of ASL are chewing gum and detergents, Golden's underwriting activities to specifically finance ASL's new computer system should not be viewed as abetting the company's tobacco business. What Golden is doing is to essentially hand over to ASL a permissible item, namely a computer system.

MARIT AYIN

At this juncture it is appropriate to consider the issue of *marit ayin* (concern for appearance). R. Barry Bressler applies this general principle of

[71]R. Mosheh Feinstein (New York, 1895–1986), *Iggerot Mosheh, Yoreh De'ah* 1:73. See, however, *Iggerot Mosheh, Orah Hayyim* 2:62.

halakhah to the issue of ethical investment. In R. Bressler's view, the *marit ayin* principle requires an investor to insure that his or her financial involvement in the company does not give the appearance of either being responsible for or approving the objectionable policies of the company. An investment that draws public attention, according to Bressler, violates this caveat. He notes that a 5 percent stake in a public corporation triggers an SEC requirement of public disclosure of the holding. A 5 percent stake in a public corporation therefore makes an individual's financial involvement with the company a matter of public knowledge.[72]

Suppose Nathan Schwartz makes a 5 percent investment in ASL. Now, if ownership of ASL shares is not widely diffused, Schwartz's 5 percent stake in the company will not compel policy-makers to take his opinion into account. Halakhically, Nathan Schwartz will not be regarded as an owner of ASL and will technically not be responsible for its policies. But, a 5 percent stake in a public company triggers an SEC disclosure obligation. Nathan Schwartz's ownership will become a matter of public knowledge. His investment should therefore be prohibited, as it gives the impression that he supports the polices of ASL, including the running of its Rawley Tobacco subsidiary. Increasing his stake in ASL to the 5 percent level should therefore be prohibited on the basis of the *marit ayin* principle.

HANUPPAH AND ETHICAL INVESTMENT

The *marit ayyin* principle, in my opinion, has limited relevancy to the issue of ethical investment. Its relevance should be confined to instances analogous to the conglomerate case just dealt with. The salient feature here is that the prospects of the firm's growth in sales and profits resulting from the new computer system are not predicated on the violation of *halakhah*. Here, making a nonsignificant but disclosure-triggering investment gives only the *appearance* that Nathan Schwartz approves the infractions involved. But, suppose the case study is not ASL, but rather Rawley Tobacco as a separate entity. Here, the company's future prospects are entirely predicated upon the *continuation* of policies that violate *halakhah*. Then, making an investment in the company entails not

[72]Please turn to p. 198 of this volume.

only an *appearance* of approval of the prohibited policies but amounts to *condoning* these policies. Consider that the regulatory environment in the United States today will work to force a shrinking domestic market for Rawley Tobacco in the future. The company's prospects for growth in sales and profits hencerely entirely on its growth prospects in foreign markets. Success in the overseas market depends, in turn, on Rawley Tobacco continuing the policies of lax or no health warnings and heavy advertising directed at youth.

Condoning the sin of evildoers violates the prohibition called *hanuppah* (prohibited flattery).[73] We take it as a given that the prohibition applies whether the evildoer is Jewish or non-Jewish. In his treatment of *hanuppah,* R. Jonah b. Abraham Gerondi (Spain, ca. 1200–1264) identifies nine different levels of severity in the violation of this prohibition. Several of the nuances are applicable to the case at hand. The most severe violation of the prohibition entails the circumstance where the transgression of the evildoer is a matter of public knowledge. Declaring to the evildoer in the presence of onlookers that "you have done no wrong" constitutes *hanuppah.* In addition, the conduct violates for the offender a particularly severe form of falsehood: "He who vindicates the wicked and condemns the righteous—both are an abomination to the Lord" (Proverbs 17:15).[74]

In his treatment of *hanuppah,* R. Eliezer b. Samuel (Metz, ca. 1115–1198) expands the parameters of the interdict to include lack of protest on the part of the observer of the evil. In the opinion of this authority, *hanuppah* is violated when the acquiescence or lack of protest to the evildoer is not rooted in a fear of suffering reprisals in his hands but rather is done out of moral weakness.[75]

In applying the *hanuppah* prohibition to the Rawley Tobacco investment, one could argue that each shareholder, big or small, implicitly communicates to the policy makers of the company: "Be assured that *I will not protest your evil.* Because I am convinced that society's moral fiber is too weak to stop you, I wish to *profit* from your evil by investing in your company."

---

[73]The prohibition of *hanufah* is based on Numbers 35:32. See *Sifrei ad loc.*

[74]R. Jonah b. Abraham Gerondi, *Sha'arei Teshuvah, sha'ar* 3, 187.

[75]R. Eliezer b. Samuel, *Yere'im* 55.

To be sure, the investment may very well manifest a libertarian philosophy on the part of shareholders that government should not involve itself in policing the morals of society. In the latter instance, the *hanuppah* involved is of a more severe genre.

Notwithstanding the *implicit hanuppah* message the investment in Rawley Tobacco entails, let's not lose sight of the fact that *hanuppah* is a *social sin*. It is violated only in the context of a *personal* communication or interaction. Here, there is no explicit communication, only an implicit one. If the shareholder is insignificant from the perspective of Rawley Tobacco, the policy-makers pay no attention to what the investor is saying. The message comes from a *stock certificate* consisting of a faceless person with no actual articulation. Add to this that one of the major rationales behind the prohibition is that *hanuppah* lends encouragement to the sinner to continue his wicked ways.[76] To be sure, the viability of Rawley Tobacco depends heavily on an active secondary financial market. But this argues no more than that the secondary financial market *as a whole or as an institution* serves to encourage Rawley Tobacco. The policy-makers do not, however, take note of the participation of a *particular nonsignificant investor* (A) in the secondary market. A's purchase of shares is hence a *non-event* as far as Rawley Tobacco's policy-makers are concerned. Given the impersonal and insignificant manner in which Rawley Tobacco views A, his *hanuppah* communication to the policy-makers should halakhically be regarded as if it were made to someone who is not really listening.

The above mitigating factors do not, however, apply when the shareholder (*B*) is significant from the perspective of Rawley Tobacco. The opinions of *B* will surely be taken into account by the policy makers of Rawley Tobacco. They will fully expect to meet with him personally in a business context. In short, *B* is for the policy-makers of Rawley Tobacco a *real* person who delivers the encouraging message "you do no wrong."

Suppose for the moment that ownership of Rawley Tobacco shares is widely diffused and a 5 percent stake in the company is significant from the standpoint of Rawley's policy-makers. Recall that a 5 percent stake in a publicly traded company triggers an SEC disclosure obligation. When all the above elements are in place, increasing one's stake in Rawley to 5 percent violates *hanuppah* in its most severe form.

---

[76]*Sha'anei Teshuvah*, loc. cit.

Let's take note that investment in a public corporation takes place through a broker. The import of this is that even the *insignificant* investor is implicitly declaring in the presence of onlookers that he or she does not regard the policies of the company as evil. Condoning action also takes place when an individual tells his friends of his investment in Rawley Tobacco. To be sure this declaration is not being made in a personal way to the policy-makers of the company, but, nevertheless, the purchase entails this declaration to third parties. Condoning the sin of an offender not in the presence of the offender violates *hanuppah,* albeit on a lesser level of severity than in the previous case.[77]

HASHKAFIC (PHILOSOPHIC) CONCERNS AND THE ETHICAL INVESTMENT ISSUE

Let's now turn to the *hashkafic* perspective on the ethical investment issue. We begin with R. Joseph B. Soloveitchik's insight into the blessing God conferred on Adam: "Be fruitful and multiply and fill the earth and subdue it" (Genesis 1:28). R. Soloveitchik understands this blessing as a divine *mandate* to mankind to subdue the earth and master the environment (henceforth, *kibbush*). In R. Soloveitchik's thinking the *kibbush* mandate amounts to a charge to man for self-actualization in realizing his godlike potential as a creative being.

Fulfillment of the mandate bids man to achieve for himself dignity but also to acquire along with it a rarified sense of responsibility.

Man achieves dignity when he reclaims himself from coexistence with nature, rising from a helpless existence to a powerful existence that is intelligent, planned, and majestic.

Coexistence with nature is undignified because man is incapable of discharging his responsibilities in a state of bondage. The more man masters nature, the freer he is to discharge his responsibilities. Therefore, dignity is not an end in itself. Without raising man's sense of responsibility, dignity has no value.[78]

---

[77]*Sha'arei Teshuvah,* op. cit., 3:189.

[78]R. Joseph B. Soloveitchik, *The Lonely Man of Faith* (New York: Doubleday, 1965), pp. 16–20.

Before the *kibbush* mandate can become operational as an evaluative criterion, the importance of the economic system in actuating the *kibbush* mandate must be noted.

The most fundamental point to be made here is that progress in subduing nature and in mastering the environment can not take place in an economic vacuum. Given the specialization and division of labor characteristic of modern society, production is impossible without the cooperative voluntary exchange of countless economic units. Professional services are the product of society's educational and research institutions. The financial underpinning of these institutions, in turn, depends on the viability of commerce and industry. The impact of these interlocking relations is to make the subduing of nature and the mastering of the environment the work of the economic system as a whole.

Moreover, dignity manifests itself in the access one has to the available technical progress. This makes income the means of securing dignity. The higher the per-capita income the more widely accessible this technical progress will be. But the single most important factor in determining society's per capita income is labor productivity. Improvements in labor productivity, in turn, result from such factors as harder work, better training, more or better equipment, and innovative technology. Economic growth hence works to propel human dignity to greater and greater heights.

Recognition of the role of the economic system plays in the dignity–responsibility formulation of the *kibbush* mandate makes ordinary livelihood activities a fulfillment of this mandate. This is so because the income earned gives the economic actor a measure of command over the technical progress of society and hence contributes to his own self-dignity. In addition, participation in the economic system frees an individual from the shackles of dependency[79] and hence raises his sense of responsibility as well.

What emerges from the *kibbush* mandate is a criterion for evaluating the *inherent worthiness* of economic activity. If an economic activity con-

[79]For the attitudes of the Sages toward human dependency, which they regarded as a deplorable situation see *Shabbat* 118a; *Eruvin* 18b; *Pesahim,* 113a; *Betzah* 32b; *Bava Batra* 110a.

tributes neither to advancing man's dignity nor to his sense of responsibility, the activity has no rationale for existence.

Illustrating a perversion of the *kibbush* mandate is the production and sale of cigarettes. This judgment is not predicated on the ability of *halakhah* to establish a clear-cut prohibition against smoking. Suppose, for the sake of argument, that a clear-cut prohibition cannot be established. Nonetheless, the causative links medical science has established between cigarette smoking and various dreadful diseases are undeniable. Far from advancing human dignity, the tobacco industry degrades human existence by causing disease, misery, and pain. Its very existence perverts the *kibbush* mandate.

In our example, Rawley Tobacco's core economic mission is to produce and sell cigarettes. While technical *halakhah* can make a case for investment in Rawley Tobacco, the investment represents a clear-cut perversion of the *kibbush* mandate and should therefore not be made.

Who at Rawley violates the *kibbush* mandate? Clearly it is not only the policy-makers but also those who are halakhically responsible for the policies. Significant shareholders of Rawley stock fall into the latter category. But consider that any investment in Rawley, whether significant or not, will be a force to reduce the investor's sense of responsibility for his fellow man. Why? Because it is events such as expanded sales and a loosening of the regulatory environment that drive Rawley stock up and the converse of these events that drive the stock down. One buys the stock both because he anticipates and hopes for favorable events, and because he hopes against unfavorable events. Successful investing at Rawley hence is a force that works to corrupt one's morals and is usually accompanied by an increase in suffering in the world. Becoming even an insignificant investor in Rawley hence violates the *kibbush* mandate.

A number of forms of investing in Rawley stock apparently meet the ethical standards we have discussed thus far. These include short selling and mutual fund investment. Let's take up each in turn.

Short Selling

In the short sale, the investor anticipates a decline in the price of the security at hand. Accordingly, the investor borrows the security and sells it immediately, anticipating that he will buy it back when the price declines and return it to the lender. If things work out as anticipated, the short seller will make money as he pays a lower price for the security than the price he sold it for.

Halakhah should apparently find no objections to short-selling Rawley Tobacco, even when it entails a significant investment. Let's see why. When the short sale is initiated, the investor (*A*) is merely *borrowing* someone else's (*B*'s) shares and is therefore not the legal owner of these shares. This being the case, *A* is not responsible for Rawley's policies. To be sure, when *A* buys back the shares, he temporarily becomes a significant shareholder of Rawley. But the terms of the short sale require *A* to return the shares to *B* as soon as he buys the borrowed shares back. Because *A*'s ownership in Rawley shares is so transient that he has no chance to control or influence the policy of Rawley, he should halakhically be regarded as no more an owner in Rawley than a permanent insignificant shareholder.

Consider that the short seller operates in the secondary financial market. This investor therefore does not take on the role of facilitator or abetter of the policies of Rawley.

Finally, consider that the motivation behind the short sale is the anticipated decline in Rawley stock. In making the investment in Rawley, *A* is hence neither guilty of *hanuppah* nor in violation of the *kibbush* mandate.

Mutual Funds

A mutual fund company pools the resources of many small investors by selling them shares and using the proceeds to buy a diversified portfolio of securities. Such shares represent a proportionate ownership in the portfolio of securities held by the mutual fund. An investor in a mutual fund does not, however, acquire direct ownership in the securities the mutual fund company buys into. Instead, the price of the shares is merely *tied* to the assets of the fund.

Suppose a particular non-Jewish–owned mutual fund company, *MF*, has Rawley Tobacco shares in its portfolio. The Rawley shares constitute only an insignificant portion of a diversified portfolio of securities. Nathan Schwartz invests in *MF*. His investment in *MF* should find no halakhic objection. Let's see why.

Consider that Nathan Schwartz's investment in *MF* acquires for him no direct ownership of Rawley shares and, in addition, Schwartz has no say in MF's investment decisions. Schwartz, therefore, bears no responsibility for Rawley's policies, irrespective of the size of his investment in MF.

Relatedly, Schwartz's indirect ownership of Rawley stock confers on him *lifnei-de-lifnei* status in relation to encouraging the policies of Rawley.

Let's now move to the *hanuppah* issue. Recall that *hanuppah* is a social sin; it is not violated unless one communicates approval to the evildoer. By investing in MF, Schwartz acquires anonymity with respect to Rawley. As far as Rawley is concerned, Schwartz is nonexistent. Schwartz's investment in MF hence communicates no message of approval to Rawley policy-makers. In respect to MF's managers, Schwartz's investment communicates implicitly only that he has confidence in their overall performance record; but communicates nothing regarding his approval of their individual stock selections.

Finally, let's take up the *kibbush* issue. To be in violation of the *kibbush* mandate, one must either be responsible for the policies of Rawley or experience a reduced sense of responsibility on account of the investment. A mutual fund investor, as previously discussed, is neither a shareholder of Rawley nor responsible for its policies. Given MF's wide diversification of asset holdings, the contribution Rawley makes to MF's profitability will hence not reduce Schwartz's sense of responsibility to his fellow man. But suppose that 3 percent of MF's assets are invested in Rawley shares. Other things being equal, tobacco news will assuredly move MF's share price. Here, Schwartz will identify with Rawley's fortunes and his ownership of MF violates the *kibbush* mandate. What this points to is an investigative responsibility for Schwartz. Before investing in a mutual fund, Schwartz should check out the asset holdings of the company to insure that its largest percentage asset holdings are not in companies that violate the *kibbush* mandate.

Let's consider one final variation. Suppose Schwartz's investigation finds that, on the basis of MF's latest report to shareholders, it had no large percentage investments in Rawley. He therefore goes ahead with the investment. In a subsequent report, Schwartz discovers that MF increased its holdings of Rawley to a relatively high percentage of its asset holdings. Here, Schwartz should be under no obligation to liquidate his investment on the basis of MF's latest report. Since Schwartz violates no technical *halakhah* by holding on to MF, he should bear no responsibility to incur a possible loss by switching to another investment.

Contributors

Barry Bressler is Dean of the Business School and Professor of Economics, Touro College. Rabbi Bressler is rabbi of Hebrew Institute Bais Medrash, Far Rockaway, NY, and Vice President and Professor Emeritus, College of Staten Island (CUNY). He is the author of numerous publications on Jewish Law, Income Inequality, and Economics, including *A Unified Introduction to Mathematical Economics* and "Arbitration and the Courts in Jewish Law" (Journal of Halacha and Contemporary Society).

Michael Broyde is associate professor of Law at Emory University School of Law and the Associate Director of the Law and Religion Program at Emory University. His primary areas of interest are law and religion, Jewish law and ethics, and comparative religious law. He has published over fifty articles in these areas. He received a juris doctor from New York University and *semikhah* (ordination) from the Rabbi Isaac Elchanan Theological Seminary.

Yehoshua Liebermann is professor of Economics at Bar Ilan University. He has published and lectured extensively on the interface between traditional economic theory and halakhah.

Jonas Prager is associate professor of Economics in the faculty of Arts and Sciences at New York University. He received his Ph.D. from Columbia University and *semikhah* from the Rabbi Isaac Elchanan Theological Seminary. His recent publications are *Applied Microeconomics: An Intermediate Text*, "Banking Privatization in Israel, 1983–1994: A Case Study in Political Economy," and "Privatizing Local Government Operations: Lessons from Federal Contracting Out Methodology."

Steven H. Resnicoff, a professor at DePaul University College of Law, is a graduate of Princeton College, Yale Law School, and Beth Medrash Govoha. Ordained by Rav Moshe Feinstein, *z"l*, has published and lectured extensively on halakhic and secular issues regarding bankruptcy, bioethics, legal ethics, *ribbit*, and other subjects.

David J. Schnall is Herbert H. Schiff professor of Management and Administration at the Wurzweiler School of Social Work of Yeshiva University. He is serving as J. William Fulbright Professor and Senior Scholar at the Baerwald School of Social Work at the Hebrew University in Jerusalem for the academic year 1999 to 2000.

Walter S. Wurzburger is adjunct professor of Philosophy at Yeshiva University and rabbi emeritus of Congregation Shaaray Tefila in Lawrence, New York. He is the author of *Ethics of Responsibility*. He served for many years as editor of *Tradition* and was president of the Rabbinical Council of America.

Index

Aderet, Solomon b. Abraham, 117, 118, 168, 240–241, 253, 283
Advertising, pharmaceutical industry, 102
Akerlof, George, 17–18
Allen, Robert, 46
Alshekh, Moses, 191
Altruism
  coercion and, 286–287
  covenantal morality, 40
  Halakhah and, 282–284
  priorities and, 287–288
  publicly traded company, 288–290
Appearances, concern for (*marit ayin*), 308–309
Appropriateness, logic of, stakeholder theory and, 13–16
Asher, Rabbenu, 252–253
Asher b. Jehiel, 78, 240
Association principle, moral misconduct, assisting in, 194
Asymmetric information, 123–146
  firm and market economy, 124–135
  Halakhah and, 135–143
  misconduct and moral education, 290–291
  overview, 123–124
AT&T specialty directory, privacy, 111–116
Auerbach, Solomon Zalman, 79, 189
Austere theory, stakeholder theory compared, 8–13

Bar Hanan, 52, 60
Basic research. *See* Research and development
Batzri, Ezra, 270
Baumol, William J., 127
Ben Buchri, 225
Benefits, employees, 66–68
Berdugo, Petahia Mordecai, 171
Berlin, Hayyim, 81
Bloi, Jacob Isaiah, 183
Bowie, Norman E., 15
Brand-name drugs, generic drugs and, customer relations, 94–98
Bressler, Barry, 308–309
Business judgment rule, *Halakhah* and, 281–282

Calabresi, G., 165
Canadian system, pharmaceutical industry, 109–111
Caro, Joseph, 163, 242
Charity, covenantal morality and, 33–34. *See also* Philanthropy
Clarkson, Max, 49
Close corporations, corporate structure, 210–211
Coase's theorem, externalities and, environment, 153–157
Coercion, corporate social responsibility and, 286–287
Collective organization, employees, 62–65
Commercial custom, validity of condition and, entity and partnership approaches, new rules, 238–242
Common good, covenantal morality and, 34
Competition, brand-name and generic drugs, customer relations, 94–98
Concern for appearances (*marit ayin*), 308–309
Conglomerates, investment and, 307–308
Consumer privacy, customer relations, 111–121. *See also* Customer relations
Cooter, R., 158
Corporate ownership, investment, 180–185
Corporate philanthropy, covenantal morality, 41–43
Corporate social responsibility
  coercion and, 286–287
  covenantal morality, 30, 34–36, 40–41
  Halakhah and, 282–284
  priorities and, 287–288
  publicly traded company, 288–290
  Wurzburger on, 285–286
Corporate structure, 203–272
  analogous commercial constructs, 206–213
    analogous structures, 212–213
    close corporations, 210–211
    professional corporations, 211–212
    public corporations, 210
  covenantal morality and, 31–32

Halakhah, 214–270
creditor approach, 254–261
entity and partnership approaches, 214–254. *See also* Entity and partnership approaches
purchaser of entitlements approach, 261–268
relationship approach, 268–270
overview, 203–206
Corporations, power of, 27
Counterbalancing principle
moral conduct, abetting of, 188
moral misconduct, assisting in, 196
Covenantal morality, 27–43
altruism, 40
charity and, 33–34
common good and, 34
corporate philanthropy, 41–43
corporate social responsibility, 30, 34–36, 40–41
corporate structure and, 31–32
education, 41
free-market economists compared, 30–31
Halakhah and, 27–29
harms, 39
health care, 40
human rights, 39
self-interest and, 32–33
stakeholders and, 31, 42
technology and, 29
unethical conduct, 37–39
wealth and, 29
Creditor approach, *Halakhah*, corporate structure, 254–261
Customer relations, 75–121
overview, 75
pharmaceutical industry
basic research, 87–89
brand-name and generic drugs, 94–98
Canadian system, 109–111
doctor's duty, 98–99
generic substitution legislation, 99–102
information channels, 102–104
laissez-faire argument, 83–87
marketing practices, 104–107
patent protection, 89–92
price information, 107–109
pricing, 76–79, 92–94
windfall profits, 79–83
privacy, 111–121
AT&T specialty directory, 111–116
commercial gain, 116–118
database industry, 118–119
self-regulation versus government regulation, 119–121

Darby, Michael R., 125
Database industry, privacy, 118–119
DeGeorge, Richard T., 32, 37, 40
Directness principle, moral conduct, abetting of, 187–188
Diversion principle, moral misconduct, assisting in, 195–196

Doctors
  responsibility of, customer relations, 98–99
  rewards to, pharmaceutical industry, 103
Donaldson, Thomas, 4, 48

Economic approaches, environment, 159–161
Education. *See also* Moral education
  covenantal morality, 41
  government subsidy, 301–303
Efficiency, private property rights and, environment, 151–153
Eliezer b. Samuel, 310
Elijah b. Solomon, 192
Employees, 45–73
  collective organization and right to strike, 62–65
  Jewish thought and, 50–55
  pay administration, 55–59
  perquisites, expenses, and worker compensation, 66–68
  severance benefits, 59–62
  stakeholder theory, 45–50, 69–73
Employment, Jewish thought and, 50–55
Entity and partnership approaches, 214–254
  analytical basis, 216–222
  corporate analogs, 222–235
  new rules, 235–254
    law of the land, 242–247
    ownership and limited liability, 247–254
    property declared ownerless, 236–238
    validity of condition and commercial custom, 238–242
  overview, 214–216
Environment, 147–173
  economic approaches, 159–161
  efficiency and private property rights, 151–153
  externalities and Coase's theorem, 153–157
  Halakhah, 161–172
  legal approaches, 157–159
  overview, 147–149
  social equilibrium, 149–151
Envy, moral education and, 296–298
Epstein, Jehiel Michel, 120
Equilibrium, social, environment, 149–151
Ethical investment. *See* Investment
Ethics. *See* Business ethics
Ettinger, Isaac Aaron, 232, 233, 234, 259, 260, 263, 268, 269
Evan, William M., 5, 15
Exclusionary clause, moral misconduct, assisting in, 191–193
Expenses, employees, 66–68
Externalities, Coase's theorem and, environment, 153–157

Falk, Joshua b. Alexander ha-Kohn, 83, 164, 165
False advertising, covenantal morality, 37–38

Feasibility principle, moral misconduct, assisting in, 191
Feinstein, Moshe, 182, 184, 188, 192, 193, 194, 195, 199, 238, 261–268
Firm, market economy and, asymmetric information, 124–135
Foodstuff ordinance, customer relations, 82, 102
Frank, Tzvi Pesach, 187–188
Freeman, R. Edward, 5, 15, 21, 24, 25, 47
Free-market economists, covenantal morality compared, 30–31
Friedman, Milton, 8, 11, 12, 13, 22, 30, 31, 36, 39, 72, 176
Friedman, Rose, 11

Galbraith, J. K., 147–148
Gantzfried, Shelomo, 183
Ganzfried, Solomon, 183
Generic drugs, brand-name drugs and, customer relations, 94–98
Generic substitution legislation, customer relations, 99–102
Gerondi, Jonah b. Abraham, 310
Gershom b. Judah Me'Or ha-Golah, 113
Gombiner, Abraham Abele, 192
Goodpaster, Kenneth E., 21, 24, 25, 72
Government regulation, self-regulation versus, privacy, 119–121
Government subsidy, family and schools, 301–303
Gratitude
  fostering of, 300–301
  moral education and, 299–300
Greed, truth and, 294–296
Greenfield, Shimon, 227

Hakkarat ha-tov. See Gratitude
Ha-Kohen, Shabbetai b. Meir, 191
Ha-Kohen, Solomon b. Abraham, 172
Halakhah. See also Law
  asymmetric information, 123–146. *See also* Asymmetric information
  business judgment rule and, 281–282
  corporate structure, 214–270. *See also* Corporate structure
  covenantal morality, 27–29, 31, 32
  drug pricing, 92–94
  environment, 161–172
  government regulation, privacy, 121
  investment and, 177, 179–180, 303–307
  pharmaceutical pricing, 76–79
  privacy, AT&T specialty directory, 112–116
  stakeholder theory and, 284–285
  windfall profits, 79–83
Ha-Levi, Aaron, 55
Ha-Levi, Hayyim David, 78

Hanuppah, investment and, 309–312
Harms, covenantal morality, 39
Hashkafic (philosophic) concerns, investment, 312–316
Health care, covenantal morality, 40
Heidenheim, Wolf, 90, 91
Heller, Aryeh Leib b. Joseph Ha-Kohen, 236
Heschel, Abraham Joshua, 19
Hildesheimer, Azreil, 263, 269
Hillel, 23–24, 30
Hirsch, Samson Raphael, 186
Hoffman, David Zvi, 263, 269
Horowitz, Isaiah ha-Levi, 293
Human rights, covenantal morality, 39

Ibn Lev, Joseph b. David, 150, 168, 169, 170, 180, 184
Income loss, severe, moral misconduct, assisting in, 194–195
Indentured servitude, Jewish thought and, 53
Independence principle, environment, externalities and Coase's theorem, 156–157
Information asymmetries. *See* Asymmetric information
Investment, 175–201, 303
  conglomerates and, 307–308
  corporate ownership, 180–185
  Halakhah, 179–180, 303–307
  hanuppah and, 309–312
  moral conduct, abetting of, 186–190
  moral misconduct
    abetting of, 185–186
    assisting in, 190–198
  overview, 175–178
  philosophic concerns, 312–316
Isaac, Solomon b., 274
Isaac ha-Levi ibn Migash, 152
Isaac of Dampierre, 78
Isserles, Moses, 106, 164, 192, 242, 243, 275

Jensen, Michael C., 12, 13, 22
Jewish business ethics. *See* Business ethics
Johnson, Robert, 46
Joseph Hayyim b. Elijah al-Hakkam, 279
Judah Loew b. Betzalel, 191, 294

Kagan, Israel Meir ha-Kohen, 192, 193
Karni, Edi, 125
Kaufmann, Walter, 28
Klein, Benjamin, 127
Klein, Menashe, 183, 199
Kluger, Shelomo, 183, 263, 269
Knight, F. H., 147
Kook, Abraham Isaac, 65, 151
Kotler, Aaron, 192, 193, 201
Krausz, Joshua, 34
Kristol, Irving, 36

Labor, Jewish thought and, 50–55
Labor costs, customer relations, 83
Labor unions, employees, 62–65
Laissez-faire argument, customer relations, 83–87

Law. *See also* Halakhah
  environment, 157–159
  unethical conduct, covenantal morality, 37–39
Law of the land, new rules, 242–247
Leffler, Keith B., 127
Levine, Aaron, 33, 36, 42, 43
Levitt, Theodore, 9
Liebermann, Yehoshva, 152, 161, 162
Limited liability
  corporate structure, 212–213
  ownership and, new rules, 247–254
Limited partnerships, corporate structure, 212–213
Logic of appropriateness, stakeholder theory and, 13–16
Luria, Shlomo b. Jehiel, 240

Maimonides, Moses, 33, 55, 120, 172, 226
Managers
  discretion of, 279–281
  role of, 273–277
Mani, 140
Mannheim, Bilha, 51
March, James, 10, 13
Marit ayin (concern for appearances), 308–309
Market economy, firm and, asymmetric information, 124–135
Marketing practices, pharmaceutical industry, 104–107
Meckling, William H., 12, 13, 22
Meir b. Samuel, 90
Meir Rottenburg b. Barukh of Rottenburg, 53, 57, 60, 68
Melamed, A. D., 165
Mendel, Menahem, 297
Misconduct, moral education and, asymmetric information, 290–291
Moertel, Charles, 92, 93
Moral conduct, abetting of, investment, 186–190
Moral education. *See also* Education
  case for, 291–294
  envy and, 296–298
  gratitude and, 299–301
  misconduct and, asymmetric information, 290–291
Moral misconduct
  abetting of, investment, 185–186
  assisting in, investment, 190–198
Mutual funds, philosophic concerns, 315–316

Nader, Ralph, 176
Nahman, 58
Nahmanides, 55, 76, 77, 152, 229, 252, 253
Nelson, Phillip, 124
Nelson, Richard R., 85
Niebuhr, Reinhold, 28
Nozick, Robert, 34

Orderly market principle, moral misconduct, assisting in, 195
Ouziel, Ben Zion, 61, 62, 65
Ownership, limited liability and, new rules, 247–254

Padua, Hanoh Dov (Henokh Dov Padwa), 181, 184, 269
Pareto, Vilfredo, 149, 150
Partnership approach. *See* Entity and partnership approaches
Patent protection, customer relations, 89–92
Pava, Moses L., 34
Payment, of employees, 55–59
Perquisites, employees, 66–68
Pharmaceutical industry, customer relations, 75–111. *See also* Customer relations
Philanthropy, corporate, covenantal morality, 41–43. *See also* Charity
Philosophic concerns, investment, 312–316
Physicians. *See* Doctors
Plato, 35
Pluralism, stakeholder theory, 1–2
Polinsky, A. M., 158
Prager, Jonas, 290–291
Preston, Lee E., 4, 48
Price information, pharmaceutical industry, 107–109
Pricing, pharmaceutical, customer relations, 76–79
Privacy, customer relations, 111–121. *See also* Customer relations
Private property rights, efficiency and, environment, 151–153
Probability principle, moral conduct, abetting of, 187–188
Professional corporations, corporate structure, 211–212
Proximity principle, moral misconduct, assisting in, 196
Public corporations, corporate structure, 210
Publicly traded company, corporate social responsibility, 288–290
Purchaser of entitlements approach, *Halakhah*, corporate structure, 261–268

Rashi, 140
Rava, 136, 138, 139
Reciprocity principle, environment, externalities and Coase's theorem, 156
Regensberg, Hayyim David, 224, 225, 226, 228, 229
Regulation, privacy, self- versus government-, 119–121
Relationship approach, *Halakhah*, corporate structure, 268–270
Religion, defined, 28
Research and development, customer relations, 87–89
Resourceful, Evaluative, Maximizing Model (REMM), 12–13
Right to strike, employees, 62–65
Rogerson, William P., 127

Self-interest, covenantal morality and, 32–33
Selfishness, truth and, 294–296
Self-regulation, government regulation versus, privacy, 119–121

Sella, Avraham, 51
Severance benefits, employees, 59–62
Severe income loss, moral misconduct, assisting in, 194–195
Shabtai b. Meir Ha-Kohen, 242
Shapiro, Carl, 127
Shimon b. Gamliel, 81
Shimon ben Meir, 228
Short selling, philosophic concerns, 314–315
Singer, Andrew, 21
Smith, Adam, 30, 32, 33, 34
Social equilibrium, environment, 149–151
Socially responsible investment. *See* Investment
Social responsibility. *See* Corporate social responsibility
Sofer, Moshe, 89, 90, 91, 106, 163, 170
Solomon b. Isaac, 81, 225
Soloveitchik, Joseph B., xxi, 24, 29, 312
Stakeholders
  covenantal morality and, 31, 42
  employees as, 45–73. *See also* Employees
  firm responsibility to, 277–278
Stakeholder theory, 1–26
  austere theory compared, 8–13
  described, 2–7
    descriptive perspective, 2–6
    instrumental perspective, 6
    normative perspective, 7
  employees, 45–50, 69–73. *See also* Employees
  Halakhah and, 284–285
  Jewish perspective on, 16–20
  limitations of, 21–25
  logic of appropriateness and, 13–16
  pluralism and, 1–2
Sternbuch, Moshe, 181, 182, 184, 199, 254, 255, 256, 257, 258, 261
Stiglitz, Joseph E., 127
Stone, Christopher, 10, 13
Strike, right to, employees, 62–65

Tamari, Meir, 33, 40
Technology, covenantal morality and, 29
Tobacco, covenantal morality, 38–39
Trading principle, environment, externalities and Coase's theorem, 156
Trani, Joseph (Moses b. Joseph di Trani), 150, 227, 276
Truth, selfishness and, 294–296

Ulen, T., 158
Unemployment, covenantal morality, 40–41
Unethical conduct, covenantal morality, 37–39
Unfeasibility principle, moral conduct, abetting of, 186–187
Universality principle, moral conduct, abetting of, 187

Valdenburg, E., 170
Validity of condition, commercial custom and, entity and partnership approaches, new rules, 238–242
Vidal Yom Tov of Tolosa, 37

Waldenberg, Eliezer Judah, 62, 65, 192
Walton, Clarence, 8, 9, 10, 13
Walzer, Michael, 22, 23
Wasserman, R., 235
Wealth, covenantal morality and, 29
Weingart, Shaul, 181, 184, 219, 220, 221
Weiss, Yitzhak Yaakov, 250, 258, 259, 263, 264
Whitehead, Alfred North, 28
Wiesz, Isaac Jacob, 183, 184, 199
Wilson, Charles A., 127
Windfall profits, customer relations, 79–83
Wolinsky, Asher, 127
Wood, Robert, 46
Worker compensation, employees, 66–68
Wurzburger, Walter, 285–286, 287, 288

Yeheil, Rabbenu, 241
Yehuda, 223
Yochanan ben Zachai, 225, 226
Yohanan ben Massya, 52
Yose, 116, 117, 118
Yosef, Ovadiah, 195

Zemba, Menachem, 223

About the Editors

Aaron Levine is Samson and Halina Bitensky professor of Economics at Yeshiva University. Dr. Levine has written widely on the interface of economics and Jewish Law. His books include *Free Enterprise and Jewish Law*, *Economics and Jewish Law*, and *Economic Public Policy* and *Jewish Law*.

Moses L. Pava is professor of Accounting and holds the Alvin Einbender Chair in Business Ethics at the Sy Syms School of Business, Yeshiva University. Among his books are *Business Ethics: A Jewish Perspective* and *The Search for Meaning in Organizations*. He is also the editor-in-chief of *Research in Ethical Issues in Organizations*.

Rabbi Robert S. Hirt has served as an administrator at Yeshiva University's affiliated Rabbi Isaac Elchanan Theological Seminary (RIETS) for more than three decades and has been vice president for Administration and Professional Education for RIETS and its components since 1985. In 1991, he was named inaugural occupant of the Rabbi Sidney Shoham Chair in Rabbinic and Community Leadership at RIETS.

Since 1985 he has overseen the "Torah U'Mada Project," the purpose of which is to explore the interaction of Torah U'*Mada* (secular studies) within the institution and raise the level of discussion about the complexities and challenges that "Torah U'Mada" poses to the community at large.

In 1987, Rabbi Hirt—who formerly directed the University's array of Holocaust studies programs—coedited Shimon Huberband's critically acclaimed book on the Holocaust, *Kiddush Hashem: Jewish Religious and Cultural Life in Poland During the Holocaust*. He is currently the series editor for the Orthodox Forum.